1997

With the exception of the occasional local case study, music-hall history has until now been presented as the history of the London halls. This book attempts to redress the balance by setting music-hall history within a national perspective. Kift also sheds a new light on the roles of managements, performers and audiences. For example, the author confutes the commonly held assumption that most women in the halls were prostitutes and shows them to have been working women accompanied by workmates of both sexes or by their families. She argues that before the 1890s the halls catered predominantly to working-class and lower middle-class audiences of both sexes and all ages and were instrumental in giving them a strong and self-confident identity. The halls' ability to sustain a distinct class-awareness was one of their greatest strengths – but this factor was also at the root of many of the controversies which surrounded them. These controversies are at the centre of the book and Kift treats them as test cases for social relations which provide fresh insights into nineteenth-century British society and politics.

The Victorian music hall

The Victorian music hall
Culture, class and conflict

DAGMAR KIFT

Translated by Roy Kift

CAMBRIDGE
UNIVERSITY PRESS

Published by the Press Syndicate of the University of Cambridge
The Pitt Building, Trumpington Street, Cambridge CB2 1RP
40 West 20th Street, New York, NY 10011–4211, USA
10 Stamford Road, Oakleigh, Melbourne 3166, Australia

Originally published in German as *Arbeiterkultur im gesellschaftlichen
Konflikt: die englische Music Hall im 19. Jahrhundert*
by Dagmar Kift 1991 and © Klartext Verlag, Essen

First published in English by Cambridge University Press 1996 as
The Victorian music hall: culture, class and conflict

English translation © Cambridge University Press 1996

Printed and Bound in Great Britain by Woolnough Bookbinding Ltd,
Irthlingborough, Northants

A catalogue record for this book is available from the British Library

Library of Congress cataloguing in publication data
Kift, Dagmar, 1954–
[Arbeiterkultur im gesellschaftlichen Konflikt. English]
The Victorian music hall: culture, class and conflict / Dagmar Kift
p. cm.
Updated and revised translation of: Arbeiterkultur im
gesellschaftlichen Konflikt.
Includes bibliographical references and index.
ISBN 0 521 47472 8 (hardback)
1. Music-halls (Variety-theaters, cabarets, etc.) – Great Britain –
History – 19th century. I. Title.
PN1968.G7K5313 1996
792.7′0941′ 09034–dc20 95–51986 CIP

ISBN 0 521 47472 8 hardback

Contents

Illustrations

Acknowledgements

This book is based on the doctoral thesis 'Arbeiterkultur im gesellschaftlichen Konflikt. Eine Sozialgeschichte der englischen Music Hall, 1840-1900', which I submitted to the Free University of Berlin in 1989. A shortened version of it entitled *Arbeiterkultur im gesellschaftlichen Konflikt: Die englische Music Hall im 19. Jahrhundert* was published in 1991 by Klartext Verlag, Essen. The present edition is an updated and revised version of the German book. I have cut out explanations which were necessary for a German readership and reintroduced some original quotations which were either omitted from or paraphrased in the German edition because their unique flavour would necessarily have disappeared in translation. Where necessary I have revised the text to take account of the latest writings on the subject. Funding for the translation was gratefully received from Inter Nationes, Bonn.

The chapter on the audience was previously published in a slightly different version in *Music Hall: The business of pleasure* edited by Peter Bailey for the Open University Press in 1986, and the section on class conflicts in Glasgow appeared as an article in *New Theatre Quarterly* volume 11, no. 43 (1995). To both many thanks.

Many people and institutions helped me greatly in the preparation of the thesis and the ensuing book and I should like to take this opportunity of thanking them warmly. I am most grateful to the staffs of the local libraries and archives in Bolton, Bradford, Glasgow, Leeds, Liverpool, London, Manchester, Rochdale and Sheffield, the Bodleian in Oxford and the British Library in London, most especially the Newspaper Library in Colindale, all of whom were very helpful and patient in assisting me in my search for sources.

Professor Dr. Hartmut Kaelble and the members of his graduate seminar at the Free University of Berlin kept me on my toes in pinning down problems and specifying my results. Thanks are also due to various people who encouraged me with suggestions and criticism along the way. These include Clive Barker, Professor Peter Bailey and Professor Dr. Heinrich Volkmann. I owe a special debt to Professor Laurence Senelick, Dr. Ulrich Schneider and Dr. Karl Ditt who read and commented upon the original manuscript. Raphael Samuel was an invaluable tutor at Oxford. His critical encouragement and support was a great spur to my researches during my year at St. Antony's.

The original thesis was funded by a grant from the *Studienstiftung des deutschen Volkes*, a grant from the British Council and a research grant from the German Historical Institute in London. I am especially grateful to Dr. Rainer Noltenius from the Fritz Hüser Institute for German and Foreign Working-Class Literature in Dortmund, under whose aegis the original edition of the book was published. The institute specialises in publications and exhibitions on many aspects of working-class literary culture and holds a unique collection of literature by, for and about working people.

Acknowledgements and thanks for the photographs are due to the following: Sheffield Archives, Bolton Reference Library, Bradford Central Library and Archives, the British Library, Manchester Local History Library and Strathclyde Regional Archives. Many thanks also to Victoria L. Cooper at Cambridge University Press and to Polly Richards for her very conscientious copy-editing.

Lastly I should like to thank my husband Roy who endured the long genesis of the original thesis and in doing so provided me with valuable insights into the innuendo and vulgarity inherent in British humour. In the course of my preparing the book for publication in both German and English he looked after the children, saw to the shopping, made the tea and did all the work for which authors' wives are usually thanked in acknowledgements. I further punished him for his commitment by persuading him to put aside his own literary endeavours for a year and translate the book into English. Although he might never want to go near it again the book is dedicated to him.

Introduction

In 1852 a Select Committee on Public Houses published the results of its enquiry into the licensing laws relating to pubs, beerhouses, dancing saloons, coffee houses, theatres and other public places of entertainment. A part of the report was also devoted to the early manifestations of a new place of entertainment: the music hall. One witness to the committee stated that many pub owners, especially in the large manufacturing towns, had begun to set up so-called 'music saloons' which offered entertainment in addition to alcohol. This entertainment consisted of music, singing in character, many forms of dancing including clog dancing, and juggling and tumbling by specially engaged performers. Some of the music saloons were already remarkably large. The three largest venues in Manchester – the Casino, the Victoria Saloon and the Polytechnic Hall – enjoyed average audiences amounting to 25,000 a week, the majority consisting of young mill hands of both sexes. The witness had undertaken random surveys in the Casino on seven Saturdays and, as a result, was able to establish the following age-structure of the audience. About 10 per cent were young people under the age of fifteen, a further 25 per cent were teenagers; 50 per cent were between twenty and thirty, and the rest were men and women over thirty. The relationship of men to women was roughly 3:1; in the Victoria Saloon 2:1.[1]

The committee was set up to enquire whether the current laws were sufficient to cope with the delicate aim of protecting both the revenue derived from alcohol taxes in the institutions under review and also public morality. Time and again the members of the commission tried to establish the influence which the various institutions had on their audiences. In this respect the early music halls made a comparatively bad impression. The above witness, for example, suspected that music saloons had only been introduced in order to promote the consumption of alcohol by keeping customers in the beerhouses for a longer period of time.

The witness's statement gives a more precise description of the sceptical public perception of the early music halls, their programme of entertainment and their audiences than the majority of the ensuing literature on the halls. Music Hall began around the middle of the nineteenth century in the industrial centres of Britain and the capital, London. At first it took place in pubs which had been extended to include a singing saloon. But before long the singing saloon developed into an independent institution in which pub gastronomy, although still playing an important role, took second place to entertainment. And singing saloons in turn gave birth to the music hall. The halls spread quickly in the 1850s, offering the inhabitants of the major conurbations a mixture of pub gastronomy and social communication with entertainment from the fairgrounds and concert rooms. As early as 1850 the Star Music Hall in Bolton (population 60,000) could boast of a capacity of 1,500; and in the 1860s the four largest halls in Manchester (population 350,000) had a combined capacity of over 8,500. London, in 1866, contained between two and three hundred small halls and thirty large ones with an average capacity of 1,500, some of them holding up to 3,500. In the 1890s the music halls developed into variety theatres catering to all classes of society. But in the early decades they catered predominantly to working-class audiences of both sexes and also to some members of the lower middle class.

The music hall can thus be characterised as an institution which was born 'from below' (i.e. from the pubs) and was rapidly subjected to a thoroughgoing process of commercialisation. In the context of this book it is regarded as a vital element in working-class culture because it catered mainly for the working classes and played an important part in their everyday life. It offered them a variety of attractions and amenities which were missing in other institutions. It was somewhere they could meet for companionship and entertainment without outside interference; a place where social trends and values could be presented and commented on by performers and audiences alike, and where social identities were shaped.

One aim of this book is, therefore, to take a closer look at the complex relationship between the halls and the working class. As C. E. B. Russell and E. T. Campagnac put it in an article on 'Poor People's Music Halls in Lancashire' in 1900: 'It is important to know what is the nature of people's work: it is not less important to know how they amuse themselves; for a man's favourite diversions provide a clue to his character and to his tastes.'[2] The book then goes on to ask how Victorian society at large perceived and reacted to the music hall as an element of working-class culture.

From its very beginnings the music hall was a socially disputed institution. It was financed by the sale of alcohol and, in many cases, the entertainment on offer did not correspond to what was regarded as socially acceptable. The halls made a mockery of middle-class interpretations of 'Victorian values' and set up their own alternatives in opposition. For this reason, during the early decades of their history, the halls were at the centre of passionate social and political disputes. And it is these disputes which form the major interest of this book. By examining the clashes between the halls and middle-class reformers, municipal authorities and the state I hope to be able to put this specific expression of British working-class culture into a larger social and political context and, thereby, establish connections between the areas of working-class culture, society and politics.

There is a large amount of literature on the halls and their history. A bibliography on the *British Music-Hall 1840–1923* published in 1981 lists over 3,000 titles ranging from newspaper articles to academic studies.[3] The latter, however, comprise only a minority of the available literature which for the most part consists of contemporary source material, more especially impressions and memoirs or selective journalistic descriptions. Despite the amount of material such writings only cover single aspects of music-hall history. Up until now the focus of interest has been almost exclusively on the London halls, their songs and their stars. Significantly enough this is true of the first general study of the halls, which set the criteria for all its successors. *Variety Stage: A History of the Music Halls from the Earliest Period to the Present Time* by Charles Stuart and A. J. Parks was published in London in 1895. Stuart and Parks were both journalists and music-hall agents and were therefore able to view their subject both as outsiders and from within. Their book is well-informed and deals with a variety of themes: the development of the London music hall, its songs and its stars, the organisations of the artists and the proprietors, the foundation of agencies, the music-hall press and the London licensing laws. Even if this is in no way a comprehensive history of the halls, the authors do throw much light onto the London scene. By comparison the great majority of their successors manage to deliver only fragmentary impressions. The ensuing literature to the end of the Second World War is dominated as a rule by subjectively tinted, journalistic memoirs whose themes are restricted to the world of the London West End variety theatres in the 1890s and the great music-hall stars of the age – not forgetting the ballet girls. In the majority of these studies the authors' youth happens to coincide with what they call the 'golden age' of the music hall and their efforts are mostly devoted to portraying the 'cheery and irresponsible life of the roaring "nineties" and early nineteen-hundreds in the square mile of London that mattered' as one witness put it.[4] The results are mostly anecdotal and confined to dealing with those aspects of the music-hall scene which were important for the authors at the time. These writings are not so much histories of the music hall as accounts of London bohemian life in the 1890s.[5] Historiographically they tend to reflect the Whig interpretation of history in that they portray the history of the halls as a continuous development from pothouse to palace; from the beerhouse with its coarse songs and rough audiences to the variety theatre with its sophisticated allusions and smartly dressed visitors. Although the halls are characterised as the *vox populi* the audiences themselves are only rarely mentioned, and even then are scarcely thought worthy of special attention.[6]

These tendencies continue in the post-1945 literature. But by contrast with earlier writings authors now devote their efforts to more studious examinations of the halls with a corresponding search for new themes and approaches. Harold Scott's *Early Doors: Origins of the Music Hall* which was published in 1946 is a descriptive portrait of the pre-history of the halls and their early years. Although its presentation is somewhat chaotic it is full of solid material and based on original sources.[7] Succeeding books are more systematic in their conception and have a wider range of themes. Particularly worthy of mention are Manders and Mitchenson's *British Music Hall: a Story in Pictures* (1965), Laurence Senelick's 'A Brief Life and Times of the Victorian Music Hall' (1971) and a collection of source material with introductory texts by David Cheshire entitled *Music Hall in Britain* (1974).[8] With these texts the history of the halls passes from managers and journalists into the hands of literary and theatre historians and, finally in the 1970s, social historians.[9] First among these are Gareth Stedman Jones and Martha Vicinus. Both writers include the halls in their researches into the history of English working-class culture, published in 1973 and 1974: Stedman Jones in a study entitled 'Working-Class Culture and Working-Class Politics in London, 1870-1900. Notes on the Remaking of a Working Class'; and Martha Vicinus in her analysis of the literary achievements of the working class, *The Industrial Muse*.[10] Both authors come to similar conclusions with regard to the music hall. They interpret it as the embodiment and affirmation of the values and norms of English working-class culture and, as such, a pillar of class solidarity. Like other working people's institutions it was resistant to outside influences and was able to preserve its relative autonomy. This autonomy, however, only had space to manoeuvre within the system and was never an alternative to it. In short the halls, as Stedman Jones puts it, remained conformist and defensive. Their character reflected the political culture of the English working class with its friendly societies, trades unions and Labour Party, all of which were orientated towards reform rather than revolution. Stedman Jones concludes that the music hall was basically 'the symbol of a culture of consolation', a thesis which succeeding historians have increasingly thrown into question.

Whereas Stedman Jones regarded the music hall as an integral part of working-class culture over the whole of the nineteenth century, Vicinus saw in its history a development from 'class' to 'mass entertainment'. This perspective also gave a boost to further research. Later studies on the history and importance of the music hall (most notably by Peter Bailey, Penny Summerfield, Hugh Cunningham and Bernard Waites) are rooted in the context of the history of leisure and popular – rather than class – culture.[11] What they have in common is a greater interest, firstly, in the role of the music-hall proprietor as entrepreneur in a rapidly expanding leisure industry; and secondly, in the question of how the State and its organs reacted to this new product of popular, urban culture. Another factor common to these studies is that they are closely tied in with the heated debates conducted amongst British social historians in the 1970s; debates concerning the reception of theoretic models from sociology, most particularly the model of social control or the Gramscian concept of hegemony.[12]

The major themes of Summerfield's essay, 'The Effingham Arms and The Empire' with its programmatic subtitle 'Deliberate Selection in the Evolution of Music Hall in London', are the London licensing laws and their application.[13] The author sees these as a framework within which managers and owners could operate, i.e. somewhere between potential state repression and the needs of the consumers. She further argues that the factor which finally defined the halls was not so much their audiences but rather a process of selection whereby certain music-hall proprietors came to the fore according to the extent to which they conformed with the intended or actual proscriptions of the state. Summerfield's arguments are basically functional in their approach and use a vocabulary of music-hall history which Peter Bailey has described as 'cultural materialism or sub Marxism', a counter-model to the Whig interpretation.[14] This approach sees an analogy between the development of the music hall from beerhouse to variety theatre and the shift from domestic to factory production and ties this in with factors such as economies of scale, division of labour and structures of domination.

Although Bailey himself was at first influenced by concepts of social control he has increasingly turned to anthropological approaches and, most recently, to analysing specific music-hall discourses and practices. He argues that the music hall should be seen as a cultural phenomenon on its own terms with its own specific content, structure and contradictions.[15] He does not dispute the capitalist features of the business – the exploitation of the performers by multiple appearances per evening, the extra burden of matinees and benefit performances and the consequent rise of trade unionism. What he does show is how these features were at the same time tempered by the persistence of traditional customs and practices.[16] Even when caterers became large scale entrepreneurs, they would still have felt duty-bound to the 'small businessman's traditions of public service and mutuality' which were part and parcel of the roots from which they sprung: the networks of the pub, the friendly society, the masonic lodge and the local vestry.[17] Using benefit performances as an example Bailey illuminates how entrepreneurial practices which were regulated by expectations both customary and modern not only gave the halls their own distinctive style but also gave proprietors and managers a social role which differed considerably from that of the traditional factory owner. Performers cannot be regarded exclusively as exploited workers as their market value was determined as much by consumer as by employer demand. And the audience refused to allow itself to be reduced to the role of passive consumers. Features such as the dialogue with the performers and the boisterous reception of the various offerings demonstrate that the audience asserted its traditional role of popular control in determining content and form. To Bailey the music hall is at one and the same time the prototype of the modern entertainment industry and an autonomous expression of popular culture.[18] Using these contradictory features as a starting point he is able to deal successfully with the music hall's own particular nexus of complexities.

Most recent research has concentrated on two particular aspects of the music hall as a popular mode of expression: its language and meaning and the relationship between text and audience. The language of the halls, for example, plays a major role in Patrick Joyce's *Visions of the People*, an analysis of how nineteenth-century labouring people saw the social order of which they were a part. Popular art is considered as central here, since it created social identities of self and other and formed a sense of belonging to a specific community and culture. Language is thereby analysed 'as a sign-system of what might be called the semiology of the social order'.[19] Joyce thus takes up an old theme in music-hall historiography – the music hall as *vox populi*. But whereas earlier scholars assumed that music-hall texts directly reflected the attitudes of the audiences, Joyce analyses the language of the halls as an expression of experience and as a factor which constituted experience. Language and content also figure prominently in Peter Bailey's 'Conspiracies of Meaning: Music Hall and the Knowingness of Popular Culture'. Bailey concentrates on 'knowingness', because it was considered to be a distinctive and also an objectionable mode of expression in nineteenth-century halls. Bailey's approach is to treat it as a discourse and practice which help us to understand the style and character of the halls as well as the culture of their audiences in a more differentiated way. After exploring what 'knowingness' actually entailed, he argues that the typical participatory style of performance and the way in which it was experienced were major factors in forming a separate identity and culture of the halls and their public. And although this culture did not question the social or political order, 'music-hall engaged its public in a more complex set of meanings than that proposed in the compensation model – the relish in knowingness suggests strongly that this was a culture of competence more than a culture of consolation'.[20]

Social historical studies of the music hall have led to changes in perspective and a broadening of themes. But there are still considerable gaps to be filled. Despite the interpretation of music hall as an institution of popular culture, the audience and its relationship to the halls and their content are subjects which still need more research. The major spotlight of research is still focused on the London halls. True, Russell and Campagnac's article appeared in the *Economic Review* as early as 1900. But subsequently regional halls quickly disappeared into oblivion. Apart from a few small contributions by local historians, a more comprehensive study was not available until 1970: G. J. Mellor's *Northern Music Hall*.[21] Although it claims to be the first complete study of the history of regional music halls, the book is in fact more a history of the 'famous halls' and their syndicates. Like many other portraits of the music hall it is notable not only for its richness of detail but also for its complete lack of footnotes and source references.

It was not until the mid 1970s that regional halls began to reappear – albeit sporadically – in studies on working people's culture. Apart from the already mentioned book by Martha Vicinus, M. B. Smith published an essay on 'Victorian Entertainment in the Lancashire Cotton Towns'.[22] These studies were followed at the end of the 1970s by case studies either of leisure in particular towns or the history of individual music halls. Amongst the most noteworthy are writings by Peter Bailey and Robert Poole on Bolton, Douglas Reid on

Birmingham, Jeremy Crump on Leicester, as well as essays by Dave Harker on the Tyneside concert hall and Chris Waters on the battle over the Palace of Varieties in Manchester.[23] Nevertheless all these contributions can only be regarded as building blocks for a future synthesis.

The approach I shall take in my book is rooted in the debates conducted by British social historians on content and methodology concerning the music hall. It conceives the music hall as a form of popular culture according to the definition adopted in these debates i.e. as a mixture of spontaneous and oppositional people's culture 'from below' and commercialised mass culture 'from above'. The concept 'popular' will be dealt with in both these senses. I shall first enquire into what made the music hall so popular. In doing so I shall not restrict myself solely to studying the songs, as has been usual up to now, but the programme as a whole and also the functions of the music hall and its role in the everyday lives of working people beyond the provision of entertainment. I shall then turn my attention to the audience, try to define its particular composition and analyse its relationship to the halls by studying its behaviour. The major part of the book, however, is devoted to case studies of local social conflicts. Music halls did not develop in a vacuum but within external frameworks such as licensing laws and building provisions, as well as recurring disputes with various groups of opponents, two of which were particularly prominent. As an element in the leisure and entertainment industry music hall represented a new form of competition to the already existing institutions, above all the theatre. And as a part of working-class culture it was inevitably bound up with conflicts involving working people.

Controversies about the halls were both vertical and horizontal in nature and involved various and varying social groups and institutions. By analysing them at a local level with its clearly visible social structures it is possible not only to pinpoint their specific features but also to illuminate the more general relationships between working-class culture, Victorian society, local government and the state – i.e. the 'big social-historical questions'.[24] I intend to examine the various forms of interdependence 'from below' (from the perspective of working-class culture) and thereby hope to throw them into a different light. The following example should give an idea into the insights to be gained by using such an approach.

Patrick Joyce's book *Work, Society and Politics* was published in 1980. Here Joyce aims to study class relationships where they were at their most intensive; at the workplace, the dominant area of a worker's life.[25] One of his major theses is that the 'culture of the factory', defined on the one hand by the social hegemony of the entrepreneur and, on the other, by the deference of the workers, intruded into the areas of family and leisure. Working people lived in dwellings provided by factory owners and made use of the latters' leisure and educational facilities. Seen in this light patterns of domination and dependence in the factory were continued outside it.[26] The primary hallmarks of class relationships, particularly in towns with a well-developed factory system, were entrepreneurial

7

paternalism and class harmony. Joyce's study was widely recognised as a new approach and his conclusions confirmed the old thesis of 'mid-Victorian stability' in the latter half of the nineteenth century.

One of the towns which Joyce takes as a model of 'the culture of the factory' is Bolton with its textile factories. The town has since been the subject of various studies from a different perspective: that of an independent working-class culture, which does not and cannot exist according to Joyce. Both Peter Bailey in his case study of Bolton in *Leisure and Class in Victorian England* and Robert Poole in *Popular Leisure and the Music Hall in Bolton* document a powerful, independent working-class and popular culture which was able to adapt to the economic and social changes of the time, and whose traditions and institutions not only remained independent of the culture of the factory but in many cases provided a counterweight to it which should not be underestimated. Their theses are thus directly opposed to that of Joyce. For Bailey and Poole Bolton is marked less by class harmony and deference than by class conflict and resistance, especially in the area of leisure. The conflicts here arose from the eighteenth-century traditions of popular culture with its wakes and fairs, its 'undisciplined' games and 'excessive' traditions of drinking which stood in direct opposition to the new industrial order. They continued in the controversies around public holidays, 'free time', and the ways and places in which this time should be spent i.e. in the controversies concerning 'St Monday', racing, blood sports, gambling, pubs and street life, common land and the annual fairs. To all these must be added the controversies caused by reforms undertaken by the state, religious bodies and private philanthropists, all of whom attempted to provide alternatives. Such reforms included restructuring the educational system and building Sunday schools, founding temperance societies, mechanics' institutes and working-men's clubs, erecting museums and libraries and introducing concerts at affordable prices as well as organised sporting activities. In all these areas conflicts arose with regard to self-determination, the control of time and territory, content and form and 'the production of meanings'.[27]

If Bailey's and Poole's 'history from below' brought fresh perspectives to the area of class relations, their detailed analysis of individual conflicts in the context of local social and power structures led to a picture of both classes – in particular the town's elite – which was more differentiated than Joyce's. Joyce portrayed Bolton's elite as a homogeneous group of traditional Anglican country squires and early industrial Tories with the addition of textile entrepreneurs who had risen to prominence in the industrial revolution. This group contained many sub-groups who had soon formed mutual associations and were bound by many cross-cultural links, one of the most important being the culture of the factory.[28] The conflicts around working-class culture, however, primarily reveal internal differences and interests individual to Whigs and Tories, Anglicans and non-conformists. These were also expressed as differences of style: the Quaker textile entrepreneur Ashworth put his paternalism into action by providing reading and school rooms in his factory, whereas the Conservative entrepreneur Ridgway preferred to celebrate with his workers in the pub.[29] But such individual interests also found expression in the town council in a more concrete manner as party disputes and power struggles. The debate on Peel Park is a good case in point. The Liberals wanted to offer the park to the workers as an example of rational recreation and an alternative to the pub. The Conservatives rejected this idea because it was a Liberal project and they succeeded in prolonging the argument for sixteen years. The dispute, however, also revealed splits within the Liberal/non-conformist camp. They were indeed unanimous in wanting to provide alternative leisure pursuits for the working class, but the sabbatarians amongst them rejected the idea of opening such amenities on Sundays which, in the case of the park, would have been practically counter to the aim.[30]

The precise alliances and composition of the ruling elite and the individual policies they followed naturally played a considerable role in the conflicts around the music halls and also focuses attention on each specific local case. My analytical approach is based on the long-standing debates on working-class culture in Britain. These debates at first took the form of social controversies in the nineteenth century. In the twentieth century working-class culture became established as an independent area of studies, an area which has been recognised as 'one of the major frontiers of social change in the nineteenth century'.[31]

The occupation with this area of studies stimulated a lively discussion on methodology amongst social historians and strengthened the change of perspective instigated by E. P. Thompson which was centred on the rejection of the Whig interpretation of history. The nineteenth century was now seen not so much as an age of progress and change, liberty and democracy, but as a period in which the old elite was able to restore its position of power by means of a comprehensive exercise of social discipline.[32] Sidney Pollard, in a report on research into English working-class culture published in 1979, noted various examples both of the repression of pre-industrial eighteenth-century folk culture and the attempts of the nineteenth-century British middle classes to shape the working class according to the former's own ideas.[33] Measures aimed at discipline and reform undertaken by religious and educational bodies as well as pressure groups like the temperance movement played a considerable role here. Looked at methodologically the choice of these specific thematic areas of interest and the perspectives from which they were studied gave rise to a discussion of sociological models of social control which a number of British historians attempted to introduce as an analytical method and theoretical framework. The high expectations which were for a while placed on sociology were however not fulfilled. In the first place the diverse concepts of social control were never precisely defined and discussed in all their implications. Even the collection of essays entitled *Social Control in Nineteenth-Century Britain* edited by Antony Donajgrodzki, whose specific aim was to introduce the application of the model developed by the American sociologist Ross as an analytical framework, used this more as a *leitmotif* than a theoretical concept.[34] And secondly a consider-able number of British social historians felt uneasy with such an overwhelmingly functionalist model.

The opponents of the concept questioned whether social history which increasingly understood itself as 'history from below' should really work with a theory which continued to put the ruling elite at the centre of events. They further asked whether it was possible to live with a theory which practically dis-qualified all actions of the subordinate classes against the system as 'deviant' behaviour, and whose main concern seemed to be how to stop such disturbances and reintroduce order and equilibrium. Alongside a number of practical prob-lems – which order and which equilibrium should constitute the starting point in view of the empirical findings that in the area of leisure new developments 'disturbed' the old order less than a new order 'disturbed' old traditions? – one basic question had to be answered: how do you tie in a functionalist model with the concept of social change? Parsons, for example, uses the category 'change', but restricts it to change within the system.[35] This means that crises and conflicts are seen by him as disturbances to be eliminated, as dysfunctions rather than contradictions inherent in the system itself which might give rise to innovatory impulses. It also follows that reforms can only be assessed as restorative mea-sures rather than the means by which social change is effected.

In the light of the concept of social control the nineteenth century took on a completely new character. As one writer put it: 'The century of change becomes the century of non-change.'[36] Critics of the concept therefore spoke out in favour of using it, at most, in a restricted manner and even went so far as to rec-ommend that it be replaced by a more dialectic and dynamic model.[37] This was partly to be found in Gramsci's concept of hegemony. By contrast with the func-tional models of social control Gramsci's concept was more dynamic and placed its emphasis on processes and change. It was also notable for the fact that it did not regard the subordinate classes exclusively as passive recipients of discipli-nary measures instituted by the ruling class but rather as participants in a two-way negotiation of 'spiritual and moral leadership' which, by definition, included transformation and modification.[38] Thus Gramsci's concept of hegemony grad-ually established itself as the key theoretical model.

Although the concepts of social control were finally rejected and replaced they had nonetheless stimulated a fruitful discourse which opened up new themes and perspectives. The debates on working-class culture can be summar-ised in the following four theses which also provide the structural framework for the approach I intend to take.

1. Many disputes in the area of working-class culture and leisure were sparked off by the social and political ruling class attempting to establish a new social consensus. These attempts took the form of various initiatives to oppose or modify traditional popular customs and stem the growth of forms of working-class culture which sprang up in the (industrial) conurbations either by banning

them completely, regulating them or reforming them. Prohibitive measures included attacks on traditional pastimes, on holidays such as St Monday, wakes and fairs and the ways in which they were celebrated. They also comprised the closing down of traditional venues of celebration such as the annual fairs and the enclosure of common land. Attacks on pub culture may also be included here.[39] Amongst reform measures may be counted the restructuring of the educational system, the erection of Sunday schools and factory schools, the introduction of organised sports with a strict division between participants and spectators such as football and rugby. Here physical training, team spirit and fair play (i.e. self-discipline and submission to set rules) provided a perfect combination. In this context the foundation of working-men's clubs and mechanics' institutes which propagated Victorian values such as hard work, sobriety, thrift and personal initiative should also be included.[40]

2. However there was not always a clear line between those exercising hegemony and the subordinate classes. This is particularly clear in the temperance question. Only a part of the middle classes were in favour of reforms. The remainder and the overwhelming majority of the aristocracy refused to support or even go along with such reforms. The working classes too were divided over the issue. Many Chartists and organised workers tended for obvious reasons to support the battle against alcoholism. Sobriety not only helped character-building and work-discipline but was also in the real interests of wives and children whose livelihood was put in danger when husbands or fathers became addicted to drink. Class boundaries are, therefore, not always clearly discernible.[41]

3. As a rule the efforts of the reform-orientated ruling class reveal a considerable gap between intention and success. Those to whom constraints and reforms were addressed refused to let themselves become passive recipients of prescriptions from above. Many such constraints could not be effectively enforced and many attempts at reform failed because working people were prepared to stand up in defence of customs and practices which they held dear.[42] Several decades of temperance campaigning failed to persuade the workers to abandon either their public houses or their drinking habits and attempts to provide counter-attractions were boycotted by a large section of the populace. Attendances at working-men's clubs and mechanics' institutes were not as great as their initiators expected whereas race meetings and prize-fighting of all types attracted thousands of visitors and gambling flourished.[43] Reform-based alternatives were mostly only accepted in a modified form. Undiluted entertainment gradually replaced character-building and instruction in mechanics' institutes which, like working-men's clubs, soon threw off the trammels of the founding fathers. Even beer sales became a part of the established order in direct opposition to the founders' original intentions.[44] In football too, ideals were swiftly replaced by patterns of behaviour which, as early as the 1890s, were perceived by the middle classes as 'unsporting': professionalisation, hooliganism, abusing the referee and other similar features.[45]

Many attempts to influence or reform matters proved two-edged. Methodism not only mediated a protestant ethic and respect for authority, its organisational structures also promoted grass-roots practices as well as spawning future working-class leaders.[46] Even the increasing number of licensing laws cannot be solely interpreted as restrictive. They also had their advantages. Building regulations for theatres and music halls contributed to a safer environment for their audiences. In fact, all measures had repercussions on their initiators: 'you cannot have "incorporation" – a word for a process much used in leisure and cultural studies recently – without the incorporated host being altered, as well as the incorporated guest'.[47]

4. 'Social control' did not necessarily result in changes in behaviour. These often ensued from adaptations to a change in living conditions and/or were the expression of authentic needs.

> There is plenty of evidence that the respectable working classes wished to be respectable not because some middle-class pundit told them to be so, but because they liked it and disapproved of shiftless and sluttish ways. Similarly, the working classes did not need to be told by the middle class that family life was important, that honest toil was better than loafing, or that saving for a rainy day was sensible.[48]

Studies on labour aristocracy in particular have shown that the presence of Victorian values such as hard work, sobriety, thrift and independence in their vocabulary is no indication that they were being assimilated into the middle classes. On the contrary such values were often important factors in the development of their own culture which understood 'independence', for one, to mean freedom from patronage and a right to their own organisation.[49] In a similar fashion Hugh Cunningham's study on the history of leisure comes to the conclusion that 'people had some capacity to make their own culture'.[50]

In part 1 I intend to present the music hall as a part of this culture by studying its history, its programme and its audiences. By contrast with other studies I shall not concentrate exclusively – nor even predominantly – on the London halls but more on the halls outside the capital, especially in those regions where they flourished most strongly: the industrial areas of Lancashire and Yorkshire. Their beginnings and the way they developed were quite different from those of their counterparts in London and accordingly stamped their mould on the form, the course and the outcome of social conflicts in which they were involved. London, as I shall show, was in no way representative of the whole scene. Where the terms 'provinces' and 'provincial' occur in the book they are intended solely as geographical references to the regions outside London and not as critical devaluations. Quite the contrary: the book is an attempt to revalue the regions which have until now been sadly and unjustly neglected in comparison to the capital. Chapters 2 and 3 consist of a summary of the current state of research into the London halls and their songs followed by my own researches into the regional halls, their programme as a whole and their audiences. Here I shall be presenting the history 'from within'. In part 2, which deals with social conflicts, I shall try to pinpoint the relationship between music hall and the outside world, i.e. between working-class culture and society. Up until now this relationship has been the subject of only a very few case studies. I have attempted to present all the most important controversies here and intend to examine not only the history of their development and their typological aspects, but also to place them in the social and political context of each particular locality.

PART I

THE ENGLISH MUSIC HALL

1

History

THE BEGINNINGS

The first major survey of the music halls in England – and one of the main sources for their history – appeared in the form of a Select Committee Report on Theatrical Licences and Regulations published in 1866. The evidence provided in the report by documents and eyewitnesses has shaped our view of the music halls to the present day. This is particularly true of a written report submitted by Frederick Stanley, the lawyer for the London Music Hall Proprietors' Association. His evidence summarises the basic features of their development. The fact that Stanley puts particular emphasis on Charles Morton's Canterbury Music Hall in London can be explained by his claims that it played a pioneering role in the history of the halls and that he was also for a time co-owner of the Canterbury.

> The first 'Canterbury Hall', which was the first music hall in London, was opened by Mr. Morton about 17 or 18 years ago. Prior to the hall being built, the house was an ordinary public-house called the 'Canterbury Arms,' situated in a narrow, unfrequented street in the Westminster-road.
>
> At this period many publicans were in the habit of holding singing meetings, generally about once a week; these meetings were attended by tradesmen and mechanics, who amused themselves by singing. This kind of singing-room was known as a 'Free-and-Easy.'
>
> Mr. Morton opened a singing-room in the 'Canterbury Arms.' The room was capable of holding about 100 persons; it was opened once a week, from about seven until twelve o'clock, and was visited by respectable tradesmen and mechanics. Subsequently it was opened twice a week. At first professional singers were not engaged, but afterwards two or three were engaged, and subsequently a larger number.
>
> The visitors continually urged Mr. Morton to open the room upon one evening each week, and admit their wives. This he did, and the place soon obtained a good reputation...
>
> Mr. Morton soon found his room was not large enough. He then obtained some ground at the back of the premises, and built a handsome hall, capable of holding about 400 or 500 persons, and having succeeded in getting a licence from the magistrates, he opened it as a concert-room. The entertainment was by

professional singers from a platform, and consisted of glees, madrigals, choruses, songs, and comic songs.

This was the first 'Canterbury Hall', and was opened about 17 or 18 years ago.

The visitors were tradesmen, mechanics, their wives and families. Children were not admitted, and it was a rule that all visitors should be properly attired.

A small price for admission was charged.

Women of a certain class did not visit the place.

A musical conductor was engaged and the glees, choruses, &c., were rehearsed, and afterwards performed before the public in a manner which soon gained for the place a widely-spread reputation...

This went on for a few years, when Mr. Morton, finding he had not room for his visitors, built the present 'Canterbury Hall', which has been open for about 12 years. It is capable of holding nearly 2,000 persons...

It has always been the steady aim of Mr. Morton to raise the character of his establishment, and with this view he added a handsome picture gallery to the 'Canterbury Hall,' at a cost of about £8,000.

...operatic selections were always kept as the leading entertainment ...

A large proportion of the public have become familiar with the music of the great masters, entirely through the selections at the music halls.[1]

Stanley not only detailed the history of the Canterbury in this paper, he also left us a prototypical account of the various stages of development of the London halls from the free-and-easies via the concert rooms or singing saloons. The free-and-easies were informal entertainments given by amateurs who generally met once a week in their local pub. They were extra attractions offered by the publicans and an integrated part of normal business within the premises. By contrast, concert rooms or singing saloons were rooms which were either structural alterations within the existing building or an additional space especially built for the purpose of entertainment. These rooms, as a rule, had a stage at one end, a bar at the opposite end and long rows of tables at right angles to both stage and bar.[2] The entertainment here was no longer provided once a week by amateurs but on a daily basis by professional singers and other performers of both sexes. Entrance charges were made, either in the form of cash or refreshment checks, and the audience took an active part in the programme either by singing along with the choruses or in amateur competitions.[3] From here it was only a small step to the music halls. Stanley's criterion for defining the difference between concert rooms and music halls were size and the fact that a music hall was not an extension built onto the pub itself but a separate building erected specifically for the purpose of entertainment. Music-hall historiography has generally adopted this distinction with some modifications as to size, architecture and the various types of entrance charges.[4]

Stanley's account of the music hall with its particular emphasis on the

Canterbury has had a strong influence on subsequent writers on the halls. Even as late as 1973 Gareth Stedman Jones claimed that the Canterbury served as a model for the regional halls which were of no great consequence because the form of entertainment was characteristically a London creation.[5] Peter Bailey was the first to throw some doubt on this assertion: 'Though important, Morton was not the solitary pioneer that music hall mythology has made him out to be.'[6] Subsequent research on the regional halls, although still fragmentary, has increasingly relativised the leading role of the capital. One of the theses I shall put forward in this book is that the development of the regional halls in no way followed the pattern of their London counterparts, not least because they came into being at the same time or even beforehand.

James Ellis, who was born in 1829 stated in his memoirs, *Life of an Athlete*, and in an interview published in the *Yorkshire Owl* two years before his death in 1893 that the first proper music hall in the country was not the Canterbury but the Star in Bolton, which he claimed was 'really the only Music Hall in Britain at that time' (the 1840s).[7] Ellis was a boxer and acrobat who performed in places of entertainment all over Britain and Europe before becoming a music-hall manager in Leeds. Before mentioning the London halls and their pro-prietors he names T. Towers's Polytechnic in Salford, Ben Lang's (later known as the Victoria) and Burton's Casino in Manchester as well as Henry Pullan's music hall in Bradford.[8] All these halls came into being either before or at the same time as the Canterbury.

Thomas Sharples opened the Star in 1832 and its success was such that he was forced to move into a larger building as early as 1840. In 1842 Henry Pullan's name can already be found as the manager of the Concert Rooms in the Bermondsey Hotel in Bradford.[9] The first reference to Towers's Polytechnic also dates back to the early 1840s and the journal of the theatre trade, the *Era*, pub-lished a review in 1848 which leads one to believe that the hall had already been in existence for some time.[10] In 1849 Henry Pullan opened the first of his halls in Bradford and Joseph Hobson opened the Casino in Leeds. Around the same time Towers took over the management of the Colosseum in Manchester to add to his Polytechnic in Salford.[11] Other early ventures include the Parthenon in Liverpool and Balmbra's in Newcastle. The *Era* reported the opening of the former in 1847 and a review of the latter appeared in the same paper in 1848. Finally there is Thomas Youdan's Royal Casino in Sheffield, which had to be enlarged only a few months after its opening in May 1849.[12] All these halls dis-tinguished themselves from singing saloons in that they were large, commercial-ised and professionalised venues which were established as a permanent business. These features also applied to Charles Morton's Canterbury.[13]

Like the Canterbury, Sharples's Star possessed a picture gallery and in addi-tion incorporated a museum and a menagerie. It had a capacity of over 1000, as did Towers's Polytechnic and Youdan's Casino. Hobson's Casino could even hold 2000.[14] Hobson was the first music-hall manager to charge cash for entry, whereas the singing saloons and many of the early halls operated as a rule with refreshment checks.[15] Like Morton, Hobson and his colleagues in Liverpool, Manchester, Salford, Bolton and Sheffield employed in the main professional artistes who performed all over the country. A case in point is the duo known as the Dempsey Brothers. In October 1849 they appeared in Towers's Polytechnic in Salford and directly afterward in Hobson's Casino in Leeds; there is also evidence that they appeared at Sharples's hall in Bolton in 1846.[16] As early as the 1840s the *Era*, which was published in London, attested to the professionalism of the regional halls and published reviews of their shows – even if only at first in small print.[17]

There is only one major difference between the early regional halls and Charles Morton's Canterbury: their proprietors and managers did not try to give their ventures a new image by naming them 'music halls' in order to distance themselves from the local singing saloons. In the 1840s Thomas Sharples either spoke of his premises as the 'Star Inn', the 'Star Inn Concert Room' or simply the 'Star'. Youdan called his Casino a 'Promenade Concert Hall' and Towers his Polytechnic a 'Concert Hall and Tavern' – this as late as 1854.[18] As owners of the largest halls in each locality and thus enjoying a virtual monopoly they clearly did not consider it of primary importance to make a distinction between their enterprises and singing saloons. In London, by contrast, the situation was entirely different.

The capital could already boast of a diverse and complex entertainment industry.[19] Hence music halls were forced to fight for their existence in the face of theatres large and small, pleasure gardens, concert rooms and song-and-supper rooms. One of the proprietors' major difficulties was to establish a distinct image for the music halls since their programme had a great deal in common with that of other rival establishments with whom there was a mutual exchange of singers and performers.[20] Morton's decision to raise his Canterbury above the rest by renaming it as a music hall was therefore a deliberate act of policy. The title was not only intended to make clear that Morton's premises had nothing to do with an extended pub, but also to awaken certain associations.

Around the middle of the century the term music hall did not mean a venue for variety entertainment but a general purpose and concert hall.[21] Such halls played an important role in the cultural life of a town, especially in the regions. In Sheffield, for example, the Music Hall which was built in 1823/4 was used as a venue for oratorios and concerts by local choirs. It also presented international stars like Jenny Lind, Paganini and Liszt. The Sheffield Music Hall, however, was not just a concert room. The local 'Literary and Philosophical Society' met within its walls and Charles Dickens and Wilkie Collins gave readings there. The Music Hall was thus mainly addressed to a middle-class audience, although its doors were not closed to the working class. The hall's management organised temperance meetings, put the rooms at the disposal of the mechanics' institutes and offered concerts at reduced prices for working people.[22]

Charles Morton also followed in this tradition at first. His programmes included the folky and the classical and his performers provided both light and classical entertainment. Moreover his singers appeared in formal evening dress. The Canterbury was not to be confused with a singing saloon. It was a concert hall for artisans and the working class. The press too regarded its early offerings in such a light. 'We are glad to notice the efforts of the proprietor (Mr. C. Morton) ... to provide music of a superior order for the Million', wrote the critic of the *Era* in 1852.[23] A variety programme of the sort which was already being offered in the regions, was only seen at the Canterbury some years later.[24]

Charles Morton popularised the original 'Music Hall' and transformed it in the direction of variety. He was not 'the inventor' of the music hall. He simply propagated its name, its image – and its mythology. Only in this context can he justly be called the 'father' of the halls.

THE LONDON HALLS

In 1866 Frederick Stanley put the number of music halls in London at over 30, 'with an average capitalisation of £10,000 and an average capacity of 1,500'.[25] True, the London magistrates had granted over 300 music licences in 1865, most of which went to music halls and singing saloons, but Stanley preferred to follow Morton's strategy of demarcation. His estimate only included those institutions offering music-hall entertainment whose owners were organised in the 'London Music Hall Proprietors' Association'.[26]

The London Music Hall Proprietors' Association was founded in 1860 as a legal aid organisation. The first music-hall agency had come into existence two years earlier and a number of trade journals already existed to keep proprietors, employees and audiences informed.[27] In the course of only a few years a new branch of the entertainment industry had been established.

The opening of Morton's Canterbury Hall was followed in the 1850s by the appearance of a number of further halls and until the end of the decade they gradually spread from the suburbs towards the city centre.[28] Morton was again first on the spot. His Oxford Music Hall was in the heart of the West End, the theatrical centre of London.[29] With the help of a new law which allowed the setting-up of limited companies, London experienced a music-hall boom in the early 1860s.[30] Even in the years of depression after 1873 the decline in the number of halls was only very slight. Indeed many proprietors managed to accumulate such profits that they were able to expand the capacity of their halls at the beginning of the 1880s.[31]

What was the atmosphere like in a London music hall in the 1870s? The following contemporary description provides a vivid, if not entirely sympathetic, picture.

> A dazzling blaze of gas; the sharp clink of pewter pots and glasses; an incessant babble of voices, male and female, talking, shouting, and laughing, blended with the loud din of a stringed and brazen band; an army of hot, perspiring waiters, napkin on arm, and laden with bottles and glasses, perpetually running to and fro between a liquor bar and an audience of impatient tipplers; an insignificant looking creature standing in the centre of a large stage and lustily stretching his lungs in the somewhat vain endeavour to make himself audible above the general clamour; – such is the appearance presented by the interior of a Music hall at the moment of entering.[32]

That the poor creature got a chance to exercise his lungs at all was thanks to the Chairman who sat at the front of the stage. He was the most important character in the early halls. He had been the leader of the amateur choirs in the free-and-easies and from there his role had been upgraded to that of master of ceremonies in the singing saloons and music halls. By contrast with the other tables in the auditorium his own table was parallel to and in front of the stage. From here he announced the individual stars, encouraged the audience to applaud, admonished them to drink and at the same time tried to ensure that matters did not get out of hand.[33] Attired in immaculate evening dress he, more than any other person in the early years, was responsible for giving the halls their tone and dignity. But the manner of his introductions and the language of his patter with its satirical exaggeration of middle-class and aristocratic speech patterns made it quite clear that he was at the same time parodying the members of those classes whose dress habits he was imitating. A high point in the life of many a visitor to the halls was to be able to share his table, as it were sitting practically in the spotlight. For it was the chairman who dominated proceedings in the halls until shortly before the turn of the century.

In 1885 the renovated London Pavilion opened its doors as a new form of music hall – the variety theatre. The Pavilion set standards of comfort and content on which all other halls, both new and converted, were to orientate themselves. By the start of the 1870s some music-hall proprietors had begun to separate their refreshment rooms from the entertainment auditorium. Their colleagues in the eighties and nineties were to continue and complete this trend. They not only moved sales of alcohol and drink completely out of the auditorium, but also replaced the rows of tables by fixed rows of seating. The internal architecture of the halls increasingly came to resemble that in the theatres. The audience was thereby made less mobile during the performance and forced to leave the auditorium immediately after the show had ended. Such measures enabled the managers to plan their programmes more easily. Given the fact that, by the 1880s, two turns an evening had become the norm in the halls, the planning of the programme and a quick and efficient turn-around of audiences took on considerable importance. The chairman too began to disappear from the scene. He was replaced by a board at the side of the stage with a list of numbers corresponding to numbers in the printed programme giving the order of the artistes' appearance.[34] With this the music hall was to lose a considerable amount of the personal character which had made it so distinctive in the early decades. Alienation also grew evident in the relationship between entrepreneurs and those they employed and conflicts became more common. In 1906 the first trade union, the Variety Artistes Federation, was formed and early in 1907 a mass strike in London music halls drew attention to the enormous tensions between variety artistes and the managements, particularly those in the larger halls.[35]

One area alone was spared from this process of rationalisation: the architectural trappings. Here proprietors and their architects attempted to reflect the principle of variety in their style and decorations. The architectural historian, Victor Glasstone describes the London Tivoli in the following fashion.

> The term 'variety' described not only the kind of entertainment available but also the choice of *décor*. The buffet, at street level, was in Indian style. A staircase in François I style led to the Palm Room (walls and ceiling decorated with palm leaves) on the first floor and the Flemish Room (oak carved in the Levant) on the second ... Plantagenet windows were separated by a giant order of French Empire pilasters, surmounted by an attic storey of Romanesque arcading and topped by a Mansard roof.[36]

Rationalised organisation and stylistic eclecticism were not the only hallmarks of the music hall in the 1890s. Up until then most halls had been in private hands or were owned by limited companies. Proprietors now began increasingly to concentrate their capital in major syndicates which built up chains of music halls not only in London but across the country as a whole.[37] Indeed this process began earlier in the regions than it did in London. Edward Moss, the son of a provincial music-hall proprietor, had already begun buying up halls in Scotland and the North of England in the 1880s. By the 1890s his chain consisted of about ten halls in ten different towns, most of them called the 'Empire'.[38] He then joined forces with Richard Thornton and Oswald Stoll, both of whom had also built up chains of music halls: Thornton like Moss in Scotland and the North of England; Stoll in Wales and the North. In a matter of years the three together made up a 'triumvirate which ruled over music halls in almost all the cities of Great Britain'.[39] But at the turn of the century the partners went their separate ways once more, after they had succeeded in getting a foothold in London. In 1900 Moss opened the London Hippodrome. He was unable to call it the Empire because the name was already taken. The Hippodrome gradually became the headquarters of Moss's business from which, by the start of the First World War – as a contemporary writer remarked – 'upwards of thirty other places of amusement are operated, in all parts of the kingdom, employing a capital in excess of two million pounds'.[40] At this time the *Era Annual* counted a total of twenty-three syndicates across the country.

Halls and variety theatres no longer catered exclusively to lower-middle and working-class audiences.[41] As early as 1891 F. Anstey described the London scene in the following terms.

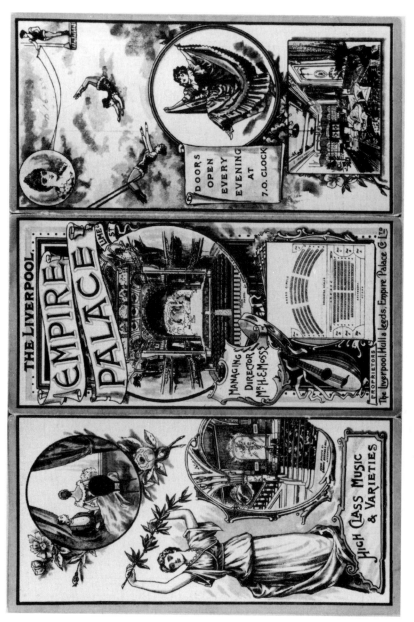

1. A programme cover for Moss's Liverpool Empire, 1900: 'Variety' in content and style(s).

London music halls might be roughly grouped into four classes – first, the aristocratic variety theatre of the West End, chiefly found in the immediate neighbourhood of Leicester Square; then the smaller and less aristocratic West End halls; next, the large bourgeois music halls of the less fashionable parts and in the suburbs; last the minor music halls of the poor and squalid districts.[42]

Had he been writing some years later he would have omitted the last category for the strict application of new building regulations by the London County Council completely wiped out the smaller halls and the pub music halls.[43]

For many years scholars – particularly representatives of the Whig version of history – have regarded the 1890s as the high point of music-hall history. In this decade they saw the completion of the transformation from pot house to palace. More recent writers do not agree with this assessment. There is no doubt that the halls had never before catered to as many visitors from all classes of the population as they did in the 1890s. However by conceding to middle-class tastes the halls had become detached from their popular roots and lost a considerable amount of vitality. The long-term consequences of this process were to be seen in the following century when the music hall gradually began to lose popularity in the face of growing competition from the new media and other forms of entertainment. Some of these were imports from the United States. Ragtime and the Charleston drew the public in droves to the dance-halls. Reviews began to be very popular. To meet the demand some halls were converted into review theatres, amongst them Charles Morton's number two hall, the Oxford, in 1917 and the London Pavilion in 1918. Moving pictures which had originally been a part of the music-hall programme – in the 1890s they were one number amongst many others – increasingly usurped the programme as a whole with the result that many proprietors were forced to convert their halls into cinemas after the First World War. Lastly the arrival of radio in 1922 meant that the BBC was able to provide entertainment for many people within their own four walls.[44] In the end such competition proved too much for the music halls, many of whose stars like Charlie Chaplin had by now moved over into film or later into radio, like Arthur Askey, Tommy Handley and Ted Ray, whose legendary series *Ray's a Laugh* ran for twelve years. But it was television which finally gave the death blow to the halls in the 1950s, although the tradition still lived on in the medium with performers like Tommy Cooper, Ken Dodd and Morecambe and Wise, and most of all in the sentimentalised version of the halls provided by *The Good Old Days*.[45]

THE REGIONAL HALLS

Whereas the London halls had to fight for a central position both economically and geographically, and showed a relatively linear development from free-and-easies and singing saloons to music halls and variety theatres, regional music

THE OLD SURREY THEATRE, WESTBAR.

2. *The Surrey Music Hall in Sheffield after the 1865 fire.*

halls developed along completely different lines and under different conditions. The early music-hall proprietors had no competition, dominated the local entertainment scene for many years and enjoyed a prominent position in their particular towns. The oldest and largest hall in Bolton was the Star which the Sharples family owned and ran from 1832 to 1860 before handing it over to a manager. In 1877 they finally sold the Star, and only then did it cease to be run as a music hall. Three years later, in 1880, the building was demolished and replaced by the Victoria Variety Theatre.[46] Thomas Youdan enjoyed a similarly dominant position in Sheffield to that of the Sharples family in Bolton. He opened the Casino in 1849 and converted it into the Surrey Music Hall in 1852. After the building was destroyed by fire in 1865 he converted the defunct Adelphi music hall, which he had bought up from a competitor in 1859 and had been using as a warehouse, into the Alexandra Music Hall. And in the 1870s he modernised the Alexandra and reopened it as the Sheffield Opera House.[47] Youdan had more competition than the Sharples for Sheffield possessed a number of other music halls. These halls, however, were continually changing hands and none of their proprietors was in a position to challenge Youdan's prominent status. The Surrey, with its capacity of 4,000, was not only Sheffield's largest music hall, it was the city's largest public building – outstanding in every respect. In Leicester the scene was dominated by two major halls for much of the period between 1863 and 1901. One of these was in the hands of the Paul family for twenty-five years, from 1863 to 1888.[48] Even before the middle of the century two music halls and their proprietors were dictating events in Leeds: Joseph Hobson and his Princess's Palace and Charles Thornton with his Music Hall, which was later known in the twentieth century as the City Varieties, a venue which became nationally famous in the 1950s as the home of the BBC series *The Good Old Days*. Thornton was the proprietor from 1857 to 1881, but at the time he was less well-known than Hobson, of whom the *Leeds Express* wrote in 1883:

> Probably there are few men in Leeds who are better known, or have been longer before the public. He has, indeed, been a very essential and important figure in our social life, and he may well take pride in the fact that during this long succession of busy years his conduct of the enterprises with which he is associated has never been called in question; while his personal qualities have gained him literally hosts of friends.[49]

Hobson had opened the Casino in 1849, renamed it the Alhambra in 1851 and changed its name yet again in 1861 to the Amphitheatre. In 1864 he turned the building into a theatre and in the same year opened the Princess's Palace which had a capacity of between four and five thousand. Hobson died in 1892 and the Princess's Palace was turned into the Tivoli Theatre of Varieties in 1898.[50] Henry Pullan enjoyed a similarly long and influential career in Bradford. Like Hobson he also started presenting entertainment in 1849 and in 1861 he opened the hall which he was to manage for more than two decades: Pullan's Music Hall. Four years later he took over the Star Music Hall in Bradford and ran that for another ten years. In 1897 the Star was taken over by the Livermore Brothers who renamed it the People's Palace. As such it became Bradford's syndicate hall.[51]

Proprietors such as Sharples, Youdan, Hobson and Pullan not only dominated the entertainment business in their towns. The manner of their presentation set the accent in content, form and tone. In his memoirs published in 1908 the Bolton journalist Robert Greenhalgh describes the Star in the following terms:

> The premises comprised a huge concert room capable of accommodating about 1500 persons, and equipped for theatrical representations, etc. Over this was a large Museum and Menagerie, with which was combined a splendid collection of waxwork, comprising likenesses of national celebrities – Royalty, statesmen, warriors, members of Parliament, and numerous other personages who had figured in history. Over the Museum was an open-air promenade and miniature garden, beautifully laid out, containing a large fishpond, statuary, and numerous ornaments. In the centre was a fully-rigged Main-mast, taken from a dismantled ship, something like 70 feet high, and a most prominent object all over the town, through its elevated position.[52]

We have already seen in Charles Morton's Canterbury that such fittings were not unusual for the period.[53] Indeed many halls reflected the personal quirks of their proprietor both in architecture and programme. After Thomas Youdan had

3. The Star Music Hall in Bolton, 1846. The picture depicts a procession of Freemasons marching past the hall in the middle of the town. The Star, bedecked with flags, is clearly more conspicuous than the church on the left – much to the displeasure of the local clergy.

completed rebuilding the Surrey in 1858 he took a whole column in the local paper to tell the inhabitants of Sheffield that: 'the whole interior has been modelled after the style of the NEW ROYAL ITALIAN OPERA HOUSE COVENT GARDEN'.[54] The programme presented in the Surrey in the late 1850s was a mixture of classics (Mendelssohn, Rossini and Verdi), comic song and dance numbers, with occasional performances by acrobats and magicians.[55] By contrast the Star in Bolton was a singing saloon in a pub and Sharples' programme was a mixture of popular culture and commercial entertainment. Amongst his performers were dialect poets and singers. On other occasions professional singers and performers were engaged from Manchester and London, and his publicity also advertised foreign artistes.[56] Whether such performers were in fact foreigners can not be established for certain, although some of them were yodellers and James Ellis's autobiography also mentions that artistes from all over England and abroad were features of the scene as early as the 1840s.[57] What is clear, in the case of Sharples, are his efforts to give the Star a mundane image. Such features were also adopted by other regional music-hall proprietors but with Sharples they were particularly noticeable.

In Bradford, Pullan differed from both Youdan and Sharples by laying consid-

erable value on the inclusion of amateurs and members of the public in his programme, either as extras, in small roles or as participants in amateur competitions, the contents of one of which was described in the following fashion:

> Singing sentimental songs with a small pig under the singer's arm, whilst seated
> upon a donkey; making a pair of boots on the stage; guessing the number of pins
> or peas in a glass bottle; hopping round the stage with a cradle in one hand and
> continually exclaiming 'I love my wife'; getting coins out of a bowl of treacle with
> the mouth, hands being tied behind the back; lacing up boots indiscriminately
> intermixed in a barrel, the one whose pair were laced up first to be the winner;
> high-kicking and walking.[58]

Thus Pullan was able to bridge the distance between stage and auditorium and
his music hall is notable for the spirit of familiarity it engendered. This feature
was further underlined by the fact that all departments of the business were
under family management. Indeed the *Bradford Observer* noted in 1886 that it
was more a clan than a family, the head of which divided his time between his
country residence in Otley and occasional visits to his music hall for the purposes
of dispensing words of wisdom and experience.

> Charley is the manager in chief; Jim is the stage-manager, four of the well-
> favoured, homely, and comely daughters officiate in the bar; and wives, sisters,
> cousins, aunts, nieces, and nephews ... have all the minor offices divided
> amongst them ... Even the members of the band are known to the audiences
> by their Christian names, and the manager himself is always alluded to as
> Charley.[59]

4. The programme cover of Pullan's Music Hall in Bradford, 1872. Just as he had done at the opening of the hall in 1869 Pullan takes great pains to emphasise its size and the comparatively luxurious furnishings in the new hall. The illustration somewhat contradicts his claims to have provided his audience with the largest and most magnificent hall in the land especially with regard to its furnishings. But such wording

Pullan followed a similar policy with regard to other halls in Bolton and Bury which he took over in the course of time.[60]

Pullan, Youdan and Sharples were music-hall proprietors the like of which could only have come to prominence outside London. Their enterprises were at the centre of affairs in more than one sense of the word for, unlike their counterparts in London, they were each situated in the heart of town. This might be obvious in smaller towns but it also holds true for much larger conurbations such as Manchester, Liverpool and Glasgow.[61]

Halls and saloons existed alongside the free-and-easies until the mid 1890s by which time the commercial music halls in London had already wiped out not only the more informal institutions but also the smaller pub-music-halls and the singing saloons. In 1891 the *Era Almanack* listed six music halls in Liverpool: in the same year the Liverpool magistrates issued a total of 325 music licences, the majority of which went to pubs and beer houses. Manchester had four listed halls: its magistrates issued 468 music licences; and 278 music licences were issued by the magistrates in Bradford with its two listed music halls.[62] True, not all these 'additional' licences went to free-and-easies, since a licence was necessary for all musical performances in public whether they were church concerts or merely an occasional piano entertainment provided by a tavern-owner. But the latter group only comprised a minority of the licences.

Unlike London the proprietors in the regions did not feel it necessary to make formal distinctions between the various types of hall and classifications were very fluid. Between November 1877 and January 1878 the *Liverpool Daily (Evening) Albion* published a series of articles on the city's music halls and singing saloons.[63] The first thing which strikes the reader is that Liverpool's two most widely known halls, the Parthenon and the Star, are not included. There is a reference to the Parthenon in 1846 which puts its ownership in the hands of the Stoll family and two generations later Oswald Stoll (1866–1942) was to control one of the major music-hall syndicates. The Star started life as a free-and-easy, changed its function to a concert room in 1847 and became the Star Music Hall in 1866, with a capacity of 1,800 to 2,000. Its interior design is said to have been modelled on the Oxford Music Hall in London.[64] At first it seems easy to see why these two halls were not included in the series, because it was conceived by the editor as a reaction to the attacks by the city's Head Constable, Major Greig, on singing and dancing saloons and free-and-easies.[65] But then again this does not explain why halls like the Alhambra, Colosseum and Gaiety should have been included. All three had a range of entrance charges and the Colosseum had a

was not meant to be taken literally. It is rather an example of the exaggerated rhetoric of superlatives typical of the music hall of the time. That said, Pullan's new hall had a capacity of 3,000 and the panelling on the ceiling was elaborately decorated. There were flower arrangements in the middle and the side walls depict allegories of the four seasons which alternate with scenes from classical antiquity, such as 'Plato as a child' or 'Amor in a rose'.

capacity of 1,600. In this respect they were no different from the Parthenon and the Star.[66] What is more surprising is the fact that the reporter on the *Albion* entitled the three halls 'Liverpool Music Saloons' and the remaining five in the series (the Constellation, the Crystal Palace, Griffith's Concert Hall, the Metropolitan and a so-called 'Unmentionable') as 'Liverpool Music Halls'. The latter five offered professional entertainment, but some of them operated with refreshment checks and none had room for more than a few hundred people. They would never have been called music halls in London. Indeed the series makes it quite clear that the criteria for 'music hall' introduced in London by Charles Morton – size and entrance charges – and adopted by the Music Hall Proprietors' Association were not applicable in the regions.

Liverpool was no exception. In its music-hall statistics for Sheffield in 1880–1 the *Era Almanack* lists the Alhambra, Fleur-de-Lis, Gaiety, London, New Star, Old Tankard (or Britannia), Pavilion, West End Palace and Criterion, most of which had been in business since the 1860s.[67] In the same year entrance charges for seven of them can be found in their advertisements in the *Sheffield Era*. The Fleur-de-Lis, West End Palace and Criterion did not charge for entrance; the Gaiety and New Star only charged on Saturdays and Mondays – 3d, of which 2d could be exchanged for 'refreshments'. Entrance to the saloon in the Old Tankard cost 3d, but seats in the gallery were free. Only the Alhambra had regular charges ranging from 2d to 1s.[68] Here too – as late as 1881 – the criteria were different from London.

The only distinction made in the regions was between free-and-easies on the one hand, and music halls, music saloons or singing saloons on the other; i.e. between predominantly amateur and predominantly professional entertainment. This principle can again be seen in the *Free Lance*, a Manchester magazine, which published a series of articles between 1866 and 1868 entitled 'How Manchester is amused'. Alongside the free-and-easies the series included articles on the city's 'three chief music halls' – the Alexandra (capacity 1,500), the London (2,000) and the People's Concert Hall (3,000) – and also on a 'lower class of music halls'.[69] According to the magazine the former 'provide facilities for obtaining beer with the music, whereas the others simply throw in music with the beer'.[70] Thus the magazine made no formal distinctions between pub-music-halls or singing saloons and the large music halls. Amongst the 'lower class of music halls' it even included the Victoria Music Hall (formerly Ben Lang's) which had a capacity of 2,000 and charged for entry, as well as four further music halls listed as such in the *Era Almanack* in 1868. Clearly the word 'lower' is not so much a reference to size as to morality. The Victoria in particular was the subject of great social dispute in the 1860s.[71] The distinction between free-and-easies and music hall and saloons can also be seen in the spread of their locations. Whereas the latter were concentrated in the city centre free-and-easies could be found in all parts of the city.

This picture was not to change until the 1890s when regional music-hall culture was further enriched by the introduction of variety theatres. This form of entertainment was regarded not only as new but also, by many people, as 'foreign' since it had been imported from the London music-hall scene.[72] Furthermore, almost all the new halls were now built in the suburbs.[73]

Suburban halls mainly belonged to a chain or syndicate. Four of the Liverpool halls were part of a chain of five owned by James Kiernan in the 1890s.[74] There was a similar picture in Manchester where Alderman William Broadhead started a chain of halls outside the city centre in Hulme, Openshaw and Colyhurst. Broadhead aimed to give his audiences 'entertainment on their own doorsteps'.[75] By the end of the century his syndicate included seventeen halls in the vicinity of Manchester. The catchment area might have remained relatively small but seen in terms of numbers Broadhead's enterprise made up quite a large part of the group of major music-hall syndicates which began to spread out, at first regionally and then nationally, in the 1890s.

Syndicates originated in the industrial cities of Northern England and Scotland. Even the best known, the Empire group owned by Moss, Stoll and Thornton, began outside London. Moss's first Empires were in Scotland. He then moved gradually down into Newcastle, Sunderland and Yorkshire from where he planned his assault on London. The Livermore Brothers, a somewhat smaller syndicate, started in Newcastle with the People's Palace and until 1900 they expanded the chain not only all over the North – Sunderland, Blackburn, Bradford, Dundee and Aberdeen – but even as far away as the ports of Plymouth and Bristol in the south-west of the country. Walter de Freece's family owned a number of halls in Liverpool in the 1870s. By 1905 he had built up a chain of Hippodromes mainly in ports and seaside resorts.[76] These syndicates had conquered a major part of the market by the outbreak of the First World War and divided it up amongst themselves. In 1914 the *Era Annual* listed seven halls in Liverpool, four of which were in the hands of three syndicates; nine halls in Manchester, five of which belonged to three syndicates; and four halls in Bradford only one of which was outside a syndicate.[77] The syndicates operating in these cities were 'Moss Empires' which comprised thirty-five halls and variety theatres by 1914; the 'Stoll Tour' with eleven halls; Walter de Freece's 'Variety Theatres Controlling Company' with nineteen halls; the 'Broadhead Tour' with sixteen halls and the 'Macnaghten Circuit' with thirteen halls.[78]

Syndicates not only dominated the regional music-hall scene until 1914. By then they had also fundamentally changed its organisation, content and style. This is most clearly expressed by the uniformity of names which were there not only to make clear that each particular hall was a part of 'its' syndicate, but that each syndicate had its own house-style and form of entertainment. Artistes were booked for the whole chain and syndicate owners managed their halls according to a set of standardised principles. A system of uniformity had now become established which, until then, had been completely alien in the regions. This process of concentration resulted in a loss of diversity, a feature which had dominated the scene in cities such as Manchester and Liverpool. In smaller towns like Bolton, Sheffield, Leeds and Bradford, halls which had been run by personalities like Sharples, Youdan, Hobson and Pullan were replaced by a wave of standardised variety theatres.[79] In the end the triumph of the syndicates, which engaged the same artistes on a nationwide basis, spelt the end of the regional music hall's close bond with folk culture, a bond which – independent of a proprietor's personality – had been its hallmark for so long and which had distinguished its programme and policies so strongly from the London halls. 'The difference in the North was that the music halls had at their disposal a wealth of folk culture on which to draw for their material and, besides, they were forced to take up this culture and adapt themselves to it in order to capture the interest of the working class public.'[80]

The great majority of the Lancashire dialect poets, composers, singers and reciters who appeared in the Bolton Star were drawn from amongst the local working population. Some of them might even have been home-weavers.[81] Their songs not only drew on traditional folksongs but also dealt with town and factory life.[82] The songs of the chairman of the Star, J. B. Geoghegan (c.1816–89) celebrated the everyday lives of the local workers, some of whom were coalminers.[83] Miners were by no means the largest group of workers in the textile town of Bolton. Nonetheless they were numerous enough to justify opening the Star for them on Monday afternoons.[84]

Sharples's programme in the Star was not the only feature directly related to local working-class culture. The museum adjoining the hall also showed strong links with local traditions and interests. It contained historical relics, parts of the human body preserved in spirits, human models which could be assembled and put back together again, a collection of technical discoveries, geological specimens, a photographic studio and stuffed animals. Amongst the latter was a leopard which had been originally intended for Sharples' menagerie, but which had killed its keeper and had then been slaughtered for exhibition.[85] In his wax cabinet members of the royal family stood alongside notorious local murderers, and in his picture gallery a portrait of the highwayman Dick Turpin hung alongside Tim Bobbin 'the Lancashire poet', Prince Albert and Napoleon.[86] All this smacks more of sensation than education. Indeed the manner of presentation shows that this effect was clearly intended. But at the same time it reflects the powerful connections with the culture and traditions of the home-weavers and the Lancashire textile workers with their interest in collecting.

> Every weaving district had its weaver-poets, biologists, mathematicians, musicians, geologists, botanists ... There are northern museums and natural history societies which still possess records or collections of lepidoptera built up by weavers; while there are accounts of weavers in isolated villages who taught themselves geometry by chalking on their flagstones, and who were eager to discuss the differential calculus. In some kinds of plain work with strong yarn a book could actually be propped on the loom and read at work.[87]

Sharples catered for such interests on a wide scale with his museum whereas his competitor Finley Frazer preferred to restrict his exhibition to butterflies.[88] In this way both men kept up local traditions, but in a new fashion: within the framework of a capitalist enterprise, the developing entertainment industry.

There is also a clear link between folk and working-class cultural traditions in the Tyneside music halls, where a number of working-class singers from Newcastle and the surrounding regions achieved national celebrity. Most notable amongst them were Joe Wilson, Ned Corvan and Bobby Nunn who lost his sight in an accident at work. To keep out of the poorhouse Nunn took a number of casual jobs, turning the lathe-wheels of cabinet-makers and making bird-cages, before trying his hand as a part-time entertainer in the evenings.[89] The careers of Wilson (1848–75) and Corvan (1830 or 1831–65) had similar patterns. Both suffered from tuberculosis and were forced to give up their jobs as printer and sailmaker respectively. As a result they tried to find some form of employment elsewhere.[90] Despite their new roles as entertainers they retained much of their old identity and in this they were typical of many others. Wilson performed in his working clothes and his songs dealt with the everyday life and problems of working people. Corvan parodied local characters and sang about the problems of survival on the edge of poverty and other working-class experiences.[91] He supported the 1851 seamen's strike and gave money from his performances to seafarers' charities. According to Dave Harker he sang not only for workers but also 'on behalf of – and, in effect, from within – that network of communities', from which he came and to which he still felt an attachment.[92] Even after they had achieved fame, Nunn, Corvan and Wilson still remained strongly attached to their roots. Some syndicate-owners, like Richard Thornton, also came from such backgrounds. Thornton's father was an itinerant musician who performed with his son around the pubs of Newcastle until they had accumulated enough money to open their own venue. From the 1890s until the end of the century Richard Thornton gradually built up a nationwide syndicate of halls, thereby contributing to the standardisation of music-hall entertainment throughout the country.[93]

2

The music-hall programme

In an article entitled 'Customs, Capital and Culture in the Victorian Music Hall' Peter Bailey has attributed the success of music halls in the nineteenth century to the fact that they managed to subsume features of pre-industrial folk culture – the pubs and the pleasure gardens, the fairgrounds and street entertainment, betting shops and brothels, and also lecture rooms and schools – and adapt them to the parameters of a new urban world.[1]

It has been difficult to recognise this richness of variety mirrored in studies on the music-hall programme to date. Most authors have concentrated their attention on comic songs and singers in London.[2] Such an approach is not entirely without justification for comic songs were the main element of music-hall entertainment from the start and their texts were the subject of academic research at a relatively early point.

One of the first studies on the halls was a German thesis written in 1929 by Eberhard Voigt on music-hall songs and public life in England. What most interested him were the laws of the 'low muse' (as he called it), especially the relationship between day-to-day politics, political music-hall songs at the turn of the century and the 'soul of the English masses'. Voigt regarded the political music-hall song as the expression of the political and literary culture of the music-hall audience: a conservative culture, 'utterly and unbearably unaesthetic'.[3] The first detailed British studies of music-hall songs appeared in the 1950s and can be divided into two groups. The first group consists of relatively comprehensive but purely descriptive portraits of the most popular songs and the roles their singers incorporated.[4] The authors identified the main themes of the songs as politics and patriotism, structures of friendship, love and marriage, the everyday life of the lower classes, work, leisure, the authorities (mainly the police) and lastly, aspects of urban life, a favourite feature of which was the transport system. The second group consists of studies of music-hall songs in relation to the overall songs of the era. The early authors also took a mainly descriptive approach and more analytic writings only began to appear around the mid 1970s.[5] The main points of interest here were either working-class features in the songs or, like Voigt, the relationship between the political leanings in the song texts and the political attitudes and behaviour of the audience.

Voigt had no problems in seeing a direct parallel between the content of the texts and the attitudes of the audience. Recent studies by Laurence Senelick,

Gareth Stedman Jones, Penelope Summerfield and Dave Russell are considerably more cautious, mainly because of the blatant contradiction between the working classes' overwhelmingly Liberal voting patterns and the conservative tenor of the songs. Some of the main questions still under discussion are: whether the songs did indeed mirror the attitudes of the audience or whether they were an attempt to influence them; who wrote the songs; and whether there was any censorship.[6] Social and literary historians like Peter Bailey and Jacqueline Bratton have also approached the subject from these points of view. Their work has been orientated on debates on models of social control, the Gramscian concept of hegemony, structuralist literary interpretations and, most recently, linguistic analyses of discourse and practices.[7]

In the first two parts of this chapter I shall try to summarise the current state of research into music-hall songs and outline the main stage characterisations in which they were presented. I shall then give a more complete picture of the music-hall programme as a whole and the way it developed. Here I shall concentrate my analysis on the programme in the regional halls as a counterbalance to the earlier parts whose sources are mostly drawn from London.

SONGS

The major theme of nineteenth-century music-hall songs has been identified as the everyday life of the working classes which was celebrated in great detail and commented on ironically, realistically and sentimentally. This can be further sub-divided into the following groups, some of which overlap: love, marriage and the family; urban life and housing conditions; work and leisure; social conditions, poverty and old age; and politics and patriotism. But, as in all genres of song, love was the favourite theme in the music halls. Here it was either portrayed as a rose-tinted dream of bliss or a comic disaster.[8] But more down-to-earth aspects of love also featured in the halls. Sex – in stark contrast to Victorian middle-class notions – was not taboo but a source of celebration and enjoyment.[9] Furthermore, music-hall songs took the subject to its logical end by dealing with marriage and family life. Here there is no more talk of bliss from either the male or female standpoint. In the songs it was mostly the women who were eager to seal the bonds of love in marriage, but when it came to singing the joys of married life, both sides were as a rule in agreement: it was a disaster.[10]

One of the favourite domestic characters was the mother-in-law. Married life was complicated enough without her. She made it even more difficult. But the humour was not simply at the expense of women. Music-hall songs often showed a great deal of understanding for their situation, particularly in their description of the problems caused by drunken husbands or ever-recurring pregnancies.[11]

Seen as a whole the prosaic aspects of everyday family life were the favourite topics in the songs: conflicts between married partners, a quickly growing

number of children which resulted in a lowering of living standards, the consequent visit to the pawnbroker and secretly moving house at night because of
failure to keep up with the rent.

Most members of the audience had direct knowledge of such problems and
the songs have been convincingly interpreted as a general expression of their
personal experiences. But scholars have also seen them as being more than just
a reflection. Jacqueline Bratton has pointed out that in the music hall at least
nobody was suffering alone. Indeed the singers took upon themselves the daily
burdens of their audience by proxy and demonstrated how such problems could
be solved or at least made bearable.[12]

This was also the case in songs about urban housing, especially in London.
The following example, as sung by Gus Elen, describes the living conditions of
the London working-class from their point of view and demonstrates how they
can be seen in a positive light.

> If you saw my little back yard, 'Wot a pretty spot!' you'd cry –
> It's a picture on a sunny summer day;
> Wiv the turnip tops and cabbages wot people doesn't buy
> I makes it on a Sunday look all gay.
> The neighbours finks I grows 'em and you'd fancy you're in
>   Kent,
> Or at Epsom if you gaze into the mews –
> It's a wonder as the landlord doesn't want to raise the rent,
> Because we've got such nobby distant views.
>
> Oh! It really is a werry pretty garden,
> And Chingford to the eastward could be seen;
> Wiv a ladder and some glasses,
> You could see to 'Ackney marshes,
> If it wasn't for the 'ouses in between.[13]

Other themes dealt with in this group were the delicate relationships between
landlord and tenants, and between tenants (particularly women) and sub-
tenants.[14]

But urban living was not confined to housing problems. The songs also dealt
with broader themes of urban living, such as the benefits of public transport or
the drawbacks of officialdom, but most of all how to turn any difficulties to your
own advantage. Here the local audience were confronted with familiar problems
and could laugh about them together. At the same time the songs enabled many
a stranger from abroad or the countryside to get to know the rules and rites of
metropolitan life. Songs about officials and civil servants offered a common
opportunity to mock those in authority, figures against which an individual was
generally powerless. The favourite scapegoat here was the policeman who,
according to Jacqueline Bratton, was the literary successor to the parson, the
major source of mockery in earlier pamphlets and ballads. But the bobby on the
beat was not simply the representative of authority. He also typified any form of

upward-climber who was trying to escape his proletarian background by taking a job, however mean, in public service.[15] People who attempted to disguise or deny their social background were particular figures of fun in the halls.

The character of the policeman illuminates a structural principle in music-hall songs: the personalisation of the general and the abstract. Songs did not deal with the police but with the policeman; not with war but with soldiers; not with work but workers. In London these included bus-drivers, milkmen, domestic servants and newspaper boys, and in the regions carters and miners.

'In music hall', wrote Stedman Jones, 'work is an evil to be avoided when possible.'[16] This is true in so far as music-hall songs clearly preferred leisure to work and a surprise legacy or a betting win to the wearisome toil to make ends meet. But the songs did not only portray work as a necessary evil. The so-called motto songs of a man like Harry Clifton with such uplifting titles as 'Work, Boys, Work and Be Contented' were highly popular with audiences. And songs which dealt with workers also expressed great pride in the work itself. The chairman of the Star in Bolton, J. G. Geoghegan, was the author of the following song: 'Down in a Coal Mine'.

> I am a jovial collier lad and blithe as blithe can be,
> For let the times be good or bad they're all the same to me;
> 'Tis little of the world I know and careless of its ways,
> For where the dog-star never glows, I wear away my days.
>
> Chorus
>
> Down in a coal-mine underneath the ground,
> Where a gleam of sunshine never can be found;
> Digging dusky diamonds all the seasons round,
> Down in a coal-mine underneath the ground.
>
> My hands are horny, hard and black with working in the vein,
> And like the clothes upon my back, my speech is rough and
>   plain;
> Well, if I stumble with my tongue, I've one excuse to say
> 'Tis not the collier's heart that's wrong, 'tis the head that goes
>   astray.
>
> Chorus
>
> At every shift be't soon or late I haste my bread to earn
> And anxiously my kindred wait and watch for my return;
> For Death that levels all alike, whate'er the rank may be,
> Amid the fire and damp may strike and flings his darts at me.
>
> Chorus
>
> How little do the great ones care who sit at home secure,
> What hidden dangers colliers dare, what hardships they
>   endure;
> The very fires their mansions boast to cheer themselves and
>   wives,

Mayhap were kindled at the cost of jovial colliers' lives.

Chorus

Then cheer up lads and make ye much of every joy ye can,
But let your mirth be always such as best becomes a man;
However Fortune turns about we'll still be jovial souls,
For what would England be without the lads that look for
      coals.

Chorus.[17]

Geoghegan's miner goes into detail about his work in the proud knowledge of its value to the nation. By so doing Geoghegan was almost certainly giving expression to the self-appraisal of a part of the audience in the Star. More particularly he was helping to upgrade the public image of the miner whose work was generally either ignored or looked down on.

Although work as a theme in music-hall songs was anything but neglected, leisure was still more attractive. Whilst there are scarcely any documented examples of songs about factory work there are countless songs about hard-won leisure activities such as the shorter working week and the free Saturday afternoon or places like the botanical gardens or beach promenades. The latter can be ascribed to the category of 'rational recreation'. But there were also songs about betting shops, horse-racing, picnics and pub visits, which naturally included the pleasures of eating and drinking. As with love the music hall confirmed and glorified forms of behaviour which were an integral part of the audience's everyday life but which were regarded as socially unacceptable by other classes. This is why some writers have perceived the music hall as the working class's most unmistakable answer to middle-class attempts at discipline.[18] Nonetheless the atmosphere in the halls was not thoroughly hedonistic. Despite the celebration of leisure, eating, drinking and other forms of pleasure the performers in the halls did not neglect the unpleasant side of life. There are many songs about poverty in all its forms: poverty in old age and as a result of having no work, forced emigration due to poverty and the social neglect of the poor. Such songs had a powerful effect because they portrayed situations which were only too well known to the audiences and which might at any moment affect them personally. The following examples give some idea of their power. The first is a sketch set in a workhouse and two men are discussing the evening meal.

Well, Jimmy, did you get it?
No, did you?
Yes – the smell of it.[19]

The dialogue can be found in the memoirs of W. Freer, the son of a hand-weaver and himself a textile worker. Freer claims it was performed in Glasgow in the 1850s and writes of the audience response:

We must, I fear, have been extraordinarily simple folks at that time, for this sort of stuff was received with shrieks of laughter and vociferous applause. Perhaps it was because we were all wretchedly poor ourselves and felt a certain comfort in knowing that some folks were even not so well off as we were.[20]

Clearly the situation described was close to the skin of any member of the working class, and yet it was resolved through laughter. This was not always the case. Nor was it a necessary precondition for success. H. Chance Newton's description of the audience reaction to Charles Godfrey's song scenes from the Crimean War also shows the importance of authenticity.

Godfrey's vigorous acting of the neglected old soldier in this sketch raised vast audiences to an almost incredible pitch of enthusiasm. Alike in London and the Provinces have I seen him move the patrons of the 'halls' to volcanic excitement and to thunders of applause!

This was especially the case when he came to the part where the now starving old tramp warrior applied for a night's shelter at the workhouse casual ward.

'Be off, you tramp!' exclaims the harsh janitor. 'You are not wanted here!'

'No!' thunders the tattered veteran. 'I am not wanted here! But at Balaclava – I was wanted there!'

So deep was the effect of this 'On Guard' sketch of Charlie's, and especially his showing up of the then all-too-prevalent neglect of many of those who had fought for King and Country, that the War Office people of the period took steps to have the sketch 'barred' in some quarters, as it threatened to be 'prejudicial to recruiting'.[21]

Music-hall songs might have lamented the social injustices in the country, but as a rule they made little attempt to propose changes to the *status quo*. Class society was accepted as a fact and anyone who attempted to break out of their class was a good subject for mockery. Policemen were not the only targets. Socially ambitious artisans and clerks and even, occasionally, working-class leaders were made objects of ridicule.

As little Tich put it, in his sketch of the gas-meter collector, 'My brother's in the gas trade too, you know. In fact he travels on gas. He's a socialist orator.[22]

Members of the upper classes were not spared either but they had no more to fear from the music hall than mockery. It is therefore no surprise that political music-hall songs never really attacked the system as such. This particular group of songs has been more researched than any other. It dealt with events and trends both at home and abroad and covered practically every theme imaginable.[23]

One of the most recurrently popular domestic themes were the conflicts between Liberals and Conservatives, symbolised in the figures of Gladstone and Disraeli. Ireland was also dealt with. The various electoral reforms and women's voting rights were very popular subjects. The latter, as might be expected, provided a good excuse for scornful and sarcastic comments. Scandals, particularly in politics, were exceptionally popular since they could be pinned on a specific

41

person rather than on an abstract theme. This was especially the case with Dilkes and Parnell where marital problems led to political scandals. In this way politics itself could be personalised. But in the main performers preferred to deal with the concrete experiences of their audiences rather than their superiors and this gave rise to songs about social politics. Samuel Plimsoll, who fought hard for better working-conditions for seafarers was as likely to appear on stage as Disraeli.

Such themes were in the political and socially critical traditions of broadsides and ballad-singers. But the halls gave them a new tone. The topical songs lacked the bite with which the broadsides and street ballads attacked social injustices. They were not only less abrasive, they were more sentimental. The audiences were meant to be driven to tears, not to the barricades. And any alternative to the prevailing state of affairs was not as a rule to be found in a better and brighter future but in the 'good old days'.

When it came to events abroad almost everything was covered. Songs dealt with the Crimean War, the Franco-German War of 1870/1, the Suez crisis, colonial policies in Africa and the Boer War. Their attitude towards such events was at the same time unequivocally patriotic and contradictory. For the protagonists' readiness to fight for their country differed considerably from song to song. This is shown most clearly in one of the best-known songs belonging to this group – and also in its parody – MacDermott's *We don't want to fight*, which introduced the word 'Jingoism' into the English language.[24]

> The Dogs of War are loose and the rugged Russian Bear,
> Full bent on blood and robbery has crawled out of his lair.
> As peacemaker old England her very utmost tried,
> The Russians said they wanted peace, but then those
>   Russians lied,
> Of carnage and of trickery they'll have sufficient feast,
> Ere they dare to think of coming near our Road into the
>   East.
>
> Chorus
>
> We don't want to fight, but by Jingo if we do,
> We've got the ships, we've got the men, and got the money
>   too.
> We've fought the Bear before, and while we're Britons true,
> The Russians shall not have Constantinople.

The song was extremely popular and it is claimed that wherever it was performed the audience sang along with such fervour that they almost brought the roof down. But the parody is supposed to have been just as popular.

> I don't want to fight, I'll be slaughtered if I do!
> I'll change my togs and sell my kit and pop my rifle too!
> I don't like the war, I ain't no Briton true,
> And I'd let the Russians have Constantinople.

> Newspapers talk of Russian hate, of its ambition tell;
> They want a war because it makes the papers sell.
> Let all those politicians who desire to help the Turk
> Put on the uniform themselves...

If MacDermott's song was popular because of its patriotic sentiments, the parody was equally so because it portrayed war from the viewpoint of the man in the street (at whose expense it was being conducted) and gave him the opportunity to voice his refusal to be turned into cannon-fodder in the interests of others. Memories of the Crimean War were still vivid in the minds of the men who had fought there. They had not only been badly fed and quartered, they had suffered from the appalling tactical errors of their commanders and been miserably treated on their return home. Such experiences had made a great and lasting impression on collective popular consciousness and they were kept alive by their re-working in the halls. Charles Godfrey's sketch has already been cited. But the author has also described an earlier version of the sketch. It gives a vivid insight into the staging of the genre and the intended effect on the audience.

> The first scene is laid in the trenches before Sebastopol, where a solitary soldier stands valiantly 'on guard' until a chance bullet from the enemy lays him low. The exterior of a village churchyard forms scene II, with a dimly-lit church in the background, from which issues the music of the organ and the choir in more or less luminous strains. The old Crimean hero, enfeebled with age and work, now enters, and after bewailing the neglect of his country whose foes he has fought so well, sinks down on a convenient gravestone, where he dies to the accompaniment of slow music and a fall of snow.[25]

Writers on the halls have described patriotic songs as both 'anti-heroic' (Stedman Jones) and 'heroic' (Bratton). They were anti-heroic because they refused to glorify war, and heroic because they sang of the heroic deeds not of the generals but of the little man. Here, as in other groups of songs, the audience was able to recognise, endorse and celebrate itself. But the equivocal nature of patriotic songs is only characteristic of the early decades of the Music Hall. By the time of the Boer War any reservations about British war-mongering activities had disappeared entirely. Songs dealing with foreign affairs were now unequivocal in their conservative opinions even though such views ran contrary to the attitudes and actions of a large part of the audiences who visited the music halls.[26]

Two explanations have been offered for this. Stedman Jones claims that as a result of the growing Liberal participation in the temperance movements since the 1860s, music-hall proprietors were more or less forced into the arms of the Tories and allowed themselves to be used as their mouthpieces. He also puts down the popularity of conservative songs to the growth – in London, if nowhere else – of the lower-middle-class element in the audiences.[27] Penny Summerfield, on the other hand, attributes the gradual change towards conservatively orientated songs to the potentially increasing pressure of the licensing authorities on

5. *The cover of the sheet music for J.B. Geoghegan's song 'England is England still'. The Union Jack topped with a crown may have pride of place but the song does not celebrate members of royalty. Its heroes are workers and sailors shown against a background of their workplaces and with their working tools. The message of the song was that England owed its economical and political power to these people. Nonetheless the crown is deliberately set in the middle. The basic attitude behind political music-hall songs was not only patriotic but monarchist.*

music-hall proprietors. As a result the latter resorted to self-censorship and took preventative action to ensure that only certain types of songs were performed, whilst others were repressed.[28]

Whether this development was spontaneous or forced, the new type of political song was a failure. It exerted no influence on the audience and gradually lost what meaning it might have had altogether. Even Voigt had noted this process of deterioration after the turn of the century and Laurence Senelick sums it up as a failure of the music hall 'to cast back an accurate reflection of the political opinions of its audiences'. This would become particularly evident in 1914, when 'the halls found themselves recruiting for a war that was against the best interest of a great part of their audiences. The result, in the early twentieth century, was a rapid decline of the music hall as a political commentator and withdrawal from major public concerns.'[29]

CHARACTERS

The following section will deal with the main characters who appeared on the music-hall stage. By 'characters' I mean the stage personae which the performers created by means of costume, make-up, accent, body language and behavioural patterns. The characters not only gave the music hall its own special style; in their dynamic interplay with the audience they presented, reflected, commented on and created images of social selves.

Characters first appeared in the halls at a very early stage, though not at first in Charles Morton's Canterbury. Here, as a matter of policy, the singers appeared in evening dress and presented their songs as in a classical concert in order to underline the respectability of the establishment. But here too it was not long before performers began to present their songs in certain roles which in turn developed into standard characters. The performers did not aim to present complex individuals but typical patterns of behaviour which were closely related to the text and which optically underlined it.[30] Performers not only sang songs from the viewpoint of a soldier, milkman or domestic servant but, to enable the audience to identify with them even more personally, they would dress accordingly. Depending on the style and approach of the song the costumes would be stylised; romanticised or exaggerated to the point of being grotesque.

It is possible to identify three main groups of characters in the music hall. The man-in-the-street and his everyday attitudes and habits at home, at work and at leisure. Ethnic characters in the broadest sense of the word: Irishmen, Scotsmen, Cockneys, Northerners (especially from Lancashire and Yorkshire) and black people. And characters based on gender. Of the second group the Irish and black people were already popular stage-figures of fun long before the music hall existed. In both cases the humour reflected attitudes which were not entirely free

45

of colonialist contempt. Black characters became known from minstrel shows which had been imported from the USA. Here blacked-up white performers presented a mainly idealised version of the everyday life and culture of American blacks in the cotton fields. As a rule there would be more dancing and singing on the plantations than work. Ulrich Schneider and Michael Pickering have pointed out that in the halls black and Irish people fulfilled differing but at times overlapping and simultaneously contradictory functions. Both suffered from massive social prejudices and were regarded as lazy, slow, ridiculous and given to drink. Given these alleged characteristics they were very easy and effective targets for an audience which was overwhelmingly white, Anglican and English.[31] But both groups also typified the quintessence of foreignness and exoticism – the emerald island and the plantation – and were for this reason additionally attractive on quite another level. This also applied to Scotsmen, with the difference that the character of 'the Scotsman' only came to the fore outside the borders of Scotland towards the end of the nineteenth century.[32]

The Irishman was not only popular for his exoticism. In cities with a high proportion of Irish immigrants like London or Liverpool the character also served as a figure of identification, someone who kept up the traditions and customs of his homeland and put them on public display. If one part of the audience regarded this as exotic, another saw in it an expression of national pride and the upkeep of traditions. This was all the more true because the character of the Irishman was not always presented as a source of ridicule and scorn. In this way it exactly fulfilled a dual function which was the hallmark of most music-hall characters. It did not simply mirror a particular section of the audience; this mirror confirmed a particular identity and simultaneously distorted it. This is especially clear in the case of characters whose humour was based on gender, whereby the presentation of female characters in particular often overstepped conventional boundaries or even publicly sanctioned such infringements. There were two major kinds of parody. The first can best be illustrated by quoting an extract from F. Anstey's *Mr Punch's Model Music-Hall Songs and Dramas*. Under the pretext of outlining a series of possible standard numbers Anstey presents us with a clichéd typology providing many basic details of the content, style and performance involved. The title of the number is 'The Idyllic' and the accompanying picture gives a reasonably accurate idea of the character-type and appearance of certain female music-hall singers.

> The following ballad will not be found above the heads of the average audience, while it is constructed to suit the capacities of almost any lady artiste.

> SO SHY

> The singer should, if possible, be of mature age, and inclined to a comfortable *embonpoint*. As soon as the bell has given the signal for the orchestra to attack the prelude, she will step upon the stage with that air of being hung on wires, which seems to come from a consciousness of being a favourite of the public.

'I'm a dynety little dysy of the dingle,'

(Self-praise is a great recommendation – in Music-hall songs.)

'So retiring and so timid and so coy. If you ask me why so
long I have lived single, I will tell you – 'tis because I'm so
shoy.'

(Note the manner in which the rhyme is adapted to meet Arcadian peculiarities
of pronunciation.)

SPOKEN – 'Yes, I am – really, though you wouldn't think it
to look at me, would you? But, for all that, -

CHORUS – When I'm spoken to, I wriggle, Going off into a
giggle, And as red as any peony I blush; Then turn paler
than a lily, For I'm such a little silly, That I'm always in a
flutter or a flush!'

(After each chorus an elaborate step-dance, expressive of
shrinking maidenly modesty.)[33]

Here we are presented with a distortion of a Victorian ideal: the shy, gracious
and well-behaved young lady. Social conventions are ridiculed and destroyed.
But at the same time such an unconventional portrayal can be interpreted as an
expression of independence and self-confidence. According to Jacqueline
Bratton the figure might have served as a source of identification and affirmation for many working-class women in the audience who likewise did not
conform to socially accepted conventions.[34]

The complementary figure to the 'shy maiden' was the 'naughty girl'.[35] The
character presented here was an ambivalent embodiment of both innocence and
experience. On the one hand she wore a little-girl costume and sang a text which
was superficially respectable. But hidden beneath both costume and text was
something distinctly more worldly and knowing. And a good performer like
Marie Lloyd was able to reveal this merely by raising her eyebrows, pursing her
lips, swinging her hips, by the wave of a hand or even a finger. It was left to the
audience's imagination to read between the lines of the text and recognise the
vulgarity beneath it. The cover of the sheet music entitled 'Our Lodger's Such a
Nice Young Man' illustrates this perfectly. It shows the picture of an apparently
innocent little girl and at the same time provides extracts from the text which
give the lie to this completely. 'He kisses mama and all of us, 'cos papa was away'
and 'At nights he makes the beds and does the other little jobs.' As Ulrich
Schneider has written: 'The typical Victorian image of the woman as a lily or a
rose, as the madonna or Mary Magdalene was much more subject to polarisa-
tion than the image of the man. The particular attraction of the naughty girl lay
in the fact that it blurred the lines of demarcation.'[36] To which it might be added
that many women in the audience also rejected such lines of demarcation in
their lives and the attractive alternatives offered in the halls only served to
confirm their views and strengthen their self-confidence.

THE IDYLLIC.

6. The Idyllic. Costume, hairstyle, face and figure give a good example of the parody involved in such 'characters'.

There is no exact parallel in the portrayal of male characters. Instead the music hall developed a character in the 1860s which for two decades was to become the most representative and popular of them all: the *lion comique*, immortalised in George Leybourne's portrayal of 'Champagne Charlie'. Although the character shared certain social features with a particular section of the audience, most importantly it personified everything the music hall stood for.

The *lion comique* was a splendid and multiplicitous figure whose outward appearance was directly descended from the 'swell', a character which had been a well-known literary and social phenomenon up until the middle of the nineteenth century. 'The dandy had been a genuine character, found in the main among the leisured classes only. Beau Brummell, though the grandson of a "gentleman's gentleman", had been educated at Eton, and ... he was (until they quarrelled) a personal friend of the Prince Regent. The feature of his dress was elegant simplicity.'[37] The dandy was the principal social model for the *lion comique*. But even in his outward appearance it was clear that the *lion comique* was a sham whose image was a far cry from elegant simplicity. The conspicuously narrow trousers, the imposing fur coat, the gloves, the large handkerchief which could be pulled from the waistcoat, the obligatory walking cane, the fat cigar, the rakish hat, the lion-like whiskers and, most important of all, glittering accessories such as monocle, golden toothpick and large diamond rings were all a part of the standard equipment of the *lion comique*. The parody lay in the exaggeration of the role model and the social group to which it belonged. It was not simply an imitation but also a vulgar appropriation. For it signalised that certain life styles were no longer the exclusive domain of the upper classes.[38]

The character not only provided many opportunities to take a swipe at the upper classes, middle-class values could also be thoroughly whipped. For the *lion comique* was by definition lazy and hedonistic and his repertoire of songs – with a few dishonourable exceptions – were hymns of praise to the virtues of idleness, womanising and drinking.[39] George Leybourne (Champagne Charlie) and his best-known rival Alfred Vance (Cool Burgundy Ben) sang their way down the complete drinks menu. And an expanding drink trade, which appropriated some of the *lions*, ensured that they also drank their way through them.[40] Both music-hall proprietors and drink manufacturers ensured that the *lion comiques* not only played out their roles on stage but also off it. When William Holland bought up George Leybourne to revive the Canterbury in 1868 he required him by contract to appear every day and at all reasonable times and places in a carriage drawn by four horses driven by two postillions and accompanied by grooms. The promotion was such a success that the *lion comique* quickly became one of the most popular characters in the halls. The fact that the performers were forced to play out their role in life also brought many of them to an early grave. Leybourne was only forty-four when he died and his death certificate indicated a probable cirrhosis of the liver. Vance died at forty-nine.[41] The way in which both characters met their end only confirmed the opinions of their critics that the character of the *lion comique* was unhealthy, raffish and vulgar: 'an exaggeration of what used to be called a "cheap gent", whose manner towards his audience is offensively impertinent and familiar, whose conversation is liberally garnished with slang, and whose experience is confined to the lowest kinds of fast life, and the worst developments of human nature'.[42] Such aversion sprang principally from the dread of the *lion comique*'s popularity and its attraction for a working-class audience. 'Critics of *lions* ... believed that they encouraged an unhealthy adulation and the wasting of money ... drove men away from steady habits, temperance, religion and other virtues necessary for getting ahead.'[43]

What made the *lion comique* so popular? Scholars have provided a number of reasons. I have already alluded to the subversive mockery of aristocratic and middle-class life styles. Furthermore the *lion comique* spoke directly to the audiences in the halls and offered them the chance to forget their every-day cares for an hour or two and escape into fantasy. By singing along in the chorus refrains the audience was able to participate vicariously in the role of the performer.[44] More basically the *lion comique* suggested to his audience that it was possible for anyone with a bit of luck or initiative to become a swell. Many performers maintained they had themselves only been given the chance by an unexpected inheritance – or a cheap tailor. And it was possible for any clerk or worker to go to a cheap tailor and play out the role of the swell in their spare time. Peter Bailey has demonstrated that the mid-nine-teenth-century swell did not only come from amongst the ranks of the upper classes. As early as the 1830s contemporary observers noted the emergence of a new sub-culture which spread predominantly amongst the lower middle-class. The counterfeit swell was especially attractive to upstart clerks and apprentices who were able to make use of cheaper mass-produced clothing to dress up in style if not in substance.[45] Swells, both real and imitation, made up a considerable part of music-hall audiences and, like many other music-hall characters, the *lion comique* with all his strengths and weaknesses was a powerful figure of orientation and identification. As such he embodied an extremely complex phenomenon which offered the audience various different opportunities for identification or rejection. Depending on your attitude he was (according to Peter Bailey) a role-model, an alternative to the middle-class ideals of abstinence and industriousness or a caricature of the aristoc-racy. The cheap imitation version also gave the audience a chance to laugh at themselves or their neighbours.[46] All these features contributed to the immense popularity of the *lion comique* who was the most loved of all music-hall characters in the 1860s and seventies. Indeed, in the end he was not so much a character as an institution. And he was treated as such. George Leybourne's offstage appearances in his coach and horses were seen as an ideal opportunity for satirical comment by his rivals, especially Walter Laburnum who was very similar to Leybourne in appearance. Much to the delight of the people of London Laburnum processed through the streets of the city in a cart drawn by four donkeys.[47]

But it was on stage that the *lion comique* was the object of most parody. And here women came into their own in the role of male impersonators. It is no suprise that the clothes and outward appearance of the *lion comique* came in for most ridicule. One of the most popular of the female swells, Nellie Farren (or Power) had a song which went:

> How d'you like the la-di-da,
>   the toothpick, and the crutch?
> How did you get those trousers on,
>   and did they hurt you much?[48]

It was only a short step from mocking the surface appearance to demasking the pretentiousness of the whole character, especially in its counterfeit version.

> And he wears a penny flower in his coat, lah di dah!
> And a penny paper collar round his throat, lah di dah!
> In his hand a penny stick,
> In his mouth a penny pick,
> And a penny in his pocket, lah di dah![49]

Nellie Power was one of the first male impersonators to exploit the comic possibilities of the popular theatre tradition of men in women's clothing by reversing it. Given the social expectations of strict gender conformity, debunking men and throwing doubt on their masculinity was not only comic but also potentially scandalous.[50] Once again it was women who overstepped the boundaries of social conformities in the halls.

That the *lion comique* as a character came in for parody thereby inspiring the invention of a new stage character is not only a sign of his popularity but more significantly points to his outstanding status in the music hall itself. Peter Bailey has summarised the swell as a 'vehicle devised to gratify the self-images of music-hall-world' because he was the embodiment of everything the music hall stood for: alcohol, bombast and glitter all in the *grande style* of the halls.[51] This self-made grandeur was also reflected in their publicity, particularly in its form of wording. A contemporary critic exposed what he saw as the inflated vocabulary used by proprietors in the following manner.

> In six-feet letters of green, on a yellow ground, the public is informed that Peter
> (the Great) Wilkins will, all next week, and till further notice, continue to
> enchant crowded audiences with his eminently successful song of 'All round my
> hat; or, Who stole the donkey?' Likewise that the Inimitable Brown, the
> Irresistible Smith, and the Delightful Robinson will variously 'electrify', and
> 'convulse' and 'occasion shrieks of mirth', amongst their kind patrons.[52]

The halls and their proprietors were never lacking in self-confidence. Joe Hobson in Leeds described the entertainment on offer as 'the Greatest Sixpennyworth in the World'. As such the *lion comique* was the personal embodiment of this self-assessment and in the 1860s and seventies its most powerful form of publicity.

In their examinations of prominent characters in the halls and the images they reflected and (re)created, recent scholars have done much to broaden our understanding of what was behind the songs. They have thrown light onto their terms of references, their relationship to literary and socio-cultural traditions, and the nature of the social relationships to which they gave expression and commented on.[53] Such research has also contributed to a much more substantial discussion of whether the music hall was indeed a *vox populi* or a manipulative capitalist enterprise and has led to a more differentiated view of the halls. Referring mainly to the work of Peter Bailey, Patrick Joyce has come to define music hall 'as a laboratory of social style and self-definition in which both old ways and new possibilities were constantly explored'.[54] This exploration took the form of a lively discourse between stage and auditorium.

In a recent article, Bailey himself has made a detailed exploration of the nature of this discourse and its consequences.[55] Almost from the start, he argues, songs and characters endowed the halls with a certain style, content and meaning familiar only to the performers and regular audiences. Thus an exclusive community was created which shared a common 'knowing' culture, practically inaccessible to outsiders. 'Knowingness' is the key word for Bailey because it worked as a 'discourse and practice' in the halls and was regarded as their distinctive hallmark outside. It 'pulled the crowd into a closed yet allusive frame of reference ... implicating them in a select conspiracy of meaning that animates them as a specific audience'.[56] It was the characters and their songs with their references to their listeners' experiences and feelings, the catch-phrases, the *ad-lib* spoken commentary and patter between the verses (where performers sometimes stepped out of character) and the commonly sung refrains which transformed shifting crowds into attentive audiences and created a particular feeling of community. In-house censorship and the proprietors' endeavour to attract new, middle-class audiences resulted in changes of style and content in the last quarter of the nineteenth century but:

> knowingness continued its ironic counterpoint to the language of respectability ... The prime device lay in the 'things of suggestion', and as control tightened and actual time on stage contracted it was the compressed code of the *double entendre* and the innuendo that signalled complicity with an audience, investing language, tone and gesture with oblique but knowing conspiracies of meaning.[57]

The purity reformers on the London County Council summed up this mode of expression in the 1890s as not so much what was said but the way it was said – or left unsaid. But when they were challenged to expose the disgraceful matters which they alleged were being left unsaid they were unable to do so without laying themselves open to the charge of being themselves dirty-minded. Their views, however, did not represent middle-class attitudes as a whole. For both Bailey and Michael Mason (in a recent study of Victorian sexuality) have pointed out that the bourgeoisie did not consist entirely of prudes and puritans. On the contrary, a substantial number rejected such attitudes and took pleasure in the mockery they incurred.[58]

Sexual allusions did, of course, play a major role in music-hall 'knowingness'. But the concept also had a wider and more practical aspect. For songs and performers continually dealt with the pitfalls and problems of everyday urban life in a rapidly changing industrial and urban environment. In doing so they not only informed their audiences of the problems and enabled them to participate in them. They also gave them a chance to come to terms with them in whatever way they chose. This aspect was not only restricted to songs and characters. It will recur yet again in the next section which concentrates on the other parts of the music-hall programme

VARIETY

In terms of both quality and quantity the songs and character-types I have examined in the previous sections were the most significant features of the music-hall programme. They were the first things one associated with the music hall and as such they gave it its distinct image. But the music hall programme as a whole was considerably more variegated and I shall now examine its structure and development between 1840 and 1900 on the basis of printed programmes, advertisements in the press and the account books of various provincial proprietors.[59] Every music-hall programme consisted of three principal components: circus numbers, music and theatre, and information and innovations. These elements were taken over from the fairs, pleasure gardens, travelling players, mechanics' institutes etc. and gathered together as a heterogeneous, but nonetheless coherent whole.[60]

Thanks to Thomas Sharples, who laid great importance on advertising, there is a good deal of written evidence on the programme in the Star Inn as early as the 1840s. To begin with the circus numbers: the Star in Bolton presented human freaks in the guise of 'man monkeys' or people who were seen as freaks like dwarfs. There were performing animals and people who dressed up as animals. Amongst the regular performers were ventriloquists, 'royal wizzards' and jugglers like 'Prof. Rivers' who, so the *Bolton Free Press* announced in 1846, would carry out 'a number of feasts [*sic*] upon 13 champagne bottles'. There were acrobats of both sexes and all types who performed on stage *and* in the auditorium. There are other reports in London of tightrope walkers and trapeze artistes who performed over the heads of the audience, and many of these also appeared in the regions.[61] Such performers were not only exhibiting artistic talents but also on many occasions their bodies in so-called living pictures: the *poses plastiques* or *poses vivantes*. In the late 1840s the Kirst family presented the labours of Hercules in Bolton in such a manner. Sharples also presented a theatrical adaptation of George Cruikshank's 'Eight Illustrations of the Effects of the Gin Bottle'. This was not without a certain irony as the Star Inn was continually coming into difficulties because of its alcohol sales. The erotic potential of *poses plastiques* was mostly recognised and exploited in London but the Kirsts in Bolton also had a number in their repertoire entitled 'Cupid and Venus' which began with 'Love unveiling'.[62] Circus numbers were not a self-enclosed section within the programme but mixed in with the rest.

The musical part of the programme was by no means limited to comic songs. The Star and other halls also offered minstrel songs, ballads, madrigals and folk songs, (particularly from Ireland or Scotland), music on wind instruments and classical music in the form of opera or instrumental solos; not forgetting the so-called 'musical eccentricities'. These were mostly instrumental artistes like Prof. Myers, 'the great German Master of the Chinese Accordion ... (who) must be heard to be believed'.[63] Superficially it might appear as if a number of colourful elements had been simply thrown together. But a more detailed examination reveals a certain inner logic. For, like the comic song, folk-songs and ballads also celebrated common folk, their everyday strengths and weaknesses, pleasures and cares and commented on them ironically and sentimentally. In all these forms the subjects of the songs are also their heroes and in the case of the music hall this also included the audience: the costumes of the protagonists were the only real difference.

Initially it is the opera which seems out of place. Operatic extracts were not a part of the music-hall programme everywhere but were mainly presented in those halls whose proprietors had a personal liking for the *genre*. The English premiere of Gounod's 'Faust' took place in Charles Morton's Canterbury and in Sheffield Thomas Youdan consistently inserted opera arias between minstrel songs, madrigals and performing dogs.[64] There was nothing in principal to prevent operatic excerpts from being integrated into the music-hall programme for everything was possible in variety. Opera, as an important component of middle-class culture, also provided an additional opportunity for music-hall proprietors to polish up their image by the presentation of 'rational recreation'. And in the nineteenth century, classical music – and especially the opera – was not the exclusive preserve of the upper classes. Working people came into contact with such music in the entertainment presented by social reformers and were themselves active in choirs, bands and orchestras. Classical music could also be heard on every street corner played by organ-grinders and other musicians.[65] For this reason it was only natural for it to be a part of the music-hall programme. Furthermore it seemed to have gone down very well. After the Surrey Music Hall was destroyed by a fire in 1865 Thomas Youdan dedicated the rest of his career to promoting his love of opera and when he opened Sheffield's first opera house it proved a great public success.

A major theatrical feature in the first two decades of the halls was the 'spectacular drama'. This was an expensively staged theatrical adaptation of sensational events, mostly catastrophes and famous battles both contemporary and historical, complete with horses, mass scenes and fireworks. The most prominent elements here were action and noise, the historical and political context being of secondary importance. In this respect there is very little difference between 'spectacular drama' and early cinema newsreels of which it can justly be claimed as a forerunner. And, looking backwards, 'spectacular drama' may be said to have followed on from and replaced the street singers in its role as a conveyor of news and current events. In 1847 the Star presented a reconstruction of the Great Fire of London, and a decade later the Bolton Millstone Concert Hall presented the Siege of Sebastopol.[66] The poster, which was full of information, advertised the show in the following terms:

TRIUMPHANT SUCCESS
of the
SIEGE
of
SEBASTOPOL

Pronounced by all who have seen it to be the most unique and striking representation of a Bombardment ever seen in Bolton

---

(...)

The Scene presents a faithful view of the Harbour, Town, and Fortification of

SEBASTOPOL

With the Allied Fleets in front; Fort Constantine, Fort Nicholas, the Quarrantine Fort, Fort Paul, various Redoubts, Batteries, &c.

Also a Bird's Eye View of

INKERMAN and the River and Heights of ALMA!
THE WHOLE PAINTED BY MR. GEORGE MARTIN, OF MANCHESTER.

The

BOMBARDMENT

Will represent the operations of the 17th October, the first day of the Siege, when the Russian works were attacked by the Allied Fleets and Armies.

The Firing Will Be Maintained by

300 CANNONS!

And a Number of MORTARS!

Conducted by Mr. T. H. MERRIDY, the celebrated Pyrotechnist, from the Bellevue and Pomona Gardens, Manchester, and the original Producer in Bolton of the memorable 'Bombardment of Algiers', the 'War in China', and other eminent Battle Pieces.

Although the Siege alone would doubtless have lasted long enough to fill the whole evening it was not the only attraction on the programme at the Millstone Concert Hall. It was followed immediately by a woman ballad singer, two further comic singers and concluded with a panorama of the Battle of Alma. The show began at 18.00 daily (Sundays excluded) and on Mondays there was an extra matinee performance at 14.00. The production costs must have been consider-

7. A poster advertising a programme in the Millstone Concert Hall, Bolton in the 1850s. The main attraction is the Siege of Sebastopol, one of the many spectacular dramas inspired by the Crimean War. The evening is rounded off by an 'explanatory address' covering military tactics, operations and gunnery and so on. Despite the great expense involved in presenting such a spectacle the sole charge for entry was by means of refreshment checks.

able. Despite this the entrance fees of 2d and 4d were still returnable in refreshments.

The panorama of the Battle of Alma was accompanied by an explanatory address by a Mr. H. S. McLeod, 'Interspersed with familiar descriptions of Military Tactics, Evolutions, Siege Operations, Gunnery, &c., and a profusion of interesting Anecdotes'. McLeod's lecture can be classified under the programme component described as information and innovations. As well as panoramas and dioramas this would also have included lectures and the presentation of new technical inventions. Sharples in particular showed great interest in such matters. In 1848 he presented a lecture on the pros and cons of emigration (complete with diorama). There were regular presentations of new inventions like the microscope or the electromagnetic telegraph. In 1844 an optician named Botten presented a panorama of Venice in the Star, which

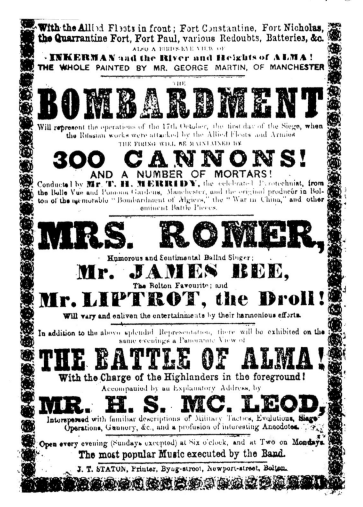

was followed by 'the astonishing MAGNIFICO DIOPTRICA, or HYDRO-OXYGEN GAS PHANTASMAGORIA; & DISSOLVING VIEWS, representing the Harbour of Hong Kong'. Mr. Botten also presented his microscope which – so Sharples claimed – was able to magnify a fly to the size of an elephant and reveal 'wonders in nature' which were hitherto hidden from the human eye, 'especially ... the innumerable tribes of Animalculae, and their voracity in devouring each other'.[67]

Sharples's endeavours were clearly oriented more towards entertainment than education for the inventions were presented more as sensational toys than as the result of scientific research. Nonetheless the audience must have received quite a good idea of how the inventions worked. And if it had not been for the music halls the working people of Bolton in the 1840s would have had comparatively little opportunity to learn about foreign countries and the latest inven-

57

tions. Sharples and other music-hall proprietors were thus able to offer some compensation for local educational deficits.

This mode of conveying knowledge (and producing 'knowingness') was in tune with more general practices in Britain at the time. In *Victorian Things*, Asa Briggs points out how easily 'novelty and innovation' were confused, and how elements of play, entertainment and fantasy were bound in with inventions and their presentation.[68] Again the music hall seems only to be reflecting trends in society as a whole. In this respect the concept of 'variety' also makes sense. At a time when world exhibitions were still intended to be utterly comprehensive and everything which existed was put on display, the halls were only reflecting on a smaller scale what was happening on the greater stage outside. And in the absence of any viable educational alternatives music-hall programmes remained many-sided and comprehensive. But in the course of time some elements gradually began to be replaced by others.

By the 1860s educational components had almost completely disappeared from the music-hall programme. This was primarily due to the improvement in working-people's educational opportunities with which the halls could not or did not want to compete. Nonetheless some links between entertainment and education still remained. William Morgan in Bradford was the manager of the local mechanics' institute before opening the Star music hall. As early as the 1870s he had begun including variety programmes amongst the courses offered by the institute.[69] By the 1890s this practice had been almost universally adopted by working-men's clubs and mechanics' institutes and the concept behind it can be said to be very similar to that of the early halls.[70] At the same time the halls tried to introduce educational items once again, but this time with fatal consequences. They were one of the first institutions to introduce film projectors to the public and by doing so invited a source of entertainment onto their premises which was later to become their major competitor. Moving pictures were at first just one among many features of the programme but after the turn of the century they gradually took up more and more performance time. The result was that many halls began to present films in the afternoons and variety in the evenings. In the 1920s halls began to be converted into cinemas and these in turn were to be killed off after the Second World War by the bingo boom.[71]

Spectacular drama also disappeared in the 1860s. Only a few halls continued to present such attractions but now they took the form of dioramas or living pictures. In February 1866 Joseph Hobson of the Princess's Concert Hall in Leeds presented a 'Historical, Allegorical Tableaux, illustrative of the very memorable BATTLE OF THE NILE and the DEATH OF NELSON in the form of a diorama'.[72] But dioramas were also decreasing in numbers. Between 1871 and 1873 Pullan in Bradford showed precisely one. As for 'spectacular drama', when it was shown at all, it was reserved for Christmas shows: and then devoid of news or information. To name but one example, in December 1866 Hobson presented a 'grand FAIRY SPECTACULAR ENTERTAINMENT' which included '100 Infant Dancers' from Leeds.[73]

The spectacular drama of the 1840s had begun to decline in popularity during the Crimean War, an event which inspired much material. The war was an era of great progress and development in the techniques of news collecting and simulated spectacular drama found it increasingly difficult to compete with factual reports and authentic photographs from the front which could be transmitted back home more speedily by means of the electric telegraph.[74] The Theatres Act of 1843 which prohibited theatrical performances was a further nail in the coffin. Theatres in the regions kept a sharp eye on the halls and the proprietors of the halls had to reckon that any presentation of spectacular drama would probably end in costly legal proceedings.[75] When these were added to the high production costs of spectacular drama with its mass scenes and spectacular effects it quickly became obvious in the 1850s that such presentations could no longer cover their costs. Music-hall proprietors, however, were reluctant to dispense with theatrical performances altogether and large spectacular shows were gradually replaced by short sketches, pantomime interludes, comedians and ballet performances.[76]

Ballet performances belonged to the repertoire of larger London music halls like the Alhambra at quite an early period. In the regions they began to appear sporadically in the 1860s.[77] In 1866 Joseph Hobson advertised a *'corps de ballet'* in the *Yorkshire Post*. There is a similar advert by Pullan in the *Bradford Observer* in 1871. And advertisements for the People's Music Hall in Manchester show that ballet companies appeared there from the mid 1870s onwards.[78] Because of the expense involved, ballet performances could only be afforded by the larger halls and variety theatres. The Manchester Palace, which opened in 1892 and was partly financed by London capital was able to boast of presenting ballet, some of which was also imported from the capital. But other halls like the Circus of Varieties in Rochdale which opened in 1882 were forced by financial considerations to concentrate their programmes more on the promotion of local culture with features like clog dancing.[79]

The remaining areas of the programme were left basically unchanged. The musical part still consisted of the classical, the folky (in the broadest sense of the word) and the comic. And circus numbers still contained jugglers, acrobats and performing animals, with local variations in emphasis. In Bradford Henry Pullan offered a wide-ranging programme of circus acts which included performances in a water-tank.[80] By contrast, the People's Music Hall in Manchester preferred to concentrate on music. Amateurs were also a part of the programme here and the hall organised many competitions for them.[81] The halls in Sheffield tended to offer a more balanced programme in the 1880s but, given the competition from Thomas Youdan's opera house, they preferred to refrain from classical music completely.[82]

The structure and content of the programme which had become reasonably

Delightful to Inhale.

ARDWICK GREEN EMPIRE,

HYDE ROAD, Corner of Ardwick Green. MANCHESTER.
(At the Tram Junction and near Ardwick Station on the G.C & L.N.W. Railway)

Proprietors	The Manchester Hippodrome and Ardwick Empire Ltd
	Managing Director - - - - - OSWALD STOLL
No. 1	District Manager - - - - - A. BULMER
	Acting Manager - - - - - H. HALL
	Assistant Manager - - - - - H. PRYME

TWICE NIGHTLY.
Monday, Sept. 9th, 1907, and during the Week.

1—OVERTURE "Banditenstreiche" ... Suppé

2—VICTORIA MONKS "John Bull's Girl." One of London's Own
Who has a style entirely her own. Don't miss "Moving Day." See the Brokers come in— See them tear the house down. The most Original Song ever produced.

3—WALTER MUNROE The Man who Struck O'Hara

4—Maggie BOWMAN & Tom J. MORTON ...
In the Comedy Duo— "She Loved a Policeman."

5—HORACE POLLOCK & Co., In a High-class Comedy Sketch
entitled—"Hester's Mystery," by A. W. Pinero.

6—GEO. NEWBURN The Popular London Mimic

7—PARK'S ETON BOYS Champion Boy Singers of the World

8—The Dieppe Motor Race, A most Sensational Picture on the
American Bioscope.

9—JOSIE MOONEY The Original "Silly Sally" and Clever Vocalist
and Dancer.

10—LEIPZIG Pronounced by the Press of England, America, and South
Africa as the Greatest Card Manipulator and Conjuror in the World.
Appeared by Royal Command at the Buckingham Palace, June 9th, 1907, before their Majesties The King and Queen of England, King and Queen of Denmark, and Prince & Princess of Wales.

The following **Local Artistes** will appear in Houses and on Dates named:

	First House	Second House
Monday.	11. Frank Hale, The Novelty Comedian.	12. Witty Will White, Character Comedian.
Tuesday.	13. Lily Hayes, Promising Comedienne and Dancer.	14. Maude Lessim, Soprano Vocalist.
Wednesday.	15. Sullivan & Edwards, Comedians and Dancers.	16. Sid Carlton, Character and Light Vocalist.
Thursday.	17. Jim Leslie, Comedian.	18. Alf. B. Millard, The Curious One
Friday.	19. Revill Hall, The Comedian at the Piano.	20. Happy Lonsdale, Coon Singer and Dancer.
Saturday.	21. Helen Mc Gregor, Scotch Contralto.	22. Frank E. Taylor, The Original Comedian.

Musical Director ... ... R. HARDWICK.
Stage Manager - - J. R. WARD. | Advertising Manager: P. BOTWRIGHT.
TWO COMPLETE AND DISTINCT PERFORMANCES NIGHTLY.
All Artistes appear at Each Performance and both Performances are alike.

FIRST PERFORMANCE:	SECOND PERFORMANCE:
Doors 6-10 Curtain up 6-50. Down 8-50. All out.	Doors 8-50. Curtain up 9-0. Down 11-0. All out.

ADVANCE BOOKING to GRAND CIRCLE, STALLS FAUTEUILS, AND BOXES AT OFFICE DAILY, 11 a.m. to 4 m., and 7 to 10 p.m.

Private Boxes, for four and three persons respectively 7/6 and 5/-, single seats 2/- Fauteuils tip-up chairs 1/6, bookable in advance; Orchestra Stalls tip-up chairs, 1/-, bookable in advance 1/3; Grand Circle, tip-up chairs, 8d., bookable in advance 9d. Pit, Rich Velvet Seating, 4d. Gallery, cushioned seats, Mondays, Saturdays, and Holidays, 8d., Tuesdays, Wednesdays, Thursdays, and Fridays, 2d. First-class Programmes and accommodation at Third-class rates.

Seats not guaranteed. Come Early. No Money returned. The right of refusing admission reserved
Seats can be booked by Post or Telephone No's. 3682 and 3680.

This Theatre is Disinfected by "JEYES' FLUID."
PLANTS &c., supplied to this Theatre by ALLEN & SONS, Smithfield Market
Manchester, and at Sale

The Stage of this Theatre is Furnished by R. S. BANKS,
Bridge Street, Manchester

PIANOS
From 2/6 Weekly at **SMITH'S**, OXFORD ROAD. 179

Wear Jackson's 3/8 Hats and 10/6 Boots.
48 & 111 Market Street. All One Price

set by the 1860s thus remained fundamentally the same for the next thirty years, the only difference being in the individual emphases and preferences of the halls. All the halls I have examined offered a mixture of music and circus numbers with or without ballet, depending on their means. However, during this period there was a radical change in the framework of the programme and the style of presentation in the halls. The early proprietors had taken almost every opportunity to publicise their entertainment in grand phrases and fantastic descriptions. Very rarely did they omit to mention the sensational, extraordinary and incredible features on offer, especially when they were somewhat eccentric. The following advertisement which appeared in the *Bolton Free Press* in May 1846, is the perfect example of their presentational style. Thomas Sharples announced the artist R.J. Hayward in the following manner:

> The great antipodean Wonder ... will tie his Body in a complete knot and will also Sing a variety of Comic Songs whilst standing on his Head.[83]

By contrast the printed programmes of the variety theatres in the 1890s were much more sober in their descriptions. They were generally restricted to numbering the order of appearance of the artistes in question with their names and a short summary of their particular speciality. Music-hall programmes were now presented in a fashion which reflected the rationalised organisation and external framework of the business. The variety theatres of the 1890s were no longer pubs with stages but theatres with fixed rows of seating. Any gastronomical and socialising needs were catered for in rooms separated from the entertainment. Performers no longer had any great say in shaping the programme along with the audience and were overwhelmingly restricted to conforming to a set time-table. Proprietors had by now transformed entertainment into a commodity. The audiences to which they catered had also changed since the 1840s.

8. The programme of the Empire Variety Theatre in the Manchester suburb of Ardwick Green, September 1907. The programme is literally divided into 'numbers', a custom which had started in the 1890s. The performers were no longer introduced by a chairman but by numbers at the side of the stage which corresponded to the numbers in the programme. Outside artistes appear in the first half of the programme, the star attraction coming immediately before the interval. The second half of the programme is devoted to local artistes. The length of the programme runs to an exact timetable (here two hours) thereby putting a curb on improvisation, encores and audience interruptions. A visit to a variety theatre like the Empire was a much more formal event than dropping into a music hall in the 1850s. There was a pause of a mere ten minutes between the first and second house. The audience was clearly warned to come on time. Anyone arriving late would risk being refused admission and their ticket money would not be refunded: an example of 'disciplining' the audience. As was usual in variety theatres there is a range of different prices, but the cheaper seats dominate. Oswald Stoll (later Sir Oswald Stoll) who owned this hall was the prime promoter of 'cleanliness' in the halls. Is it purely coincidence that the very first words at the top of the programme indicate in no uncertain manner that the hall has been fumigated? There is yet another explicit reference to 'disinfection' further down the page.

3

The audience

COMPOSITION

In 1910 an article on music halls and their audiences appeared in *The Times*, part of which read: 'Today, in place of the obscure supper-room or the hall attached to the tavern, we have a large number of comfortable, handsome buildings ... [and] in place of an audience of men only, or of men accompanied by the least creditable of their female acquaintances, we see amongst the audience the family'.[1] *The Times* was not alone in its assessment. It reflected a historiography which interpreted the history of the halls as a development from pothouse to palace with a corresponding change in audience composition from an all-male gathering of roughs to a respectable assembly of all classes and both sexes.

We have already seen that F. Anstey divided the London music halls into four groups; the aristocratic halls in the West End, the smaller and less aristocratic West End halls, the large suburban bourgeois music halls, and finally the minor halls in the poorer parts of the city. Such a structure had been in place well before 1890 and was a particular hallmark of the London scene.[2] There may not have been 'bourgeois' halls beforehand but those in the West End had always attracted an audience of aristocrats, bohemians and students. The third category of hall, which Anstey rather euphemistically described as 'bourgeois' included the Metropolitan in Edgware Road, the Canterbury in Lambeth, the Winchester in Southwark, Wilton's in the East End and, more centrally situated, the Middlesex in Holborn. Such halls tended to draw their audiences from the immediate neighbourhood. They were therefore relatively homogeneous and consisted of small tradesmen, shopkeepers and their assistants, mechanics and labourers, as well as soldiers and sailors.[3]

The differences in the London halls are mirrored in their admission prices (see table 1).[4]

Whereas the bottom range of prices overlap there are considerable differences in the top range which point to a socially differentiated audience. Certain suburban music-hall proprietors such as James Robinson of the Eastern, John Wilton of Wilton's and Charles Morton of the Canterbury also attempted to attract a more broadly based audience to the halls in the south and east of the

Table 1.

Admission prices in some London music halls			
Decade	Music hall (category according to Anstey)	Price range	
		Seats	Boxes
1860s	Alhambra	6d–4s	1gn
1870s		6d–5s	1–2 gn
1870s	Oxford	6d–1s6d	10s6d–1gn
1860s	Canterbury	6d–1s	–
1870s		6d–1s6d	–
1860s	Wilton's	4d–8d	1s
1860s	Boro' Music Hall	3d–6d	1s

city. Their advertisements in the newspapers (even *The Times*) not only stressed their respectability but included train and bus connections to and from the centre. But they were not very successful. Members of the upper classes did undertake the odd safari into the jungles of the working-class suburbs but by and large there was no basic change in the regular clientele and the social structure of the audiences in the halls remained constant.[5] Nor were there any great changes in the nineties. An LCC inspector, reporting on the composition of the audience in the Canterbury wrote that it consisted principally of mechanics, primarily tradespeople and their wives, working men, lads and girls.[6]

The London music-hall structure with its distinctions between socially mixed halls in the centre and working-class halls in the suburbs had no parallels in the regions. Almost all the halls outside London were in the middle of town and scarcely any of them catered for mixed audiences. Nor did they attract them. It is possible to make a partial reconstruction of their composition from reports on fires and panics, which also contain lists of the casualties involved. Between 1858 and 1896 there were panics in six halls in various cities which gave rise to public enquiries. The subsequent reports contain the personal data of 203 men and women (mostly name, age, address and occupation) who either died during the events or survived to give witness at the enquiries. The panics took place at the Surrey in Sheffield in 1858, Springthorpe's in Dundee (1865), the Victoria in Manchester (1868), the Colosseum in Liverpool (1878), the Star Theatre of Varieties in Glasgow (1884) and the People's Palace of Varieties in Aberdeen (1896). All the panics, apart from the last where a fire broke out, were caused by a false alarm.[7] In the United Kingdom as a whole there were eighty-seven fires and ten panics in music halls between 1850 and 1900, most of which were also caused by false alarms. Of the fires, only the one in Aberdeen resulted in considerable casualties; by contrast, precisely half the panics gave rise to injuries and fatalities. These panics occurred when the audience trying to escape the halls encountered inadequate exits, narrow staircases and steep and worn-out stairs.

Five of the six halls in question were structurally unsafe. Local authorities were, as a rule, aware of this but could do nothing about it owing to a lack of local licensing regulations; on the other hand they made little effort to ameliorate matters by applying for such regulations, even after the disasters. But the case of the Surrey in Sheffield demonstrates that panics could and did also lead to fatalities in structurally safer buildings.

That staircases were the scene of most accidents points to the fact that the victims came from specific areas of the halls – apart from Springthorpe's in Dundee which had no internal divisions. In Liverpool, Manchester and Aberdeen the victims came from the galleries, in Sheffield from one of the two galleries and in Glasgow from one gallery and the pit. Nonetheless the evidence provided by witnesses at the inquests and differing admission prices make it possible to come to an overall assessment of the audience composition in these halls. The Sheffield, Dundee and Aberdeen halls can be regarded as representative since they were the largest, if not the only music hall in these towns at the time.[8] In Manchester and Liverpool the unlucky halls can be compared with other halls in the same city by referring to their respective admission prices; and further information on the music-hall scene in both cities can be gleaned from newspaper reports published around the time of the panics.[9]

In all cases the composition of the audiences mirrors the occupational structure of the city in question. Thus in Sheffield 75 per cent of the victims and witnesses whose occupation was given worked in the cutlery trades as grinders, filesmiths and razorsmiths, as scissor filers, filecutters and edge-tool fitters; and in Dundee eleven out of thirteen were textile-factory workers. In the larger cities, Manchester, Liverpool and Glasgow, the occupational structure was naturally more diverse. A third of the victims in Manchester and a quarter of those in Liverpool worked in building and heavy industries. A further and larger proportion consisted, as in Glasgow, of day-labourers, drovers, street hawkers, apprentices, warehousemen and message boys and girls. Nonetheless the specific industrial structure of each city is recognisable. Two fifths of the victims and witnesses involved in the panic in Manchester were textile workers (where an occupation was given). As for the two ports; in Liverpool a quarter, and in Aberdeen a third, came from seafaring trades and allied occupations such as sailors, dockers and sailmakers.

Women were present in all cases – amongst the victims and also as witnesses. Their occupations are variously given as message girls, domestic servants, textile workers, scissor filers, potters and housewives. Nowhere in the reports on the disasters is there a hint that any of them might have belonged to the 'least creditable' part of the female population. Although it is undeniable that music halls everywhere were meeting places for prostitutes clearly not all women visiting the halls before 1890 were prostitutes. Indeed the sources make clear that there was a close connection between women in employment and women who visited the halls. The proportion of women in the audience was particularly high in those cities which offered paid work for women; like Manchester with its textile factories or Sheffield where the cutlery trades, even in 1858, were still based on domestic industry and small-scale workshop production. And it was women above all who integrated many a music-hall song into industrial folklore.[10]

A large part of the audience consisted of youths and children. Indeed they were predominant in the cheapest seating areas. It was here, in 1868, that a panic broke out in the Victoria Music Hall in Manchester. Amongst the thirty-four dead and wounded were twenty-three between 15 and 21 years old, and ten between 10 and 14. In 1875, ministers in Glasgow estimated that at least 2,000 children under 13 and 5,000 young people between 13 and 17, a quarter of whom were girls, regularly visited the city's halls. Whilst conceding that in each age group this was only 10 per cent of the total numbers the ministers stressed that the remaining 90 per cent were equally familiar with the music halls and their songs. There was not a single message boy who was completely ignorant of the songs. By contrast there were fewer than 600 boys and girls enrolled in the official evening institutes.[11] The picture was very little different in the 1890s. Of the twenty-eight dead and wounded in the 1896 Aberdeen disaster, there were fifteen young people between the ages of 15 and 19 and eight children between 10 and 14.[12]

As with women, young people in the halls were a considerable headache for the middle classes. Young people who spent the evening in places offering both drink and dubious entertainment and who were neither accompanied nor supervised by their parents were more in danger here than anywhere else imaginable.[13] Such fears were confirmed by enquiries in Bolton in the 1860s. Young offenders who were asked how they had got into crime stated that they had first been led astray by visiting the Star; and that they had taken up theft in order to pay for admission to the hall.[14] The stereotypical nature of the interviews at this point, however, leads one to suspect that the interrogators were putting the answers into the mouths of their interviewees. It is highly probable that the young people were only too willing to put the blame on the Star if that was what their questioners wanted to hear. After all the Star was a very suitable and convenient scapegoat. As for the interrogators, such evidence was an ideal confirmation of their own prejudices.

Most young people did not regard music halls as breeding-grounds of vice and crime. They simply preferred them to Sunday School or evening institutes. Here they were offered entertainment and a chance to participate in an adult lifestyle. Their sole supervision and guidance from above came from the proprietors and managers of the halls who were compelled from time to time to remind their youthful visitors that certain rules had to be observed. When the Star was opened in Bradford in 1875, William Morgan directed a part of his speech to his 'juvenile but demonstrative friends in the pit' pointing out 'that the strictest order will be enforced; that while every reasonable liberty will be allowed them of showing their approbation or disapprobation in a legitimate way, the very objectionable custom, so very often resorted to in music halls of whistling and shouting will be firmly and rigorously put down'.[15]

Some young people might have resorted to crime to pay for their entertainment in the halls. Another, and very popular, alternative was to try to sneak in unseen. Several proprietors tried to meet their younger patrons half way by offering them reduced admission prices.[16] For music halls, unlike the middle classes, regarded young people as an integral part of their audience. One witness put it to the Select Committee on Public Houses in 1852–3 that if boys were allowed to earn their living in mills and factories and 'made premature men of in that way, I submit to the Committee the gross injustice of excluding them from their amusement in the evening'.[17] Parents took a similar attitude. There were some who disapproved of their children going to the halls in the evening. But others took them along with them.[18] Here, as in the question of content and programme, working-class attitudes once again differed from those of the middle classes.

Nonetheless music-hall audiences were not exclusively working-class, even in the industrial regions of the North, as can be seen from a comparison between the disaster halls in Liverpool and Manchester and other halls in the cities (see table 2).

Table 2 shows that the Victoria and the Colosseum were the cheapest halls in town, although the price range in the Colosseum was considerably larger than in the Victoria. The reports on the panics indicate that both were solely working-class halls. But there was some social segregation in the Colosseum. The pit, which cost 1d, 'was made up of working men of the lower class ... dock labourers and labourers engaged in the varied labour of this great port'. And the 6d gallery was occupied by seamen and artisans.[19] Seating areas costing more than 1s as in the Liverpool Parthenon were 'not wholly composed of the working or labouring class' but included a 'fair sprinkling' of commercial travellers, clerks and shopmen. The same held true for the London and the Alexandra in Manchester.[20] Of all the halls in Manchester and Liverpool during the 1860s and 1870s, only the Star in Liverpool deliberately set out to attract an audience which went beyond the working and lower-middle class. Modelled on the London West End halls, it used its somewhat metropolitan ambience to distinguish itself from the ordinary provincial hall, and it was the only hall which advertised in nearly all the Liverpool literary weeklies and middle-class entertainment guides throughout the 1870s. Nonetheless it remains questionable whether the middle class – given their attitude towards the halls in general – did in fact patronise the Star. Indeed, clerks seem to have been more in evidence there than their employers. Manchester's Alexandra did attract the 'sons of wealthy merchants and manufacturers', but their presence can be attributed less to a desire to share in working-class cultural activities than to enjoy the company of prostitutes for which this hall was renowned in the 1870s. In general, however, the middle class tended to leave the halls to the working class and those sections of the lower middle class (artisans, tradesmen and shopkeep-

Table 2.

Admission prices in Manchester and Liverpool Music Halls		
Manchester 1868 (capacity)	Liverpool 1878	
Victoria 2d.–3d.(2,000)	Colosseum	1d–6d
Peoples's 2d.–6d. (3,000)	Alhambra	1d–1s
London 6d.–1s. (2,000)	Gaiety	2d–1s
Alexandra 6d.–1s. (1,500)	Parthenon	6d–1s
	Star	6d–1s6d
	Constellation	free
	Crystal Palace	free
	Griffith's	free
	Metropolitan	free

ers, as well as their assistants and clerks) who continued to share a common cultural context with them.[21]

It has been suggested that during the nineteenth century the lower middle class increasingly separated and protected itself geographically, economically, socially and ideologically from the working class. But this is not equally true for all sections of this class, and becomes more valid only towards the turn of the century, by which time the lower middle class as a whole had already become an integral part of music-hall audiences. Although they enjoyed a somewhat 'better' status and income, many members of the old lower middle class – shopkeepers and artisans – continued to share their living quarters with the working class during the early decades, and remained close to their style of life, especially since there was still a certain amount of social mobility between artisans and (skilled) workers, and between workers and traders. Geographical, social and economic proximity to the working class equally applied to many members of the new lower middle class, the clerks and shop assistants. Consequently both groups chose to participate in working-class rather than exclusively in middle-class cultural activities. They did not, however, share the same seating areas. In Manchester's Alexandra the workers sat in the galleries, and the body of the halls was occupied by shopkeepers, clerks and artisans.[22] But these divisions overlapped with other internal areas of differentiation, such as age groups. The decisive factor is that various social groups all shared in and celebrated a common entertainment. And the idea of the local community, which found its expression in the halls, was considered far more important than the maintenance of status and separation.[23] Indeed for some sections of the lower middle class, music halls were considered a thoroughly acceptable and respectable, if not the only, form of entertainment.[24]

It was not until the 1890s that the middle class as a whole – employers, civil servants and clerks in higher positions, and tradesmen who were not rooted in the locality – began to visit the halls with their families in any great numbers. But now they were visiting variety theatres, whose architecture and fittings were modelled on 'straight' theatres, with bars separated from the auditorium. By this time the halls were less foreign to middle-class families for nurses and nannies had long since introduced their charges to the songs performed in the halls. And from the 1880s the annual Christmas pantomime began to be a source of direct contact with music-hall stars.[25] Here again admission prices and seating areas give a good idea of the composition of the audience. In 1868 the Alexandra in Manchester had two seating areas. In the nineties it was renamed the Tivoli and comprised six areas with seats costing between 6d and 3s, and boxes between 10s6d and £2.00. At the newly-built Palace the price range was even greater: seats cost up to 5s and boxes up to 2 guineas.[26] Here the management was aiming at a very socially differentiated audience and took care to ensure that they did not come into touch with each other. Where possible each seating-area had its own entrances and exits.

But in the main socially mixed halls like the Tivoli and the Palace were the exception rather than the rule, even in the 1890s. The regular audiences at the overwhelming majority of halls continued to be drawn from the working class and the lower middle class. Of all the halls in Liverpool only the Star raised its prices in the top area of seating. Admission prices in the remainder stayed constant. And it was on these halls rather than the socially mixed variety theatres that the proprietors of new halls in the suburbs tended to orientate their business. Kiernan's halls in Liverpool and those belonging to Broadhead in Manchester make this only too clear. Their admission prices ranged between 3d and 1s.[27]

BEHAVIOUR

The composition of the audiences might have remained relatively homogeneous in the 1890s. What did change during this time was their behaviour. This resulted from alterations in architecture and organisation. In the 1890s a visit to the halls was generally confined to a certain period of time and made for a definite purpose. Two performances an evening with officially fixed starting times meant that the auditoria had to be cleared at the end of each performance and made ready for the next. This in turn meant that people were only allowed to stay on the premises for the purposes of entertainment. To this end tables were now replaced by rows of seats facing the stage. This change in fixtures and fittings also ensured that the audience was relatively immobile and only 'consumed' the offerings on stage.

The older type of halls with their mix of entertainment and gastronomy had been considerably more varied in their attractions. They not only offered, but enabled, more communication amongst the audience and between audience and performers. The tables in the auditorium were an encouragement to conversation and mobility. But in the new halls and variety theatres visitors had to resort to the bars for such purposes. Such changes were bound to alter the relationship between audience and performers. In the traditional halls the performers were not welcomed by applause from a silently expectant audience but had to fight for attention and convince their audiences they were worth listening to. This was particularly difficult for performers who were unknown to the audience, as the following account makes clear:

> On the night that I was present, there occurred a great disturbance. 'Joss Jessop, the Monarch of Mirth', a gentleman evidently high in local request, was, for some reason or other, not forthcoming, and, in his place, the management proposed to offer a female performer on the zither, one Signorina Ballatino ... Here a voice from the gallery requested to know what had become of 'Old Joss', and was greeted by loud cries of ''Ere, 'ere.' The chairman, ignoring the interruption, continued: ' – the world-renowned performer on the zither' – 'on the whoter?' came in tones of plaintive enquiry from the back of the hall. 'Hon the zither,' retorted the chairman ... 'A hinstrument well-known to anybody as 'as 'ad any learning.' This sally was received with much favour, and a gentleman who claimed to be acquainted with a family history of the interrupter begged the chairman to excuse him on the ground that his (the interrupter's) mother used to get drunk with the twopence a week and never sent him to school ... 'Blow yer zither', here cried out the gentleman who had started the agitation, 'we want Joss Jessop'. This was the signal for much cheering and shrill whistling, in the midst of which a wag with a piping voice suggested as a reason for the favourite's non-appearance that he had not been paid his last week's salary ... Then Signora Ballatino, clothed in the costume of the Sunny South, where clothes are less essential than in these colder climes, skipped airily forward, and was most ungallantly greeted with a storm of groans and hisses.

Given the Chairman's inability to quieten the audience the 'signorina' herself had to step in.

> Calling the chairman 'an old messer', and telling him for — sake to shut up, if that was all he could do for his living, she came down to the front, and took the case into her own hands. She did not waste time on the rest of the audience. She went direct for that coalheaver, and thereupon ensued a slanging match the memory of which sends a thrill of admiration through me even to this day. It was a battle worthy of the gods. He was a heaver of coals, quick and ready beyond his kind. During many years' sojourn East and South ... he had gathered together slang words and terms and phrases, and they came back to him now, and he stood up against her manfully. But ... At the end of two minutes he lay gasping, dazed, and speechless. Then she began. She announced her intention of 'wiping down the bloomin' 'all' with him, and making it respectable; and, metaphorically speaking, that is what she did ... For five and three-quarter minutes by the clock she spoke, and never for one instant did she pause or falter ... At the end, she gathered herself together for one supreme effort, and hurled at him an insult so bitter with scorn, so sharp with insight into his career and character, so heavy

with prophetic curse, that strong men drew and held their breath while it passed over them, and women hid their faces and shivered. Then she folded her arms, and stood silent; and the house, from floor to ceiling, rose and cheered her until there was no more breath left in its lungs. In that one night she stepped from oblivion into success. She is now a famous 'artiste'.[28]

More timid, or unlucky performers might have been greeted by jeers and hisses, followed by hails of eggs, tomatoes and other vegetables. But if they managed to survive the first few minutes they could forge a bond with the audience during the choruses and create a feeling of togetherness between stage and auditorium. Chorus singing and the boisterous response to the offerings are the two most striking features of audience behaviour. These are even mentioned from time to time in the earlier literature on the halls, which is not notable for its interest in the audience.[29] These two elements were to leave a lasting stamp on the special atmosphere of the halls. At first they were accepted as a natural part of the entertainment until – as we have seen in William Morgan's speech above – managers and proprietors began to make a distinction between legitimate and illegitimate expressions of disapproval in the 1870s, and to pursue the latter as a matter of policy.

In the following years there was a considerable increase in newspaper reports about 'riotous behaviour' and the attempts to stamp it out. This might have been connected with the fact that managers wanted to make their new policies publicly known. But it might also have been the consequence of these policies, which only served to provoke 'riotous behaviour'. 'Serious disaffection of sections of the audience' can also be seen as an expression of alienation. And at times this escalated into full-blooded acts of violence.[30] In the 1880s the *Era* reported that a band of youths had blackmailed performers into 'donating' sums of money under the threat of disrupting their acts if they refused to cooperate. And in 1890 a stage manager in Birmingham was beaten up and killed for refusing free admission after the management had withdrawn its practice of free passes.[31]

Incidents of this sort were responsible for the bad public image of youthful audiences in the halls. The audience as a whole was considered to be rowdy but high-spirited; the young people however tended to be written off as hooligans. More modern and anthropologically orientated methods of research into youth culture have since attempted to shed a different and more accurate light on 'deviant behaviour' by examining it from the perspective of a popular jurisdiction of ritual.[32] The starting-point for such analysis was the behaviour of music-hall managements. Peter Bailey has shown that as they 'became more officious, so the sanctions of popular control became cruder and more obtrusive'; and that, from about the 1870s, 'what once may have been tolerated as custom was now redefined as delinquency' and vigorously pursued by those in charge of the halls.[33]

Chorus singing and riotous behaviour were two sides of the same coin; two forms of popular control of the performers. In the early years of the halls such control was considered natural; and for certain sections of the audience it continued to be seen as such. After all the main subject of the songs and sketches were the characteristics and peculiarities of the audience and the give-and-take between performers and audience was very fluid. The audience helped to shape the programme by taking part in the chorus singing, and were even given the chance to perform from the stage when amateur competitions were held. Many a famous name was discovered in this way. Harry Lauder, for one, began his working life at the age of twelve as a textile worker in 1882. A year later he went to work in a coal mine. He sang in a temperance choir and appeared at church fetes and football club parties, as well as taking part in several singing competitions. These were the launching pad for a career in the halls which was to take him to the very top and even earn him a knighthood.[34] Nonetheless he never made any bones about his origins and for the audience he always remained 'one of us'. And anyone who was considered 'one of us' had to submit to popular control.

The definition of 'riotous behaviour' was a direct result of the campaign of discipline instituted by the managements as music-hall business became increasingly commercialised and premises grew larger. 'Commercial organisations needed orderly conditions and security for their property' not only to satisfy the licensing authorities: they were also trying to attract new audiences.[35] Commercialisation also affected audience behaviour and visiting patterns. For, as we have seen, an evening in the music hall in the 1890s was very similar to an evening in the theatre. The audience went there to see a definite programme and stayed there only for the duration of the programme. In earlier times, however, visits to the halls had been determined neither by content nor time; less undertaken with a particular aim in mind than as an integral part of the rhythm of work and leisure.

> 'I work in a foundry', explained one of the witnesses at the enquiry into the panic at the Liverpool Colosseum in 1878, 'and sometimes I and others go to the Colosseum just as we leave work. We stand at the rear of the pit ... the pit is more convenient for us just to drop in for a little during the 'first house'.[36]

This man did not visit the hall to see a complete show from beginning to end. He clearly saw the place more like a pub, somewhere to drop in for a short time on the way home from work. It would be wrong to say that all music-hall visiting patterns were as informal as this before the 1890s but they did have a close connection with the rhythm of work. The halls in Manchester, for example, were always packed on a Friday because Friday was pay day in the textile factories. But it was the new day off for the workers, Saturday, which was to become the main day for visiting the halls.[37] And it was Saturday which gradually replaced Monday as the traditional workers' day off, although this development was irregular both geographically and chronologically. We have already seen elsewhere that Monday was the favourite day for the miners in Bolton to visit the Star. Monday was also important because this was when the new programme was first presented. The singer, Vesta Tilley, tells of a town in Lancashire where a gaffer was sent out by miners to check out the entertainment on offer so that they could decide whether or not it was worth visiting the hall with their families.[38]

Visits to the halls had a collective character. They were seen as 'monster convivial parties' (as one contemporary witness put it in 1866) involving 'multitudes of men and women, who, while the singing or dancing proceeds upon the stage, sit at tables or lounge about, munching, drinking, smoking, chattering, laughing'.[39] The audience came in groups, knew each other from work or had the same circle of acquaintances, neighbours or families. Many of the victims of the panics lived in the same street or were related to each other. An audience observer in Pullan's Music Hall in Bradford wrote in 1886 that 'children in arms are freely admitted, and cackle, and laugh, and cry at their own sweet will – the crying, if I must speak the truth, being the predominant baby sound'.[40] Visits in family groups were not a later phenomenon but one of the hallmarks from the start. One witness at a Manchester singing saloon in the 1840s remarked that a third of the audience consisted of women 'young and old – a few of them children seated in their laps, and several with babies at their breasts. The class of the assembly was that of artisans and mill-hands. Almost without an exception, men and women were decently dressed, and it was quite evident that several of the groups formed family parties.'[41] Such patterns of behaviour can also be found in the popular concerts which were specially aimed at the working classes. Babies, of course, were not tolerated here.[42]

There are many references to families visiting the halls. Nonetheless these should not be overrated. For the larger the family, the less likely it would be to visit the halls as a unit. A larger family not only meant more demands on the wife in terms of child care and housework, but more heads to feed and clothe. Consequently there was less money to go round. This is why most sources refer to young families, or mothers with babies. And it also explains the differences in the pattern of attendance between women and men. Whereas men of all ages could be seen in the halls, women's visits were more irregular and closely followed their changing patterns of life and work. The largest group of women in the halls were young, single and employed. They would tend to go along with their neighbours or friends from work. In Bradford, a centre of the textile industry, one writer who visited Pullan's in 1872 tells of his surprise at seeing more members of the 'weaker sex' than he had expected. He also noticed that some of the women were accompanied by husbands or lovers but most of them were unaccompanied by men at all.[43]

After the young, single and employed, the largest group of women consisted of young wives and mothers with babies. By contrast there is scarcely any documented evidence of the presence of older women with adolescent children in the halls. The statistics on the panics in the halls confirm this. Only two women

9. *A colliers' pub in Wales, 1873. The picture indicates the informal entertainment probably provided by the customers themselves. Such a supposition is further strengthened by the instrument on the wall and the fact that the performers are dressed no differently from the audience. Note that this was not an exclusively male gathering, as witness a young couple and a family.*

were over twenty-five; one was forty-two and the other fifty-eight.[44] It would be rash to make a definite judgement on so little evidence but one may suppose that women's pattern of attendance would change once more as soon as their children had grown up and found employment. For mothers would now have more time and money for themselves and their leisure activities and could start visiting the halls once again. For, in principle, they regarded the halls as belonging as much to them and their children as to their husbands. The music hall was consciously aimed at all members of working-class families and was one of the few institutions of the age which was open to them all. It was precisely this aspect of the halls which roused the deepest expressions of disapproval from amongst the middle classes. They believed that women and children should not be in the halls at all.

Another controversial aspect of the halls was the content of the programme and the values being put across by the performers, most of which stood in direct contrast to those of the ruling culture. Opponents of the halls did not restrict their efforts to demonstrations. They aimed to close them down or impose strict regulations on them. But if the halls were attacked for the above reasons audiences and management were quick to close ranks in their defence. For an attack on the halls was seen as an attack on their culture and life-style as a whole.

Just as the audience defended their halls where necessary so did the halls come to the support of their audience in times of crisis. For the halls also played an important social role outside opening hours. They were not simply a service industry but regarded themselves as an integral part of the local, working-class community. As such, managements had certain duties and responsibilities to their audiences, which they were ever ready to put to the proof 'with benefits and subscriptions for the victims of local and national calamities – the painter who broke his leg, the victims of colliery disasters, the unemployed Lancashire workers in the cotton famine'.[45] Proprietors threw tea parties for the elderly or put on charity shows for the benefit of the needy. Here the main beneficiaries were the veterans of the Crimean War, schools and hospitals.[46] Joe Smith, the proprietor of the Rochdale Circus of Varieties, was one of many owners who were members of charity organisations.[47] One of his charities was known as the Syndicate and its aim was to feed and entertain the elderly and the children of poor out-workers during the winter months. Such efforts were rewarded not only in terms of prestige. Some of the fund-raising was clearly undertaken for ulterior motives, especially when the proceeds were donated to funds for police orphans. It would be cynical to say that such benefit performances were purely self-seeking. The proprietors did feel a sense of social responsibility and expressed it not only in the form of charity but also political solidarity. Here the beneficiaries were working-class organisations. Joe Wilton in London donated money to Friendly Societies, others such as Henry Pullan in Bradford opened their doors for meetings of striking workers.[48] And when it came to the crunch this could indeed reap dividends. In 1891/2 the licence of the Liverpool Grand was under threat until the city's first working-class magistrate and the Trades Council came to the rescue. Since the manager, J. T. Roach had often helped the workers in their struggles they felt it only right to repay that support. Roach's licence was renewed.

PART II

CULTURES IN CONFLICT

4

1840–1865: rivalry in leisure

Conflict was the main feature of the first decades of music-hall history until the halls became socially acceptable in the 1890s. Music halls were conspicuous for several reasons and inevitably became the centre of public interest. Regional halls were concentrated in the city centres and in many cases the size of the buildings alone was enough to make them remarkable, even in the larger conurbations. The main source of irritation, however, was not their architectural but their cultural dominance: the fact that they diverted the attention of the workers from the alternative leisure opportunities offered by philanthropic and religious reform groups.[1] Most seriously of all, the values propagated in the halls were anything but the Victorian values of hard work, sobriety or respect for marriage and the family. And if such values were propagated they were interpreted in a different manner from that of the ruling classes. The popular figure in the halls was not the hard-working teetotaller but the dandy. The moral tone was not conducive to wholesome and sober recreation, for the stage was dominated by scantily-clad dancers and acrobats. Marriage was not presented as something to be strived after but as a disaster. The fact that the predecessors of the halls were the pubs only fuelled the arguments of their opponents. They regarded pubs as potential places of depravity which corrupted their visitors with alcohol and played a major part in the social misery of the age. The two main bones of contention concerning the halls were therefore their form of business – in which alcohol was an important source of income – and their programme.

Music-hall research to date has paid little attention to these controversies, the main interest being directed towards the anti-music-hall attitudes of the middle classes in general or to individual conflicts. As with all other aspects of music-hall history more attention has been paid to the situation in London than in the regions. This has resulted for the most part in individual case studies of isolated events.[2] I shall attempt to redress the balance here by putting the individual controversies into a national context over a larger time-span.

I have elicited these controversies from reports in the *Era*, the weekly paper of the trade. Further source material has come from police reports and documents recording the annual licensing applications in the areas I have researched. Here objections to applications meant that conflicts were inevitably given an airing. I intend to present the conflicts chronologically in order to give a clear picture of their development, using case studies to illustrate specific types of conflicts. There are two reasons for presenting the case studies in such a way. Firstly, even where national thematic connections are evident the disputes surrounding the halls were local in nature. Secondly the particular constellation of supporters and opponents, the course of the controversies and their outcome can in many cases only be explained by the unique character of the place in which they occurred, its particular history and, above all, its social and administrative structure. There is no unifying factor here because of the peculiar nature of English urban history and urban administrative structures.

The Municipal Corporations Act of 1835 – along with the 1832 Reform Act and the 1834 Poor Law – counts as one of the fundamental reforms made by the new middle-class order in Britain. Until 1832 the middle class involved in trade and industry had been excluded from political power. It was only after they had pushed through the 1832 electoral law reforms and helped a Whig government to power in the following elections that restructuring of political power on a national level was succeeded by debates on the fossilised structure of urban administrations.

> It had been the policy of the aristocracy to cripple the municipal spirit and the municipal constitutions for Parliamentary and political purposes. It was the policy of the middle classes, now that they had obtained political power, to reform the authorities and to bring the law into conformity with a higher standard of public order and public health.[3]

There were not only political reasons for this. The growth of population and urbanisation as a consequence of industrialisation had resulted in a new set of social relationships which the framework of the old system was incapable of dealing with. The incoming Whig administration had scarcely come to power before it initiated a Royal Commission to investigate the corporations of England and Wales, their constitutions and administrations and put forward proposals as to how these might be reformed.[4] The Commission presented its report in 1835. The ensuing Reform Bill was presented to Parliament and came into force in September of the same year. The old self-perpetuating corporations were abolished and replaced by democratically elected city councils.[5]

The Municipal Corporations Act of 1835 has been generally regarded by historians as a local government revolution. Indeed, as far as the older corporations were concerned it did lead to a basic change in local power structures and, particularly in the North, to a removal of the old Tory elite and its replacement by representatives of the Liberals and of the non-conformist industrial middle classes.[6] Nonetheless the significance of this particular reform has been somewhat overvalued. It only applied to the 179 corporations which the Royal Commission had investigated and therefore did not cover even all the incorporated municipalities. The Commission had given London a wide berth. It might even be asserted that its members had simply capitulated in the face of the jungle of power-relationships in the capital. Neither the non-incorporated municipalities nor the rural areas were taken into account, despite the fact that the former included large industrialised cities like Manchester which, in 1831, had a population of 202,000.[7] Rural areas had long since begun the process of urbanisation and many were in urgent need of municipal administration. The best that could be hoped for in all these cases was a 'Local Act' allowing for incorporation and presented in Parliament on behalf of the municipality as a private member's bill. In order for this to be done, however, a majority of the citizens had to be in favour. Until 1877 these citizens also had to meet the considerable expense involved in such a process. Therefore they often rejected the idea of incorporation out of hand.[8]

Thus the Municipal Corporations Act did not at first result in a comprehensive change in the English municipal landscape. It simply laid down the preconditions for such changes provided a majority of local inhabitants were in favour. This in turn led to a change in the elite within the reformed municipalities and to a gradual reform of the administration. The main aim of the act was to abolish corruption and inefficiency and introduce a democratic and effective system of administration. Its main effect however was to strengthen the principle of local democracy – with the emphasis on 'local'. Each municipality was now able to determine for itself how it should be administered. Its taxpaying citizens – not Westminster or Whitehall – were now able to decide what form this should take, whether within the framework of the old system or on the basis of a new reformed municipal constitution. The 1835 Act contained only enabling provisions.[9]

The nature, form and extent of change depended on the widely differing social structures and power relationships within each municipality. English industrial towns were as a rule based on particular branches of industry and the resulting economic structures threw up specific social and power structures peculiar to each town. These structures might differ considerably even in immediately adjoining conurbations.[10] The political elite in Bolton with its textile factories was recruited from amongst the factory owners. But in Sheffield, where grinders' and toolmakers' workshops predominated, political power sprang predominantly from a radical worker and artisan culture.

The composition of local elites and the policies they followed played a decisive role in the conflicts involving working-class culture. In Sheffield, whose political elite was rooted in a working-class culture, and in Bolton where the ruling elite was plagued by internal disputes there was no systematic intervention by the local authorities. Attempts to regulate working-class leisure can, however, be found in Leeds, whose political elite was drawn from the middle classes and consisted overwhelmingly of Liberal non-conformists. It is within these specific local configurations that I shall attempt to investigate the disputes around the music halls.

BOLTON 1840–1860: PUBS AND MUSIC HALLS

The first reports of social conflict involving music halls appeared in Bolton in the 1840s shortly after the first halls came into business. In 1840 Thomas Sharples had enlarged the Star and two years later a so-called anti-singing-saloon movement began a broad campaign against Sharples and other music-hall owners. Their aim was 'to destroy the demoralising effect of singing-rooms'.[11] The choice of words and the fact that the vicar of Bolton, Canon Slade, was involved, seem to indicate that the campaign was of middle-class origin. However it was not the town elite which took action against the halls in 1842 but the pub owners of Bolton, organised in the Licensed Victuallers, because they feared the business competition inherent in a combination of alcohol and entertainment. The middle-class form of words had been chosen for tactical reasons. Canon Slade was involved in the campaign not on ethical or moral grounds but because of his connections with the town's 'drink interest'.[12]

The people of Bolton were quick to see through the contradiction between packaging and content with the result that the campaign met with little success at first. Indeed the sanctimonious accusations provided an ideal counter-argument for the saloon owners, who could now seriously claim that the *saloon* was not the dominant element in their offerings, but *singing*. And since it was generally recognised that music had a moralising effect, what they were providing in their saloons fitted in perfectly with the ideas of the social reformers. Music, according to Finley Frazer, one of the owners of the halls under attack;

> has a strong tendency to allay, if not destroy, a great deal of the natural
> moroseness of some minds, and the asperity of feelings in others ... It has often
> been my lot to witness persons, certainly not of the richest cultivation of mind,
> drawn from the use of low and vulgar language, and indeed riotous conduct, into
> some submission after hearing a good sentimental song.[13]

The Licensed Victuallers then attempted to beat the owners of the halls at their own game and considered opening a theatre 'upon terms which will supersede the necessity of attending Singing Rooms at Public Houses'.[14] Sharples's immediate reaction was to apply for a theatre licence himself but his application was rejected. Despite this he persisted in presenting plays in January 1843 and legal proceedings were initiated against him.[15]

By this time his opponents had mobilised their friends in the magistrature. Consequently Sharples not only failed to get his theatre licence but in 1844 his alcohol licence was not renewed, along with that of Finley Frazer. The official reason for this was that Sharples and Frazer had violated the Lord's Day by allowing music to be played on Sundays, opening their museums and demanding money from the public to see their collection of curiosities.[16] This again was no more than a pretext. For it was difficult to argue that the singing-saloon opponents who consisted mostly of pub owners were honouring the Lord's Day by serving alcohol. Indeed the magistrates did not come down against Sharples and Frazer for reasons of piety but because several of their members were themselves pub owners.[17] There would normally have been no legal grounds for suspending their licences since in 1844 there were no opening-times laid down by law but merely a general understanding that pubs should remain closed during church services. The magistrates could, however, attach conditions to a licence and in this case they had forbidden public entertainment in Bolton on Sundays and Sharples and Frazer had chosen to ignore this order.[18]

Sharples and Frazer were deeply affected by the loss of their alcohol licences because singing saloons were to a great extent financed by income from the sale of alcohol. It was not yet usual to demand an entrance fee for entertainment, admittance being generally by means of a refreshment check. Theoretically, Sharples was the sort of person who would have been perfectly capable of thinking up alternative methods of generating income. He had already introduced entrance fees for his museum and his clientele might well have been willing to buy tickets for the entertainment too. Since many of them took along their own supply of drinks with them the absence of an alcohol licence would not have put a restraint on their drinking habits. And in any case there was nothing to prevent him applying for a beer licence from the Excise, over which the magistrature had no authority.[19]

But Sharples preferred to meet the challenge directly and in 1844 he took active steps to defend himself against what he considered to be the duplicitous decisions of the magistrates. It is one of the singularities of the controversies in Bolton that not only the Tory magistrates and the pub owners adopted the arguments of the temperance movement. The lawyer and future district coroner John Taylor, who represented Sharples and Frazer, was also a prominent member of the temperance movement and was later to oppose the issuing of any new alcohol licences on principle. According to Taylor's autobiography he was a theatre-lover and took part in amateur dramatics. This might have been one reason why he took up the cause of the singing saloons.[20]

Taylor's arguments were both defensive and offensive. He pleaded that Sharples and Frazer had already agreed to the magistrates' order forbidding performances on Sundays. And as there was nothing dearer to their hearts than to meet the wishes of the magistrates the two had also ceased to allow the consumption of drinks in their concert rooms. (Later sources, however, suggest that this was only a temporary measure.)[21] Furthermore Sharples was prepared to keep the part of his museum which contained living animals closed on Sundays 'and he understood if the animals were covered from public view, that no objection would be made to the charge of a penny to view and inspect the inanimate portion of the museum'.[22] Indeed to forbid him to charge for entry to the rest of the museum was scarcely in the interests of general morality because it was the price of entry which prevented any Tom, Dick and Harry from visiting the museum. This was a very spurious argument as a botanical garden intended especially for the working class was opened in Birmingham a year later in 1845 with exactly the same entrance charge: one penny.[23] Taylor closed his plea by noting that it had cost a great deal of money to set up the museum, that there had been no objections to it thus far and therefore it had a right to exist on the basis of common law. This was enough to convince the magistrates who, in September 1844, revoked the decision they had made a month earlier. Considering the configuration of political power in Bolton it might be that the magistrates – and perhaps even the combatants – had realised that it was not in their long-term interests to have Tory pub owners in a clinch with Tory singing-saloon owners with the almost inevitable involvement of the magistrature. Perhaps they had also recognised that the rise of the singing saloons was irreversible.

Frazer and Sharples reacted in different ways to this decision. From the start in 1842 Frazer had tended to bow to the opposition rather than to fight. Consequently he kept to his word and his advertisements in the local newspapers illustrate this only too clearly. 'F. Frazer wishes it to be distinctly understood that he WILL NOT ON ANY ACCOUNT give Prizes ... on the Lord's Day ... In reference to his MUSIC ROOM, he begs leave to observe, that the only days for Music are SATURDAYS AND MONDAYS.'[24] But even Frazer was not completely free of the irony which so characterised Sharples. His advertisements also thanked the members of the Total Abstinence Society for their kind assistance in strictly supporting the new rules of conduct which he imposed in his saloon. Sharples, by contrast, pushed the whole matter into the realms of the ridiculous. In his advertisements he announced that he had acquired a weighing-machine 'by means of which visitors may have a correct ticket of their Height and Weight taken every day, except Sunday'.[25] Around the same time he began to insert the motto of the Order of the Garter – *Honi soit qui mal y pense* – in the star which embellished his newspaper advertisements.

Thus the first phase of the conflicts involving music halls in Bolton came to an end. It was essentially characterised by competition in the leisure industry in which the ruling elite were involved as direct participants and only indirectly in their role as municipal authorities. For the authorities as such were not yet in a position to take any decisive action in such conflicts.

Bolton was not one of the towns covered by the reforms of 1835. It was only incorporated in 1839 at the instigation of the Liberals and non-conformists in the face of considerable opposition from the traditional Conservative elite. The Tories at once put all their energies into obstructing the work of the new town council. This proved relatively easy. The Liberals might have been alone on the town council as the Tories had boycotted the first elections: the problem was that the new council had relatively few powers and very little scope for action. Hence it was forced to depend on the cooperation of the Tories, which was not forthcoming.[26] Things were made more difficult by the fact that, by contrast with other towns, both groups were roughly equal in size. The 1850 census shows that the inhabitants of Bolton consisted of 41.7 per cent Anglicans and 44.3 per cent Non-Conformists, the remainder being mostly Catholics.[27] The result was a stalemate for many years. It was not until 1850 that the council began to assume more powers. In the same year the city administration began to show a clear majority of Liberals. Liberals also began to dominate the magistrature which until then had been a Tory domain for years.[28]

Such political developments inevitably had their effect on working-class culture in the town, above all on the pubs and music halls. Immediately after the Liberals had gained control of the magistrature in 1850 they began to revise the existing practice of alcohol licensing. Until then the Tories had granted almost all new applications. The Whig magistrates, by contrast, decided to grant no new licences whatever. Like many Liberal municipal authorities those in Bolton were of the opinion that, by acting in such a manner, they could damp down the consumption of alcohol in the town. In this they were much mistaken as a reduction in the number of public houses generally led to a corresponding rise in the number of beer-houses which were outside their control. But at least the magistrates were sending out a signal.[29]

The second area in which the political changes in 1850 made themselves noticeable were the music halls. Here again the question of alcohol consumption was prominent. The Star was destroyed by fire in August 1852 and a few weeks later, in order to prevent its reopening, the magistrates suspended Sharples's alcohol licence along with the licences of most other singing saloons in the town.[30] Such measures were hardly consistent with the prevailing licensing practices whereby all new applications were rejected but any existing licences would be renewed even where the licence-holder had been guilty of minor contraventions of the law.[31] The singing-saloon owners could not even be accused of the latter. There were other reasons behind the magistrates' decision: firstly, the increased social activity of the various reform and pressure groups above all the opponents of alcohol; and secondly the particular configuration of power in Bolton.

In 1853 opponents of alcohol had joined forces in a new movement, the 'United Kingdom Alliance for the Suppression of the Traffic in All Intoxicating Liquors'. Its aims and tactics differed considerably from those of its predecessors. Earlier temperance groups like the 'British and Foreign Temperance Society' (BFTS) had, in the 1830s, tried to influence and convert the supposedly drunken masses by means of propaganda and personal example. The policies of the Alliance, however, were directed towards state intervention in the form of prohibition – in direct contrast to the general economic doctrine.[32] On a national level the immediate aim was a change in the law. Locally there were attempts to influence the licensing practices of the magistrature. In Bolton, as in other municipalities, protest demonstrations took place at the annual licensing sessions and resolutions were read out in court immediately following the police reports.[33]

The non-conformist middle classes played a leading role in the new movement. Even the churches, which had previously been more concerned with souls than livers, began to put aside their scruples and involve themselves in the movement.[34] All the same, neither before nor after 1850 was the movement entirely middle-class. Alongside the hierarchically organised BFTS in which philanthropists and church reformers held sway, a radical organisation known as the Temperance Movement or Teetotallers had been set up in the 1830s. Its supporters were mostly drawn from the working classes and their aims were different from those of the BFTS. Whereas the BFTS wanted to promote sobriety and maintain moderation amongst the sober the Teetotallers' aim was total abstinence which, they argued, could only be achieved by direct contact with drunks and alcoholics. They could see no solution to the problem by simply preaching moderation without dealing directly with those affected. Thus their activities were not restricted simply to propaganda meetings. Instead they began to set up an alternative, 'respectable' working-class culture with its own clubs, publications, opportunities for further education, leisure activities such as tea-parties and excursions, and even its own hotels and restaurants.[35] The middle classes were deeply shocked by the radical nature of these demands, the methods of propaganda and the target-group which the teetotal movement addressed. Huge assemblies of the proletariat with spectacular mass conversions using the language of the workers and music-hall type acts were as alien to the middle classes as they themselves were to the consumers of alcohol.[36] Another important factor was that the meetings made no attempt to instil a middle-class way of life into their audience but propagated self-help amongst the workers. Even so the working classes remained divided on this question as the efforts of both the BFTS and the teetotallers only reached a minority.[37]

The campaign of the United Kingdom Alliance against alcoholism was firmly in the hands of the middle classes. Although it modelled its alternative institutions on those of the Teetotallers its organisational structure, like that of the BFTS, was strictly hierarchical. What made the Alliance different was not only its strategy (protectionism instead of individual conversion) but also its aims and target group. The main objective was no longer to support the sober and reform drinkers but prevention. And this meant addressing a different age-group. Young people now became the objects of special attention, the idea being to keep them clear of alcohol from the start.[38] This was also the aim of the principal opponents of the Star in Bolton in 1852, some of whom were members of the Alliance.

Four weeks after the Star was destroyed by fire and shortly before the annual licensing sessions a group of 'Christian ministers, Sabbath-school teachers, parents and guardians of youth, and the friends of religious education'[39] – amongst them factory owners – called a meeting for the 19 August 1852 to decide on how to oppose the Star. It was agreed to send a delegation to the magistrates with a resolution demanding not only an end to Sharples's establishment but to all singing saloons in Bolton.[40] The grounds for such action were that singing saloons were 'flood-gates of vice and licentiousness'[41] and highly danger-ous to young people – two arguments which were to crop up time and time again in the conflict between reform groups and the music halls. The saloons, they argued, had an almost magic appeal to young people who, in addition, visited them without parental supervision. Worst of all the immoral character of the entertainment was likely to corrupt the young people entirely. The system of refreshment checks and the whole atmosphere of the saloons was an invitation to excessive consumption of alcohol. And this, in turn, would inevitably ruin the young people's health and lead them to thieving and prostitution.[42] As proof of this the opponents were able to make use of the minutes of conversations between the chaplain of Salford Gaol and young prisoners from Bolton in which the latter put the entire blame for their misfortune on the Star. For they had only turned to thieving in order to finance their visits to the Star.[43]

This line of argument was entirely to the taste of the magistrates who used it as grounds for suspending the licences. There may have been no special protec-tion for young people in 1852 but the justices were not bound to any particular set of rules when allocating licences and could therefore make their decisions in an entirely arbitrary manner. Nonetheless the magistrates cannot be said to have acted exclusively as a quasi-executive of the temperance movement nor in alliance with the social and political elite of the town. For there was no common agenda amongst these groups to discipline the culture of the local working class. The most notable feature of their decisions was that the Liberal magistrates did not suspend the licences of all the singing-saloon owners but only those of the Tories. Their own friends and partisans were spared. As the *Era* reported:

> It may also be further mentioned ... that Mr. Sharples and Mr. Nightingale, whose licenses are suspended, voted at the late election for the defeated Tory candidate ... and that every magistrate on the bench on the occasion of the suspension, were warm supporters of the successful Whig radicals. The only license spared, whose holder gave singing in any shape, was Mr. Grimshaw's ... and a reference to the poll books will shows that he voted on the same side as the presiding magistrate.[44]

The only new licence granted at these sittings also went to a partisan of the Whigs.

The most noteworthy feature about the disputes in Bolton was that they were not a matter of class conflict or even conflicts between working-class culture and the authorities but that they ran through a cross-section of both groups. Of course people were sincerely disturbed by the problem of alcohol and deter-mined to reduce drinking amongst the lower classes. But in the final analysis the magistrates only acted against the Conservative singing-saloon owners.

The music-hall camp also closed ranks over and above the boundaries of class. The Star in particular, which was Bolton's largest and most popular hall, was defended from two different sides. Firstly the town's working classes insisted on being allowed to choose the form of entertainment which suited their own tastes, especially since there was scarcely any alternative to the singing saloons because the authorities were unable to agree on a uniform policy regarding public leisure activities. The workers were particularly indignant that factory owners had complained to the magistrates about the allegedly pernicious influence of singing saloons when it was a well-known fact, documented in parliamentary reports, that factories were both physically and morally damaging to the health of the working population. Furthermore it was not right to regard and exploit young people as adults in the factories during working hours and afterwards treat them like children. And to claim that singing saloons promoted alcoholism was nonsense. Quite the contrary: people visited the saloons primarily for entertainment not to get drunk, and since every Englishman had a basic right to a glass of beer no one should be allowed to deprive them of such a harmless pleasure.[45]

Sharples's other group of supporters came from Bolton's traditional Tory elite who sided with him partly for political and partly for social reasons. It was true that Sharples expressly catered for the working class. But he was also the embodiment of the old-style pub-owner in whose rooms persons from all strata of society could meet, celebrate and rekindle the slowly disappearing spirit of Merrie England unmolested by the puritanical attitudes of the Liberal and nonconformist middle classes and the demands of factory discipline.

The following report of William Sharples's wedding reception in November 1844 gives a good impression not only of Thomas Sharples's connections with the Tory establishment but also of the high opinion in which the family held itself. It is difficult to believe that the staging was accidental.

> On Thursday evening upwards of 80 of the friends of Mr. Sharples, sat down to a sumptuous supper in the large Concert Room ... the floor was elevated by a platform covering, and the effect presented on the stage appeared like scenes recorded in Eastern story – the scene representing a wood, in which several beautiful living parroquets and cockatoos were perched. At the front of the stage were the letters V.R. in gas, with other beautiful devices ... The health of 'The Queen', 'Prince Albert and all the Royal Family', 'Long Life and Happiness to the Newly-married Pair', 'Mr. and Mrs. Sharples', and 'prosperity to the Star of Bolton', &c., &c., were drunk with rapturous applause. The band played many select overtures. &c., in exquisite style; and the company enjoyed the sparkling glass and harmonious song until a late hour.[46]

There are other indications that the Sharples family neither belonged to a subculture, nor was generally regarded as such. Like others of similar economic standing they took an active part in charitable enterprises in the town and the acknowledgement of their donations is a sign of their social acceptance. In 1852 Thomas Sharples tried to donate one day's takings from the Star towards the establishment of a dispensary. Unhappily this act of generosity was turned down on the grounds that it might be construed as an attempt at bribery, coming as it did in the middle of the controversies concerning the Star. But by 1859 circumstances had changed. In that year Sharples's son, William, organised a charity concert in aid of the construction of a new 'ragged' school, which was attended by a number of distinguished Liberals despite the vehement protestations of other members of the same party.[47]

As a pub-owner Sharples and his family were simultaneously members of the working class and of 'society'. They were therefore able to mobilise enough supporters for their cause in any disputes which involved them. In September 1852 the magistrates were forced to bow to pressure from both the public and the police, who also sided with Sharples, and revise the decision they had made only a month before.[48] As one of Sharples's friends wrote: 'The public are not all Sunday School teachers or teetotalers, nor are they ever likely to be.'[49]

In the following years William Sharples took great pains to cultivate public opinion – with great success as is shown by his 1859 charity concert. Even the confessions of the young offenders from the Salford House of Corrections incriminating the Star in their downfall in 1860 were not enough to turn the general mood of the magistrates against him. They were dealt with within the framework of a 'private inquiry ... relative to the influence of the Star upon the morality of the people'.[50] In April of the same year William Sharples applied for and was granted a theatre licence for the Churchgate Theatre which he had recently acquired. In doing so, with the help of a report from Superintendent Harris, he succeeded in presenting the Star as one of the best run houses in the country and its opponents as a temperance minority.[51] At the same time he let it be known in a pamphlet distributed to mark the rehousing of the museum collection in a new building, that he was well aware that in some quarters of the population strong prejudices existed against amusements of all kinds on the grounds of their being morally objectionable. As to whether there was any basis to the accusations he was not prepared to venture an opinion. He was, however, convinced that the working man could enjoy himself in a decent and reasonable manner in the Star and trusted that his efforts would always be 'directed to ... provide a place for the public, in which not only rational amusement may be found to relieve the monotony of daily industry, but in which also a taste for the beautiful may be encouraged and the mind improved'.[52] This was why the Star had been so successful and even enjoyed the support of the municipal authorities.

So it was that Sharples succeeded in playing off the authorities against the reform groups. That he was able to do so is one of the characteristic features of the early disputes involving the halls. It also demonstrates that these conflicts were not so much between the authorities and working-class culture but rather between competing sectors of the leisure industry on which the authorities were either called upon to sit in judgement or were themselves personally involved. The conflicts in Sheffield not only confirm this but shed more light on further aspects of the early controversies around the halls.

SHEFFIELD 1850–1865: THEATRES AND MUSIC HALLS

The early music-hall controversies in Sheffield were very similar in their constellation to those in Bolton, consisting basically of conflicts between two competing sectors of the leisure industry each of which enjoyed the support of a section of the authorities. In the case of Sheffield the halls were supported by the town council, and their competitors by the magistrates. However there are two essential points of difference between Sheffield and Bolton.

Thomas Youdan's Surrey Music Hall, the centre of most disputes, was not competing with the local pubs but the theatres. True, Youdan sold beer and operated with refreshment checks. He did so, however, not with an alcohol licence from the magistrates but a beer licence from the Excise. Thus campaigns like those in Bolton were impossible. Nor were they necessary. The Surrey Music Hall was not conceived as a singing saloon but as a music saloon cum theatre. Consequently the main opposition to the Surrey and its most stubborn competitor in the 1850s was the local Theatre Royal. In Bolton the theatre had been reduced to insignificance with the arrival of the halls. This was not the case in Sheffield.[53]

The second difference between Youdan and Thomas Sharples was that Youdan's problems were not caused by his allegiance to a particular social and political grouping or because he sought to uphold traditions which were under attack from reform groups. He himself was to blame for most of the conflicts involving the Surrey because he sought to extend his business activities without regard to the law. The Sheffield magistrates were frequently called on to intervene against him, in particular by informants acting on the instigation of the Theatre Royal.

Youdan and Sharples were, however, alike in that neither operated outside the mainstream of society despite the fact that they came from different social backgrounds. Whereas Thomas and William Sharples were part of the old Tory society Youdan, who was born in 1816, projected himself as the prototype of the self-made man. His rise to riches and social respectability was not due to his connections but to ambition and a measure of unscrupulousness. He had started as an agricultural day-labourer. He then took a job as a silver stamper and followed this by a spell as a beerhouse-keeper before setting up his own business in the Surrey. At this point he became involved in politics, was appointed a workhouse guardian and in 1858 crowned his social climbing with a seat on the town council. Some time later he became the proprietor of Sheffield's first opera house and in 1874 retired back to the country as a landowner.[54]

This rise to prominence was not as smooth as it might seem. An examination of the year 1858, when Youdan was elected to the town council, makes this only too clear. On 13 September a panic broke out in the Surrey Music Hall which was attributed by certain witnesses to a pistol-shot fired by one of Youdan's opponents. Other witnesses claimed there had been a gas explosion. Youdan, for his part, was utterly convinced that the panic had been caused deliberately and claimed that the motive for the crime was to damage his business as he had just completed rebuilding and enlarging the premises. By this he implied that the Theatre Royal was the prime mover behind the plot. The dispute was given wide coverage in all the newspapers, which were likewise divided in their opinions. The subsequent judicial enquiry was also unable to reach any definite conclusions.[55] Some time later, shortly before his election to the council, Youdan appeared before the courts on another matter: to dispute a paternity suit. It was alleged that he had raped a fifteen-year old barmaid during the previous winter and as a result she had given birth to a son. Youdan regarded himself as the innocent victim of a witch hunt. His protestations, however, were not sufficiently convincing and he was condemned to pay a weekly alimony of 2s6d for the next thirteen years.[56] The reports of the legal proceedings portray him as a thoroughly unscrupulous character who would stop at nothing in the pursuit of his aims. His approach to business matters was, in principle, the same and this was generally the cause of the many disputes between himself and the Theatre Royal or the magistrates.

Although most of the conflicts were caused by Youdan's violations of the law, some activities which the law defined as illegal were local traditions in Sheffield and were regarded by most people as utterly legitimate. The following two cases provide a good example. On 2 December 1854 the Theatre Royal lodged a complaint against Youdan on the grounds that he had contravened the Theatres Act of 1843.

> There were three informations, the first charging Mr. Youdan with keeping a house for the public performance of stage plays without being legally authorized, and the second more specifically alleging that he had permitted a piece called 'The Battle of the Alma' to be performed. The third was against Mr. G. H. George, one of the performers in 'The Battle of the Alma', for unlawfully acting in a place not legally authorized for the performance of stage plays.[57]

The case was clear and Youdan was ordered to pay a fine of £15. He was not the only manager of a music hall to fall foul of such complaints. Other examples can be found in Manchester (1850 and 1853), Leeds (1852), Liverpool (1858), Portsmouth (1865), Birkenhead (1872) and Birmingham (1881).[58] In Youdan's case, however, this was not his first breach of the Theatres Act nor was it to be his last.[59] In 1862 he declared to the magistrates that even if he was refused a licence, he would go on playing in spite of them and was quite prepared to pay the fines.[60]

In January 1858 he got himself into difficulties with another law when he held a form of lottery as an extra attraction to his Christmas seasonal entertainment. This was nothing new as he had held similar lotteries in previous years. The *Era* of 6 January 1856 reported:

> The spirited proprietor of this popular concert hall ... has ordered a monster twelfth cake, weighing four tons, which he advertises to sell at 1s6d per lb. Inside the cake is to be distributed indiscriminately 154 small medals, which are to answer to money prizes amounting to £200, divided into 154 different sums.[61]

The 1858 cake was a clear contravention of the law against gaming and lotteries – or so the Theatre Royal asserted. For it was the Theatre Royal which again lodged a complaint.[62]

Gambling, like alcohol, had become a social problem in the nineteenth century and was the object of several parliamentary enquiries.[63] In this respect Youdan was not the only music-hall proprietor who got into difficulties. Although complaints outside London against lotteries were not as numerous as those against illegal theatrical performances, there is evidence that music-hall owners in Manchester (1879) and Nottingham (1880) were also reported to the authorities for such offences.[64]

Youdan was again found guilty by the magistrates. In 1854 he had been dismissed with a fine but now he was sentenced to a week in gaol. Luckily for him he was spared the humiliation thanks to public protests and an intervention from J. A. Roebuck, the MP for Sheffield.[65] In both cases Youdan had quite clearly contravened the law. Nonetheless a great many citizens of Sheffield regarded the magistrates' decisions as unjust – not simply because of the harsh sentence handed down in 1858 but on principle. Youdan's actions in 1854 had been in direct contravention to the 1843 Theatres Act, many of whose provisions were outdated and were regarded not only by those affected but by many impartial observers as unjust. And the law against lotteries on which Youdan's 1858 conviction was based was in complete contradiction to the custom and traditions prevailing in Sheffield at the time.

The 1843 Theatres Act had been originally introduced to regulate internal conflicts in the theatre world which had become so bad that a Select Committee was set up in 1832 to enquire into the matter with the aim of doing away with the antiquated regulations.[66] These took the form of two Royal Patents dating from the seventeenth century – which permitted only the theatres in Covent Garden and Drury Lane to produce 'legitimate drama'. The Lord Chamberlain, who operated simultaneously as the public censor was, in theory, empowered to grant other theatre licences. But in practice this rarely happened. The result was that Covent Garden and Drury Lane enjoyed a virtual monopoly. Numerous theatres had come into existence by 1832, many of which were named saloon theatres after their locations. The scope and content of their performances were severely restricted by the provisions of their particular licence so that they were reduced to presenting melodramas and other 'lower forms of the drama'.[67] Amongst the recommendations of the 1832 Select Committee were the abolition of the exclusive privileges enjoyed by Covent Garden and Drury Lane and the introduction of free competition between the theatres.[68] However it was not until 1843 that the law was changed. From now on every theatre in the land could apply for a licence, depending on their location either to the Lord Chamberlain or to the local Justices of the Peace, and present whatever they wanted – within the bounds of censorship. The new Act deliberately defined a stage play in very broad terms: 'to include every Tragedy, Comedy, Farce, Opera, Burletta, Interlude, Melodrama, Pantomime, or other Entertainment of the Stage, or any other Part thereof'.[69] At the same time there was a line drawn between theatre and pub entertainment. Henceforth all saloon theatres had to decide whether they wanted to apply for a theatre or an alcohol licence. It was deemed impossible to have both as the general opinion was that the consumption of Shakespeare and beer had little in common.[70] Indeed it was not until 1859 that theatres were finally given permission to sell beer. But drinking and smoking were still forbidden in the auditorium – by contrast with the halls.[71]

The Theatres Act and its definition of 'stage play' was to prove a great burden to the music halls and the continual disputes led to further parliamentary enquiries in 1866 and 1892.[72] It was not as if music-hall proprietors wanted to put on complete plays. This would not have fitted in with their programmes which consisted of a series of separate numbers. What the theatres complained of as 'illegal' was 'the other entertainment of the Stage or part thereof' which for them included sketches, scenic ballets (i.e. ballets with a story-line), the singing of operatic arias in costume with scenery and spectacular dramas.[73]

But the principal argument of the theatre proprietors was that since they were forbidden to sell alcohol they stood little chance of economic survival against halls which could offer similar theatrical entertainment at lower prices subsidised by the sale of alcohol. On this point there is very little evidence to show that regional magistrates acted on their own initiative when the law was contravened. Indeed many of them were of the opinion that theatrical *intermezzi* only served to improve the programmes of the halls.[74] The Sheffield magistrates would probably have taken no action against Youdan in 1854 if the Theatre Royal had not complained.

They were not always as strict in their interpretation of the act. In 1862 they received another complaint from the Theatre Royal that Youdan had presented a melodrama in the Surrey, which was without doubt a 'stage play'. This time the complaint was rejected. And on highly remarkable grounds, namely: 'that the occupancy of Mr. Youdan had not been proved'.[75] True every child in Sheffield knew that Youdan had been the owner of the Surrey for the last twenty years. The magistrates also openly admitted the fact. But, as one of them argued: 'it is my duty sitting here as both judge and juror, to act not on my own private knowledge but on the evidence adduced before me'.[76] One year later Youdan was finally granted the theatre licence he had been after since 1851.[77]

In 1854 and 1862, Youdan had violated a law which most of his contemporaries – theatre people apart – regarded as too narrow in its definition and never conceived to be used against the halls. By contrast, in 1856 and 1858 he broke a law which was perceived as a crass contradiction to local customs. His Christmas lottery had little or nothing to do with gaming as it was a traditional form of festive charity. The town council viewed the matter in the same light and expressed its opposition to proceeding against the matter in such a literal fashion. As one of the council members put it:

> They would never be able to pull the strings so tight as to put down a raffle for a paltry piece of beef, or for blankets for widows ... that old Christmas should be kept as usual... and that the law should not be strained but left to take its course ... He [Mr Harvey] had put in for a goose at Christmas time – (laughter) – and considered there was nothing immoral in it.[78]

The magistrates too needed several nudges before they were willing to proceed against – and condemn – Youdan. A local informer had lodged a whole series of complaints. Because these had been ignored he took the matter to the Home Secretary who, in turn, referred it back to the magistrates. Only then did the magistrates feel compelled to take up the case.[79]

Youdan, of course, did not have to distribute his Christmas presents in the form of a lottery. He was partly following a well-worn custom. But, true to character, it was not his practice to go about matters unobtrusively by distributing money in sealed envelopes. All his charity performances were carefully, effectively and spectacularly staged and even when they were only a part of the programme, like the Christmas lottery, they gave the impression of being a self-contained show. A typical example of this was a 'monster tea party' for 2,000 old ladies (minimum age fifty-eight) which was organised by Youdan in June 1856 to celebrate the ending of the Crimean War. The *Era* reported that he offered special tickets to 600 or 700 further people simply to view the proceedings; and that later in the evening a further 8,000 to 10,000 people joined in dancing to bands stationed in various parts of the premises.[80]

In the years that followed Youdan organised further such parties. In 1857 he donated the profits from ticket-sales to the Indian Patriotic Fund. In 1858 he scaled down the tea party and held it on the roof of the Surrey. Since this was too small to contain 2,000 old ladies at a time, they were divided into three groups and catered for on three separate days.[81] Charity events themselves were nothing out of the ordinary. William Sharples had also held a tea party for 200 elderly ladies in Bolton to celebrate the reopening of the Star; and from then on the event was repeated annually.[82] It was Youdan's presentation which made the Sheffield parties so remarkable. And in this he was celebrating his own particular style.

In both towns the attitude of the local inhabitants to such events sheds an important light on the social standing and acceptance of the halls and their proprietors. Youdan's public activities not only won over the good will of the town council and the elderly. There is evidence that he was a much-loved figure amongst the working people of Sheffield as a whole and enjoyed a good relationship with representatives of the local trades union branches. In 1856 George

Powell, president of the table-knife trade was guest-of-honour at a banquet given by Youdan for 126 waiters and waitresses who had served at his tea party.[83] Furthermore he seems to have been on good terms with the churches. The *Era*, in its report of the 1858 tea party, mentions the presence of the Rev James Langhey, who gave a short and impressive speech alluding to 'the substantial repast which, through the blessing of God, had been provided by Mr. Youdan'.[84]

Seen in this light Youdan's election to the Sheffield town council in 1858 scarcely comes as a surprise. His success in this respect – by contrast with Sharples in Bolton – cannot be attributed simply to his personal merits, or the fact that the Star was surrounded by scandal and the Surrey not. It had also to do with the different economic, social and political structures which prevailed in the two towns. Bolton was a town typical of early industrialisation. It was dominated by the cotton industry which was one of the first to be taken over into the factory system. Hence the town consisted for the most part of factory-owners and workers. Engels had visited Bolton in the early 1840s as part of his researches for *The Condition of the Working Classes in England*. His descriptions show clearly how these social opposites were reflected in the architecture of the town. Bolton and similar industrial towns consisted almost solely of 'large working-class areas, only interrupted by factories and a few main streets ... and relieved by a few highways on which the gardens and villas of the factory-owners were built'.[85]

Sheffield, by contrast, was a town of forgers and grinders, file-makers, saw and tool-makers whose workshops dominated the town even after the middle of the century. Its social structure reflected this. There were few large manufacturers and the transition between workers, artisans and 'petty mesters' [*sic*] remained fluid.[86] 'Sheffield lacked large manufacturing enterprises, a powerful Anglican hierarchy, a substantial professional and mercantile establishment.'[87]

The first attempt to incorporate the town in 1838 was a failure because of its egalitarian social and political structure. Many people disliked the idea of creating an official elite and a great deal of workers were against such a move because it would probably result in an increase in taxes. It was only when the West Riding Justices tried to take control of the Sheffield police that opinions in the town began to change. The majority of the people of Sheffield now began to speak out in favour of incorporation and this was achieved in 1843.[88]

The most influential faction in the new town council were the manufacturers in the iron-and-steel industry. In controversial questions class conflicts were only too clear and council decisions were often met with public demonstrations of protest organised by the workers.[89] Nonetheless two Chartists were elected to the council as early as 1846 and three years later Chartists held 22 of the 56 seats on the council.[90] Notwithstanding the economic and social disparities the council as a whole presented itself as a politically radical body. As examples of this Sidney Pollard mentions the petition for the liberation of Kossuth, petitions of solidarity to the London Peace Conference and proposals to the government with the aim of reducing the National Debt.[91] But when it came to dealing with conditions in Sheffield itself the council's radical fervour was somewhat less in evidence. A good case in point were the sanitary conditions in the town. It was not until after an outbreak of cholera in 1849 that the council even began to consider the matter. Extensive propositions for improvement were worked out, only to disappear into office drawers as soon as the epidemic began to die down. Indeed, it was not until 1903 that the council began to deal seriously with the sanitary problems of the town.[92]

This lukewarm attitude towards reform is also noticeable with regard to working-class leisure activities. The sort of factory paternalism which Joyce has noted in the Lancashire textile towns did not and could not develop in Sheffield. Nor did the council – as in Bolton – attempt to offer anything as a substitute. And in 1853, unlike Manchester, Sheffield could boast no public parks, no libraries and no museums.[93]

Several factors prevented the authorities in Sheffield from undertaking the reforms which other towns had introduced. Incorporation had not resulted in a clear and effective distribution of competencies. Even as late as 1850 there were several institutions responsible for the sanitary conditions.[94] These were problems which other authorities also had to deal with but elsewhere there were local politicians – like Chamberlain in Birmingham – with enough ardour for reform, vision and stamina to get things moving. Sheffield lacked such personalities.[95] Significantly, it took until 1897 before they got round to building a town hall: some forty years after Leeds.[96] A large proportion of Sheffield's inhabitants regarded urban centralisation and its accompanying hierarchy with a good deal of scepticism. These included the Chartists on the council whose leader, Ironside, was a strong advocate of grass-roots suburban democracy.[97] Such a notion fitted in well with the dominant social and political structures of a town which was, in the 1860s, still essentially little more than a collection of villages, each branch of production being largely situated in its own close-knit community, whose workers were organised in trade societies offering comprehensive patterns of welfare and support. Within this culture the workers' social, political and leisure activities were centred on the local tavern.[98]

Thomas Youdan's career as a music-hall owner began in such a tavern. Youdan, a former silver-stamper, had his roots firmly planted in the working-class culture of his town. Although he ended his life as the proprietor of an opera house he never severed his early connections. He provided not only entertainment for the workers and artisans of Sheffield but also supported their organisations with benefit performances principally in aid of trade and friendly societies. But Youdan's roots in working-class culture did not keep him isolated from the rest of society. On the contrary, the particular economic and social structures of the town were an important factor in enabling him to take his place amongst the local political elite. The presence of a clergyman at Youdan's 1858 tea party gives some idea of his acceptance in church circles, whose representatives did not

generally show themselves alongside music-hall proprietors in public. In circumstances such as these it is not surprising that there is little documented evidence of anti-music-hall campaigns by reform groups in Sheffield, despite their
considerable activities.

As early as the 1830s the local temperance movement had begun to attract a
considerable amount of support in the town. It had even survived the encroach-
ing radicalisation in the middle of the century without the resulting split into
moderates and radicals as in other towns. One of the main reasons for this can
be attributed to the fact that James Silk Buckingham, the first MP for Sheffield,
was himself a teetotaller and, even if he did not stress this in his politics, gave
radical teetotallers such an appearance of respectability that they seemed
acceptable even in the eyes of middle-class reformers.[99] Indeed the movement
in Sheffield in the 1840s not only consisted of many workers but also included a
number of influential members of the middle class.[100] In the 1850s the United
Kingdom Alliance enjoyed a surge in its membership in the town and in 1854,
with the support of church representatives, a local section was set up. During
this period many national organisations also held their annual conferences in
Sheffield and in 1880 the town even became the headquarters of the British
Temperance League.

By 1852 the Temperance Movement had become so influential that the
council initiated an enquiry into drunkenness in Sheffield.[101] The ensuing
report, issued in January 1853 recommended, amongst others, a tighter control
of beer-houses, the prohibition of the sale of alcohol to under-seventeens and
the ending of the custom of paying wages in public houses. As an alternative it
also proposed the provision of cheap 'moral' amusements.[102] None of these proposals was put into practice but, nonetheless, the Sheffield magistrates decided
from now on as a matter of policy to issue no further alcohol licences. In the following decade the mayor of Sheffield was to send resolutions from the council
at regular intervals to the Home Secretary demanding a change in the licensing
laws.[103]

None of these actions, however, affected the music halls in Sheffield. By contrast with Bolton they were not accused of promoting drunkenness although
they did serve alcohol. The Sheffield reform movement concentrated its efforts
more on promoting alternative leisure institutions and activities such as day-trips
and concerts – not forgetting tea parties of course. The churches – Anglicans,
Quakers, Unitarians and Congregationalists alike – were most active in the area
of adult education.[104]

Youdan with his tea-parties and his bent for opera fitted in perfectly with such
ideas. For this reason an attack on all places of entertainment in Sheffield undertaken by a solitary Quaker in 1861 in the *Sheffield and Rotherham Independent*
came to nothing apart from a few indignant readers' letters.[105] Unlike the 1852
controversy over the Star in Bolton there was no resulting debate on the pros
and cons of such places of entertainment in Sheffield. In 1865 the Surrey Music

Hall, which was by now a theatre, was destroyed by fire; and when a clergyman publicly declared that the theatre employees who had lost all their belongings and their place of work could only hope for help and support if they resolved to turn away from the theatre and follow the path of virtue, his suggestion met with little sympathy and understanding in the town. Indeed a broad cross-section of Sheffield citizens joined forces in favour of Youdan and his people.[106] Charity organisations appealed for donations, reminding people of Youdan's own generosity.[107] The mayor summoned a meeting of the council in which it was resolved to set up a committee to support the unemployed and destitute actors and stage-hands. Likewise the workers of Sheffield held meetings of support. Youdan himself did not count explicitly amongst those deemed worthy of aid as he – unlike his employees – was insured. All the same the meetings assured him of their greatest sympathy. Even Charles Pitt from the Theatre Royal came down handsomely on the side of Youdan and organised a benefit performance, although it must be added that this was not a spontaneous gesture on his part but rather the result of demands from his company. The theatre in the neighbouring town of Rotherham also participated.[108]

For Youdan the loss of the Surrey, in which he had invested more than twenty years of his life, was a painful blow. Especially so, because in 1865 his life's work was due to be crowned by the patronage of the Social Science Association which had planned to hold its annual conference in the theatre – even if the real reason for the choice of venue, according to some of the participants, was simply the size of the auditorium. For had there been any suitable alternative the association would never have chosen to meet in a music hall.[109] Youdan did, however, find a way of staging the event in another of his venues. Some years previously he had acquired the lease of the Adelphi Theatre, a defunct music hall which he used as a warehouse for his props. When the Surrey burnt down in 1865 he promptly renovated and reopened the Adelphi, renaming it the Alexandra Music Hall. Operatic performances were the dominant feature of the programmes presented there, and in due course it came to be considered as Sheffield's first opera house. It boasted the largest stage outside London, an audience capacity of 4,000 like the Surrey, and was known to the locals as 'Tommy's'.[110]

The conference of the Social Science Association marked the opening of the Alexandra and the President of the association, Lord Brougham was there to grace the occasion. For Youdan this was indeed a very special honour. The prominent Whig politician belonged to the political and intellectual elite in mid-Victorian Britain. He had trained as a lawyer and made his name as a contributor to the *Edinburgh Review* before taking his seat in Parliament in 1820. In 1835 he became Chancellor of the Exchequer. He was a reformer by conviction who had not only helped to carry through the great advances of the period, such as the 1832 Reform Act and the municipal reforms of 1835, but also supported movements such as the Mechanics' Institutes. Although he was a member of the Alliance, he was not personally a teetotaller. Indeed he was clearly liberal enough in his attitudes to feel free to appear on the stage of a music hall.[111]

To conclude: despite the considerable differences in the economic, social and political structures in Bolton and Sheffield and the different types of controversies aroused by the halls, there are two structural factors common to the disputes. Firstly, competition between different leisure institutions; and secondly, a disunited local authority whose support was split between both sides. The fact that councils opposed magistrates and some magistrates opposed others, that neither Tories nor Whigs sided with one particular party and that even the Church was often unable to put up a united front are grounds for concluding that this was probably also the case in other urban centres.

There are two basic reasons for such a conclusion. The object of dispute was still in an early stage of development and – leaving aside the views of rigid puritans – the question of exactly how to classify it had not yet been resolved. True there were clear connections between the halls and pub culture. But even in the 1850s the pubs had not been exclusively discredited despite the efforts of the teetotallers. The pub was the traditional meeting-place of working people and played a prominent role in their culture, not only for alcohol and entertainment but also as a focal point for trades unions, friendly societies and clubs, as a library, unemployment agency and sometimes even as a second home.[112] JPs and councillors would meet there and choirs would hold their rehearsals in such buildings.[113] Most music halls had developed from pubs and continued their traditions. Where proprietors offered their entertainment under the guise of 'rational recreation' they did not use the term merely as a propaganda ploy or because they wanted to seduce more people into alcoholism. By erecting museums and galleries and including classical music in their programmes they did indeed come very near to the idea of 'rational recreation'. And they did so in a period in which there were very few alternatives. Their charity events also give the lie to the accusation that the halls were nothing but very cleverly disguised dens of vice.

The second reason was the fluid state of development of both halls and local authority administrations. The Municipal Corporations Act of 1835 had, in many towns, not led to an undisputed takeover of power by the Liberal middle classes and the internal power-relationships in the towns were often still in a state of flux. Even where municipal administrations were under the control of the Liberal, non-conformist entrepreneur class they were more concerned with tackling more urgent problems like sanitation or slum clearances. On the whole at this time it is difficult to discern any interest on the part of the middle classes to shape the working class according to the former's own ideas.[114] Indeed, notwithstanding the campaigns of a few groups, the way in which they dealt with the music halls in the early decades of their development is rather more a sign of indifference. One indication of this is the fact that scarcely any town outside London bothered to regulate these new institutions by means of law and licensing provisions as they were required to do in respect of pubs. Thus the relationship between the authorities and the halls at this time was neither clearly defined nor fixed. This situation was to change in the 1860s when a number of towns began to introduce licensing laws for music halls and related institutions.

5

1860–1877: the 'demon drink'

Between 1860 and 1888 controversies around the halls were most affected by two developments. Firstly, debates on music halls were subsumed into nation-wide debates on temperance and moral reform; and secondly, the structural conditions of the controversies changed as municipal authorities gradually took over responsibility for licensing their local halls.

Debates on alcohol dominated the social conflicts around the halls until the mid-1870s. These were accompanied by campaigns by the temperance move-ment to persuade municipal authorities to introduce licensing laws in order to control the halls, especially with respect to the consumption of alcohol. As early as 1851 the *Era* reported from Manchester that:

> A respectable meeting had been held in the Town Hall ... Resolutions were drawn up, which ... are to be submitted to the magistrates, and then the legislature appealed to for an act to give legal authority for the manner of conducting performances in establishments where ballets, singing, and dancing take place, and strong drinks are sold ... The movement ... is likely to have numerous, influential, and strong supporters.[1]

It was not until the start of the 1860s, however, that the first successes were recorded. During this decade there was a sharp increase in the number of towns requesting the Home Secretary to introduce licensing laws, amongst them in 1865 alone, Norwich, Bury, Huddersfield, Preston and Leeds. Birmingham (1861), Cardiff and Salford (1862), Swansea (1863), Oldham (1865) and Leeds (1866) actually did introduce such legal controls.[2] Furthermore, in Leeds the temperance movement was particularly active in trying to influence the Justices of the Peace in the issuing of music licences.[3] In this chapter I intend to use Leeds as a paradigm in order to examine how municipal authorities dealt with such exter-nal pressure. I shall then look at the alcohol question from the point of view of music-hall culture – with the help of a dispute in Liverpool in 1877 – and try to determine what role the consumption of alcohol actually played in the halls.

LEEDS 1866–1876: TEMPERANCE AND LICENSING

In February 1865 Leeds Town Council requested the Home Secretary to intro-duce a bill for the licensing of music halls. Their request was strongly supported by the Leeds Temperance Society which also made representations to the Home Secretary a month later.[4] The subsequent Improvement Act which provided that 'no room, garden or place shall be kept or used for public dancing, music, or other entertainment of the like kind without a licence ... first obtained from the justices' came into force in November 1866. The Temperance Society clearly hoped that such an act would result in a decrease in the number of music halls and singing saloons in the town and, ideally, that they would disappear completely.[5] Given the social structures and power relationships in Leeds such hopes were not entirely unjustified.

Leeds had been incorporated in 1626. Its administration fared quite well when compared to other corporations mentioned in the 1835 Royal Commission Reports on Municipal Corporations. It was not considered corrupt and the decisions of the justices were overwhelmingly accepted as fair. Nonetheless in 1835 there was a change in the town's political elite. Until then the corporation had been dominated by Tories and Anglicans and drew its membership from the old established merchant families of the town.[6] Non-conformist Liberals and members of the new industrial elite – those manufacturers in the wool, flax and engineering industries which sprang up in the Industrial Revolution – had been excluded from the corridors of power.[7] In the nineteenth century this Tory/Anglican elite was no longer representative of the majority of the town's inhabitants. In 1851 two thirds of the population were non-conformists and most of these were Methodists.[8] But until 1835 they had only had access to the lower levels of urban administration, such as the Vestry or the Improvement Commissions.[9]

Not unexpectedly, the first elections after 1835 led to a radical realignment of power in the town. Of the sixty-four members of the new council, only six had previously been members of the corporation, whereas fifty-one came from the Liberal camp. This realignment was gradually followed by the 'liberalising' of other municipal institutions which had previously been in Tory hands.[10] Of the twenty-two justices who were nominated in 1836, nineteen were Whigs and three Conservatives: fifteen of the twenty-two also sat on the council.[11] The policies which they now pursued were simultaneously Liberal and non-conformist. The first Lord Mayor was a Baptist, the second independent, the third a Unitarian, the fourth a Catholic and the fifth a Wesleyan. The 1850s also saw an increase in the influence of the temperance movement.[12] In 1854 only two members of the council belonged to the Leeds Temperance Society. By 1868 this number had risen to fifteen and teetotal non-conformists had also begun to make their presence felt in the magistrature.[13] From the early 1860s the magistrates' policy began to draw a clear line between alcohol consumption and music or entertainment. Thus, in September 1862, they suspended the alcohol licences of some pub owners who had erected singing saloons on the premises.[14]

Such interference in the realm of working-class culture had given rise to massive protests amongst the townsfolk of Bolton ten years before; and if the

Sheffield elite had attempted to impose similar restrictions they would surely have been greeted with a similar storm of protest. In Leeds, however, there was scarcely any noticeable resistance in 1862: not so much because the working people saw themselves confronted by a strong and unified authority, but because they shared a common culture with their masters, a culture which in many areas transcended the barriers of class.

A century earlier the non-conformist middle class in Leeds had begun to develop a middle-class municipal culture by means of philosophical and literary societies and clubs, musical circles, bookshops and several daily newspapers. In the early years of the nineteenth century they made their first attempts to introduce this culture to the working people of the town. They were actively engaged in adult education, arranged exhibitions, opened the gardens of the Zoological Society or the Botanical Society, and set up several choirs which were to be the foundation for Leeds' reputation as one of the most important centres of choral music in the 1850s.[15]

All these activities were propagated with the aim of bridging the gap between the classes, at least on a cultural level. They were also clearly intended to impose middle-class hegemony in the area of culture. The conditions for fulfilling such aims were particularly favourable in Leeds. On the one hand Wesleyanism, which counted a great many working people amongst its members, was a strong factor in unifying the classes. And in a town which was expanding both commercially and industrially, what the middle class had to offer in the area of culture was well suited to the thirst for education felt by a comparatively prosperous working class.[16] The rapid growth in the choral movement, which was generally strong in the industrial North and particularly so in Leeds, is only one indication of this.[17] True in the 1830s the working class in Leeds was reputed to be particularly radical but this radicalism never extended to the system as a whole.[18] Its aims were to share power with the ruling class, not to bring it down. The Chartists were to experience this particularly strongly. Their extreme wing in Leeds was notable only for its failure to build any basis amongst the workers.[19] In the area of culture, however, there were strong links between the Chartists and the Liberals. Here again the non-conformists played an important role in bringing them together, as witness such organisations as the Hunslet Union Sunday School which was 'conducted jointly by Teetotallers and Chartists' or the Leeds Total Abstinence Charter Association.[20]

In view of the fact that working-class and middle-class culture in Leeds had so much in common and that the two overlapped in so many ways it is at first surprising that licensing laws were introduced in 1866 at all. Especially so because the town's music halls – unlike in Bolton – had not until then been the centre of any scandals which might have provoked the authorities. Some of the causes for the introduction of licensing came from outside the town. A major factor was a nationwide wave of agitation initiated by the teetotallers which reached its climax in the mid 1860s. During this period it was not only pubs which were regular targets of propaganda but also music halls, which were seen as a special form of pub.[21] The new non-conformist town administration, which comprised a large number of teetotallers, did not remain untouched by the wave of agitation.[22]

How did the justices in Leeds handle the licensing laws in practice? And how much influence did the teetotallers wield in the long run? In November 1866 the magistrates met for the first time to discuss the new licensing laws and decide on the necessary provisions for carrying them out. These comprised:

(a) setting the dates for the licensing sessions on the first Friday in January, April, July and October
(b) specifying the opening hours for licensed institutions from four in the afternoon until eleven at night daily, except Sundays, Good Fridays and other days of 'Public Fast or Thanksgiving' when they were to remain closed all day, as well as prohibiting dancing on Christmas Day
(c) prohibiting the presence of drunken and disorderly persons and prostitutes on the premises, gambling, and the tolerance of obscenities and profanities
(d) obliging the licence-holder to allow the police right of entry at any time and to display the form of licence (music, dancing or both) in a clearly visible form in the entrance.[23]

Anyone offering entertainment without a licence would, henceforth (or respectively, six months after the passing of the laws) risk a fine of £5 per day; and any person contravening any of the terms of the licence would have to reckon with his licence being withdrawn at the next sessions.[24] Furthermore the magistrates demanded a form of police report on any applicant, as was usual for the granting of alcohol licences. Thus, from a legal point of view, the conditions were laid down for a comprehensive control of the music halls both in quantity and quality. How did this look in practice?

The first licensing sessions took place on 4 January 1867. Of the eleven justices present, one was the current mayor and three were former mayors and members of the town council. At least another four justices had made themselves a name in the town for their activities in the non-conformist reform movement and philanthropic work, in particular for their parish and missionary work – missionary in this case referring to their work amongst the native 'savages' of Leeds – in Sunday schools, mechanics' institutes and other projects concerned with education; and for their work with young people, in the Young Men's Christian Association and the rehabilitation of prisoners. Some were also active in poor law administration. There is explicit evidence to show that a number of them were opponents of alcohol, and it may be presumed that they were all of like opinion.[25]

Given the composition of the bench it is surprising that the mayor announced that they intended to proceed in a liberal fashion and, should this prove false, they would revise their decisions at the next sessions when police reports would be available. Nonetheless only twenty-one of the thirty applicants were granted a licence.[26] The police report gives no reasons for the rejections. Three of the unsuccessful applicants had in the past contravened certain sections of their alcohol licence, but this also applied to seven of the new licence holders. Other applicants like Charles Thornton, who as early as 1862 had numbered amongst those whose alcohol licence had been suspended for setting up a singing saloon, were met with a protest resolution submitted by the local residents. These 'observed that as there was only one means of exit from the establishment, the street, which was a very narrow one, was almost completely blocked up ... The hall was also very insufficiently provided with sanitary accommodation, and hence the stench in the street at night was an intolerable nuisance.' Despite this, Thornton's application was granted, on condition that he built a second exit and improved the sanitary arrangements.[27]

It is only on studying the police reports of 5 April 1867, when eight of the unsuccessful January applicants again applied for a music licence, that the reasons why five of them again failed in their applications become clear. All their institutions were described as 'resort(s) of Thieves and Prostitutes' and 'low company', or their premises were assessed as unsuitable.[28] The remaining three applicants were granted a licence. On the whole the justices dealt with the applications before them in a very liberal manner. In April 1867 they granted 116 of the 122 applications, and at the third sessions that year only three of the twenty-three new applications were turned down. Table 3 shows that this upward trend was to continue in the following years.[29]

Not all licences were for music halls or singing saloons. The Leeds Music Hall (which was in fact the town's concert hall), the town hall, the circus and the Band of Hope all needed licences for music and dancing. This also applied to mechanics' institutes, parish halls, hotels, clubs and schools which offered entertainment on a regular basis. However, in the 1860s and 70s most licences went to pubs and music halls. There is no discernible trend in Leeds towards either a quantative or qualitative control of these institutions where the granting of licences is concerned. This is not only clear from the number of successful licence applications but also from the reasons for the rejections, which were in many cases spurious. Of the thirty-two unsuccessful applicants in January 1870, twenty were turned down because they neither turned up at the sessions, nor sent a representative; and a further nine were rejected because the application was submitted too late. Five of the seven persons who failed to obtain a licence in October 1870 had not even applied for one, and in January 1871 again eighteen applicants failed to show up.

There was, nonetheless, some control of quality. Normally police reports on the applicant and his establishment contained the remarks: 'a very respectable man & good house well conducted'.[30] But anybody whose rooms were inadequate, who allowed entry to persons of dubious character or disregarded the opening hours was likely to find his application rejected. There were also cases

Table 3. Music Licences in Leeds, 1869–71

Month	Year	Application for or renewal of licence	Granted	Annual total
Jan.	1869	142	120	
Apr.		105	99	
July		95	92	
Oct.		48	44	
				355
Jan.	1870	271	239	
Apr.		102	94	
July		49	33	
Oct.		28	21	
				387
Jan.	1871	401	370	
Apr.		38	28	
July		33	28	
Oct.		26	19	
				445

where a respectable applicant would be turned down simply because his house was in a disreputable area. On the whole, however, the controls were no more extensive than for pubs or other institutions which needed a licence for alcohol or dancing. Given the fact that there were no checks or objections to content or texts, although the law made provision for such precautions, it may be concluded that the music halls were controlled much less rigorously than the theatres which were subject to the vagaries of the Lord Chamberlain.

The teetotallers had not imagined that licences would be granted in such a fashion. As early as 1868 they were complaining that 'licenses have been granted almost indiscriminately to publicans and beersellers, to the utter ruin, it is to be feared, of a vast multitude of mere boys and girls who frequent these hells'.[31] And in 1869 they protested strongly against the magistrates' decision to extend the opening hours.[32] Music-hall licensing was not the only area of friction between the temperance movement and the magistrates at this time. The Leeds Temperance Society Annual Report of 1870 noted with satisfaction that the magistrates' first action on taking over the licensing of beer houses was to close ninety-four pubs; the following year's report noted with regret that they had failed to continue such a restrictive policy.[33]

The magistrates were evidently not willing to act as the tools of the temperance movement. Instead they tended to follow a pragmatic policy of non-intervention on principle with occasional shots across the bows, the more so towards the end of the 1860s when the movement's influence, which had been so strong in the middle of the decade, began to wither. It was also suffering from internal crises. The annual report of 1868 contains appeals to the conscience of the membership to keep up with their payments and refers to the sinking income from this source. The executive committee also complains that wealthier members had ceased to participate in the day-to-day work of the organisation and bemoans the lack of support from the churches.[34]

Whether the temperance movement would have had a more long-term influence over the magistrates if it had been stronger, is, however, questionable. The non-conformist Liberal elite in Leeds might have seemed relatively homogeneous but beneath the surface there were quite considerable internal tensions. As A. Taylor has noted:

> The Liberals in Leeds were a many-sided party, frequently at odds among themselves and in no way reticent in airing these internal disputes in the public arena. For many years before 1870 the party had been in the play of the forces of voluntaryism and teetotalism, which, while they appealed to and indeed largely sprang from the interest of radical Dissent, were less welcome to those of more moderate persuasion.[35]

The practice of music licensing in Leeds demonstrates that radical reform groups and teetotallers failed to exercise any comprehensive influence on the magistrates' decisions, despite their undeniable and immense influence in the town. There were two main reasons for this. Firstly there were considerable fluctuations in their own strength; and secondly they could not count on the unanimous support of the magistrates, the majority of whom were not opposed to the music halls as such. They might have been strict in their determination to forestall any link between alcohol and music in pubs in the early 1860s. But on the whole they enjoyed a fairly good relationship with major music-hall proprietors: men such as Joseph Hobson.

Hobson's career in entertainment began with the opening of the Casino in 1849. The fact that he obtained the land from a local MP leads one to conclude that he enjoyed good connections with at least some of the authorities.[36] The magistrates, too, were not unfavourable in their attitude towards him. When Hobson got himself entangled with the Theatres Act in 1852 he was summonsed to court and although the magistrates were duty-bound to convict him, they handed him down the mildest sentence within their powers.[37] He in turn showed his willingness to cooperate with the authorities by substituting entrance tickets for refreshment checks.[38] Like Youdan in Sheffield Hobson was after a theatre licence. But he too had to wait several years because Leeds already had two theatres and the justices were unwilling to license a third. There are no records of disputes between the theatres and the halls at this time. On the contrary Hobson was occasionally allowed to present theatre performances and was finally granted his licence in the mid-sixties.[39] In 1866 he presented a concert by the Christy Minstrels in the town hall, and organised several concerts featuring famous artists at which the mayor and members of the town council were regular guests. This friendly relationship continued undisturbed until the mid 1880s.

Even Mr Tatham, the radical teetotal mayor of Leeds, who forbade the drinking of wine at official banquets during his time of office with the result that dignitaries preferred to accept official invitations to breakfast, found nothing wrong in accepting the proceeds from Hobson's benefit performances.[40]

To sum up, it may be stated that there were no long-term disputes in Leeds of the type which occurred in Sheffield or Bolton. Nor were the licensing laws applied in a restrictive manner. Significantly enough the one major conflict between the music halls and the magistrature, which arose in 1876, had nothing to do with any differences between the two but, like the introduction of the licensing laws ten years earlier, was connected with a new, major campaign organised by the temperance movement.

The teetotallers now aimed, once and for all, to achieve the demands which they had put forward on the introduction of the 1872 licensing laws: to establish a definite relationship between the size of the population and the number of alcohol licences; and to be granted some say in the granting of licences.[41] With this in mind they began organising a series of local actions in various towns.

In Bradford temperance organisations conducted an enquiry in all districts of the town, with the aim of collecting and presenting evidence of violations of the law in pubs and beer houses, such as the serving of drunks and children, gambling, the presence of thieves, prostitutes and the like, the bribing of policemen and operating without a licence. Such duties were clearly the responsibility of the police but, according to the teetotallers, they had been blatantly neglected.[42] The action was not simply intended as a practical criticism of the authorities. It was meant to 'prove' that there was a direct relationship between the amount of alcohol abuse and the number of licensed houses and consequently, to force a reduction in the number of the latter. A 'Permissive Bill', allowing inhabitants to have a say in determining the number of pubs would thus be introduced by the back door.

There was a similar action in Liverpool organised by local inhabitants who were convinced that there was a close relationship between alcoholism and crime and who were dissatisfied with the way the police and the authorities were applying the 1872 licensing laws. This dissatisfaction reached such a pitch in 1875 that they took the law into their own hands and set up a Vigilance Committee.[43]

The authorities in Birmingham, on the other hand, were very receptive to the arguments and worries of the teetotallers: not least because Joseph Chamberlain, who was mayor in the early 1870s, was strongly committed to the cause and made it official policy during his term in office. In 1876 he began a campaign to introduce the so-called Gothenburg system. This was accompanied by informal measures such as teetotallers visiting the homes of those who had been found guilty of drunkenness or the supplying of alternative drinks in markets and other public places.[44]

Leeds was not left untouched by this new wave of actions, particularly since the town's elite had undergone another change in its composition. From the mid

1870s until 1890, merchants and manufacturers on the town council were gradually replaced by men 'who were by vocation small tradesmen, by political persuasion Liberal and by religious affiliation Nonconformists'.[45] Many of the new councillors were members of the Leeds Temperance Society, whose influence on the council began to increase once more. In 1868 the teetotallers accounted for fifteen members on the council: by 1882 their numbers had grown to twenty-two. In reality their influence was even greater for when it came to critical votes they could, as a rule, count on the support of more than twenty-two for their cause. The election of several radical teetotallers to the office of mayor brought the group further prestige, and there were corresponding – if more gradual – changes in the membership of the magistrature.[46]

In 1850 the teetotallers had adopted demands for prohibition. In 1875 they again followed a pattern of action which had been tried out in the United States: the so-called women's crusades. Here women were in the forefront of the action since their appeals were considered to be especially impressive and effective, as witness the following report in the *Leeds Monthly Record of Current Events*:

> Mrs Gott (wife of the vicar,) read a petition from the wives, mothers, daughters and sisters of Leeds as follows: 'To the worshipful Magistrates of Leeds, sitting in Brewster Sessions ... Your memorialists respectfully remind your Worships that women and children form a large majority of the population, and that these (often without fault of their own) are exposed to the most bitter suffering and wrong from the evils of the Liquor Traffic; and further that large numbers of women themselves are led astray by the facilities for obtaining drink. On behalf of all such we earnestly beseech the Licensing Bench to reduce the excessive number of public houses, and thus lessen the temptations to drunkenness, and do away with much of the crime, pauperism, and other evils which afflict the community.' The petition was signed by 12,910 persons.[47]

Other towns also witnessed women's crusades in 1876.[48]

From this time on there was scarcely any increase in the number of pubs and beer houses in Leeds. There were 365 pubs in 1879 and nine years later this number remained the same. The number of beer houses even declined – from 447 in 1879 to 425 in 1888. At the same time the population of the town increased from 310,000 to 340,000.[49] As early as 1876 the Chief Constable was able to state that 'since the adoption of the present system of supervision, much greater care is taken by publicans and beerhouse keepers generally in preventing the supply of drink to drunken persons, and in prohibiting drunken persons from remaining on their premises; and although a number of licenses still sail very close to the wind in this respect, I am convinced that a gradual improvement is taking place in the management of licensed houses generally'.[50] The same officer was responsible for ensuring that the music halls were also included in this new policy in 1876. By contrast with other towns, chief constables in Leeds regarded themselves as natural allies of the temperance movement.[51]

In 1876 the Chief Constable presented a detailed and critical report on the music hall scene in the town. He began with an overview of the number of music and dancing licences in 1875, and the institutions to which they were granted. These included twenty-four institutions which did not have a licence for alcohol, amongst them ten British Workmen's Institutes, four Temperance hotels, ten 'mechanics' institutes, refreshment rooms, schoolrooms &c', and 338 pubs and beerhouses, of which 221 according to the Chief Constable did not require a music licence. The owners had not applied for one 'for the purpose of enabling them to carry on any regular musical or other entertainment, but simply because they deem it a safeguard in the event of their having occasional parties, suppers, concerts, &c.'.[52] Indeed in the following year many owners did not apply for an extension of their licence.[53] The remaining 117 consisted of five concert halls with professional singers and 112 free-and-easies.

The Chief Constable confirmed that most licence-holders ran their houses well and that instances of excessive drinking within them were comparatively rare. Nonetheless he was of the opinion that programmes of music led many people – particularly young people – to alcohol. This was especially true for the free-and-easies which had no entrance charges and therefore depended on sales of alcohol for their livelihood. Other institutions did not escape criticism either. Some of the twenty-four which did not have an alcohol licence were reprimanded for the manner of their entertainments and enjoined to improve them. As for the five 'concert halls' (meaning music halls), the two largest and the only two which charged for entry, Hobson's Princess's Palace and Thornton's Varieties were described as regular meeting-places for prostitutes. The remaining three – the Seven Stars, the Angel Inn and the Rose and Crown – not only had unsuitable accommodation but were badly run. Here the report goes into into more detail:

> In these places it has been a common practice for the professional singers, as soon as they have finished their turn upon the stage, to take their seats in the midst of the audience in their stage dresses (which are not always of the most unquestionable description), and to partake of drink in company with any of the youths who may be disposed to pay for it for them. This practice has become a nightly one, and when the ages and characters of the youths generally found at these singing rooms is taken into consideration, it will readily be believed that the influences to which they are thus subjected cannot fail to have a baneful effect.[54]

The Chief Constable objected to the extension of the three licences on the above grounds and the magistrates acted accordingly.[55] Interestingly they took no steps against the free-and-easies, although similar arguments could have been used against them. The magistrates were clearly interested in making an example of the three music halls, thereby making it clear that what they were prepared to tolerate in small and semi-professional establishments would in all certainty not be permitted in the larger, commercial music halls. For this reason the magistrates had picked on the very three halls which still charged for refreshment checks instead of entrance tickets. They clearly wanted to deal a death blow to this old system of sales which only offered music and entertainment in association with the consumption of alcohol.

All this was very much to the taste of the temperance movement. Nonetheless they still considered that the magistrates could have gone further, not only because two of the three music halls later reapplied for a licence – and at least one of them was successful – but because the free-and-easies came off largely unscathed in 1876.[56] True, a few of their licences were not renewed, but that was the case at most sessions for various reasons. Basically the magistrates allowed everything to remain as it was, despite the fact that they had obtained new powers which would have allowed them to act in the public interest – rather than that of certain groups – against the smaller halls.

Building regulations were introduced for the first time in 1876. Up to then it had been merely laid down that the premises had to be 'suitable'. Now the magistrates decided 'not to grant any new licenses for music or dancing in respect of any room which has a less superficial area than 400 feet, and a less height than ten feet'.[57] Such decrees were certainly in the interest of public safety. They also had the advantage of being a potential method of restricting the number of music halls, particularly at the lower end of the scale; the singing saloons and the free-and-easies. It is not possible to say for certain whether these were the real intentions behind the new regulations in Leeds because the licensing documents for the years 1877–84 are missing. The only evidence available shows that the number of free-and-easies in the town halved between 1876 and 1877. The *Leeds Mercury*, commenting on this, did not however attribute such a reduction to a rigorous application of the building regulations – something which it would surely have underlined since its editor was one of the leading Liberals in the town. The newspaper simply explained that the reduction was due to the fact that those owners who did not need a licence had not applied for a renewal, and that other free-and-easies had since been discontinued.[58]

Another nine years passed before it sank into the heads of the authorities and the public that fire regulations were no bad thing considering the many fires in theatres and music halls. In 1886 the magistrates in Leeds set up a committee to systematically control the execution of the now more detailed building regulations.[59] In the following years the committee took its duties very seriously indeed, but music halls were not dealt with any more strictly than other public buildings, including those belonging to churches.[60]

All things considered – with the exception of the events of 1876 – relationships between the municipal authorities and the music halls in Leeds were relatively free of conflict between 1866 and 1888, despite the nonconformist majority on the council and the varying degrees of influence wielded by the teetotallers on their policies. The authorities did not leave the music halls to their own devices. Their attempts to register and control them by means of licensing are evident. Nonetheless the regulations were not out of the ordinary, as witness the ban on prostitutes and drunks. Nor were they applied in an excessively rigorous manner in respect of building regulations and censorship. The music hall proprietors in turn played their part by striving to keep a low profile. In Leeds there was no equivalent to Thomas Sharples or Thomas Youdan. Nor would such characters have survived very long in the town. Hobson and Thornton, on the other hand, were rather successful in winning over public opinion. Even the Liberal *Leeds Mercury* took a reasonably tolerant view of the music halls in spite of their negative aspects. A commentary published by the paper in January 1876 stated that:

> So long as the popular taste demands such places of entertainment, it is necessary, in the interest of the public, that they should be conducted in strict obedience to the law. We fear it must be admitted that prostitutes cannot be altogether excluded from these places without creating a still greater evil, but the public have a right to insist that neither managers nor the police shall allow these halls to become mere decoy places for immoral assignations.[61]

Both sides could live with such an arrangement. The only party dissatisfied with the compromise were the teetotallers who failed, even in a town like Leeds, to wield any comprehensive influence on the authorities. Because of the licensing laws, the situation in Leeds with regard to music halls might have been different from that in Sheffield and Bolton. Nonetheless neither the politicians nor the magistrates allowed themselves to be used as a tool by the reform groups for a concerted and unified attack on the culture of the working people.

LIVERPOOL 1877: MUSIC HALLS AND ALCOHOL

One year after the interventions in Leeds the Head Constable of Liverpool, Major Greig started a campaign against the music halls and singing saloons in the town which – as in Leeds – was also connected with an extensive social debate on the problems of alcohol.

In 1877 Parliament ordered a select committee to enquire into the effects of the 1872 Licensing Laws and once more investigate the problem of intemperance. The committee's enquiries lasted over two years and their reports filled nearly 2,000 pages.[62] They were also concerned, if only incidentally, with the music halls. Amongst the subjects under discussion were the possibility of giving magistrates more stringent powers of control and the desirability of separating entertainment from alcohol. In its final report the committee recommended the former and came down in favour of licensing music halls.[63]

Major Greig had given evidence to the committee in February 1877. In his annual report the following November he attacked not only the singing and dancing saloons but also the free-and-easies in the town for allegedly exercising an unduly baneful influence on young people of both sexes, and demanded that they be subjected to rigorous controls by the authorities.[64] He must have been exceedingly grateful for the incentive provided by the select committee. The anti-music hall campaign also gave him the opportunity of polishing up his image which had been severely dented in 1875 when discontented citizens formed an action group to persuade the police to deal more severely with alcoholism in the town. The public were so sensitive to the problem that he was confident of broad agreement with his proposals. He also received strong support from one of his subordinate officers, Inspector Rogerson, who had come to attention on several previous occasions because of the fervent ardour he brought to bear in his struggle against alcoholism and the halls. In 1875 he had reported the owner of the Star Music Hall for allegedly serving alcohol outside official hours. Unfortunately for him the allegations were subsequently dropped because he was unable to provide any substantial proof since the officers accompanying him were unable or unwilling to confirm the allegations. In 1877 however, Rogerson was successful in preventing the owner of the Colosseum Music Hall, Mr J. Goodman, from being granted a theatre licence.[65]

As in Leeds (but not in Bolton) the Liverpool police occasionally had considerable doubts about their music halls. What they lacked, however, was any support from the authorities such as the Chief Constable of Leeds had enjoyed in 1876. Neither could they rely on the local press for the sort of support given in Leeds by the *Mercury*. True, in 1877, the *Liverpool Daily (Evening) Albion* at first supported the views of its Head Constable and confirmed the wisdom of his condemnation stating that:

> The ordinary singing saloon attached to a public house is simply a decoy for drunkenness and worse ... Two things should be considered in this matter. First the danger of associating public amusements with opportunities for drinking; and next, the importance of amusements of the people ... public amusements should be under public control, and all efforts to bring about this end will meet with the support of all social reformers.[66]

Not satisfied with this the newspaper then sent a reporter to investigate the matter further. The resulting assessment was entirely different from that of Major Greig. The reporter visited several of the incriminated establishments. In only one singing saloon was he able to confirm Major Greig's accusations. Even then he objected to Greig's putting them all in the same boat.[67] In the town's other singing saloons – including Griffith's Concert Hall, a favourite haunt of sailors – he was unable to come up with anything offensive. Although drinking took place in all of them: 'There was no drunkenness and no disorder, for the proprietor knows too well the value of his license to permit either the one or the other.'[68] To top it all, Liverpool's three music halls – the Colosseum, the Alhambra and the Gaiety – did not even possess an alcohol licence. The reporter was forced to conclude that, although there was some room for improvement, Major Greig's accusations were for the most part nothing but hot air and pure denunciation.[69]

This all served to confirm Mr J. Goodman's accusations against Inspector

Rogerson who had opposed the granting of a theatre licence to the Colosseum a few weeks earlier. Goodman maintained that Rogerson in his ignorance was only interested in spreading malicious gossip in order to be able to interfere in harmless and legitimate expressions of working-class culture. 'The only crime that would have been committed' he told the magistrates in November, 'was that I was giving too cheap an entertainment to the working class'.[70] Several weeks later Goodman again applied for a licence. This time he was supported by a petition signed by neighbours and 'influential tradesmen of the neighbourhood' amongst them a Vestry member.[71] This stated that:

> ... Mr Goodman had been a well-known resident in the neighbourhood for ten years. Seamen, labouring men of the poorer classes who were unable to pay a high rate of admission, went to the Colosseum, and the style of entertainment was creditable to the house, not having in a single instance exceeded the bounds of modesty and decorum. There were no drinking tables in the body of the theatre, and it was generally closed before eleven o'clock. The Colosseum drew from the streets and the public houses seamen and others, and induced the promotion of quietness and sobriety.[72]

The petitioners' praises were almost certainly exaggerated and failed to convince the magistrates. But the authorities did not believe Major Greig either. The magistrates refused to support his cause and no action was taken against the halls.

Press report or no, Greig's campaign would probably not have been successful. Unlike Leeds, Liverpool was not a town of nonconformists with a strong teetotal component but a Tory stronghold where brewery owners wielded considerable social and political influence. Only once did the town bring itself to adopt Liberal attitudes and that was, notably enough, when the authorities abandoned controls over the market for alcohol and granted licences to all applicants across the board.[73]

This seems the right point to shed a more precise light on the role which alcohol really played in the music halls. It was doubtless considerable as the opponents of the halls alleged. The singing saloons, which had no entrance charges and therefore relied for their income on the sale of refreshment checks, depended entirely on the sales of alcohol to cover their running costs and pay performers and singers. Thus employees, from waiters to the Chairman, were duty-bound to encourage the guests to order drinks. The same applied to the singers. In London George Leybourne and Charles Vance regularly sang their way down the drinks menu; and J. B. Geoghegan who was for many years a chairman and manager in Liverpool, Manchester, Bolton and Sheffield put a high value on the rather more proletarian ales native to Lancashire and Yorkshire.[74] Here economic forces were strongly bound up with the traditional culture of the pubs and the sort of 'merrie olde England' sociability promoted by Thomas Sharples in Bolton. For such people the consumption of alcohol had nothing to do with the teetotallers' visions of alcoholism, sickness and social misery. It was rather a sign of healthy living and as such every man's basic right. Geoghegan put this message across in several songs.[75] One of them puts it like this:

> John Barleycorn is a hero bold
> As any in the land,
> For ages good his fame has stood.
> And will for ages stand.
>
> The Lord in courtly castle
> And the Squire in stately hall:
> The great of name, of birth and fame,
> On John for succour call.
> He bids the troubled heart rejoice,
> Gives warmth to natures cold;
> Makes weak men strong, and old ones young,
> And all men brave and bold.
>
> Give me my native nut brown ale,
>   All other drinks I scorn;
> The English cheer is English beer,
> Our own John Barleycorn.

This form of patriotism could not resist taking a dig at outsiders and the particular target here were the French.

> So, lads need no persuasion,
> But send your glasses round:
> We'll never fear invasion,
> While Barley grows its ground,
> May discord cease and trade increase,
> With ev'ry coming year;
> With plenty crown'd, content and peace,
> I'll sing and drink my beer.

Thus the ideas of entertainment and propaganda, beer and patriotism were all emphatically and successfully brought together.

Visitors to the halls were supposed to drink. And they did so. But this did not automatically turn them into alcoholics. As Brian Harrison has put it: 'The Victorians often failed to distinguish between alcoholism, drinking and drunkenness. Temperance reformers argued that drinking inevitably led to drunkenness, and society at large failed to distinguish between drunkenness and alcoholism.'[76]

The fact that the teetotallers failed as a rule to provide any concrete evidence to back up their assertions that a) the singing saloons and music halls had a corrupting influence on their audiences; and b) more alcohol was consumed in these places than in pubs, beerhouses or gin palaces precisely because of the entertainment on offer, shows that there were real points of difference. These are confirmed by insiders who maintained that the audiences in the halls could very well distinguish between social and narcotic drinking.[77] The reporter on the

Liverpool Albion in 1877 was able to find very few people not drinking in the halls. On the other hand he witnessed very few cases of drunkenness – and this in a large port. Other sources confirm this positive picture and portray the halls as places where men could drink with their wives and families (as opposed to getting drunk alone in a pub) and that the presence of such womenfolk was a strong force for moderation. Furthermore the main attraction of the halls was not drink but the entertainment.[78] And proprietors had little interest in promoting drunkenness and thereby risking their licences. The same can be said for the clientele who were interested in enjoying the entertainment without being disturbed by drunks who were, in any case, quickly thrown out.[79]

As time went by alcohol played an ever-decreasing role in the halls. As early as the 1870s, as the examples in Liverpool and Leeds have shown, many proprietors did not offer alcohol at all. Others gradually began to separate their bars from the auditoria.[80] J. P. Weston who succeeded William Sharples in Bolton is reported in 1873 to have removed the bar and all tables from the auditorium and to have forbidden the sale of alcohol.[81] Such changes were only partly due to real or anticipated pressures from outside such as the teetotallers, or from above like the magistrates. They were much more an expression of an increasing drive for respectability and a consequence of the growing professionalism which distinguished the halls from pubs. As independent producers within a growing entertainment industry their most important source of income came from entrance charges. Income from alcohol sales, although still important, no longer played a pre-eminent role.[82] This growing perception of the music hall as music hall, however, gave rise to new and different types of disputes.

6

1875–1888: programmes and purifiers

In the mid-1870s disputes around the music hall began to take on a new quality. There were three main reasons for this. First, the question of programme and presentation now came to the forefront of public discussion. In August 1874 the *Dublin University Magazine* published an article suggesting that a thoroughgoing debate on the halls was inescapable because 'these establishments are now so numerous and popular ... that their influence cannot but be great upon the minds of a large portion of the people'.[1] Other newspapers agreed.[2] Second, a new generation of music-hall critics now began to examine the halls more closely from within. Such procedures would have been regarded as superfluous by their teetotal predecessors for whom the halls were nothing more than extended pubs. Last, the disputes began to take on a definite class character, something which was almost entirely missing in the alcohol debate where the opposing fronts cut right across all classes. From now on music halls were to become the ground for a clash between middle-class and working-class culture.

I shall begin this chapter by looking at the controversy on the music-hall programme in Glasgow in 1875, which can be seen as a paradigm for this new type of conflict. I shall follow this by examining the licensing practices in Bradford and Sheffield, where – as in Leeds – I hope to shed some light on the relationship between the controversies under social debate and the actions of the municipal authorities. Neither of these two towns introduced licensing laws until the 1880s and in both the question of programme content played a considerable role in the issuing of licences. Licensing practices, however, were not the only way in which middle-class reformers attempted to 'improve' the tone of the halls. I shall therefore conclude the chapter with a discussion of the concepts and policies of the so-called 'counter-attractionists'.

GLASGOW 1875: MIDDLE-CLASS OBJECTIONS

In February 1875 a number of influential Glasgow citizens began a campaign against the local music halls. After they had paid several visits to various halls, in particular the Whitebait Music Hall, they made an appeal to the local press for help in shedding light on the 'problem'.

> During the past week several correspondents drew our attention to an entertainment which for more than a fortnight had been disgracing one of the principal music halls in our city ... Our dramatic critic visited the hall one evening last week, and his report bore out the statements ... as to the thoroughly objectionable and immoral tendency of the entertainment.[3]

A public meeting was called for 24 February which was well attended. After discussing the subject in detail those present decided to submit a petition to the city magistrates. The initiators must have had considerable problems not only with their reports to the meeting but also in the ensuing discussion and the wording of the petition. For the gentlemen considered that what they had witnessed in the Whitebait Music Hall was so shameful as to be literally unspeakable. For that reason they had taken the precaution of hiring an artist for their tour of inspection who had 'sketched' the most important details so that every member of the meeting could at least see what it was about: in particular young women 'so scantily clothed as to be almost naked dancing upon stages before crowds of men, sitting drinking beer and spirits, and smoking cigars and pipes, whilst men sang songs both blasphemous and filthy, containing, as they did, suggestions of a coarse and indecent nature'.[4] The meeting closed by demanding that the magistrates make stricter use of the law which provided penalties for 'indecent behaviour' (£10 or sixty days imprisonment); and also, that they draw up in cooperation with the petitioners further and more effective methods of controlling the content of the halls.

The petition was signed by forty-nine people including the main initiators of the campaign, John Burns, Principal of the Cunard Shipping Company, a member of the School Board, two directors of the City Mission, as well as several ministers and lawyers.[5] At the time none of them seems to have been a member of the council or magistrature.[6] The city authorities reacted with alacrity and, on Saturday 27 February, sent two police officers to inspect the music halls.[7] On the following Monday a meeting took place between the petitioners and the magistrates, the Lord Provost and the Chief Constable. John Burns and a number of ministers who were professionally involved with youth and educational work again pleaded their case with much fervour. What was in dispute was not only the character of the music-hall programme but above all its allegedly negative influence on the audience, especially the young, who were liable to be morally corrupted and tempted into crime. John Burns had had his eye initially only on shop and warehouse lads and young clerks, but such concern was now extended to include young people as a whole.[8] As a result the circle of people who were considered to be in moral danger became much greater than originally perceived.

Given the fact that it was in the 1870s when the growing group of white-collar workers first came to be regarded as a problem in the public eye, there are good grounds for suspecting that originally John Burns' main concern was not the music hall at all. A few years before, B. G. Orchard had published a study of 'the clerks of Liverpool'. The study was highly critical of clerks as a group whilst at the same time claiming that they had been neglected by society. The clerks were accused not only of a lack of readiness to organise but also – and here the parallels with Glasgow become apparent – of morally doubtful leisure pursuits, extravagant clothing and above all, music-hall visits.[9] In the latter respect Orchard's conclusions agreed with the opinions of the employers with regard to their workforce. John Burns might also have been one of those employers who instituted an enquiry into the leisure pursuits of (his) clerks and in doing so came across the music halls. Here, however, he would not only have noted a 'cultural deviation' on the part of his employees but also the existence of an alternative culture which was not only highly attractive to the lower classes but also diametrically opposed to the culture of the middle classes.[10] To the reverend gentlemen who had joined Burns's campaign this was nothing new. They had long been painfully aware that working-class youth would turn their backs on middle-class attempts at socialisation whenever possible and head for the music halls.[11]

The magistrates noted all these points but reacted with much less alarm than the petitioners, arguing that although it was their privilege and duty to oppose vice and immorality at all times, the matter had been dealt with by the police and, in any case, the offending show had been discontinued. Any citizen could of course object to the granting or renewal of a licence. But since the magistrates' duty was to judge, they could not also take the role of prosecution. Nonetheless they were thankful for the concern and commitment of the petitioners.[12]

The one step taken by the magistrates against the Whitebait in April that year was to refuse an alcohol licence to its proprietor, a Mrs Shearer.[13] In this respect the course of events in Glasgow and their outcome show a similar pattern to previous controversies in other towns. In content, however, they represent an important turning-point in the history of the disputes around the music halls. The major point of contention was now not alcohol but the programme. The opponents were now not teetotallers but moral reformers. And it was the constellation of these two new factors which was to define the nature of the disputes for the next twenty years.

As in Glasgow, the new opponents of the music halls were as a rule middle-class reformers and philanthropists, amongst them many clergymen. Despite this, they could not always depend on the support of the authorities. Indeed, depending on their viewpoint, they regarded most authorities as lacking the necessary commitment or fanaticism, at least until around 1890. Up to this point there are clear parallels with the previous disputes about alcohol in the halls and some of the moral reformers must certainly have also been teetotallers. What was new in this case was that the opponents were now divided on class lines. Where formerly the opposing fronts had been divided into 'respectable' (teetotallers) and 'not respectable' (drinkers) irrespective of class, the struggle was now between middle-class social reformers on the one hand and workers (including some clerks) on the other. Although working-class culture had absorbed many Victorian values it was not content to be a mere imitation of a middle-class way of life or let itself be influenced to any considerable degree by middle-class attempts at socialisation. It wanted to be independent and stand on its own feet. The disputes in Glasgow clearly illustrate that Disraeli's two nations had also developed two cultures, and just how alien and inconceivable working-class culture was to certain sections of the middle class. John Burns and his friends could only find strong words of horror and rejection for what they had witnessed in the Whitebait and the other halls of Glasgow.

But what had they in fact witnessed? According to a review in the *Era*: the 'Francis Parisian ballet troupe' with a can-can programme, and the 'Sisters Ridgway, the clever duettists and dancers'.[14] Two further police reports, under-taken on orders from the magistrates, show that Lieutenant Andrew found nothing offensive about the performance; and that although Superintendent Brown found nothing directly obscene in the offerings of the can-can dancers, their costumes were at the least unseemly, if no more so than those normally to be seen at the theatre or in a circus. He did, however, have certain objections to the costumes worn by the Sisters Ridgway, describing them as follows:

> Rose wears a dress which consists of a flashy blue silk body with light trimmings & akin tights disclosing the form of her legs & thighs up to her hips, in fact the skirt scarcely comes down to her private parts but is quite modest as far as the upper part of the body is concerned. She appears to be a model in a figure & in her performance she throws up her legs in such a manner as to cause an impression on the minds of her audience that it is done for the purpose of showing off her figure to the best possible advantage, & gains great applause. In my opinion her conduct is very unbecoming of her sex. As regards her sister Helen, she is dressed in a short skirt reaching to the knee in the same style as ballet girls are dressed at Pantomimes.[15]

Not content with a verbal description the Chief Constable ordered further information in the form of a drawing from the director of Brown's Music Hall. (see illustration).[16]

Both the police reports as well as some of the readers' letters to the newspapers emphasised that neither the can-can dancing nor the comic songs with their often ambiguous wording played a dominant role in the evening's entertainment. Lieutenant Andrew's report on the events on the evening of 9 March 1875 names many elements of folk music, such as ballad singers, a 'Scotch comic', 'Highland Dancers', an Irish duo and an Irish comedian alongside the standard music hall offerings. One of the letter-writers was anyway of the opinion that comic song:

> is entirely thrown away on the hard-headed Glasgow artisan. On a recent visit to one of the most respectable of these places here, I thought I had discovered that the ruling passion of the ordinary Glasgow singing saloon frequenter was clog

I may explain, "Trunks" are simply "coloured under-Draws" puff'; as worn by Clowns, Acrobats, &ᵉ :

Niel Ballets: dresses, can always be put on decently, but I am of opinion that Can Can - Dancing should be dispensed with - and even the music/which is

10. *'Coloured under-draws' [sic] as worn by can-can dancers in Glasgow, 1875.*

dancing. Full two dreary hours were consumed in the different varieties of this amusement...[17]

So what was all the fuss about?

Irrespective of the question as to how much of the programme was dominated by the can-can and comic song – and there was general agreement that the rest of the programme was not really so bad – the problem was that the objectionable numbers were allowed to be on the programme at all. For it was these offerings which Burns and his friends accused of poisoning the whole atmosphere and dragging down the rest of the programme to their level. The Glasgow citizens were not alone in their condemnation. The author of the article in the *Dublin University Magazine* in 1874 had made almost exactly the same point. Despite certain acceptable, even excellent, numbers and songs the music-hall programme was regrettably overshadowed by 'boisterous vulgarity and outstanding absurdity, unrelieved by humour, and often flavoured with indecency'.[18] Representatives of the middle class seemed to have suffered a form of culture-shock on entering the halls. At home they had been accustomed to high-buttoned clothing and bowdlerised editions of the classics. And suddenly they were confronted with short skirts, tights and ambiguous texts; forms of sensuality which had been repressed in their own lives and which were here on open display. The *North British Daily Mail* hit the nail on the head exactly in one of its articles: 'The literature of past ages is sometimes very impure. One would scarcely recommend Rabelais, or the Decameron of Boccaccio for penny readings, and even Shakespeare is none the worse of being edited by Bowdler for the family circle, or judiciously excised for the stage.'[19] Nonetheless these were cultural achievements which the music hall had not yet reached, the paper contin-

119

ued. Quite the contrary: 'the most sensual imaginations of Boccaccio have now come to be out-heroded on the Music Hall platform'.[20] Worse still, according to the *Glasgow Weekly Mail*, the Music Hall was a frontal attack on basic Victorian values and even made a mockery of them: 'all chivalry, all honour, the purity of women, the sacredness of marriage, and every private virtue have been defiled, and the very Bible itself made a text-book for ribaldry, whilst vice and profligacy have been wantonly displayed, and made themes for familiarity and mirth'.[21] Furthermore topics like sex and prostitution were freely bandied about.[22] That they were part of an otherwise acceptable programme was clearly the most dangerous factor of all. 'Where the impropriety is gross and palpable respectable young men stay away. It is in the semi-correct institutions that the taste first becomes vitiated, and afterwards the decline is rapid, the appetite growing with what it feeds on.'[23]

Such points of view were completely alien to the audiences in the halls, who did not divide the programme into 'good' (folky) and 'bad' (sensual) but regarded both as part of a unified whole. The events in Glasgow show that the music hall was firmly established as a third power amongst the workers and clerks, alongside the pubs and traditional entertainment on the one hand, and 'rational recreation' on the other. Here the folky element was particularly noticeable: comic songs, Scottish and Irish songs and dances and offerings, such as jugglers, acrobats and magicians, which had their origins in the fairs.

The music hall satisfied the needs of its audience for uncensored entertainment, culture and information. Its folkiness addressed their feelings for tradition and local pride, and the comic songs gave expression to contemporary topics. This, more than any other, was the area where the audience could see their lives and problems (love, marriage, family, work and leisure, social ambitions and failures) mirrored on stage and could put them in an ironic perspective. Sensuality was not repressed and was therefore not regarded as a moral foible. In 1875 the *Glasgow Weekly Herald* asked its readers: 'Do these crowded singing saloons indicate the week-day revolt of the Sunday church-goer, or are they the expression of an out-and-out rebellion against a church-going which fails to interest, whether on account of its good qualities or its deficiencies?'[24] The answer, presumably, is both.

BRADFORD AND SHEFFIELD 1882–1883: MUNICIPAL REACTIONS

The events in Glasgow mark a turning point in social attitudes towards the music halls in an ever-increasing number of towns. This change was not restricted solely to a minority of middle-class reformers but gradually took a grip on municipal administrations.

Bolton's magistrature began to be infiltrated by the teetotal and Sunday school lobby in 1873. As a result it introduced licensing laws for its music halls and in 1876 ordered the owners of the halls to submit the texts of the songs and sketches which were to be performed during the following week for censorship every Monday.[25] Since performers tended to improvise with the audience it is questionable whether there was in fact any effective control over the programme. There is no documentation to prove the case either way but these measures do demonstrate the amount of concern caused to the authorities by the music-hall programme.

This concern is also manifested in a fresh licensing boom in the 1880s. The first such boom had been in the early sixties in the course of which at least seven towns had introduced licensing laws for their halls. This had slackened off by 1870 and in the following years only Bolton took the opportunity of taking statutory control of its halls. After 1875 the numbers began to increase again. Wakefield in 1877 was followed by Birkenhead (1881), Bradford and Manchester (1882), Sheffield (1883) and Leicester (1884).[26]

Not all of this increase can be attributed to the events in Glasgow. In many cases the control of the halls may only have been a by-product of the growing bureaucratisation of urban life. But from time to time it was more than this. At the very first licensing sessions in Bradford the town's magistrates used arguments against their music halls which were very similar to those put forward in Glasgow in 1875. By means of the powers granted to them by the licensing laws they attempted to intervene in the form and content of working-class culture and impose their own preconceptions on it.

The controversies in Glasgow had been sparked by the differing views of culture held by two classes and had been dealt with by a bench which was for the most part neutral. In Bradford, by contrast, the dispute was between music-hall culture and the magistrates themselves who, because they adopted the line taken by the middle-class reformers, can also be said to have acted on class lines. Bradford was not alone in such matters. A less striking but still noteworthy example can be found in the first licensing sessions in Sheffield. The magistrates did not at first take such a definite stand against the halls. However the opponents of the halls assumed, quite rightly, that their chances of success would be considerably increased if they put forward 'middle-class' objections instead of pushing their own particular interests.

It cannot be maintained that until then the magistrates had stood above the classes. In many areas there is solid proof to show that they had not, especially in the administration of the Poor Law and the application of the game laws. But intervention in the business of the music halls had been rare and when it did occur the magistrates had refused to let themselves be reduced to mouthpieces for pressure groups like teetotallers or middle-class reformers. In the 1880s this began to change. Some of the changes, as in Sheffield, can be attributed to a shift in power within the town's elite. But there was also a growing tension between the classes, which is characteristic of the 1880s as a whole, and which in 1891

121

culminated in the founding of the Independent Labour Party in Bradford.

The first licensing sessions in Bradford were held on 18 January 1882.[27] Even before the magistrates met it was no secret in the town that some of the smaller pub music halls would have difficulty in gaining a licence, if at all. Four days earlier the *Bradford Daily Telegraph* had reported that: 'the Bradford Justices have had an inspection made of some 230 licensed houses ... and measurements taken of the structural arrangements ... We understand some opposition will be offered.'[28] Objections to the suitability of some premises were certainly justifiable. Nonetheless this was not to be the main subject for discussion in the sessions. The reason for the change was an intervention by the council in the person of the Town Clerk, Mr Mossman. Mossman's concerns were not really to do with the buildings as his attitudes towards culture and class were very similar to those of the music-hall opponents in Glasgow in 1875. He was intent on reforming the working-class culture of the town; more precisely in repressing certain expressions of this culture by means of the authorities. And his arguments left no doubt that this was the main reason why the council had introduced the licensing laws.[29] His objections to the granting of music and dancing licences were aimed essentially at three types of establishment. First – and primarily – against the pub music halls which employed women as pianists. The lawyer for the music-hall owners stated that Mossman had made it clear to all applicants that if they wished to have a licence they should sack their lady-pianists, and named twenty such cases to support his argument.[30] Second, there were objections to those music halls – as a rule the smaller ones – where itinerant musicians performed. And last, objections were raised to pubs and hotels which organised dance evenings for working people.[31]

Women performing in pubs was a double affront to the Victorian ideal of womanhood. That these women were not working at home was bad enough; to make matters worse they were employed in public houses, which were by definition 'male' areas associated with alcohol. The bench was quite open in concurring with Mossman on this point and gave voice to their disapproval of young women performing in pubs. Hence the majority of applications for licences were refused.[32] There was probably little difference in the magistrates' attitude to women performers in the large music halls. Nonetheless these applications were dealt with in a somewhat different manner, presumably because here the women were at least separated from the audience by a stage, unlike in the pubs where they sat amongst the male drinkers and might not be employed solely for their fingerwork on the piano.

Mossman also objected to the dance evenings on the presumption that there was a link between alcohol and contact between the sexes which was difficult to control. Alcohol, bodily contact and music were regarded by many members of the ruling classes as a highly explosive mixture which only served to undermine the allegedly loose morals of working people even further. It cannot be an accident that, during discussions on a licence application for the Fox and Goose

Hotel where dances for working people were held, Mossman pointed out that, although alcohol was not served in the dance-hall itself, it was easy to obtain at the nearby bar. Not content with that, he drew the magistrates' attention to his misgivings about a cheap lodging house directly adjoining the hotel. 'It was in such places, where invitations, seductions and allurements to wrong were held out to young people', and for that reason the leisure activities of working people should be put under sharper control.[33] As for itinerant musicians this was also a question of control: control over informal and spontaneous elements of working-class culture which might lead to disorder and confusion.

By contrast the large music halls in Bradford had no difficulty with their licensing applications at the first sessions. Pullan's Music Hall and Morgan's New Star were not even mentioned. Their size, the character of their proprietors and the way they were run seem to have been regarded as a guarantee of order and surveillance. Pullan and Morgan belonged to a completely new breed of music-hall proprietor, some of whose successors would even receive knighthoods in the decades to follow. The sort of working-class culture they presented seemed acceptable, even respectable, in the eyes of the magistrates and, more importantly, the municipal authorities.

The music-hall audience, for their part, made no distinction between large and small halls; nor even amongst themselves. The dancers at the Fox and Goose did not regard themselves as 'roughs' but as decent women factory workers and 'respectable artizans'.[34] The itinerant musicians and female pianists in the pubs also regarded themselves as respectable, a view which was shared by the local press. The *Yorkshire Busy Bee*, a satirical weekly, took up the cause of the itinerant musicians in particular, describing in moving terms the case of a seventy-six-year-old blind fiddler who was:

> thoroughly sober and respectable, and trying manfully, in spite of all manner of misfortunes ... to earn a decent livelihood. Now, by a Pharasaical and Puritanical act he is deprived of his means of earning bread, except by tramping many weary miles beyond the borough and then tramping back after the public houses have closed at night ...

The magazine was not only highly critical of the town's licensing laws. It was particularly harsh on those who introduced and applied them. At first it published a biting satire on the 'anti-licensing-sessions ... under the Woolford Milk-and-Water and Chadband Act' and soon after denounced the town's magistrates as 'a few bigoted Pharisees beyond the means of enjoying themselves' who had committed a 'glaring injustice'.[35]

The *Bradford Observer* also took up the cause. On 2 February 1882 the paper published a letter to the magistrates from a woman who had been a pianist for three years in the town and who had 'always behaved myself as a Lady and given satisfaction to my employers'. Writing as the mother of five who depended on her for support she had heard that after 2 February:

lady pianists ... will not be allowed to play in the town, even in those places where licences have been granted. It seems very hard that a respectable married woman is debarred from making a living honestly. May I hope that you will give some official intimation ... whether my surmises are correct? ... if so, it will throw me out of employment, as also other married ladies who are similarly placed...

Both the above cases have a touch of sentimental melodrama about them and were clearly picked out by the press for that reason. Nonetheless they were probably genuine and highlight the fact that Mossman's campaign did not so much hit the rough end of the market as the informal and semi-professional area of music-hall culture. This area was important because it provided entertainment in the neighbourhoods outside the town centre and at the same time was a source of employment for those who, for reasons of health, family or age, would otherwise have scarcely been in a position to earn a living. By adopting the council's reservations based on differences in class and culture, and in many cases using them as guide-lines in their decision-making, the magistrates helped to destroy these functions. It would take many years before they were restored.

At the first licensing sessions on 18 January 1882 19 applications were rejected and 17 granted, and in the first year of operation a mere 112 out of over 200 applicants received a licence. Only in a few cases were the magistrates willing to look favourably on applications for special licences for events such as club parties or annual meetings.[36]

The decisions of the magistrates in Sheffield in the following year were less drastic in numerical terms. And the issues they dealt with were, at first sight, different from those encountered by their colleagues in Bradford. In the first place pub music halls were not the centre of interest. On 5 September 1883 the bench granted 59 of the 62 applications and a week later 104 of the 116. Of the remaining twelve, four were postponed and six of the further applicants failed to appear. In short, only two were rejected. On 17 October of the same year the magistrates considered a further twenty-six applications, most of which were granted.[37] Secondly, when it came to the licensing laws, Sheffield town council made no attempt to force through a restrictive policy with regard to the music halls. Indeed, during the debate on the introduction of the new licensing laws the mayor of Sheffield went out of his way to allay the fears of the music-hall owners by assuring them that, provided their premises were suitable, they were assured of a music licence.[38]

All the same, the Sheffield administration was susceptible to arguments which touched class perceptions of culture in general and working-class culture in particular. Preeminent amongst the groups who exploited this susceptibility were the teetotallers. One of the movement's umbrella organisations, the British Temperance League, had moved its headquarters to Sheffield in 1880. This gave them a fresh impetus to intensify their campaign against alcohol abuse and music halls were inevitably affected.[39] On 20 September 1883 the Sheffield magistrates dealt with a licence-application from the Star Music Hall. During the proceedings the lawyer for the Star read out a newspaper report on a meeting of the Good Templars, where 'a grant of money was made in aid of the funds for the opposition to licences at brewster sessions. Regret was expressed that the magistrates had not used the power they possessed to reduce the number of licences.' There was also opposition to the Gaiety Music Hall. The person behind the scenes who orchestrated this opposition was a neighbour of the tenant, Frederick Mould, and an active member of the United Kingdom Alliance. Mould's lawyer stated that he had definite evidence that this man had gone about stirring up as much animosity against Mould as he could, even to the extent of offering money for witnesses to come forward with their objections. The teetotallers were not motivated simply by noble principles. According to the *Independent* the group also had 'two places sailing under total abstinence colours' with music and dance licences and would have been only too glad to have seen off some of the irksome competition in this way.

It was mainly due to the lawyers for the halls that all this came into the open. For the teetotallers' strategy was to run a low-profile campaign – for good reasons. Experience had taught them that competitive envy would never be accepted as a valid argument against a music licence and there was not much promise of success in bringing sales of alcohol into question. There was also the specific factor of Sheffield to be taken into account. In a town where the partic-ular conditions of work made drinking almost a professional necessity, teetotal arguments would not make much impression on a bench consisting mostly of manufacturers in metal industries.[40] Hence the teetotallers made no effort to thematise the question of alcohol which was probably an important, if not the main, reason for their interference. Their lawyer W. E. Clegg's strategy was to put forward only such arguments which would be effective in persuading the magistrates to refuse licences to the three largest halls in the town, the Gaiety, Star and Britannia. And it was only in the course of the hearing that he was forced to admit, albeit reluctantly, that he was active in and acting for the United Kingdom Alliance. Clegg's strategy was to steer clear of alcohol and concentrate his attack on the cultural aspect of the halls, their content and programme. In this he was at first successful. He accused both the Star and Britannia of allow-ing entry to young people thereby exposing them to bad company; for these venues were clearly not patronised by respectable society. With respect to the Gaiety, he brought up arguments against those aspects of working-class culture which – as we have already seen in Glasgow and Bradford – were regarded by the middle classes and sections of the ruling elite as particularly disturbing. First he drew the attention of the bench to the fact that young people were not only to be seen amongst the audience at the Gaiety, but also had access to a separate room in the building where dancing took place. In this he intended to arouse precisely those fears which Mossman had exploited in his arguments to the Bradford magistrates. Furthermore he pointed out that in the Gaiety 'songs of an indecent and immoral character were sung by – above all people – women', and offered to provide two police constables as witnesses, one of whom 'knew that half-a-dozen women of ill-fame were there'.[41] Last he succeeded in portraying Frederick Mould, the tenant of the Gaiety, as a person whose moral character made him utterly unsuitable to run such an establishment. Mould, he claimed, had been involved in a public slanging-match with his wife who had suspected him of having a relationship with one of his singers.[42] Given such circumstances, and the numerous and serious affronts to the moral values of the authorities, it is no surprise that Mould's application for a licence was rejected.

Clegg's attack took the town's music halls by surprise. The proprietors and their legal representatives had assumed the only point at question was the suitability of the buildings and were not prepared for arguments aimed at programme and content. By alluding to the cultural differences between the town's ruling classes and the working population their opponents had struck at a vulnerable area and produced the desired effect upon the magistrates. At the sessions of 5 September 1883 the latter had been of the opinion that satisfactory premises were sufficient for the granting of a licence. But scarcely three weeks later, on 21 September, they considered that a licence depended much more on 'innocent recreation', 'good order and good morals'.[43] The lawyer for the Gaiety was quite correct in calling such arguments 'class opposition'.[44]

But in the end Clegg's strategy proved a failure. The Star and Britannia succeeded in applying for a postponement of the hearings in order to prepare an effective defence. This not only exposed Clegg's attacks as a manoeuvre on behalf of the temperance movement but also managed to mobilise the music-hall audiences in the town. The halls were also aided by the fact that Clegg's allegations against the Star and Britannia – by contrast with those against the Gaiety – lacked any substance. Without providing any hard evidence he had simply claimed that both the halls and their audiences were, by definition, 'not respectable' and that young people visiting the two venues would be in danger of moral corruption. The music-hall scene had always managed to refute such allegations. In Sheffield too, both proprietors succeeded in mobilising the town's working people to defend their culture, assert their own feelings of respectability and make clear to the bench that they had no right to intervene in any way whatsoever.

Both proprietors, Alfred Milner of the Star and Arthur Pogson of the Britannia had been in the business for almost twenty years; since 1864 and 1866 respectively. Indeed Pogson's hall had been in the family's hands since 1840, Pogson having inherited the reins from his father. The two men underlined their integrity by pointing out to the magistrates that they had never had any serious clashes with the authorities in all that time. The same applied to their programmes which had never given cause for objection. Milner could further claim to his advantage that for years he had allowed the Star to be used as a venue for religious concerts by the Sheffield Choir. In this he was even supported by one of his competitors, E. R. Callender from the Theatre Royal, who regarded the programme offered in the Star as 'somewhat rough ... but educational'. As for the audience: 'Those whom he had seen in the hall ranged from eighteen to seventy years of age. Whenever he had been there the utmost order prevailed' and he 'had never seen any drunkenness or any bad characters there'.[45]

But neither Milner nor Pogson confined their arguments simply to what they thought would be acceptable to the bench. Both took the view that the halls were there for working people who had a right to be entertained in the way they considered to be acceptable and correct, whether that coincided with the ideas of the authorities and middle classes or not. And when it came to women in the audience Milner did not mince his words: 'If a girl respectably dressed came to the place he should let her in, and if she called for it she would be supplied with drink.'[46] Both proprietors had brought along members of the audience to help them plead their case. One after another, craftsmen, tradesmen and workers lined up to give evidence to the bench. For example:

> William Derbyshire, 34, Carver street, optician, said he and his wife had visited the Britannia once or twice a week, and he considered the performances of the highest character and the place well conducted. – Charles Thomas, scissor manufacturer, Furnace hill, said he had taken his daughters to the hall, and he should not have so had he not thought it a fit and proper place. – Mr. Marshall, cutlery manufacturer, Exchange street, gave similar evidence.[47]

In the end the only serious point of contention was the presence of under-fourteens in the audience. And here neither the magistrates nor the owners were able to agree on a clear and unified line of approach. On the one hand they were not all that enthusiastic about children and young people visiting the halls. On the other hand the seating arrangements in the Britannia demonstrated that it had always been customary for them to do so. Married couples sat in the stalls, unmarried youths occupied the balcony and those under eighteen years of age went into the top gallery. The young people themselves were not content to be shut out and were always finding ways of getting into the halls. The magistrates, for their part, were able to understand this. One of their members, Mr Blake, was of the opinion that although the bench considered that 'sufficient care had not been taken relative to these boys, still they did not intend to make that a ground for refusing the licence'.[48] The upshot was that both music halls were granted their licences.

The case of the Gaiety was quite a different matter. Here the allegations were more serious and substantial. Similar charges against 'good morals' in the past had been relatively easy to ignore. In 1858 Youdan had even had no problem in being elected a councillor shortly after losing his paternity case. But now Mould was regarded as having disqualified himself from the tenancy of a music hall simply as a result of a marital row over an alleged relationship. In Glasgow in 1875 some people had been willing to stand up in defence of the can-can act in the Whitebait but eight years later in Sheffield no-one even attempted to argue that the character of the songs presented there was simply a matter of interpretation. The proprietor of the Gaiety, Louis Metzger, was forced to rely on his spotless personal reputation and the evidence of several witnesses – including artisans, tradesmen and several musicians – who maintained that the programme in the Gaiety was neither indecent, improper, or 'immorally suggestive'.[49] All this failed to impress the bench. Even suggestions that Mould was the victim of a secret agenda on the part of the teetotallers proved fruitless. In the end the bench were only willing to grant a licence on three conditions: that Metzger promised to get rid of Mould and take over the management of the music hall himself; that he would stop all dance evenings; and that he would pay a police constable to be present at all evening performances.[50] Metzger had no alternative but to agree and was finally granted his licence at the fourth sessions in November 1883.

Clegg and the teetotallers may have lost their battle. Nonetheless they succeeded in showing what potential lay in arguments against the halls based on content and cultural differences between rulers and ruled. This was now even possible in Sheffield because the gap between the classes had widened considerably between the 1860s and the 1880s. It is no accident that disputes about content and cultural differences dominated the first licensing sessions in the town and eventually spread to include a general confrontation between the authorities and working-class culture. Nor can this be solely explained as an expression of increasing social concern with music halls. In Sheffield it also indicated a change in the political constellation of power and increasing tensions between the classes. The economic, social and political changes over the preceding quarter of a century now meant that the attitude of the authorities towards working-class culture was considerably less tolerant in 1883 than it had been in 1858.

In the 1860s steel manufacture in the town began to expand and it quickly became a major industry. Although traditional forms of production and organisation managed to survive until the turn of the century heavy industry now predominated.[51] Expansion in the steel industry was accompanied by changes in the social and economic structure of the town which in turn led to political changes. The steel industry did not grow out of the old industries but was an independent development, separated both geographically and personally. The major steelworks and the settlements which grew up around them were situated in the north-east of the town in Attercliffe and Brightside, their capital and labour being to a considerable extent brought in from outside.[52] Thus a new Sheffield gradually came into being whose large enterprises had little in common either with the forms of production and the decentralised structure of the older industries, or with the working-class culture centred around the neighbourhood union branches. The new Sheffield did not develop alongside the old but in competition with it. And from the mid 1870s relationships between the town's traditional radical working class and the overwhelmingly conservative steel magnates began to deteriorate.

The growing antagonism between the parties made itself most noticeable in the town council.[53] Only a few years previously several of the councillors had been Chartists. In 1885 the council rejected a petition on behalf of the Federated Trades that representatives of the working people should be elected to the magistrature, and in 1891 it voted against a proposal for council meetings to be held at times which enabled working people to participate without loss of earnings.[54]

It is highly probable that these new social and political relationships were behind the introduction of the licensing laws. They were certainly responsible for the new character of the disputes around the music halls in Sheffield. Youdan would have had no chance of becoming a councillor in 1883. Clegg, on the other hand, who was both a lawyer and chairman of the British Temperance League in 1883, represented the Attercliffe ward and was the town's mayor in 1885.[55]

Internal power relationships also played a central role in the disputes about working-class culture in Bradford in 1882. But these were more widely connected with national changes in class relationships. Bradford, along with Leeds, was the centre of the Yorkshire woollen industry. Although the two towns had much in common, there were nonetheless considerable differences. Whereas Bradford's existence depended chiefly on the worsted industry – hence the nickname 'worstedopolis' – Leeds could boast of mechanical engineering and the clothing industry in addition to wool. Not only was the structure of employment different. Until 1840 the number of hand-loom weavers in Leeds threatened by economic and technical improvements was comparatively insignificant, whereas in Bradford it was not only relatively high but supplemented by a large number of Irish immigrants. Accordingly the political culture in Bradford was more radical than that in Leeds.[56]

This explains why 'law and order' played a major role in the battle for incorporation. For only incorporation could ensure that Bradford would have effective control over its police-force. Because of strong resistance from radicals who, in this matter, joined forces with the Tories, incorporation was not achieved until 1847.[57] In the following years tensions in Bradford gradually eased off. This was not only due to the strengthening of local authority controls as a result of incorporation. There was a general upturn in the state of the economy with the introduction of the factory system which undermined the basis of the working-class radicals. Furthermore the town's ruling class was able to accommodate working-class demands within the activities of the Liberal party.[58] This phenomenon was not limited to Bradford alone but was nationwide. Working-class politics in the latter part of the nineteenth century were for the most part conducted within a Liberal framework not only at Trades Union level but also in Parliament.[59]

The relative harmony between the classes, expressed in the Lib-Lab pact, began to crumble in the 1880s when Liberalism gradually ceased to function as a model for class integration. The depressions of the 1870s and 1880s not only

129

undermined the belief in steady economic and social progress accompanied by a continual improvement in the lot of the workers – one of the basic tenets of Liberal faith – they also undermined the confidence of working people in their leaders. The Liberals seemed able to offer little to combat the crisis, their main concerns being for the interests of the middle classes. There was also dissatisfaction with the policies of the Trades Union Council which, at first, tried to maintain the Lib-Lab pact.[60]

In this situation the working class had only two alternatives. First to join forces with the Conservatives with whom they had formed occasional alliances in the past – in their struggles for the introduction of factory legislation, or against incorporation. Indeed the Conservatives now experienced a considerable increase in support at both local and national level. But here the Irish question was probably of more significance than the break-up of the Lib-Lab coalition.[61] The second alternative arose from developments within the working class itself which attempted to create its own forms of political representation. The movement had its seeds in the radical workers' clubs and was an amalgam of the relics of Chartist self-confidence and socialist thinking. This found its expression in 1883 when the Democratic Federation, which had been in existence for only two years, was renamed the Social Democratic Federation. Furthermore a large number of new socialist societies and clubs came into being, one of which was the Fabian Society in 1884.[62] These clubs formed alliances with a new form of unionism in the 1880s. The 'New Unionism' of the decade no longer consisted mainly of skilled workers but addressed itself to the interests of the unskilled and semi-skilled, rural and dock workers, workers in the gas industry, and general labourers. Where the old unions had pursued a policy of free negotiation between owners and workers, the new unions were more intent on campaigning for state intervention on behalf of the economically weaker of the two parties.[63] As G. D. C. Cole has written: 'Out of the Socialist propaganda of the 'eighties had come the "New" Unions; now out of the "New" Unions came a new political movement ... ready to pursue an independent policy based on socialist ideas.'[64]

And in 1891 Bradford was once again involved: in the beginnings of the Labour Party. The direct cause was a five-month long strike in Manningham Mills in which unskilled and semi-skilled workers of both sexes were in opposition not only to their boss, Mr S. C. Lister but also to the Liberal town council which came out openly on Lister's side.

> Defeat at Manningham, and the precarious nature of the partial organisation achieved elsewhere, were a spur to political action – and for three leading reasons: First, the bitter indignation aroused by economic oppression and social injustice, against which industrial action appeared to provide no effective remedy, was bound to break out in the demand for an independent class party opposed to the parties of the employers. Second, if the causes of poverty could not be removed, its effect could be tackled by resolute independent action in the

field of local government ... Third, the complexity and subdivision of the textile industry, and the preponderance of women and juvenile workers ... all these gave overwhelming point to the demand for the Legal Eight Hour Day. Political action was seen as the only effective remedy for industrial grievances.[65]

The potential for an independent worker's party was there: in Yorkshire's cooperatives, unions and friendly societies all of which were still coloured by Chartism. The factor which was missing in the 1880s and which now acted as a catalyst was the new, militant unionism which would transform self-help into campaigning for socialism. And the immediate impulse was the failure of a large and bitterly fought strike.[66] The founding of the Independent Labour Party put the seal on the break-up of the Lib-Lab Pact which, in many areas, had already begun to crumble in the 1880s. The first licensing sessions in Bradford in 1882 are an expression of this.

In this context, music-hall licensing was only a small skirmish on the fringe of a major battle. Nonetheless it can be interpreted as an early sign of increasing tensions between the classes, and between working people and the authorities. These tensions would have a political outcome scarcely ten years later in the Manningham strike and result in a final break. By then tensions between the Bradford administration and its music halls had long since been laid to rest. The council no longer intervened in the licensing sessions and the number of music and dance licences granted by the bench rose continually.[67] These were mostly licences for pub music halls. And those which advertised in the newspapers in the 1890s did so for a programme which the council had so vehemently campaigned against in 1882: a programme of informal grass-roots culture, free-and-easies and women artistes.[68]

Once again working people were able to defend and assert their culture. Even though the remainder of the decade was comparatively free of conflicts the political gaps which had opened in 1882 were not to be bridged again. It is of more than symbolic significance that the men and women strikers from Manningham Mills held their meetings in the Star Music Hall and the strikers' battle songs consisted of a mixture of hymns and music-hall songs.[69]

THE COUNTER-ATTRACTIONISTS

By 1885 debates on music halls and their programmes had become so heated that several more municipal authorities had introduced licensing provisions for their halls. Nonetheless this was still less than half of the twenty-four largest towns in England (those with more than 100,000 inhabitants). There is no documentary evidence to suggest major licensing conflicts apart from in Bradford and Sheffield, and even these were restricted to the first sittings.[70] In most towns music-hall licensing seems to have been a by-product of a growing bureaucracy, rather than a deliberate policy.

The social reformers who had sparked off the debates in 1875 with their demands for sharper licensing controls were as disappointed with the results as the teetotallers of the 1860s had been during the first licensing boom. Consequently several of them decided to switch their hopes away from state control and concentrate their efforts on beating the music halls at their own game.

The seed of the idea can be traced back to the temperance movement but it really only began to take root during the 1870s when the prohibitionist aims of the United Kingdom Alliance finally came to grief at the hands of parliament. Whilst there was general agreement on keeping to the same strategy some members of the movement now proposed a new approach: the carrot rather than the stick. They sought to provide a series of coffee-houses offering soft drinks, in many cases cheap food and in the course of time even inexpensive overnight accommodation and programmes of entertainment. Given the commercial potential inherent in such an idea it was not only reformers and philanthropists who belonged to the self-styled 'counter-attractionists' but also 'railway promoters, coffee-house proprietors, soft drink manufacturers and even publicans and brewers' and the like.[71] Each approach complemented and extended the other as we have seen in Birmingham where the introduction of the Gothenburg system by Chamberlain in the 1870s was accompanied by the setting-up of coffee-houses.

The 'Reformed Public-House Movement' first saw the light of day in Leeds where, in 1867, coffee taverns opened their doors to the public. By 1878 the city could boast of over ten British Workman Houses (as the coffee taverns were known) and seven cocoa houses. And in Liverpool in 1879 the British Workman Public-house Company presided over no fewer than thirty-three houses catering for 7,000 customers.[72] The coffee-house societies often cooperated with the working-men's club movement which had been set up in 1867 and whose founder Henry Solly had realised at an early stage that preaching alone was not enough to keep working people off the streets and out of the pubs.[73] Unlike the mechanics' institutes which concentrated their efforts on adult education, working-men's clubs set out to provide entertainment. In the early stages they operated a strict no-alcohol policy and the coffee houses seemed to provide a natural partner. Indeed, both institutions were often housed under the same roof.[74]

Leading lights in public life, amongst them the Earl of Shaftesbury, supported the movement and it quickly spread throughout the land. A form of interim report drawn up by its historian, E. H. Hall, counted fifty-three societies in England alone, and seventy or eighty when Wales, Scotland and the Channel Islands were included. When entertainment was finally added to the original offerings of soft drinks, cheap food and overnight accommodation – in Leeds for example, free-and-easies were held on Saturday evenings – it was but a short step to the setting-up of alternative music halls.[75]

In the summer of 1879 a number of illustrious names including the Dean of Westminster and his wife, gathered together to found a Coffee Music Hall Company. Several of the founding members were probably most interested in the commercial aspects of the enterprise, amongst them Carl Rosa, who ran his own opera company, the composer Arthur Sullivan and John Hullah, one of the best known choral conductors of his time. The aim of the society was: 'the establishment of Music Halls, the special features of which will be the substitution of non-intoxicating drinks for those usually sold in such places, and also such a supervision of the entertainment given as shall free the programme from the unworthy style of song and other attraction offered in too many of the existing Halls'.[76]

At Christmas 1880 the first Coffee Music Hall, the Royal Victoria Coffee Music Hall in South London, formerly the infamous Old Vic Theatre, opened its doors to the public. Its manageress, Emma Cons had formerly worked in the coffee house movement, but her background had more to do with social reform and philanthropy than with business administration or the entertainment industry.[77] The Royal Victoria was undercapitalised and its management more notable for its moral integrity than its commercial expertise. Within a matter of months it had piled up considerable debts and was unable to afford any first-class artistes who might have saved the enterprise let alone make it a serious rival to the large London halls.[78] This was not only due to the lack of capital but to a wrong-headed policy with regard to entertainment. Instead of providing attractive and genuine alternatives like the coffee house movement or the working-men's clubs, the new society put more value on moral edification and instruction. 'At the Victoria', said one complainant, 'you were likely to get, not art, but a huge illuminated diagram of a liver of a Drunkard.'[79] Clearly this was no way to see off the music halls, and in retrospect it is easy to see why the society was unable to engage a professional from the entertainment industry to manage its enterprise. Failure could not be attributed alone to the lack of alcohol, since there were quite a few successful 'dry' halls in the north of England. But the combination of soft drinks and propaganda for moderation and reform was simply too much for the run-of-the-mill working person.

The magazine *Punch* had already prophesied its downfall. In 1879 it remarked dryly that the fact that the average Cockney visitor could not get a beer there was not exactly ideal, but that 'the recreation would perhaps be even more out of his way than the refreshment'.[80] And in 1895 the magazine published a further satire on a similar project, the 'Progressive Music Hall' with the following imaginary dialogue.

> 'No singing allowed in the entertainment?' queried the visitor.
> 'None at all,' was the reply; 'we consider that music is a mistake. Of course some songs are good, but as others are bad it is better to prohibit them altogether, and thus escape the risk of a mistaken choice.'
> 'And no dancing?'

'Of course not. That would be entirely contrary to our principles. If people require exercise they can walk or run.

. . .

You see our object is to have an entirely new entertainment, and consequently we reject all items that have figured in other programmes.'

. . .

'Of course it won't be an entertainment in the usual sense of the word. It can't naturally be an entertainment – I should have said a performance.'
'But we give neither entertainment nor performance.'
'Why not?'
Then came the answer, which was more convincing than surprising – 'Because, my dear Sir, we can't get an audience.'[81]

That was, in a nutshell, the problem of the Royal Victoria Coffee Music Hall, which finally shut down in 1884. Nonetheless the history of the Coffee Music Hall Movement cannot simply be dismissed as an insignificant episode in music-hall history. For this was when reform groups first came on the scene as rivals to the London halls: a clear signal that the capital city was now included in the controversies which had hitherto been mainly confined to the regions.

7

The special case of London, 1840–1888

The music-hall controversies in London differed from those in the regions in three ways. First, there was more competition in London within the various sectors of the entertainment business. Second, the issues of contention were different. In the regions, debates, for the most part, concentrated on the role of the halls in promoting alcohol abuse and the extent to which the programme was responsible for moral corruption. In London, by contrast, the first disputes centred around the question of how much the halls were responsible for encouraging debauchery by their (alleged) tolerance of prostitution and 'provocative' dance performances. Third, the London authorities were considerably more involved in the controversies surrounding the halls as licensing provisions for places of entertainment had been in existence since the middle of the eighteenth century and these automatically applied to music halls. London did not come into line with the regions until the 1880s when alcohol and the contents of the programme began to play a role in the debates. This alignment was further strengthened by the introduction of a new national licensing law in 1888 which applied to all towns alike.

AREAS OF CONFLICT: MORALITY AND BUSINESS

The conflicts in London were different from those in the regions because of the economic, social and political structures specific to London's role as the capital city. The Industrial Revolution had scarcely affected London. The new industries, above all textiles, heavy industries and ship-building, had developed in the North. London's economy, on the other hand, was still based on clothing, shoes, furniture, publishing, metal goods and luxury articles. When the building industry is included, 70 per cent of its workforce was employed in such occupations in 1851, almost all of whom worked in small production units – workshops, sweat shops or at home. Workers were either skilled artisans or unskilled labourers. Larger places of work for ship and machine building like the arsenals in southwest London came into existence at a later stage or arose from the needs of the service sector like the gasworks or the docklands.[1]

Given this particular economic structure two social groups which played an important role in the regional disputes were missing in London – non-conformist manufacturers and female factory workers. The consequences of the former were that the temperance movement found it almost impossible to make progress against London's influential breweries;[2] and there were no debates in the early years about alcohol consumption in the halls. London, for its part, was the scene of controversies which were unknown in the regions until the end of the 1880s, and which can partly be explained by the lack of a female factory proletariat. At question was the presence of women in the halls unaccompanied by men. It was assumed that such women could only be prostitutes and the question was whether the managers of the halls promoted such activities. There was no such debate in the northern industrial cities. It might not have been socially acceptable for young women to be seen in the halls without a male companion. Nonetheless people had learnt to accept that women who earned their living in a factory by day had some right to decide for themselves how they should spend their leisure hours. It was quite usual for women to spend their time away from home and the idea occurred to no-one that women who visited places of entertainment could only be prostitutes.

Women factory workers were practically unknown in mid-nineteenth-century London. The overwhelming majority of women were employed as domestic servants, washer-women or in sweated industries.[3] Any woman who dared to leave her home in the evening unaccompanied by a man in order to go to a place of entertainment was automatically presumed to be a prostitute. Such assumptions were based on two social facts. First, many casual and domestic workers were underpaid and their employment was often only on a seasonal basis. Many women, therefore, had no option but to turn to prostitution in order to survive. Indeed unskilled and semi-skilled women were the largest source for the recruitment of prostitutes.[4] Second, London was especially notorious for its prostitutes. A national analysis of police reports on prostitutes and brothels has shown that there were comparatively few in industrial centres, particularly in those with textile industries where many women were employed on a relatively secure basis. But in ports and seaside resorts where there were no such employment opportunities for women and where the male population was overwhelmingly mobile, the instance of prostitution was very high. This was particularly true in the case of London which was not only a major port but offered few opportunities for women to earn a basic living. The main areas of work for prostitutes were places of entertainment such as pleasure gardens, theatres, cafés and the music halls.[5]

In addition prostitution was a 'social evil' which the authorities in London had traditionally regarded with concern and where they had closely co-operated with reform groups since the early years of the eighteenth century. Unlike alcohol, social evil was regarded as a potential political evil. Here the French Revolution was held up as an example of the demoralising effects on a society when law and order are destroyed. This – or so it was presumed – inevitably led to lasciviousness and irreligion.[6]

136

For all these reasons it is hardly surprising that in London particular attention was paid to the question of prostitution in the music halls. Indeed the level of preoccupation with the problem can be measured by the occasional over-reactions on the part of the authorities which were out of all proportion to the realities of the situation. In the 1870s, for example, it was the general policy of magistrates to regard unaccompanied women in the halls as prostitutes; and this alone was reason enough for them to withdraw the licences from certain music halls. The music-hall owners themselves were not immune to the general wave of hysteria. Instead of arguing the case that such women were not necessarily prostitutes they preferred to put up signs prohibiting entry to women unaccompanied by gentlemen and were constantly emphasising the fact that the majority of their female visitors were respectable married ladies – likewise a distortion of the real picture.[7]

The disputes about prostitution were not restricted to the level of debate. As early as 1857 the magistrates had refused a licence to the Argyll Rooms on the grounds that they promoted 'great social evils'. And it was only with great difficulty that the owner regained his licence a year later.[8] In 1871 there were objections to the renewal of the licence for the Oxford Music Hall on the grounds that it had become a meeting-point for prostitutes; objections which were many times repeated in the following years.[9] The Oxford was one of the smarter West End establishments with a widely-known reputation for prostitution and inevitably came under the scrutiny of the authorities. But such scrutiny was not restricted to the West End. From 1881 churches and reform groups began to draw attention to the halls in the East End and made a particular example of Lusby's Music Hall. Supported by a petition signed by 1,400 inhabitants including the Suffragan Bishop of London and almost all the clergymen of the area, the MP Mr Firth opposed the granting of a licence on the grounds that the hall was badly conducted and a resort of 'disreputable women'. Similar petitions were also brought before the magistrates in the following years.[10]

Nonetheless the majority of music halls retained their licences and those which lost them did so only temporarily, although many justices would have preferred it otherwise. The magistrates were faced with two problems. Any person – and that included prostitutes – was allowed by law to visit the halls, theatres or pubs. The owners of such institutions were only breaking the law if they tolerated prostitutes who were clearly there other than for entertainment or the consumption of alcohol, i.e. for soliciting or loitering on the premises longer than was necessary for the purpose of their visit.[11] It was not only difficult for the police to assess such behaviour accurately. The magistrates' job was made even harder by the fact that the London force was not particularly interested in doing so. By contrast with their colleagues in Leeds and Liverpool, the London police tended to adopt a pragmatic stance on questions of morality. This was particularly true of Sir Richard Mayne, one of the two Metropolitan Police Commissioners in the 1860s. Mayne's force was not only understaffed, he personally saw no reason to intervene as long as prostitutes kept a low profile. The fact that they were to be seen in public places of entertainment was equally no thorn in the eye. For it was Mayne's opinion that, given the structure of Victorian society, the phenomenon of prostitution was inevitable and he preferred to see prostitutes in theatres and cafés than out on the streets.[12]

The magistrates took entirely the opposite attitude, but they were unable to suggest any alternative solutions. Their only remedy was to try to put pressure on the police but this was more difficult than it might seem. The metropolitan police force was answerable to the Home Office and not, as in the regions, to the local authority. Furthermore the Home Secretary tended to support the police rather than the magistrates.[13] In 1879, for example, the magistrates complained to the Home Secretary that the police were not acting energetically enough to combat prostitution in music halls. The complaint conveniently disappeared in the sands of bureaucracy. Other complaints led to a lengthy exchange of correspondence but no action was ever taken.[14]

Indeed, relations between the police and the magistrates were far worse than those between the police and music-hall proprietors, who often called in the police at their own expense, if not to keep the peace or restore order, at least to give the impression of doing so. Officers, for their part, were rewarded with presents like the 'two hampers of wine' which the proprietor of the Oxford Music Hall presented to 'his' local officers for Christmas 1870. Other proprietors organised benefit performances for police organisations, one of the favourites (because of the good publicity it generated) being in aid of police orphans. This shaded at times into bribery and was also regarded as such by the general public and some newspapers. Indeed corruption amongst the lower ranks, like the moral pragmatism of the leadership, was for many years regarded as the hallmark of the metropolitan police.[15] Such a situation was particularly favourable to the music halls since the police, as a rule, sided with the proprietors rather than the magistrates in disputes about the presence of prostitutes in the halls. In 1871 the police confirmed that, prostitutes or not, they had no objection to the manner in which Mr Syers conducted the Oxford Music Hall; and in 1878 an Inspector Crook noted that 'he had seen prostitutes there, but not disorderly prostitutes, and it was not the resort of prostitutes'.[16] In 1881 an East London police inspector, reporting to the magistrates on Lusby's Music Hall, remarked that the hall was well-conducted, that the number of prostitutes to be seen there was 'not more than the average at such places' and that 'the audience he had seen contained a large number of respectable women'.[17]

Although most halls were able to keep their licences the Argyll Rooms, by contrast, did have its licence withdrawn. But here the issue was different. The Argyll was not a music hall in the strict sense of the word and the presence of prostitutes was not the only problem. Up to 1849 the Argyll had specialised in *tableaux vivants* or *poses plastiques* which were regarded by the authorities of the day as 'indecent exposures'. From then on it began to specialise in musical entertainment and gradually gained a reputation as London's most notorious dancing saloon: notorious because, in the 1860s and 1870s, the Argyll was *the* meeting-place for the cream of London's prostitutes. Although the hall was by no means exclusively devoted to the promotion of sexual activities, the respectable side of its business was of little interest to the general public and the authorities.[18] The magistrates regarded it with particular disapproval because it combined two evils, each of which was regarded as promoting the other: prostitution and dancing. In our survey of the disputes in the regions we have seen that dancing, with its mixture of music and bodily contact often under the influence of alcohol was particularly suspect to Victorian officialdom. The London authorities too were under no illusion as to the precise nature of the moral danger.

> These girls went up to the Music and Dancing places, and waited outside till a young 'gentleman', of course took them in and danced with them. Then there came a waltz, which excited their feelings and passions. By looking into the local newspapers it would be seen from the Coroners' Inquests ... that an awful amount of infanticide existed. ... The number of women brought into the workhouse to be confined was alarming, and these young women might never have fallen but for the Dancing Saloons.[19]

The twin problems of dancing and prostitution under one roof in the Argyll finally proved too much for the magistrates and the saloon lost its licence in 1878. Two years later the management tried to reopen the premises as a music hall under a new name, the Trocadero, but the magistrates remained convinced that even under a different name the premises would once again become a meeting-point for all 'that was vicious in this great metropolis'.[20] It was not until 1882 that they finally relented.

For this reason other institutions which offered their clientele the chance of dancing or other means of informal contact quickly fell into difficulties. This was particularly true of the pleasure gardens. In 1846 Cremorne Gardens opened its gates to the public. Amongst its several attractions were Chinese pagodas, Indian temples and Swiss chalets, not to speak of a theatre, concert-rooms, a circus and menagerie, a shooting-range, a bowling alley, a restaurant and – inevitably – a dancing saloon. Not surprisingly the venue had problems whenever its licence came up for renewal and it finally closed in 1877. Highbury Barn, which was also known as a place of entertainment, had already succumbed to a similar fate in 1871 after several years of controversy.[21]

Such institutions were not music halls in the strict sense of the word. But dancing saloons, pleasure gardens and music halls were all treated alike with a combined licence for music and dancing. Anyone who was granted a licence was therefore free to present both. Even in the early years of the halls this was extremely disagreeable to the magistrates. In order to prevent music-hall owners from erecting dancing saloons on their premises they threw all their energies into changing the law so that they could themselves decide whether to grant a music and dancing licence or simply one for music. Their efforts bore fruit as early as 1850 and after this time there was a noticeable change in the outcome of licensing applications. In 1850, under the old rules, the magistrates had renewed sixty-one licences but granted only eleven of the eighty-seven new applications. In the years to 1857, under the new rules, the total number of licences grew to over 300, a fact which can be attributed to the rapid rise in the number of licences solely for music – 255 out of 308.[22] Nonetheless the rule separating music from dancing proved to be a mixed blessing to music-hall pro- prietors. The magistrates might have become more liberal in their approach to the granting of music licences and, in any case, the majority of proprietors were not interested in holding dances. Nonetheless if they presented dancing on stage they were duty-bound to apply for a dance licence. The majority of such applica- tions were refused because, had they been granted, the halls would have been free to hold public dancing as well.

The magistrates were very wary about the idea of dancing on stage in the first place. When Charles Morton applied for a dance licence in addition to his music licence in 1865 he asked the magistrates to clarify 'whether the word *dancing* meant dancing by the public, or both dancing by the public and exhibitions of dancing by professional dancers'.[23] He received neither an answer nor a licence, although he had expressly stated that he was applying for a licence solely for stage performances. Other music halls which did receive dance licences fre- quently lost them very quickly. In 1868 the magistrates refused to renew the dance licence for the London Pavilion because of a can-can performance 'which a Mr. Inspector Bacon thought indecent'.[24] The Oxford Music Hall which finally received a dance licence in 1868, lost it again in the same year; and the Alhambra suffered the same fate in 1870.[25]

It was the large halls which were mostly affected by such measures, just as it was the large halls which were mainly accused of promoting prostitution. They were also at the centre of a further problem which distinguished the London conflicts from those in the regions – competition from within the entertainment industry, not only from theatres but from other music halls. These conflicts played a considerably greater role than they did outside the capital. The entertainment sector in nineteenth-century London was for the most part commercialised and the size of the market when compared to the regions was considerable.[26] Any new enterprises which might be a source of competition to those already existing were regarded sceptically and, where possible, their plans for development obstructed. Business interests might therefore take prece- dence over any cultural and social differences between the entertainment indus- try and the authorities. Opposing parties sometimes tried to mobilise the municipal authorities against possible rivals with the help of social reform argu- ments. In 1860 the owner of the Alhambra, Mr E. T. Smith, applied for a music and dancing licence. This was met with a counter-petition from John Buckstone, the lessee of the Royal Haymarket Theatre, from the lessee of the New Royal

Adelphi Theatre, Ben Webster and a list of other theatre tenants and managers, who claimed: 'that the number of Music Halls are now becoming so great that your Memorialists consider that they are not only detrimental to their interests as Lessees and Managers but to Public Morality'.[27] With this in mind they begged the bench not to grant any further such licences.

Such opposition to unwelcome competition was furthermore strengthened by a clause in the licencing provisions (the 'wants of neighbourhood' clause) stating that a licence could be refused if the number of licences already granted was sufficient to cover the needs of any particular district. This paragraph was used against many applicants, including Charles Morton when he tried to open a second music hall, the Oxford, in the West End in 1860.[28] His opponents promptly claimed that there were already three theatres and five music halls within a half-mile radius of the Oxford. Nonetheless the magistrates usually came down on the side of the applicant. The 'moral' arguments of the competitors were too transparent and the magistrates did not feel themselves duty-bound to protect the commercial interests of one businessman against another, particularly since it was in the interest of the local vestry to promote new business because of the considerable income to be derived from commercial rates.[29]

Commercial rivalry in London was not simply restricted to the area of licensing. The programme offered by the halls was a source of considerably more friction and the resulting conflicts between theatres and the halls were to go as high as Parliament.[30] The cause of the disputes can be found in the highly unfortunate wording of the licensing laws for theatres and music halls. The music-hall licence allowed for 'public dancing, music, or *other public entertainment of the like kind*',[31] whereas paragraph twenty-three of the Theatres Act of 1843 provided that 'every Tragedy, Comedy, Farce, Opera, Burletta, Interlude, Melodrama, Pantomime, or *other entertainment of the stage, or any part thereof* constituted a theatre play and had to be licensed by the Lord Chamberlain. There was clearly an overlap here. While the music-hall owners tried to stretch the interpretation of their legal provisions to the limit, the theatre owners insisted on a literal interpretation of the law as laid down under the Theatres Act. Conflict was inevitable and representatives of both parties were to meet at regular occasions in the law courts.

One of the first major legal confrontations took place in 1860–61 when Ben Webster, described by the *Era* as 'one of the most distinguished actors, and one of the most successful managers, in the dramatic world', took Charles Morton to court for contravening the Theatres Act.[32] The cause of the conflict was a so-called pantomimic duologue named 'The Enchanted Hash', half of which according to the statements of several witnesses consisted of songs and a 'fair proportion of dancing'. Two actors portrayed ten different characters in a tale of two young lovers whose courting was at first disturbed by devils and then protected by good fairies 'and ultimately developed into Clown, Pantaloon, Harlequin, and Columbine' – in other words characters from the *Commedia* dell'Arte.[33] The arguments used by the opposing sides give a clear insight into the lines of dispute. The theatre folk claimed that anything called a 'pantomime' was indisputably a theatre play within the terms of the Theatres Act. The fact that there was a stage, costumes, characters and a story-line were further proof of it being a play 'or any part thereof'. The music-hall supporters, on the other hand, strongly denied the existence of a story-line or plot and maintained that the other elements alone could not possibly constitute a play because basic elements such as scenery and scene-changing were missing. These might have been interesting arguments as criteria for a new theory of the drama but they were of little practical help in solving the immediate problem.

Given the wording of the two laws, conflicts about what constituted a play or not were inevitable. The theatres already felt themselves threatened by the halls because of the novelty of their attractions and the fact that the audience were able to eat, drink and smoke during the performances. If the owners of the halls were further allowed to present theatre plays, so the theatre owners protested, they might as well shut up shop immediately for they had nothing to offer which the music halls did not already possess. Needless to say the owners of the halls considered themselves likewise at a disadvantage. On the one hand society accused them of providing nothing but trivial entertainment like performing poodles, obscene songs and racy sketches. But when they attempted to present anything more demanding or educational they were promptly brought before the courts by the theatre owners. After all, they were doing no more than acting within the provisions of their own licences and following the tradition of pub entertainment – a tradition which, before 1843, had never discriminated between musical and theatrical entertainment.

The court in the Webster-Morton controversy was only too aware of the dilemma. Morton was convicted but given only a comparatively minor fine. In 1864–5 he was fined again following an intervention by the theatres, this time for presenting a 'hotch potch optical illusion' called 'The Ghost Entertainment'.[34] The basic problem remained. Law suits continued to be prosecuted and were even sought after by both sides. In 1865 John Hollingshead, who was both a theatre and a music-hall manager and as such a supporter of more liberal licensing laws, presented a short play in the Alhambra entitled 'Where's the Police?' The men in question soon put in the appearance Hollingshead had hoped for, since his ulterior motive was to provoke a test case and settle the matter once and for all. In this he was using the same tactic as many theatre owners. And this is the reason why the theatres continually targeted the same few music-hall proprietors when many others could also have been prosecuted for contravening the law. It was no accident that Webster, the doyen of the London theatre chose to pick on Charles Morton, the 'father of the halls'.

But none of these court cases succeeded in setting a definite legal precedent. On the contrary, disputes became more rancorous, any attempts at conciliation failed and the number of cases coming up before the courts rose constantly.

Matters came to a head in 1865 when not only Morton was summoned before the courts but also Frederick Strange from the Alhambra, another leading figure on the scene. Whereas Morton had been constantly hauled up before the courts for putting on mini-plays and sketches, Strange's case highlights a second major area of conflict: the ballet. For theatre owners were of the opinion that ballet was not always the same as ballet. They drew a distinction between 'ballet d'action' (a ballet with scenery and a story-line such as 'Giselle') and 'ballet divertissement' which had no plot. The ballets which Strange presented at the Alhambra clearly belonged to the first category. Nonetheless, by contrast with the Webster-Morton judgement, the court came down in favour of Strange by judging that 'the ballet in question was not a stage play'.[35]

In the end both camps were forced to conclude that the problem would never be effectively solved by litigation since the decisions of the courts in almost every case were based on different criteria.[36] The only satisfactory solution was a change in the law. To this end Frederick Stanley, the lawyer for the London Music Halls Protection Society, had contacted the Home Secretary Sir George Cornwell Lewis as early as 1861 with a series of proposed amendments to the Theatres Act.[37] Unfortunately Lewis was replaced by Sir George Grey before he could take up the matter and the proposals were never put before Parliament. Stanley, however, persisted in his efforts with the Home Office and in 1866 Parliament set up a select committee to enquire into theatrical licenses and regulations.[38]

Both sides reiterated their respective standpoints to the committee. The theatre owners insisted on how much they would suffer if the halls were allowed to present 'dramatic offerings' – possibly even uncensored – in addition to all the other advantages they were allowed like the consumption of food, alcohol and tobacco in the auditoria. For good measure the theatres also threw in an aesthetic argument by asking the committee to consider the negative effects not on the theatre but on art as a whole; for art was in no way compatible with banal activities like eating, drinking and smoking. As a logical consequence the theatre owners were only willing to concede to a change in the licensing laws if the halls were made subject to the same restriction as the theatres when they presented theatre plays (in the broad definition of the act of 1843). These restrictions naturally meant censorship and the banning of any form of refreshments in the auditoria. The proprietors of the halls, on the other hand, were of the opinion that the theatre owners were deliberately deflecting from the real theme. The argument was not really about the pairing of Lear and beer, as the theatre people maintained, for the halls never intended to present theatre plays in their entirety. The point at issue was the legalisation of dramatic-type numbers which were neither full-length nor even genuine plays but which, nevertheless, fell under the broad definition of the Theatres Act. By this they meant scenic ballets, pantomime interludes and sketches which could never be seen as competition to Shakespeare. The public was mature enough to decide for themselves whether they wanted to visit the halls or the theatre.[39]

In principle the committee members agreed with the arguments of the music-hall proprietors. But nonetheless they proposed the extension of censorship.[40] As so often in the past, however, no new law resulted from the select committee's report. Parliament obviously had more important matters to consider and licensing-procedures at the time were purely a local matter which most municipal authorities considered to be of secondary importance. The only group for whom the subject was of any interest at all were music-hall owners and only a small proportion of these – the proprietors of the large London enterprises – had any interest in reform.[41]

Nothing changed. The halls continued to present scenic ballets, operatic excerpts and sketches, for which they were regularly brought before the courts and let off with small fines.[42] But this situation in no way succeeded in allaying the tensions between the halls and the theatres. Quite the contrary, matters became even worse. In the years which followed the many forms of theatrical genre presented in both theatres and halls became so mixed and fixed – both on a personal and institutional level – that the legal status quo was inevitably called into question once again.

For all their insistence on art the theatres had for a long time included variety elements like dancing and songs in their programmes. The borrowing of music-hall elements made further ground when theatre managers began engaging music-hall artistes either as entertainers in their own right or for the annual Christmas pantomime where they were a fully-integrated part of the show.[43] In the halls, on the other hand, sketches gradually became a permanent feature of the programme. Sketch-artistes were in a particularly precarious legal situation since their every appearance could be seen as a breach of the Theatres Act. Furthermore they regarded themselves as superior to the run-of-the-mill music-hall entertainers since they were presenting 'art'. Some of them were even stage actors who claimed they had been driven out of the theatres by music-hall entertainers.[44] In the 1880s the sketch-artistes and the proprietors of the halls were the two most vociferous groups demanding a reform of the licensing laws. To this end, in 1889, they sent a deputation to the newly-constituted licensing authority, the London County Council (LCC), which in turn came out in favour of legalising sketches.[45] This proposition was put to the opposing parties but fell through because they could not agree on the maximum length of a sketch. The only suggestion which found common approval was the setting-up of another select committee.[46]

Proposals for a reform of the law had also been forthcoming from a third party. The MP Mr Dixon-Hartland had busied himself with the problem for some years and put forward several outline bills between 1882 and 1887. All of them proposed that the London theatres and music halls be put under the control of the Home Office. This at least found favour with the music-hall proprietors who were not on the best of terms with the magistrates.[47]

The Select Committee on Theatres and Places of Entertainment finally met in March 1892 and from then until the end of May interviewed both magistrates and police officers, music-hall and theatre proprietors, performers, singers and actors from London and the regions. The argument about sketches was now different from that in 1866 since the theatre-owners had given up their opposition in principle. What they wanted to prevent at any cost was that sketches, in respect of their duration, technical needs and size of cast, might be mistaken for 'legitimate' theatre plays. They therefore supported the proposals put forward by the LCC in 1891 which would have restricted the maximum length of a sketch to twenty minutes with a cast not exceeding six persons. The music-hall owners, for their part, whilst agreeing with the cast-size, wanted to extend the possible duration to forty-five minutes.[48] The committee finally came down in favour of the halls, recommending they be allowed to present ballets and sketches under the terms of their own licences but – in order to accommodate the theatre owners – that such offerings be restricted to a maximum duration of forty minutes and a cast of six.[49] Once again however, as in 1866, no subsequent law was forthcoming. It was not until 1912 that sketches, the number of which a 1910 contemporary assessed at approximately 150,000, were finally legalised.[50]

But the 1892 enquiry was no mere replay of its predecessor in 1866. The arguments had moved on from then, not simply with regard to the sketches. It was now generally acknowledged that laws which took no account of the real circumstances would not be respected and that they had to be adapted to accommodate such realities, even if it took a further twenty years. Another major difference was that the dispute had now extended to include not only the owners on both sides, but also the performers and even members of the audience. In 1889 one of the largest working-men's clubs in the East End distributed a petition to other clubs in the capital asking for signatures in support of music-hall proprietors who were trying to prevent the LCC from banning sketches and dancing from the music-hall stage. At the same time the petitioners took the opportunity of making known their views on another problem which was at the forefront of disputes in London – the question of prostitution:

> It would be cruel and utterly monstrous ... to deprive those who have the misfortune to be prostitutes of their right to enter a place of amusement; and because in practice it would be impossible for the doorkeeper to decide who were and who were not prostitutes; and, moreover, that if 'immoral' women have to be excluded, 'immoral' men should be excluded too.[51]

Thus the London public demonstrated its solidarity with the halls in defending both issues under attack. The attitude of the metropolitan authorities, by contrast, was rather more ambivalent. They were strictly opposed to the composition of the audiences and the programmes on offer. But when it came to legal battles between theatres and halls their role was more of an umpire, although they tended to side more with the halls even when they were compelled by law to act against them. Despite the many differences, it would be fair to say that relations between the owners of the halls and the authorities were relatively good. After all, it was the halls who continually turned to Parliament for help, thereby demonstrating a tenacious faith in the institutions of the state in spite of the many setbacks they were forced to endure. For its part Parliament tended to show a distinct lack of interest and dismissed any proposals for reform which might have resulted in direct state intervention in music-hall programmes.

For all that, it should not be forgotten that London had possessed licensing laws enabling the authorities to regulate the halls from the very beginning. In the regions such laws had only come into force over a considerable period of time and with great local variations. Thus the London disputes were not only thematically different. They also took place within a different institutional framework.

LICENSING PRACTICES: THE MIDDLESEX MAGISTRATES

There was a law for licensing music halls in London long before they even existed. The Disorderly Houses Act had come into force in 1752 with the three-fold aim of 'preventing Thefts and Robberies, and for Regulating Places of Entertainment, and punishing Persons keeping disorderly houses'.[52] It was valid within the area of 'the cities of London and Westminster, or within twenty miles thereof'.[53] The Justices of the Peace of London and the adjoining counties were responsible for its implementation. London had no central administration until 1888 so the areas north of the Thames – with the exception of the City, which was autonomous – were administered by the county of Middlesex and those south of the river divided between Surrey and Kent.[54] Since most music halls were situated in the Middlesex area and the Middlesex justices were the only ones who actually sat in London, the great majority of research (including the present study) has been concentrated here.

The Disorderly Houses Act was intended to bring all public places of entertainment which were not otherwise dealt with (such as theatres) under control. The wording of the act, however, with its references to 'riotous plea-sures', 'the habit of idleness' and 'mischief' meant that any new places of entertainment were inevitably pushed into a twilight area of crime. Thus, right from the start, music halls were tarred with the same brush as eighteenth-century places of entertainment and a considerable number of magistrates, par-ticularly those with no personal experience of the venues, regarded them with disapproval. In particular the reports to the 1866 select committee show that they thought that music halls were potential hotbeds of vice and crime. It was not considered necessary to go into the matter more closely, for 'one does not want to taste poison to know that it exists in a chemist's shop'.[55]

The act of 1752, as its full title reveals, had three main objectives. But a closer examination shows that it was not equipped to deal equally with all three. Any places of entertainment frequented by the criminal underworld could be closed and their proprietors severely punished. If they had a licence they were duty-bound to allow the police right of access at any time; and once they had a record they were highly likely to lose their licence. If they then persisted in keeping their premises open they would be hounded by the law and heavily fined: which in turn meant gradual and inevitable ruin. Prosecution was not in the hands of the police alone, because there was no police force in the modern sense of the word.[56] For this reason paragraph V of the Act also allowed private persons to report unlicensed houses. Thus the regulation of crime was adequately covered. By contrast there was scarcely any regulation of more day-to-day affairs and the content of the music-hall programme.

In addition to granting the police a right of entry licence-holders were bound only to display a notice by the entrance stating that a licence had been granted, and to inform customers of the opening-times. Apart from that they were free, in principle, to do what they liked. The shortcomings of the Disorderly Houses Act had been recognised as early as 1850 by John Adams, a JP in Middlesex for many years. At this time the magistrates' practice was to licence practically all premises which were remotely to do with entertainment. These included plea-sure gardens, pubs, singing saloons, free-and-easies and even hotel rooms with pianos which provided occasional and irregular entertainment for guests.[57] In an open letter Adams criticised the act for being simultaneously too harsh and too weak. Too harsh because it forbade any concert, even the most respectable, before five in the afternoon; and too weak because it prevented the organs of the state from performing their primary duty in the public interest, which was the 'strictest surveillance and control' of the programme and the audience.[58] Adams was of the opinion that the law was out of date and should be replaced.

Police representatives were also to express their dissatisfaction with the law to the 1866 select committee. They confirmed Adams's criticism that they had very few powers to control what went on in the halls. They were merely required to ensure that opening-times were adhered to and that audiences were not 'dis-orderly', even though nobody had ever bothered to define 'disorderly'. This was no guarantee that police could ensure law and order in the halls. Their presence doubtless had a calming effect but it did not prevent all types of disturbance. When there were disputes between performers and the audience it made no difference whether the police were present or not. And even if they were on the premises they tended as a rule not to intervene unless expressly requested by the manager to do so. The police made a distinction here between 'disorderly behaviour' and 'popular control' and, when in doubt, sided with the audiences.[59] Theoretically they could have intervened under the terms of the 1843 Theatres Act. But given the discussions on the act which tended to get lost in the most obscure technicalities they felt this was beyond their capacities.[60] And when it came to controlling performances or the premises they had no legal authority whatever.[61] This was first made possible in 1878 by the Metropolitan Building Acts Amendment Act and a year later by the Children's Dangerous Performances Act. But even then questions of content or moral aspects of performance were still not covered.[62]

Despite its many shortcomings scholars have held the 1752 Disorderly Houses Act in comparatively high regard. Hugh Cunningham is of the opinion that it provided the state with increased powers to regulate the provision and content of leisure, and that the organs of the state lost no time in protecting and upholding public morality within the bounds of market forces.[63] Penelope Summerfield, in an extensive study of licensing practices in Middlesex has argued that the magistrates had a strong interest in controlling the development of the halls from the outset; and that their decisions ensured that only a certain type of hall – variety rather than the pub – could survive. 'Music hall was becoming the dominant form, not through a linear development caused by changes in popular taste, but through a process of selection, caused primarily by the removal of other forms as a result of the authorities' use of the licensing laws.'[64] Her conclusions are based on the following points. Firstly, between 1848 and 1850, a period of Chartist activity at home and revolution abroad, the magistrates had extended music licensing to include pubs with the aim of controlling working-class activities and meeting-places. Secondly, magistrates had consciously granted licences on a selective basis with a view to restricting the density of pubs in working-class and immigrant areas and thereby exerting control over alcohol consumption and prostitution. Any persons contravening any part of the terms of their licence would automatically have it withdrawn.[65]

But there is no clear evidence from licensing records and newspaper reports either to support the thesis that the Middlesex magistrates operated a stringent policy of control over the halls, or that there was a uniform line of continuity between the policies of the Middlesex magistrates and the LCC in respect of singing saloons and variety theatres. The argument that there was a relationship between the extension of licensing and Chartist activity is unconvincing for the simple reason that such a relationship would have been revealed most clearly in the bastions of Chartist activities. But here in the North of England nobody considered it a matter of particular urgency to license music halls or even pub music halls. In London, by contrast, pubs which offered entertainment were required by law since 1828 to apply for a licence, as Summerfield herself points out. That an increasing number of licences were issued after 1848 can be attributed quite simply to the fact that this was the nascent period of the music halls. For that reason there was a distinct increase in the amount of pubs offering entertainment.[66] There is also no documentary proof that pubs in working-class or immigrant districts were systematically discriminated against. The most that can be said here is that the magistrates' decisions were inconsistent.[67] There is no doubt that anyone who breached the terms of their alcohol or music licence had to reckon with losing one or both licences. But did magistrates really use this clause to systematically decimate the smaller halls?

It is useful at this point to examine the Middlesex licensing procedure in more detail. The first step taken by magistrates was to invite applications for new licences or renewals. These applications would then be made public in order to enable anyone to lodge an objection. At the same time the magistrates issued a circular letter to the police and JPs in the parishes or boroughs asking them to sound out information about the applicants. As time went by these letters became increasingly more detailed in their enquiries: in 1840 the magistrates only wanted to know the names of licence holders and applicants with previous convictions or against whom objections had been lodged. By the 1860s they were demanding information on the size of the premises, lighting, heating, ventilation and exits, and also asked whether the 'public requirements of the locality demand the grant of such licence'.[68] With such information to hand and given the co-operation of the police the magistrates would now have been able – had they wished – to rid themselves of any disagreeable music halls in a most elegant and easy manner. Building regulations especially could have provided a convenient pretext, particularly after they were extended to include all public buildings in London by the Metropolitan Management and Building Acts Amendment Act of 1878.

This was the theoretical framework. But how were matters dealt with in practice? In the decade after 1850, when music and dancing licences were dealt with separately, the overwhelming majority of all licence applications were granted by the magistrates. In 1850 71 per cent; between 1851 and 1856 90 and 95 per cent; and in 1857 74 per cent; and the total number of licences issued in this period rose from 72 to 331.[69] Renewals, however, were dealt with in a different manner from new applications. Between 90 and 95 per cent of all applications for renewal were granted. Most of the remainder failed simply because no application for a renewal had been made. In the case of new applications this was almost the reverse despite the dramatic rise in the number of licences granted. In 1854 67 per cent, in 1856 75 per cent, and in 1857 93 per cent of all new applicants were refused a licence by the magistrates.

Exactly why licences were refused or not renewed can only be established by looking at each case individually. Formal reasons played a large part here: applications either arrived too late or applicants failed to show up at the sessions. Infringements of the provisions of the licence also led to applications for renewal being rejected.[70] Further reasons for rejections were due to counter-petitions and objections by local authorities (see table 4).

Even where there were objections they did not automatically result in applications being rejected. In one case in 1854, five in 1855, two in 1856 and eight in 1857 (of which one was a complaint from the police) the magistrates decided to grant a licence despite objections. Nor were the rejections final as shown by the number of successful reapplications. All in all, despite the high proportion of

Table 4 *Reasons for a licence refusal*

Year	Total number of refusals	Formal errors	Counter-petitions	Police objections
1854	7 renewals	4	3	
1856	2 renewals		1	1
	21 new applications	5	7	
1857	7 renewals	1	5	
	69 new applications	10		

unsuccessful new applications between 1851 and 1856 the magistrates granted on average 79 per cent of all applications. These had, as a rule, been made by pub music-hall owners in a period when the number of halls in London more than trebled.

The upward trend came to a halt in 1860 and there was a marked fall in the total number of halls between 1860 and 1865. The pub music halls were the main victims here, whereas there was a clear growth in the number of music halls. A few new pub music halls came into existence but these were greatly exceeded by the number which went out of business. Here, as in the 1850s, the number of owners not reapplying for a licence was higher than those whose applications were unsuccessful, but the total amount of applications was still significantly higher than in the previous decade.

There is nothing here to point to the fact that magistrates deliberately discriminated in favour of the large music halls. The rise in the number of rejections for pub music halls is even less dramatic when looked at in relationship to the total number of applications for renewal. In 1862, for example, the year with the most rejections, the number of unsuccessful applications for a licence renewal from pub music halls amounted to just over 4 per cent of the total. In 1863 it was 3 per cent and in the following year, 2 per cent.[71] It is interesting to note that intervention was at its greatest in 1862, the year *before* the magistrates began demanding more information about individual applicants.

Nor did the more detailed enquiries, introduced in 1863, lead to any reduction in the number of halls. The 'wants of neighbourhood' paragraph could easily have been exploited here. As it is, it played no decisive role either in respect of new applications or renewals. As in previous years, when magistrates were considering renewals they were far more likely to base their rejections on licence infringements such as staying open after hours, the presence of prostitutes and 'bad characters' on the premises, or complaints from the neighbourhood. As for new applications, most failed either on formal grounds, because the applicant had a criminal record or had committed offences like presenting musical performances without licence.[72]

The fact is that the magistrates rejected very few applications for renewals.

Indeed they granted new licences to a whole series of pub music halls in the 1860s. According to *The Times* there were seventy-two new applications for music and/or dancing licences in 1864. The newspaper published the results in forty of the cases: one application was withdrawn, twelve were rejected and twenty-eight granted.[73]

Finally, pub music halls played a very minor role in the controversies of the period. A few of them were shut down by the magistrates in 1861–2. But so were two notorious haunts of the upper classes, the Coal Hole and the Cyder Cellars.[74]

The most likely explanation for the numerical fluctuations in the early 1860s is the fact that this was a boom period in the history of the London halls. Because competition was so great many fledgling enterprises met an early death. Given their general reaction to hostile authorities, it is unlikely that any music-hall proprietors were deterred from applying for a licence merely for fear of a refusal. On the contrary the figures show that a considerable number of applications for renewals were made – and granted – precisely during the period of the early 1860s.

It was not until 1868 that the number of pub music-hall applicants who unsuccessfully applied for a renewal of their licence exceeded those who decided, of their own accord, not to reapply. The same goes for 1870 and 1872. For the most part this can be attributed to the fact that the number of licence holders who voluntarily went out of business was comparatively small between 1866 and 1879. Only in 1868 do the records reveal a relatively large number of rejections for pub music halls. Nonetheless by 1870 they did not amount to even 2 per cent of all applications for renewal.[75] The 1870s were as a whole a relatively quiet decade of consolidation. There were scarcely any newcomers and even fewer halls went out of business. It was only in the early 1880s that the number of licence rejections began to rise again, and even here this cannot be attributed to a change of policy on the part of the magistrates towards pub music halls. Nine of the eleven rejections for such premises in 1883 were made on the grounds that the licence-holders had made little or no use of their music licences.[76] As I have already indicated, after 1868 the magistrates could have made more use of the new Building Act. But here again it is significant that they did not do so.

The Metropolitan Management and Buildings Acts Amendment Act was the first act to lay down safety provisions for public buildings. With regard to music halls, its most important requirements were that premises above a minimum size had to have certain walls built in brick; that stairways and corridors be fire-proof and free of chairs or rubbish; and that there were sufficient water supplies and emergency exits with doors opening outwards. At first the act only applied to new buildings but in the course of time the regulations were extended to include all existing structures.[77] The Metropolitan Board of Works and the Middlesex Magistrates were jointly responsible for implementing the act. It was not until

1882, however, that the magistrates began to perform their duties; and then only reluctantly.[78] In 1868 they had drawn up their own safety provisions but the 1878 act had made these redundant. For this reason the magistrates needed some time to overcome their feelings of resentment before they were willing to co-operate.[79] After that they were only prepared to issue licences on condition that applicants provided a certificate from the Board of Works or that positive information was forthcoming from the said Board.[80]

Nonetheless comparatively few halls were closed on the basis of the new act. Diana Howard's figures show that in 1885 and 1887 respectively only one music-hall proprietor went out of business because of the building provisions; and that on the same grounds the magistrates refused to renew a mere four licences between 1886 and 1888.[81] Nor was the Board of Works able to make many changes in respect of existing halls, for proprietors had a right to reject any requirements which proved too expensive.[82] The Board, therefore, attempted to extend the range of its powers but still failed to make any inroads against the combined forces of the proprietors of both halls and theatres.[83]

For all these reasons it is difficult to agree with the theses of either Cunningham or Summerfield. State powers did increase in the course of the nineteenth century but up to 1888 these powers were still quite restricted. Certainly the Middlesex magistrates were never slow to intervene in order 'to maintain public safety and uphold public morals'.[84] They might have discussed such issues but they never used all the powers at their disposal to implement them, let alone to pursue a deliberate policy of eliminating the pub music halls.

The magistrates' one clear maxim was not to tolerate unlicensed places of entertainment. In 1850 John Adams had asserted that there were twice as many unlicensed premises in London as licensed. Such assertions would not have been valid in 1880. But even then the magistrates did not grant all new applications. Here it is difficult enough to establish a logical pattern behind the decisions. And it is even more difficult to find even a trace of a guiding principle behind the licensing procedure as a whole – other than a uniform and persistent line of inconsistencies.

This was also the contemporary view. What disturbed people most of all was the magistrates' capriciousness.[85] In 1850 John Adams had written that he could not understand the principle behind licensing decisions.[86] And in 1868 the *Era*, whilst conceding that there should be some control over the halls, remarked that:

> the granting, withholding or forfeiting of licences should be governed by
> principles of equity and common sense which is certainly not the case in the
> administration of the law by the Justices (?) sitting in Session at Hicks's Hall....
> the Middlesex magistrates ... are not consistent in their decisions, and what
> appears to be an offence in the Haymarket is not an offence in Marylebone,
> what may be perfectly correct in St. James, Westminster, is perfectly incorrect in
> St. Mary's Islington.[87]

These remarks had been sparked off after the Alhambra in Westminster had been granted a licence whilst the Oxford in Islington had not, although both halls were equally respectably conducted. The Pavilion in the Haymarket lost its dance licence and came very near to forfeiting its music licence for presenting can-can girls. The very same girls then went on to perform in the Metropolitan in Marylebone, both of whose licences were renewed without a murmur. On several occasions the *Era* pleaded for a change in the law to relieve magistrates of their licensing duties and replace them by more competent persons or institutions. This view was shared by the 1866 select committee whose proposals even found favour with several high-ranking justices, amongst them Henry Pownall, Chairman of the Middlesex magistrates, Sir Thomas Henry and the Hon George Chapple Norton.[88]

Nonetheless nothing was done to change the status quo and in the following years the *Era* was to summarise its reports and comments on the annual licensing chaos under the headline, 'The Magistrates' Muddle'.[89] The reason for the headline was simple: the justices did not seem to know what they were doing as they would 'vote this way or that as the humour seizes them'.[90] In many cases the remarks were quite justified. However, the magistrates cannot be held completely responsible for the chaos because they were themselves at the mercy of the procedures. The cases on the agenda were not chosen by the magistrates alone but also proposed by outsiders, who were even able to manipulate the voting procedure. For when it came to a vote the issue was decided by the majority of those present. Here the guiding rule for applicants seems to have been to 'get some assistance among ... friends who have influence with the magistrates'.[91]

In 1880 the theatre manager John Hollingshead was to write of the Middlesex magistrates: 'Here is a body, over four hundred strong, representing in its working majority every form of fussy respectability, narrow-minded bigotry, hopeless ignorance, wrought-iron prejudice, sour sectarianism, puritanical zeal, and well-meaning obstinacy.'[92] It is easy to understand his outburst since he had suffered at their hands on several occasions. Nonetheless he was wrong. The Middlesex magistrates might have been unpredictable and their judgements often seemed to lack rhyme or reason. But most of them were in no way prejudiced or puritanical. The justices who gave evidence to the 1866 select committee were quite divided in their opinions about the music halls. Those who were acquainted with them through their daily work in the neighbourhood tended to take a favourable view; whilst those in the upper ranks, most of whom had never set foot inside a hall, were for the most part antipathetic.[93] But as a body, when it came to decision-making they were for the most part acquiescent. Nonetheless not a year went by without some wretched proprietor falling foul of their inconsistencies and the transfer of powers to a new authority, the LCC, in 1888 was greeted with general relief by the halls. The *Era* alone had misgivings about the new authority and called on the proprietors of both halls and theatres to get elected to the new council or in some other way ensure that their interests be represented. The correctness of this warning was soon to become all too clear.

8

Controversies in the 1890s

Until the end of the 1880s music-hall controversies had been mainly determined by local factors. Looked at broadly there were two distinct areas of discussion. The disputes outside London mostly centred on alcohol, but from 1875 these were supplemented with controversies about the programme. They were provoked by a broad reform movement in which teetotallers played a leading role. In London the abstinence movement was very weak which explains why alcohol at first played such a small part in the disputes. The main problems here were perceived as prostitution and dancing which allegedly led to promiscuity. And, by contrast with their counterparts in the regions, the London authorities were directly involved in the conflicts because of the metropolitan licensing laws.

These distinctions were to fade away in the 1890s when the same themes began to concern the nation as a whole and after the 1888 Local Government Act had introduced a uniform framework for licensing. At the same time licensing policies began to change as social reformers gradually increased their influence over local authorities. Nevertheless local peculiarities and traditions were not fully eliminated by the new developments and the particular social constellations which had been one of the main reasons for the differences between the regions and London between 1840 and 1890 continued to prevent a complete alignment.

NATIONAL TRENDS

Signs of a trend towards uniformity in the subject of the disputes had begun to be apparent in London in the 1880s in the form of a campaign led by Mr Frederick Nicholas Charrington whose character and methods were typical of a new breed of music-hall opponent. Charrington was born in 1850 and his family owned the largest brewery in the East End. By religion they were evangelicals, but Frederick differed from rest of the family in that he was unable to reconcile his religious education and his commitment to social reform with the income from the production of alcohol. These severe inner conflicts eventually led him to break with his family. Charrington severed all ties with the firm, renounced his heritage and proceeded to dedicate his life to social work in order to make amends for the damage which he believed his family had caused.

In the 1870s he became involved in innumerable reform projects. He joined the Methodist Tower Hamlets Mission and carried his mission to the East End poor with bands, public assemblies and prayer-meetings. He taught in a church-run evening institute for workers and organised campaigns to feed the hungry.[1] His greatest efforts were, however, directed towards the elimination of two evils which he considered to be the principal causes of the social misery of the time: alcoholism and prostitution. He was a man of heartfelt compassion, resolute commitment and fanaticism, qualities which he shared with many of the social reformers of the age. He distributed pamphlets in pubs calling on drinkers to turn to God and instituted legal proceedings against the brewers, his own family included.[2] He also instigated legal actions against innumerable brothels in the East End and sought them out personally in an effort to save as many prostitutes as he was able. And, if his biographer is to be believed, he was thoroughly successful in his efforts. It was he, more than any other, who 'joined purity with temperance' and merged the long-standing London debates on prostitution with those on alcoholism which, although not new, had up to then played only a minor role in London.[3]

In Charrington's eyes the music halls nurtured both these evils and they were at the front line of his campaign in the early 1880s, a campaign which was to go down in history as the 'Battle of the Music Halls'. His principal target was Lusby's Music Hall. The choice was probably deliberate for Lusby's had been the venue for his religious rallies in the 1870s. Since 1879, however, the building had been exclusively used as a music hall and this conversion was regarded by Charrington as the symbolic triumph of evil over good.[4] Charrington's attacks on Lusby's, like all his campaigns, were conducted on two levels: formally through the law, and personally by direct action. On the one hand he worked closely with other music-hall opponents to persuade the magistrates to withdraw the licence by denouncing the evils of prostitution, a tactic which he considered to be more effective than an attack on alcohol consumption. On the other hand he conducted a personal crusade outside the premises. It was here that he thundered against the dangers of alcohol and attempted to turn the public back from the doors.[5] The broad strategy was clear: to turn Lusby's into a social leper. But the way he went about it and the fact that he was using Lusby's as a scapegoat for a phenomenon for which the hall could not be held directly or indirectly responsible only succeeded in rallying support for the proprietors. Charrington was assailed with flour, paint and rubbish and – if his biographer is to be believed – beaten up by a hired mob in the pay of Lusby's.[6] Contemporary reports tend to belie this assertion. It is probably nearer the truth to say that he was attacked by local residents and music-hall visitors who felt insulted by his words and angered by his pamphlets.[7] In his excess of zeal Charrington had damned all visitors to Lusby's as sinners, an opinion which they could scarcely be expected to share. A number of working-men's clubs also protested against Charrington's methods and assertions.[8] And even the police felt unable to support his opinions or approve of his actions. They took the view that if Charrington would only stop molesting the people outside Lusby's every night the continual aggravation would cease: for 'disturbances always took place when Mr. Charrington walked about outside'.[9] At the licensing sessions police representatives would speak out in favour of Lusby's and the hall was further supported by local councillors. This was enough to persuade the magistrates and year for year they renewed the licence of the two proprietors, Crowder and Payne, to the delight of large crowds of sympathetic supporters.[10] Charrington had a further setback in 1883 when he was forbidden by the courts to distribute pamphlets outside the hall. The fact that he continued to do so until the hall was destroyed by fire a year later scarcely improved his position in the eyes of the authorities. The building had scarcely been rebuilt and reopened under the name of the Paragon than he was on the spot once again.[11]

Charrington has gone down in music-hall history as a moral apostle whose only aim was to prevent his fellow citizens from enjoying harmless entertainment. This judgement is not completely fair. He showed great personal commitment in his resolute campaigns on behalf of the weaker members of society. And if he did spoil the evening for one or two drinkers, he possibly saved a part of the housekeeping money for the rest of the family. Nor did he confine his struggle against prostitution to preaching but endeavoured to provide alternatives to enable women to escape from the deadly spiral of unemployment, poverty and prostitution. However his opponents were correct in their opinion that he was a sour-faced reformer who measured everybody by his own austere and ascetic standards. For it was Charrington's rigid puritanism, more than any other factor, which marked him out as a typical representative of the Social Purity Movement.

The movement was one in a long line of reform movements against prostitution in London and, in the 1880s, it was to become the most powerful and important of them all. It had grown out of the campaign against the Contagious Diseases Acts of 1864, 1866 and 1869. The acts were primarily intended to control the spread of contagious diseases in the armed forces.[12] The problem was that they were not so much addressed to men as against women. All prostitutes and women who were assumed to be so – the latter had to prove that they were not – were compelled by law to undergo medical examinations and had to reckon with the possibility of nine months' detention in hospital. This was blatantly unjust. That the acts were utterly unsuited in practice to the fulfilment of their medical aims only served to arouse widespread public resistance. The opposition was further fuelled by the fact that the acts appeared to condone prostitution. As Josephine Butler, one of the most ardent campaigners, put it: 'The acts not only deprived poor women of their constitutional rights and forced them to submit to a degrading internal examination, but they officially sanctioned male vice.'[13] The main bodies behind the opposition were religious organisations, non-conformists and Anglican evangelicals, the Salvation Army and working-class leaders, all of whom joined hands in a 'National Association' in 1869. Women were the major force behind the movement. Although they were at first excluded from the association and forced to set up their own parallel body, 'The National Association of Women', it was they who provided its radical edge and paved the way for its success. This was above all due to the efforts of Josephine Butler who denounced the acts as a 'blatant example of class and sex discrimination' in favour of middle-class male double morality.[14] Not all her supporters were willing to go so far in their criticism. Nor were they willing to support her efforts to transform the struggle against prostitution into a struggle to help prostitutes rather than simply condemn them.

A new social purity movement, organised in the National Vigilance Association in 1885, took a different and far more repressive line against the prostitutes. Its aims went far beyond a simple crusade against prostitution. Its members wanted to raise the standards of social morality in general by repressing sexuality and promoting chastity. Their activities became even more intensive after 1886 when Parliament repealed the Contagious Diseases Acts. Now the purity reformers began to organise sex education campaigns and also launched a comprehensive attack on 'obscenities' in society, arts and entertainment.[15] Music halls with their dance performances and songs full of innuendo inevitably fell into the reformers' field of vision. As a result of contacts with other campaigns like Charrington's Tower Hamlets Mission the association also took up the cause against alcohol.[16] By 1890 all the various strands had consolidated into a broad-based social reform front which was determined either to reform the music halls in their entirety or to destroy them.

This development was not confined to London alone. Just as London had taken up the theme of alcohol which had been the main source of contention in the regions for so long, so the regions extended their traditional spectrum of complaints against the halls to include those problems which had marked out the disputes in London until 1890. In 1889 reform groups in Manchester, whose recruits were drawn mainly from the ranks of the temperance movement, took up arms against the Palace of Varieties even before the building was completed. On the surface this was just another traditional campaign: to prevent the city's first variety hall, which was completed in 1891, from being granted an alcohol licence.[17] But the reformers' ulterior target was 'variety', which they associated with a certain category of London halls whose atmosphere was charged with bohemianism and prostitution. Such dens of vice, they suspected, might also take root in Manchester. One only had to look at the name of the new hall and consider that the capital for such a venture had been raised by London stockbrokers and speculators. Worse still, the hall was run by the manager of the notorious London Empire and its programmes were to be based on those presented in the capital. The citizens of Manchester were neither willing to be bought up by London capital nor to be corrupted by it. A variety theatre such as the Palace was an 'affront to the honour and dignity of the city'.[18]

In 1891 another controversy broke out in Liverpool. The focus of attention here was the Grand Theatre and its theatre licence. And the controversies which it aroused demonstrate even more clearly the role which prostitution now played in the disputes outside London. The Grand had a theatre licence; but according to the *Era Almanack* it was run as a music hall and perceived as such by contemporaries since its programme traditionally consisted of a mixture of music-hall entertainment and theatre sketches.[19] After 1890 there were repeated objections to the renewal of the licence. But these objections were no longer based on the old argument that the Grand's theatre licence made it possible for the lessee and manager, John Roach, to obtain a beer licence from the Excise. Now it was claimed that the Grand was one of the major meeting places for Liverpool's prostitutes.[20] These objections were put forward by a new reform movement dedicated, like its London counterpart, to social purity. Following the social reform traditions in the regions, its members were mainly drawn from the temperance movement. But these had now extended their sphere of action to include the battle against prostitution. One of their leaders, the Reverend R. A. Armstrong, had gone public in 1890 with a widely noted pamphlet on 'The Deadly Shame of Liverpool'. In it he not only attacked the usual social evils but even took up cudgels against the city's administration for holding their protective hand over alcoholism and prostitution over the years.[21] The reformers' interests were also shared by the Liberal Party which had instituted its own 'purity campaign' against the city's brothels in 1889.[22] The Liberals won a majority on the council in 1892 and Roach promptly lost his licence. The events in Liverpool thus show a further parallel with developments in London. In both cases reform groups not only put their arguments before their respective licensing authorities but co-operated with them and eventually operated from within. This was made possible by the second major local government reform of the century.

The Local Government Act was passed in 1888.[23] By contrast with its predecessor in 1835 this act covered all towns and it was the first to include the counties which up until now had been entirely untouched by administrative reforms. A single unified system now came into force to deal with the chaos which had resulted from the many differing and overlapping administrative units. In this connection there was now a uniform system of music-hall licensing.[24] The new act provided that in counties and county boroughs with more than 50,000 inhabitants, county councils would in future be responsible for licensing procedures. And a further law passed in 1890 underscored the nationwide compulsory licensing obligations.[25]

The Local Government Act did not merely ensure a unified framework. It was the expression of a more intensive striving for local reform and many new authorities made it the basis for a broader and more extensive reorganisation of their administrative powers. This was particularly true for those cities which, like London, had been untouched by the 1835 act and whose organisation was long overdue for reform; or in cities like Liverpool where, despite the 1835 act, there had been little change in traditional structures of power or social problems.

Liverpool's council had been under the continual and undisputed rule of the Conservatives for almost the whole of the century (bar the years 1835–42 and 1892–5) and in this respect it was almost unique. The conditions for a Liberal takeover in the city were highly unfavourable. Unlike Manchester, there was scarcely any potential reservoir of Liberal voters amongst either its manufacturers or its workers. It was basically a port, dominated by long established, Conservative, business, merchant and shipping families who had brought wealth to the city in an enterprise which was strenuously opposed by the Liberals: the slave trade. For this reason the Liberals had little of interest to offer the citizens of the city, not only with respect to slavery but also in their attitude to the problem of alcoholism.[26]

Between 1862 and 1866, whilst the rest of the country was considering prohibition, the Liverpool council was busy introducing its so-called 'free licensing policy' which allowed licences to anyone with reasonably suitable premises. The policy was even supported by a few teetotallers who hoped that, despite the risk of an initial rise in alcohol consumption, free market forces would soon regulate and reduce it once more. Quite the opposite occurred. In 1862, the number of pubs in Liverpool was already comparatively large. By 1866 the total amount had grown to 366. And by 1874: 'Liverpool boasted 1,929 public houses, 383 beerhouses ... and 272 off-licences and refreshment houses. They outnumbered all grocery, provisions, furniture, chemist, and stationary shops.'[27]

The administration was not simply following a policy of laissez-faire. Many of its members were also considerably involved in the drink trade. In 1877 one of the leading magistrates in the city personally owned seventy-seven pubs. And in 1880 he was accused by Alderman John Hughes, an influential member of both the Watch Committee and the Bench, of profiting from alcoholism and prostitution. The corporation too did not only profit from the brothels in terms of rates, it even managed some.[28] There were several temperance-led campaigns against the city's licensing laws in the 1860s and in 1875 a citizens' vigilance committee was set up. But this had no tangible effect until 1890.[29] This was not simply due to the intransigence of the authorities. The campaigners could seldom agree with the police on a unified approach to the problem. Whereas the teetotallers adopted a policy of 'all or nothing' the city police, whose aims were very similar in principle, were more pragmatic in their approach. They considered the demands of the teetotallers completely unfeasible and as a result supported them on very few occasions.[30] Given this division, any effective opposition to the authorities was impossible. Only in the mid 1880s, when teetotallers and the Liberal Party began to co-operate more closely, did things slowly begin to change.

Up till then relations between the two had not been entirely free of problems. Although there were more Liberals than Conservatives amongst the ranks of the teetotallers neither the leadership of the party nor even the majority of its members had supported the reform movement for fear of becoming too closely identified with its narrow aims. Indeed, until the 1870s the teetotallers had

sought support from both parties.[31] But during the 1872 election campaign the
Alliance conducted an enquiry specifically aimed at discovering the attitudes of
the various candidates towards prohibition. The replies, which were published,
showed that there were considerably more prohibitionists amongst the Liberals
than the Conservatives. From then on the temperance movement initiated a
deliberate policy of infiltrating the Liberals with a view to making them a vehicle
for their own legislative plans. At the same time – after the extension of the fran-
chise – the Liberals began to recognise the increased voting potential amongst
the ranks of the temperance movement which enjoyed considerable support
amongst workers in the industrial cities of the north: and, in turn, they became
more open to the aims of the teetotallers.[32]

At the end of the 1880s the two sides joined forces when the Liberals in
Liverpool set up a 'moral campaign for temperance and civic purity'. The campaign not only adopted traditional regional attitudes towards temperance reform
but was closely associated with the new purity movement of the 1890s.[33] Its
activities extended to include the 1890 local elections, but the results in
Liverpool failed to produce a Liberal takeover and structures of power within
the city remained unchanged. Nonetheless reformers did succeed in infiltrating
a part of the administration and were instrumental in helping to carry through
new directives to the police. This was to be the start of a series of repressive measures against brothels in the city.[34]

Music halls were for the most part unaffected by these directives. But after
the Liberal victory in the 1892 election the halls came under the scrutiny of
zealous reformers on the new council. The Grand Theatre was not the only
victim of the new broom. All the city's music halls were to suffer. Between 1892
and 1895 the number of music and dance licences issued by the magistrates, who
were now also under Liberal influence, fell considerably.[35]

The 1888 Local Government Act had an even more incisive effect on the halls
in London. Here a group of outspoken opponents of the halls succeeded in
gaining a foothold in the newly constituted London County Council (LCC) and
a strong position on the licensing committee. The LCC was dominated by the
so-called 'progressives', a broad-based movement of committed social reformers whose spectrum embraced liberal intellectuals, socialist working-class
leaders and Fabians, amongst them John Burns and Sidney Webb. They adopted
a wide-ranging social and political reform programme which expressed the
hopes of many Londoners that the LCC would be 'not merely ... a huge administrative board but a genuine Parliament ... for the Metropolis'.[36] Their programme contained a broad series of traditional measures aimed at improving
housing and domestic conditions and bringing the city's infrastructures up to
date by means of modern 'municipal socialism'. These and many other policies
were not only formulated for the benefit of consumers. They also took account
of workers in the service industries with a view to improving their wages and
working conditions.[37]

Not all reform measures proposed by the LCC met with popular support. One among these was an ambitious programme to 'purify' the music halls.[38] In principle the council as a whole was responsible for such measures. But in practice they were implemented by the licensing committee whose composition differed in one decisive way. Rather than mirroring the overall composition of the council it was a sectarian reservoir of purity reformers. Over a third of its twenty-one members either belonged to or sympathised with the National Vigilance Association (NVA). Even Frederick Charrington, who had been banned by the magistrates only a few years previously from distributing pamphlets outside Lusby's, was a voting member. Another prominent personality on the committee was John McDougall, 'known as Muck Dougall and the Grand Inquisitor ... a prominent Methodist who later became Chairman of the LCC'.[39] In addition his father-in-law, George Lidgett was a member of the Methodist Connection and married to a leading activist in the NVA and British Women's Temperance Association.[40]

The controversies surrounding the London Empire were to become a test case for the effective co-operation between reformers in and outside the new administration, and the accompanying waves of publicity were even to be felt abroad.[41] The Empire was situated in the heart of the West End, in Leicester Square, one of the main centres of prostitution in the nineteenth century. Inevitably the hall became a favourite haunt of high-class prostitutes who would parade up and down its promenade every evening plying their trade to wealthy visitors. The Empire was not a music hall in the traditional sense of the word but a new form of variety theatre. What set it apart from other halls was its audience which was dominated by members of the upper class and the bohemian set. To them the Empire was more of a club than a music hall; more a meeting-place for persons of similar class and outlook than a place of entertainment.[42] The controversies surrounding the Empire were, therefore, not only a test case but also a trial of power between reformers and the Establishment. They began in 1894 when the prominent social reformer, Mrs Ormiston Chant, objected to the renewal of the licence after informal discussions with the manager of the Empire had come to nothing. She was supported in her efforts by the National Vigilance Association, London's Methodist network and a series of temperance organisations, for the most part female. Since representatives of these organisations (women apart) also sat on the Licensing Committee it did not take long for them to decide that such an obvious centre of prostitution could no longer be tolerated. The committee decided to withhold the Empire's licence until such time as the manager, Mr Edwardes, could find other uses for its promenade and stop the sale of alcohol in the auditorium. Edwardes appealed against the decision immediately but his appeal was rejected and the Empire was forced to close in 1894.[43]

Contemporaries in particular have described the Empire controversy as a massive campaign of sanctimonious bigots and Mrs Chant as a po-faced enemy of the halls.[44] This is unfair to Mrs Chant. True, she was part of the temperance and social purity movement. But when it came to the question of prostitution she was at one with the opinions of Josephine Butler that this was just as much a problem of female exploitation and male double standards as it was of morality. Her attitude to the halls was also radically different from that of Frederick Charrington. She was in principle well-disposed towards the halls and regarded them as suitable places of entertainment for the working classes. She even went so far as to plead for Sunday opening. But she was strictly against places such as upper-class variety theatres being misused for the purposes of prostitution, and their toleration by public bodies such as the LCC.[45]

The LCC took a similar view of the matter. But they grossly underestimated the broad range of public opposition to the closure. Theatres offered themselves as venues for protest meetings. Members of the Stock Exchange publicly dissociated themselves from their colleagues on the LCC. Workers and liberal clubs protested. Most outraged of all were the business and trades people in Leicester Square; the cabbies, variety and other unions, and the several charity organisations for music-hall artistes, all of whom had an interest in the fate of the Empire.[46] Nonetheless, taken as a whole, the working-class movement in London was divided over the question. The supporters of the Empire were doubtless correct when they argued that prostitution would not be abolished or even reduced by closing down the Empire, the more so when such a decision meant that four hundred ballet-dancers would be thrown on the streets. They were also right in pointing out that the sole effect of closing the hall, if any, would be to put its employees out of work. On the other hand as Mrs Ormiston Chant herself protested, neither she nor the LCC was to blame for the state of affairs in the Empire. And it was John Burns, the working-class leader on the LCC, who emphasised this point more than anyone else during the licensing sessions.[47] Both Burns and Mrs Chant pointed out that the Empire had not been closed down for good. All that was required was a short period of reconstruction. They therefore argued that an organisation which paid out dividends of 75 to 80 per cent could well afford to keep its employees on the books during rebuilding if it really wanted to. And anyway, why should the working-class movement devote its energies to defending the amusements of the wealthy when it had much more important things to fight for? For the Empire most definitely did not cater for working people.[48]

The anti-capitalist aspect of the dispute which Burns took up has been largely disregarded or even ignored. Nor can Mrs Chant's campaign be simply dismissed as a puritanical crusade typical of its age. For the campaign introduced new elements into a controversy which has appeared to date to be nothing more than a fusion of traditional components. It demonstrates very clearly the split which had developed within the music-hall scene as a result of the rise of large variety theatres in London. The halls were no longer overwhelmingly or exclusively institutions of working-class culture and as such, deserving of their support. Capitalist variety-theatre impresarios had, therefore, no right to reckon with the automatic solidarity of the workers. Nor was Burns alone in this opinion. It was also shared by Mrs Chant and a significant part of the reform movement. Before the 1890s they had, as a rule, restricted themselves to doctrinal and moral arguments. But now their opposition began to show some signs of criticism of the capitalist system as a whole.

The Empire was, indeed, only closed for a very short period. It opened its doors once again on 3 November 1894 with a new wall dividing the bar from the auditorium as required by the LCC. However it was built in such a fashion that it practically invited destruction. In this respect young Winston Churchill was able to distinguish himself by devoting his maiden speech in Parliament to the matter.[49] The following year the LCC gave up its opposition to the Empire and henceforth dispensed with any conditions for the licence.[50] It was not until 1916 when the Bishop of London pointed out that the ladies of the Empire were not exactly the most salubrious influence on young soldiers on leave from the Front, that the promenade was finally closed down for good.[51]

The Empire controversy is not the sole gauge of the effectiveness of the co-operation between social reformers and the newly reformed local authority. The LCC might have lost the power struggle against the variety theatres and its supporters. But it was thoroughly successful in its efforts to 'clean up' working-class culture in London by getting rid of the pub music halls. Historians have claimed that one of the results of the 1888 Local Government Act was to put music-hall proprietors under increasing pressure from the authorities. By contrast with the magistrates before them, elected councils had to take account of public opinion, and thereby the reform organisations.[52] It is certainly correct that the authorities in the nineties made life more difficult for music-hall owners. But to say that this was due to more pressure from outside or below is not convincing.

The main reasons lie elsewhere. First, many municipal authorities delegated responsibility for music-hall licensing back into the hands of the magistrates – as foreseen by the act. But the magistrates continued to be nominated, not elected, and were therefore not dependent on the wishes and opinions of the electorate.[53] Of the three authorities dealt with in this section only the LCC took direct control of licensing its halls. In 1890 the *Era* estimated that the majority of licensing procedures were still in the hands of the justices. And this was confirmed by the 1892 select committee.[54] Second, it made no difference whether licensing procedures were dealt with by an elected or a nominated body. The cases in London and Liverpool show that after 1888 the restructuring of the municipal administrations led to a corresponding shift in the social constellations of power (including the magistrates) in the various cities. Thus it very often happened that members of pressure groups themselves were elected to the councils or nominated to the bench. They were therefore no longer entirely dependent on applying pressure from below when they were able to do so directly from within. On the other hand some magistrates, like those in Manchester, who were independent of election pressures adopted new policies of their own accord. In the framework of his research into the controversies surrounding the Manchester Palace of Varieties at the beginning of the 1890s Chris Waters has put forward the thesis that this was the consequence of social reformers who increasingly turned 'to the state, hoping that it might succeed where philanthropic efforts had failed – and commercial efforts could not hope to succeed – in promoting a more moral culture'.[55] But this is only partially correct. In the case studies I have examined we have seen that English reform groups had tried to enlist the help of the State at a much earlier period. As far as the halls were concerned, the 1890s mark the end rather than the start of a development.

The beginnings can be seen in Glasgow in 1875 and the first successes – admittedly minor – were achieved in the 1880s in Bradford and Sheffield. True, the restructuring of the municipal authorities after 1888 did lead to a comparatively more effective cooperation between social reformers and the state. But the culmination of this development also marked its end. The case of the London Empire was not only the most powerful combined intervention of reformers and the authorities, it was also the last such case. In this respect it gives a convincing insight into the (new) limits of such interventions. Where earlier moral attacks on the halls had failed due to a lack of interest by the authorities, intervention on the part of the authorities was now to fail before the protests of a broad-based public drawn from all classes, who had come to accept music-hall culture as a part of their national heritage. In the end this form of pressure proved to be stronger than that of the reformers.

LOCAL DISCREPANCIES

The 1888 Local Government Act may have introduced national, compulsory licence duties but it did not lead to a unified licensing procedure since the framework of the act allowed individual councils considerable freedom to shape their own practices. Therefore local discrepancies arose merely at the question of which authority was responsible for licensing the halls. We have seen that, of all the municipal authorities mentioned in the previous section, only the LCC took direct responsibility for music-hall licensing in its area. The majority of councils in the regions delegated duties back into the hands of the magistrates. Further differences come to light when examining the form of entertainment licence granted by the individual authorities. From 1892 onwards Manchester granted some of its halls theatre licences thereby allowing them to put on sketches, a measure which the LCC was unable to carry through.[56] Manchester and Liverpool differed from the capital in other ways. Premises where music and singing (especially by amateurs) took place only on an occasional basis did not require a licence at all: but pubs which offered music and singing on a regular, commercial and professional basis had to apply for the normal music and singing licence. Establishments which wanted to offer a mixed bag of music-hall and theatrical entertainment could apply for a combined licence. In this case they were duty-bound to relinquish their beer licence from the Excise (which premises with only a theatre licence were allowed to hold) or risk the loss of their music licence. Furthermore they were disqualified from applying for a spirit licence from the magistrates.[57]

Although the act enabled each authority to deal with licensing in its own way, regional licensing methods had many common factors which set them apart from London. They suggest that informal working-class culture, traditional halls and pub music halls were not at the centre of reform efforts. Although there might have been a common theme to the disputes around the London Empire, the Manchester Palace and the Liverpool Grand, there were differences in emphasis due to the differing opposing parties and the fact that the struggles were not conducted along the same class lines.

The LCC licensing committee is particularly renowned for its practices. Its programme of reforms included measures to make music halls both 'purer' and 'safer'. 'Purer' meant not only ridding the halls of prostitutes but cleaning up – or censoring – the offerings on show. This included abolishing satirical invective in the texts of comic songs and the traditional unscripted dialogue with the audience, one of the original features of the halls and something which gave the performer a good opportunity to indulge in innuendo and slip in the occasional dubious gag.[58] The committee's aim was to replace such features with music-hall sketches which, because they were drawn from the realm of drama and therefore 'Art', were thought to have an edifying effect on the audiences.[59] 'Purifying' the programme, in the extended sense of the word, also meant that halls would now be safer for the new and growing middle-class audiences whose aesthetic and moral sensibilities would be protected from offence.[60] But safety was not confined to the area of morals. It found its main expression in a plethora of building rules and regulations. Given the outcome of numerous panics and fires, more stringent regulations were clearly in the interest of the audiences.[61] At the same time, however, the LCC licensing committee used them as a pretext for pushing through its anti-music-hall policies which were indeed directed against the smaller halls, as Penelope Summerfield has argued. The regulation which provided for bars to be separated from the auditoria was intended to lead to an indirect reduction in the consumption of alcohol. And the vast amount of building directives which were in the main imposed on the proprietors of pub music halls were not so much intended to make the premises more safe as to drive them out of business. These small music halls were a bugbear to the members of the licensing committee. They regarded them as little more than extended pubs which, because they were difficult to control, were potential and inaccessible hot-beds of working-class culture. The ideal solution was therefore to eliminate them in favour of the larger and more socially mixed music halls. And here the LCC was successful. Only a very few proprietors had the financial means to carry out the innumerable reconstruction measures required by the licensing committee.[62]

If building directives alone did not suffice, the committee had other means at hand. Charrington and his friends had no scruples in going beyond the scope of the act. In 1890 they sent an unauthorised inspector to 'find' prostitutes in the Queens Arms Music Hall. The man did his duty and duly found some. The committee's official inspector, on the other hand, stated some time afterwards in an official report that he had never seen prostitutes there at all.[63] The fanaticism of the committee's purity wing can be seen at its most blatant in the case of two pub music halls in the East End: the Angel and Crown, and the Rose and Crown. Both were music halls where the audience could also dance, they were favourite haunts of sailors and their proprietors had foreign names (John Akkersdyk at the Angel and Pedro Femenia at the Rose). Thus they were a thorn in the eye to certain members of the committee for several reasons.[64] At first routine procedures were adopted. An inspection of the buildings showed up several grounds for improvement without which the licences could not be renewed. The ensuing repairs cost Akkersdyk £1,000 and Femenia £1,135. There then followed an alleged report which hinted that both halls were not being correctly conducted. The committee took no action on the basis of this report. Nor did it warn the two proprietors as it should have done.[65] Some time later when it came to the licence renewals the committee anounced without prior warning that, repairs or no, the licences would not be renewed because the proprietors tolerated prostitutes on the premises and were therefore promoting prostitution. This decision was all the more surprising to the proprietors since not even the police inspector responsible for the area was able to confirm the allegations. On the contrary he disputed absolutely that the women under suspicion were prostitutes and tried to explain to the committee that they were dealing with a culture which might be different from their own but nonetheless had its own ideas of respectability and lived according to them. The halls were not meeting places for prostitutes. Most of the audience came and went in couples. The couples were not as a rule married but enjoyed a stable, if in many cases temporary, relationship. The women might have been kept by the sailors but that did not mean they were prostitutes.[66] The inspector did not consider this offensive. He furthermore stated, in favour of the two proprietors, that they had never contravened the licensing laws and had always conducted their halls in an orderly manner. 'Many a respectable woman goes there' added a heckler and this was even confirmed by the committee's official inspector.[67] But the majority of the committee remained obdurate and recommended that both licences be withdrawn. The LCC approved the recommendations and the upshot was a huge law case. Here it was established that the procedures adopted by the committee and the LCC had been incorrect. As a result the LCC instituted another formal and legally correct procedure which again resulted in the licences being withdrawn.[68] The ensuing publicity triggered off a broad discussion on the licensing practices of the LCC which resulted in an internal purging of the committee, one of whose victims was Charrington.[69]

None of this was to prove much help to the city's pub-music-hall proprietors as most of them had already gone out of business. But the LCC's reputation was also damaged for quite some time.[70] In 1893 Alderman Routledge, himself a member of the LCC, accused the Theatres and Music Halls Committee of being 'the only Committee of the Council whose deliberations and recommendations had brought ridicule on the work of the Council'.[71] Nonetheless chroniclers have tended to portray its overall licensing policies as a long-term success. For they managed to destroy the traditional link between alcohol and entertainment which had been the hallmark of the halls for years, and resulted in a definite improvement in the tone and content of the programme.[72]

Most contemporary historians do not concur with this assessment. Edward Bristow has claimed that moral aspects of the programme never played a great part in licensing procedures despite the massive pressure from the purity faction; and that, as a result, proprietors were not forced to take preventative measures.[73] He is supported in his thesis by Ulrich Schneider who, in respect of the Empire, was the first to document the failure of a morally based policy of intervention and with whose conclusions I can only agree.[74] Susan Pennybacker even goes as far as to argue that the main aim of the LCC was not intervention, either directly or indirectly, but co-operation with the halls, a policy which it also pursued with regard to other industries.[75] But there is no hard evidence to show that the LCC had an interest in co-operating with the London halls. However, the majority of researchers do in principle agree that the moral pressure exercised by the LCC, no matter how it was applied, had no far-reaching consequences whatever. The general tone of music halls might have been raised; but this can be attributed to the actions of the proprietors who had an interest in attracting a more broadly based audience, and also to a change in public taste.[76]

Long before the LCC took power, music-hall owners in and outside the capital had pleaded for a moral 'improvement' in the programme and had attempted to achieve this by putting pressure on their performers. This was even the case in those towns which had not yet introduced licensing procedures.[77] The pivotal factor in all these cases can scarcely have been fear of state intervention. Far more crucial to the changes were the internal developments within the halls themselves. It is no accident that the majority of those managers and owners who introduced house rules to discipline their employees were drawn from the larger halls and the new variety theatres. These rules were accompanied by an increasing rationalisation of the programme, the establishment of the two turn system and the multiple engagement of artistes. Indeed the majority of such rules were concerned with punctuality and sobriety, the nature of the costumes and penalties for breach of contract. And only a small proportion dealt with censorship measures and instructions with regard to content.[78] Here the rules were mainly intended to make the larger halls and new variety theatres with their socially different seating arrangements more acceptable to a new audience. Broadening the social base of the audience beyond the traditional and narrow confines of workers and lower middle-class clerks was therefore very much in the proprietors' own interest.

But managers and proprietors could not simply 'raise' the quality of the programme over the heads of their traditional audiences.[79] As early as 1863 there were reports in the *Era* about arguments between managers and singers over the tone and content of their performances. The managements accused the singers of bringing the halls into disrepute with their disposition towards obscenity. The singers replied that they were only providing what the public wanted and accused the management of hypocrisy for demanding respectability whilst profiting from the opposite.[80] Both sides were of the opinion that audience reaction was the crucial factor in deciding the shape and content of the programme for the audience did not hesitate in making their feelings known. Thus the trend away from open vulgarity towards innuendo in the 1870s has also been attributed in great part to a change in public taste.[81] But even then the occasional performance went too far for some audiences. In 1873 a group of dancers was hounded from the stage of the Canterbury Music Hall in London because the audience felt their self-respect and sense of morality had been offended.[82] And in 1884 a singer who wanted to make a name for himself in Bradford with risqué jokes was soon back in the dressing-room at Pullan's.[83] Thus it is clear that state intervention on the part of authorities like the LCC was not the prime factor in promoting a rise in the tone of the halls. The subject was discussed long before the LCC existed and even before 1875 when the spotlight of public attention began to be directed at the halls and their offerings. The changes before 1890 resulted from a decade of internal discussions between management, artistes and audience independent of outside demands. And they would not have tolerated such interference even if it had existed.[84]

It should be added here that the outcome of these discussions in no way conformed to the wishes and expectations of the purity campaigners. The early historians of the LCC are wrong on both points when they assert the halls were 'clean' in 1892 and that this was the sole result of intervention by the LCC. The capital's halls were as diverse as their audiences and each hall correspondingly devised its programmes to suit the particular composition of its audience.

Of Anstey's four categories of London music halls it was the third – halls for middle-class men and their families – which corresponded to the ideas of the LCC. But these particular halls had not been reformed under pressure from the authorities. They were there precisely as a result of the wishes of both audiences and proprietors. One of the latter, Oswald Stoll, the owner of the Coliseum, was to become a byword for 'family music halls' at the turn of the century. He started his career in Liverpool at the Parthenon (which was managed by his mother) and built up a chain of halls in ports around the country before moving into London. He culminated his career as the director of the Stoll Circuit which owned a series of major London halls, and in 1919 he was knighted for his services to the industry and to charity.[85] Stoll's biography thus exemplifies a line of evolution from the nineteenth-century locally based pioneers to the syndicate impresarios with their chains of halls throughout the nation. On a personal level he had most in common with men like Pullan and Morgan, although the latter would have had no chance of being knighted in the 1880s. Stoll was a teetotaller and non-smoker and dressed like a cross between a priest and a bank manager.[86] Where possible he always attended performances in his halls, not however to enjoy the show – he allegedly never laughed – but to observe the reaction of the audience.[87] The Coliseum was reputed to be a monument of respectability. Expletives and innuendo were expressly forbidden under threat of strict punishment.[88] Stoll needed no encouragement from the LCC for 'purer' and 'safer' halls.

But the sort of halls run by Stoll were not representative for London in the 1890s. At one end of the scale were the 'unreformed' (and unreformable) variety theatres patronised by the upper classes and bohemians whose frivolity was an expression of their conscious opposition to the narrow confines of Victorian society.[89] The pretensions and programmes of the working-class East End halls were also entirely different from their bourgeois counterparts in the suburbs. They may have had little in common with the frivolities of bohemian taste but they were equally out of touch with the staid and conventional middle-class atmosphere which pervaded the Stoll type of halls. These differences can be seen most clearly by examining the career of one of the greatest stars of the age, Marie Lloyd.

Lloyd was born in the north-east of London and in 1885 began her music-hall career at the age of fifteen. Within a very short time she had shot to the top of her profession. She was a master of innuendo, double entendre, suggestive remarks and gestures, techniques which she raised to the level of perfection.[90] Her career flourished primarily in the atmosphere of the West End variety theatres and, according to many anecdotes, she suffered quite badly from the shock of discovering that her style was not to the fancy of the working-class audiences in the East End. Nonetheless her popularity was not confined to the West End alone. She was the darling of the public all over the country not only for her innuendo but also for the accuracy of her characterisations which were drawn from her observations of the daily life and work of ordinary people. And it was the ordinary working people with whom she shared her riches and who regarded her as one of their own; someone who had made it without forgetting her origins.[91] The fact that her suggestive style was not to the taste of East End audiences should not be taken to indicate that they only wanted 'clean' songs, but that they preferred up-front humour to sophistication. Marie Lloyd too was all for vulgarity in the halls and pubs, according to one of her biographers.[92] It is noteworthy that she was never engaged by Stoll. Nor was she invited to perform at the first Royal Command Performance in 1912. When she died in 1922, 100,000 Londoners accompanied her coffin to the grave and she is still revered as one of the greatest stars of the music hall.[93]

By this time the LCC and its licensing policies had long fallen into oblivion.[94] This was partly due to their lack of success and partly because the policies pursued in London were exceptional rather than, as has been asserted up to now, representative of those pursued in the rest of the country. Scarcely any other authority based its licensing policy on a comprehensive programme of social reform and no other body showed such intensive, even fanatical, interest in the halls as the licensing committee of the LCC. Even the new reform-minded council in Liverpool was more reticent in its procedures than the LCC. It did indeed drastically reduce the number of pub music hall licences in the city but this should not automatically be interpreted as the expression of a deliberate policy. One of the factors behind it was a decision by the local justices only to license those premises which regularly offered entertainment and charged for it.[95] This was still not the case in many pub music halls. Nor is there any evidence in Manchester that the authorities took active steps to target the pub music halls. Rather the contrary. In 1892 the *Era* reported that the number of pub music halls in Manchester had grown by 120 per cent over the previous nine years.[96]

London did not only differ from the regions in licensing policies and practices with regard to pub music halls. In the case of the London Empire the council intervened to stop an abuse of traditional activities and protect the moral behaviour of its audience. The Empire could not in any sense be regarded as a bastion of working-class culture like the pub music halls. It was a meeting place for the upper classes, part of whose entertainment consisted of the exploitation of women. The disputes around the Liverpool Grand and the Manchester Palace were entirely different, although they were also concerned with prostitutes. Opponents of the halls equated the Palace in particular with the London Empire. This misunderstanding can be attributed to the first owners of the Palace who were tactless enough to name the Empire as the model for their new hall. It was never their intention to grace Manchester with a clone of the notorious Empire. They simply intended to base their programme on that of the Empire and, where possible, book some of its artistes. The Palace was aiming to appeal to a completely different audience. Not for nothing did it advertise itself as Manchester's first variety theatre for the 'classes and the masses'.[97] This was a new type of music hall for Manchester. Just as in Liverpool, the majority of halls in the city were traditional working-class venues with admission prices between 1d and 6d.[98] One exception was the Folly Music Hall which, like its Liverpool equivalent the Star, had four seating areas (not counting the boxes). Here admission prices ranged from 6d to 2s (the Star) and 6d to 3s (the Folly).[99] The Palace too had four seating areas (not including the boxes) and charged between 6d and 5s.[100] Thus its top price ranges were aimed at attracting a more affluent audience whilst its bottom prices kept it competitive with other halls in the city. This was a deliberate policy. For all its efforts to attract a more broadly-based audience the management was well aware that in order to survive it had to be regularly patronised by workers and their families. They were the people for whom the Palace intended to provide wholesome entertainment within pleasant surroundings; and it was they to whom the Palace appealed for support in their disputes with the magistrates.[101] Nor were their hopes disappointed. In February 1891 – the Palace was completed but not yet open for want of a music licence – a reader's letter in the *Manchester Courier* protested that it was impossible to understand a bench which handed out licences to every dingy pub and then refused one to the Palace which would have been much easier to regulate. If this was not changed workers and their families would have no alternative but to spend their evenings in pubs. A month later the *Manchester Courier* reported that a petition with 20,000 signatures in favour of the licence was presented to the city authorities; and other papers put the number as high as 60,000.[102] The socialist movement in the city was also firmly behind the Palace, above all Robert Blatchford's weekly newspaper, *The Clarion*. Blatchford was only too aware that the Palace was a capitalist enterprise. Nonetheless it was one which 'treated workers as respectable consumers, capable of differentiating wholesome from disreputable pastimes'.[103] The ensuing debate in the paper lasted five weeks and of the letters to the editor discussing the pros and cons of the Palace, there was a clear majority in favour. The magistrates could not but be influenced by such pressure and when the Palace again applied for a licence at the end of March 1891 they reversed their February decision and granted the application.[104] On 18 May the Palace opened its doors to the general public, three days after giving an invited preview for local dignitaries, church leaders and temperance reformers. Even *The Manchester Guardian* which had tended to oppose the Palace commented on the opening that the theatre did indeed provide good entertainment.[105]

The Palace had managed to integrate itself into the existing social structures of the city. Unlike the London Empire, it had not broken the bond between the halls and working-class culture; a culture which, anyway, had always been more strongly developed in the regions than in London. In this respect Manchester was not alone. The Grand in Liverpool received similar support from working people in its disputes with the authorities, not only because it aimed to provide the working class with good, clean entertainment but also because it was the city's oldest working-class music hall. It was the successor to the Colosseum which had stood on the site of a Unitarian chapel since 1851 and was closed after the panic of 1877 because of its state of disrepair.[106] The magistrates' refusal to grant it a licence led to massive protests in the city. Within a very short time John Roach, the manager and lessee of the Grand had received a list of 12,000 signatures in his support. This was followed a week later by a petition signed by 47,000 workers.[107] By this time Roach had put in a fresh application for a licence and when it came to the hearings in November over one hundred witnesses turned up to testify to the respectability of both Roach and the Grand. These consisted not only of regular members of the audience but also artisans, traders, journalists, a lawyer and even a manufacturer who allegedly visited the Grand with his family and servants. The most persistent support, however, came from the organised working-class movement in the city. The former President of the Trades Council, Philip Harris, testified that working people regarded the Grand as their theatre and even took their wives along with them. As such they could see no reasons for its closure.[108] Harris was not the only working-class representative to testify in support of Roach. One month before, in October, another former President of the Trades Council, William Matkin, had also spoken out in Roach's favour.[109] In his capacity as a magistrate – he was the working-class member of the Liverpool Bench – he championed Roach's cause from within, while the Trades Council was mobilising support from amongst the population as a whole. Immediately after the licence was refused they passed a resolution stating the reason why they were so committed to Roach's cause: 'That we gratefully remember the kindness of Mr J. T. Roach in lending his theatre on behalf of the Scottish Railway servants and the Garston dockers, when the members of these societies were struggling to obtain what every fair-minded man considered them justly entitled to.'[110] In the face of such broad support the Liverpool magistrates finally gave way and in December 1892 partially revised their decision of the previous October. Roach was granted a music-hall licence with the remark that he could not reckon with a spirit licence from the bench. He was further directed to arrange the auditorium more clearly and get rid of the dark corners.[111] Roach duly complied with the instructions but the following year went bankrupt.[112]

To sum up. There were two main factors which contributed to the continuing existence of local discrepancies in the disputes concerning music halls in the 1890s. Both ran counter to the trend towards a unification of the themes under discussion and of the administrative framework. Firstly the reception and consequences of the 1888 Local Government Act were different in London than they were in the regions. This was principally due to the different conditions in every city at the time the act was passed. The act might have provided for unified municipal administrative structures throughout the land but it failed to demand a unified system of compliance. In cities such as Manchester and Liverpool there was comparatively little change. London's administrative structures, on the other hand, were altered from top to bottom. Whereas the act only brought about minimal adjustments in the regions and at most only the majority relationships were changed at the top, it granted London its own central municipal administration for the very first time. The LCC did not therefore view itself merely as an institution whose duty was to maintain the status quo whilst ridding the city of a few of its more unwholesome aspects. Its administration and reform were rather orientated towards a broad programme of completely new local policies. As far as the halls were concerned this programmme resulted in licensing practices which not only aimed at a fundamental reform of the number and type of music halls in the capital, but were as different from those of its predecessors, the Middlesex magistrates, as they were from the practices in the regions. The regional authorities did not view the act as a complete break with tradition. They therefore saw no grounds for developing, or even introducing, policies. This was even the case in Liverpool, whose new council was for a time particularly disposed towards reform. It was the changes in the music-hall scene itself, in particular in the growth of new types of music halls, which were responsible for stirring up changes in licensing procedures outside London.

Which brings us to the second factor: each municipal authority had to decide on the stance it would take towards its own halls and the culture they embodied. In London such a culture was socially differentiated and had taken diverse forms even from the start. In the regions it had maintained much of the social homogeneity which had been its hallmark from the start. Thus it was not 1888 which marked a break in regional licensing practices but the early years of the 1890s when new types of hall began to come into existence. These halls were based on London models but were primarily rooted in their local context. Their audiences were more broadly based but still consisted overwhelmingly of members of the working class. Thus, with regard to the social constellations, the disputes which arose around the halls were no different from those in previous years. Even the new variety theatres were at first a part of each city's working-class culture and were defended in the same manner as the traditional halls. The battle around the London Empire was not only different in the course it took. It is a paradigm for a new stage of development in the disputes around the halls. The workers who sprang to the defence of this variety theatre were no longer drawn principally from the audience. It was theirs, only because they were directly employed by the management or in some other way economically dependent on it.

Conclusion

Vox populi, a capitalist enterprise, an autonomous formation of popular culture with its own specific compound of custom and modernity, a culture of consolation, a laboratory of social style and self-definition, a culture of knowingness and competence – these are some of the terms which have been used to characterise the music hall over the last decades. The terminology also expresses the historiography of the various approaches, common to which is an endeavour to analyse and understand an institution which – despite all differences in interpretation – has come to be regarded as significant in the formation not only of modern British working-class culture but of the culture of the nation as a whole. The main emphasis to date has been on the following questions: What exactly was the music hall? How did it work? Who worked there and for whom? What does it tell us about its audiences, their expectations, attitudes and visions?

In this book I have looked at the music hall from a somewhat different perspective. I have asked, what happened after the music hall established itself as a powerful element of working-class culture? How did Victorian society in general – and which groups in particular – react to the halls, their messages and their success? What were the repercussions within the working class? What was the nature of the conflicts which arose between supporters and opponents of the halls? And what do these conflicts tell us about classes and cultures, society and the state and – on a different level – about local, regional and national cultures?

It was not until the 1890s that music halls began to appeal to society as a whole. Before then audiences were almost exclusively recruited from working-class neighbourhoods. Between 1840 and 1890 they consisted overwhelmingly of casual workers, day labourers, dock workers and carters, message boys and girls, apprentices, domestic servants, soldiers, sailors and workers of both sexes in and outside factories. At the top of the social hierarchy were members of the working-class aristocracy and those members of the lower middle class who lived and worked in working-class neighbourhoods or had their roots there: skilled workers, artisans, trades people, owners of small businesses and (young) clerks. The music hall was a community-based institution which catered for both the working class and the lower middle class, the two being separated only by different areas of seating. It was in no way 'almost exclusively ... a male culture'.[1] It appealed to both men and women alike, single persons as well as families and more than any other institution it served as a communication centre for family groups and circles of friends, neighbours and workmates of both sexes.

Music halls offered their audiences a variety of attractions which other institutions were unable or unwilling to provide. Unlike pubs the halls could offer more than alcohol. Nor did they restrict themselves to instruction like adult education institutions. They offered food and drink, entertainment and instruction, sociability and space, a place where one could be oneself without being disciplined and 'improved' by one's superiors – and all this at a reasonable price. But there were three more essential points of attachment between the halls and their audiences. The halls rescued and transformed essential elements of pre-industrial popular culture into a modern urban setting and thus maintained traditions which otherwise would have been lost. But the halls not only referred back to the past; they also reflected contemporary life and presented new images and orientations. The comic song in particular celebrated the culture and life-style of the 'little man' – and woman. In doing so it raised the self-esteem of a social group which at work were reduced to the status of 'hands' (i.e. to that part of their body which was necessary to dealing with tools and machinery) and who, outside work, were generally regarded as uncivilised savages and targets for middle-class reforming efforts. In the halls, by contrast, they were accepted and welcomed for what they were. Instead of having to reckon with patronising instruction they were confronted with a positive confirmation of themselves and their way of life. Thus the comic song reflected, shaped and strengthened the audience's experiences and identities as a group and gave public expression to them.

The immense significance of the music hall is confirmed by the acceptance it found amongst working people. Although data on attendances is sparse, 25,000 visitors a week in the music saloons of Manchester in the 1850s, or 4,000 visitors per performance in the Rochdale Circus of Variety (a town with only 40,000 inhabitants), speak for themselves. It was precisely this popularity which made the music hall so vulnerable to attack. The values propagated in the music hall – hedonism, ribaldry, sensuality, the enjoyment of alcohol, the portrayal of marriage as a tragi-comic disaster, and the equality of the sexes at work and leisure – all these were diametrically at odds with those propagated by and attributed to the Victorian middle class: asceticism, prudery, refinement, abstinence, a puritanical work ethic, marriage and the family as the bedrock of social order with the woman's role as housekeeper and mother. Hence, many Victorian contemporaries did not portray the halls so much as capitalist businesses but rather as manifestations of a somewhat dubious counter-culture.

Patrick Joyce has recently argued that the visions and identities which were created and propagated in the halls should be termed 'popular' rather than class-orientated because the making of 'culture', even of a separate culture, was not the same as the making of 'class': 'the consciousness of a class need not be the consciousness of class'.[2] Nonetheless there was a strong element of 'class' in the controversies surrounding the halls. They were viewed by their critics as institutions which either corrupted the working classes or gave public expression to their lack of morals and respectability. The halls in turn were also defended in terms of class.

The music hall was one of the most controversial institutions of English working-class culture. Nonetheless a closer look at the opposing sides in particular controversies frequently reveals that they were not composed along clear-cut class lines but consisted of temporary and shifting coalitions of even the most disparate groups across these lines. A good deal of the controversies – despite the rhetoric involved – consisted of rival battles within the leisure industry: between pubs and music halls in Bolton in the 1840s, between music halls and the theatres in Sheffield in the 1850s and in London over the whole period. The majority of the conflicts were very closely related to the major social questions of the time: temperance and social purity, issues which were also not debated on class lines alone but within each class.

Outside London, as early as 1850, the temperance question led to disputes in Bolton, Manchester and Liverpool about the sale of alcohol in the halls. And in the capital itself the problem of prostitution gave rise to heated debates on the presence of women in the halls. In this connection there arose a further discussion on dancing licences because dancing was associated with physical pleasure, bodily contact and illicit sex, i.e. prostitution. This in turn gave rise to debates on the music-hall programme, which were to develop at a later date in the regions and for other reasons. The first debates began in Glasgow in 1875 when a lobby of middle-class reformers and local VIPs decided to investigate the halls from within and came face to face with songs, sketches, performances and forms of communication whose easy-going freedom appeared to express contempt for middle-class values and demonstrated a huge gulf between working and middle-class cultures. What had earlier been debates about class now shifted to confrontations between classes.

Opposition on class lines was accompanied by a change in the tactics adopted by music-hall opponents in putting forward their arguments. The failure of the temperance movement had demonstrated the futility of trying to win over the authorities with anti-alcohol arguments. So, after 1875, middle-class opponents of the halls began to woo their favours by shifting the emphasis of the argument onto their common background and culture. Even the temperance movement refrained from using alcoholism as an argument against the halls in Sheffield in 1883, preferring instead to stress the problems of culture and class, a tactic which came very close to success. A group of middle-class reformers and town councillors in Bradford – not teetotallers – were more successful. In 1882, they took up cudgels against certain pub music halls in the city and temporarily succeeded in winning the support of the licensing magistrates. But here it should be pointed out that these conflicts took place against a general background of increasing class tension. Conflicts of this sort were unknown in London before

1888. But they developed all the more intensely after the Local Government Act of 1888 led to the first democratically elected London local authority and enabled middle-class members of reform movements to get a foothold amongst the political elite and directly influence the policy of music-hall licensing.

Regional differences in the themes of disputes involving the halls had gradually lessened during the 1890s. By this time reform groups had put the alcohol question on the agenda in London and the growth of variety theatres in the regions had led to concern about 'London conditions' – in particular prostitution – spreading to the provinces. Moreover all these disputes were now conducted within a unified administrative framework after the introduction of the first national system of music-hall licensing between 1888 and 1890. Until then licensing powers had been in the hands of individual local authorities whose policies were dependent on their degree of interest and commitment. Licensing provisions were present in London from the start because a law for the regulation of places of entertainment was already to hand a century before music halls came into existence. Many other cities – prominent amongst them Liverpool – had no provisions for licensing until 1888. Other cities gradually introduced licensing laws over a lengthy period of time.

There was often a link between the social disputes concerning the halls and the introduction of provisions for their licensing. This was evident in the 1860s at the height of the temperance campaign against national drink laws and in favour of licensing the halls. Such a link can be seen once again in the 1880s when social and purity reform campaigns led to a second, if smaller, boom in licensing. Here the point at issue was morality and the music hall programme rather than alcohol. Despite a general tendency towards uniformity, regional and local variations remained, even in the 1890s. If licensing practices were now nationwide and the same topics of discussion were argued throughout the nation, they were neither practised nor argued everywhere in the same way. Indeed the disputes continued to retain their specifically local character. Even when a dispute was part of an overall national controversy, its cause, progress and outcome were directly associated with its particular locality, and its specific components depended on the socio-cultural relationships and the political structure in which it developed.

In regional terms the most glaring differences in the nature of the disputes was between London and the industrial North. This cannot simply be explained by the particular conditions which set the capital apart from other major conurbations. The decisive factor – and the cause of the different nature of the conflicts – was the differing economic and social structures. In London the secondary sector had been very little affected by the industrial revolution. As a result London lacked the non-conformist industrialists and workers who made up the backbone of the temperance movement in the regions. This explains why there were hardly any discussions on alcohol in the London halls in the early years. Furthermore there were very few women factory workers in London. In the North they had set the tone for women's social attitudes and behaviour in a fashion unknown in London. That women could spend an evening in places of entertainment alone or with other female companions was socially accepted in the North and gave rise to very little discussion. But in London such behaviour was associated solely with one particular group of women. Thus prostitutes were a major topic of contention in the London halls. It is possible to discern differences between London and the regions even in the 1890s. Outside the capital there was no basic change in licensing practices following the 1888 Local Government Act. Inside London the act gave rise to a very reform-minded city council which deliberately set out to 'purify' the halls. By contrast, the authorities in the regional cities had very few objections to the status quo. The one area where they did react in a critical fashion was the modernisation of the music-hall scene and the introduction of the new variety theatres.

Neither was there any unified character to the disputes outside London. The conflicts in Bolton and Sheffield in the 1840s and 1850s, and those in Leeds and Liverpool in 1876–7 were all between music halls and the local authority. And – with the exception of Leeds, where in 1876 a non-conformist magistrature at the height of a wave of temperance agitation actively intervened to stop the serving of alcohol in some halls – the lines of conflict were not between the halls on the one side and a unified ruling class on the other. In Liverpool in 1877 the chief of police mobilised an action against alcohol in the halls but failed to gain the support of the local magistrates who had more connections with the alcohol lobby than the temperance movement. There are similar constellations of interest which cross class lines in the conflicts in Bolton in the 1840s and Sheffield in the 1850s. In Bolton the magistrates acted against the halls because several of their members were pub-owners and felt their businesses seriously threatened by the growing success of the halls. In Sheffield the magistrates sided with the theatres which were under threat from the halls, whereas the council backed the music halls. There were not only cultural but political reasons behind the shifting alliances. In 1852 several music halls in Bolton, including the Star, lost their alcohol licences. The magistrates did not act against the halls on class lines but as Whigs against Tory music-hall proprietors, a constellation which had arisen as a result of a bitter power struggle between Whigs and Tories following Bolton's incorporation. The political structure of a town not only played a role in each particular conflict but also in the question of music-hall licensing. Leeds, where a majority of the ruling elite came from a Liberal non-conformist background, introduced licensing as early as 1866. Liverpool, which was Conservative, only brought in licensing controls after the 1888 Local Government Act. But other factors also played a role. Not all cities with a Liberal majority were in a hurry to introduce licensing. Manchester waited until 1882 since the local authority considered there were more important problems to deal with than controlling the halls.

An investigation of the conflicts at local level reveals that the nexus of relationships between the halls and their socio-political environment was particularly complex. The basic constellation was generally the same: reformers against the halls. But as soon as municipal or national institutions became involved alliances were thrown up which varied from conflict to conflict and place to place. In Bolton in the 1850s membership of a political party was the decisive factor in the attitudes and actions of the magistrates when dealing with the halls. In Liverpool in 1877 the authorities were divided in their attitude to controlling the halls because justices and the police chief differed in their attitudes to the the question of temperance. This phenomenon was to be repeated again and again. Only very rarely did the police, the local council and the magistrates form a unified front against the halls. The police and the magistrates took completely different attitudes to the halls in Liverpool in 1877, as they had in Bolton in the 1850s. But whereas in Bolton it was the police who had defended the halls against the magistrates, in Liverpool the situation was the other way round. In Leeds the police and the magistrates worked hand in hand in licensing the halls, whilst in Glasgow neither institution showed much interest in strengthening controls over the halls even after demands from leading businessmen and clergy in 1875. Attitudes not only differed between police and magistrates but also between magistrates and the local council. There are examples when the two worked together in the question of licensing as in Manchester or Bradford after 1882. But these must be set against other cases like Sheffield in the 1850s where a certain disharmony is evident. The police had the broadest range of attitudes, extending from support for the halls, through indifference, to inspection and attempts at intervention. Their reactions not only differed from town to town but might also depend on rank. This was particularly true of the London force whose attitude mainly depended on the type of contact they had with the music-hall scene. If bribery occasionally played a role it was only a minor one. When discussing the problem of prostitution in the 1860s Police Commissioner Richard Mayne defended the halls against the magistrates not because he was in the pockets of the music-hall industry or had an interest in promoting immorality. Given the discrepancy between the overall work-load and the number of constables at his disposal in London, Mayne thought it best to take a pragmatic attitude towards the problem rather than adopt morally 'correct' but impracticable solutions. Constables at street level also defended the halls, if from a different perspective. In 1891 one police district inspector came to the defence of the Angel and Crown music hall which was under threat from the LCC licensing committee. The committee was convinced that the hall was a meeting-place for prostitutes whereas the arguments used by the local inspector were not, like Mayne's, pragmatic but socio-anthropological. Seen in the context of local culture the Angel and Crown was not a centre of prostitution but a perfectly normal music hall. The inspector's attempt to impart his knowledge of local customs and morality to the committee nonetheless came to grief. The licensing committee was neither prepared to view matters from the perspective of another culture, nor was it capable of doing so.

Thus it can justifiably be argued that there was no clear relationship between the authorities and the music hall either at a national or local level, but rather a multiplicity of relationships depending on the specific social and political structure of each locality. In this context the 'two-way' social standing of those music-hall proprietors who dominated the local scene was also of importance. In principle each proprietor fulfilled two social roles. On the one hand he produced and promoted working-class culture in the sense of culture for the workers, especially in the early years. (Thomas Sharples propagated his Star in Bolton as being explicitly 'under the patronage of the working classes'.) On the other hand music-hall proprietors were also capitalist entrepreneurs belonging to a different class and culture. Each of the proprietors dealt with in this book can be taken as a paradigm for other entrepreneurs of his age and background. Sharples was a traditional pub-owner and as such part of the Bolton Tory network in the 1840s, with whom he was closely associated. Thomas Youdan in Sheffield can be described as the prototype of the self-made man of the industrial age. He exploited the economic and political egalitarian structures of Sheffield in the 1850s to climb the social ladder to a place on the council. Hobson in Leeds, and Pullan and Morgan in Bradford were equally successful in business terms. But in non-conformist Leeds Hobson was merely tolerated, whereas Pullan and Morgan, in the 1870s and 1880s, were socially accepted as well. Morgan in particular was a product of the workers' education movement which was promoted by the middle classes. As such he presented and represented an uncontroversial form of working-class culture. It is significant that in 1882 both Pullan and Morgan kept themselves at arms length from the owners of the smaller halls in their conflicts with the council and the magistrature. The situation was very similar in London in the 1890s when the proprietors of the larger halls showed no solidarity with those of the pub music halls who were under attack from the LCC. The typology of music-hall entrepreneurs culminates with the owners of large syndicates at the turn of the century. They not only created a music-hall business equivalent in scale to their industrial counterparts but were likewise rewarded for their services to their industry by knighthoods and other forms of social recognition.

Music-hall proprietors, no matter what they offered and propagated, were entrepreneurs and taxpayers. They did not hesitate to demand the same treatment from national and local authorities as industrialists; and as a rule they got it. Most cities were in no particular hurry to license their halls, often only deciding to do so following strong pressure from campaigners or after middle-class social reformers had infiltrated the local administration. The same applies to central government which was reluctant to intervene in the entertainment sector until 1888. Thereafter it simply unified already existing local laws and made music-hall licensing compulsory on a national level. It did not however interfere with the content of the entertainment. In this respect Hugh

Cunningham's thesis of increasing state intervention seems too strong. It would be more accurate to say that the halls were affected by a lengthy and uneven process of increasing bureaucracy. This is admittedly also a form of intervention in that it imposes rules and regulations. But in the case of the halls there was no underlying deliberate policy to change, reform or control either their form or content. If anything it was the music-hall proprietors who, after 1866, continually demanded intervention from the state; all to no avail. The music hall did not attack the dominant system. If it can be called political at all it was conservative and patriotic. For this reason the state was in the main willing to let it define its own cultural policies and attitudes, even if they hardly reflected those of the ruling class.

Middle-class reform groups were much less tolerant towards the halls. They considered they had an exclusive right to dictate how other people should live and were not prepared to tolerate any rival influences, groups and institutions. They were particularly hard on those who hindered their efforts to gain access to the working class for such people practically wiped out what little chance they might have had of exerting any influence. The basic conflict surrounding the halls can thus be described as being between a hedonistic and somewhat unbridled working-class culture and middle-class social reformers organised in temperance and purity movements; industrialists, executives, the clergy, academics and Sunday school teachers. It was they who embodied at their most extreme what is commonly known as 'Victorian values'. They made no distinction between sobriety and abstinence, respectability and repressive sexuality, diligence and endless labour, working for a living by day and devoting one's leisure to personal improvement. Their idea of leisure had nothing to do with rest and relaxation. 'Rational recreation' was the very opposite of the leisure propagated in the halls: the enjoyment of sex, food and drink, the right to idleness and pure entertainment. The reform groups were only too aware of these counter-cultural elements and condemned the whole institution out of hand as 'perverse' and 'criminal'. The content of the music hall was not the only bone of contention. The habitual forms of communication in the halls also contravened Victorian norms as they were understood within the context of the exaggerated morality of the reformers: young people going to the halls unaccompanied or unsupervised by their parents; the very presence of women, often without male companions; the easy-going contact between the sexes in the halls, which might even result in them dancing together. Both these aspects – content and forms of communication – drove a wedge between the music halls and middle-class culture. Indeed, in the eyes of the reformers, the halls disqualified themselves from any definition of culture and respectability whatsoever.

Respectability was the central concept in the arguments of the reformers. That this was allegedly missing in the halls justified any and every external intervention. But it was 'respectability' which simultaneously played a central role in the defence of the halls. Just as music-hall culture accepted the system so it also accepted its basic values – albeit not in the way they were understood by the reform groups. The halls may have been critical of Victorian morality in its extreme puritanical form, they may have viewed it ironically or mocked it, but they did not refute 'Victorian values' as such. They did, however, reserve for themselves the same right as the reform groups to interpret these values in their own fashion. And as such, what was offered in the halls was indeed deemed 'respectable' by their supporters. Selling beer in the halls did not mean promoting alcoholism. For beer was as much a part of traditional English culture as roast beef and Yorkshire pudding, and every Englishman had a right to his daily pint. Managers and members of the audience might have had their doubts about some of the songs but they insisted they could deal with this themselves without any need for outside intervention. Some of the texts were admittedly rather daring and coarse but that did not make them obscene or dirty. And anyone who interpreted the songs in such a way must have a very vivid imagination. As for the attacks on the sacred institution of marriage: what was wrong with portraying everyday problems, large and small, from time to time? Or was it only respectable to glorify such an institution? And since women and young people were treated in the same way as men during working hours they had a right to the same entertainment in their leisure hours. And the fact that they might happen to go out alone did not mean they were not respectable.

All the arguments which came from the music-hall camp were based on an assertion of their own respectability and their right to interpret the word according to their own lights. This not only applied to proprietors but also to performers and especially the audience. They did not back the proprietors merely out of solidarity or because they wanted to protect an institution which greatly enriched their everyday life. In times of dispute they turned up in large numbers at the halls, were present at law courts and licensing sessions, wrote letters and petitions because they regarded any attack on the halls as an ill-informed and unjustified attack on their own values and behaviour. And by defending the halls working people and members of the lower middle class were able to rebut the attempts of the middle-class reformers to intervene in the interest of their own hegemony. The audiences' struggle was simultaneously a struggle for cultural self-determination, based on the defence of traditional rights and, not least, on the promises inherent in the system itself. If the ideology of government was devoted to non-intervention and laissez-faire then this had to apply to all. The course and outcome of the controversies show that this line of argument was successful.

Thus social stability in the mid-Victorian epoch cannot be explained simply as a result of the infiltration of the 'culture of the factory' into all areas of life nor as a successful attempt of the middle classes to impose hegemony. Seen as a whole the middle class was not interested in comprehensive controls. And those groups within it which *were*, failed to win over the necessary support from the state for such measures. The fact that the state rarely intervened on the side of the middle classes but stayed true to its ideology by leaving the conflicting parties to their own business no doubt played a considerable part in strengthening its legitimation in the eyes of working people – thus ensuring 'a non authoritarian social stability'.[3]

Recent research has maintained that the comparatively late development of an independent Labour party was mainly due to two factors. On a regional and national level Liberalism and the Lib-Lab pact 'functioned' for the working class. And on a local level the working class managed to build up a comprehensive network of grass-roots organisations based around charities, friendly societies, co-operatives and local trades union branches in parishes, neighbourhoods and at work which proved strong enough to fend off middle-class attempts at interference and to solve class conflicts within the community.[4] Increasing social, political and economic tensions between the classes undermined this social regulatory mechanism in the 1880s and led to the break-up of the Lib-Lab pact and the development of a new party. The Labour Party did not however develop from above as a rival to working-class culture but sprang out of the network of grass-roots organisations and community-based cultural institutions. The music hall was a part of this network. Its proprietors supported working-class organisations, unions and charities with benefit performances and opened up their premises for strike meetings. The main achievement of the halls was the propagation of a culture which strengthened both the self-confidence and the consciousness of the working class. This might not have been class consciousness in the classic Marxist sense, but it was about class and about separate identities. And when the Labour Party was finally founded in the 1890s it was able to build on this culture and consciousness.

Notes

INTRODUCTION

1 Parliamentary Papers 1852–3 (855) XXXVII, Select Committee Report on Public Houses, pp. 271–2.
2 C. E. B. Russell and E. T. Campagnac, 'Poor People's Music Halls in Lancashire', *Economic Review* (1900), pp. 289–308.
3 L. Senelick, D. Cheshire and U. Schneider, *British Music-Hall 1840–1923. A Bibliography and Guide to Sources, with a Supplement on European Music-Hall* (Hamden, CT, 1981).
4 J. B. Booth, *'Master' and Men* (London, 1927), p. 5.
5 Booth was the main representative of this tendency and published countless memoirs between 1925 and 1957: *Old Pink 'Un Days* (London, 1925); *'Master' and Men* (London, 1927); *London Town* (London, 1929); 'The Old Music Hall', in Booth (ed.), *Fifty Years Memories and Contrasts* (London, 1932), pp. 77–86; *Pink Parade* (London, 1933); *A Pink 'Un Remembers* (London, 1937) [ed.]; *Life, Laughter and Brass Hats* (London, 1939); *The Days We Knew* (London, 1943); *Seventy Years of Song* (London, 1943); *Palmy Days* (London, 1957). Similarly W. Macqueen-Pope: 'The Men Who Wrote the Songs', in J. B. Booth, *Seventy Years*, pp. 67–70; *Carriages at Eleven* (London, 1947); *An Indiscreet Guide to Theatreland* (London, 1949); *Ghosts and Greasepaint* (London, 1951); *The Melodies Linger On* (London, 1951); *Queen of the Music Halls* (Norwich, 1957).
   More detailed and from a broader perspective are the memoirs of H. G. Hibbert, *Fifty Years of a Londoner's Life* (London, 1916); and H. Chance Newton, *Idols of the 'Halls'. Being my Music-Hall Memories* (London, 1928). And especially J. Hollingshead: *My Lifetime*, 2 vols. (London, 1895). Hollingshead was not a journalist but a theatre and music-hall manager and had direct experience of the halls from the start. My list is incomplete here. For a full list of authors see the above noted bibliography by Senelick, Cheshire and Schneider.
6 Peter Bailey (ed.), *Music Hall. The Business of Pleasure* (Milton Keynes, 1986), pp. xiii-xiv.
7 H. Scott, *The Early Doors: Origins of the Music Hall* (London, 1946).
8 J. Manders and J. Mitchenson, *British Music Hall: A Story in Pictures* (London, 1965); L. Senelick, 'A Brief Life and Times of the Victorian Music Hall', *Harvard Library Bulletin* 19 (1971), pp. 375–98; D. Cheshire, *Music Hall in Britain* (Newton Abbot, 1974).
9 The most important literary analyses are by E. Voigt, *Die Music-Hall-Songs und das öffentliche Leben Englands* (Greifswald, 1929); C. Pulling, *They were Singing* (London, 1952); M. W. Disher, *Victorian Song* (London, 1955); C. MacInnes, *Sweet Saturday Night* (London, 1967); P. Davison, *Songs of the British Music Hall* (New York, 1971); L. Senelick, 'Politics as Entertainment: Victorian Music-Hall Songs', *Victorian Studies* 19 (1975–6), pp. 149–80; J. Bratton, *The Victorian Popular Ballad* (London, 1975); U. Schneider, '"Let's all go to the Music Hall": Die Music Hall and ihre Songs', *Anglistik und Englischunterricht* 15 (1981), pp. 85–102; same, ' "That exquisite sense of the frivolous". Die Music Hall im England der neunziger Jahre', in M. Pfister and B. Schulte-Middelich (eds.), *Die 'Nineties'. Das englische Fin de Siecle zwischen Dekadenz and Sozialkritik* (München, 1983), pp. 342–57; same, *Die Londoner Music Hall und ihre Songs 1850–1920* (Tübingen, 1984); same, 'Joyce und die Music Hall', in U. Bertram and D. Petzold (eds.), *Erlanger Anglistik und Amerikanistik in Vergangenheit und*

Gegenwart (Erlangen, 1990), pp. 295–309; same, 'A Rollicking Rattling Song of the Halls: Joyce and the Music Halls', in R. Bauerle (ed.), *Picking Up Airs: Hearing the Music in Joyce's Texts*, (Urbana, 1993), pp. 67–104; M. Raab, *The Music Hall is Dying: Die Thematisierung der Unterhaltungsindustrie im englischen Gegenwartsdrama* (Tübingen, 1989).

From the point of view of music and theatre history: S. McKechnie, *Popular Entertainment Through the Ages* (New York, 1969, 1931, repr.); P. A. Scholes, *The Mirror of Music 1844–1944*, 2 vols. (Oxford, 1947); W. Bridges-Adams, *The British Theatre* (London, 1947); R. Nettel, *Music in the Five Towns 1840–1914* (Oxford, 1945); same, *The Englishman Makes Music*, (London, 1952); same, *Seven Centuries of Popular Song* (London, 1956); E. D. Mackerness, *A Social History of English Music* (London, 1964); E. Lee, *Music of the People* (London, 1970); same, *Folksong and Music Hall* (London, 1982); R. Pearsall, *Victorian Popular Music* (Newton Abbot, 1973); P. Beaver, *The Spice of Life. Pleasures of the Victorian Age* (London, 1979); R. Middleton, 'Popular Music of the Lower Classes', in N. Temperley (ed.), *Music in Britain* (London, 1981), pp. 63–91; Ian Watson, *Song and Democratic Culture in Britain* (London, 1983); J. Bratton, *Performance and Style* (Milton Keynes, 1986); D. Russell, *Popular Music in England, 1840–1914. A Social History* (Manchester, 1987).

For (social-)historical works on the halls, part of which deal exclusively with the halls and part with the halls in the context of the history of leisure, local history or the history of working-class culture: G. Stedman Jones, 'Working-Class Culture and Working-Class Politics in London, 1870–1900. Notes on the Remaking of a Working Class', *Journal of Social History* 7 (1974), pp. 460–508; M. Vicinus, *The Industrial Muse* (London, 1974); P. Bailey, *Leisure and Class in Victorian England* (London, 1978, reissued with a new introduction 1987); J. Walvin, *Leisure and Society 1830–1950* (London, 1978); H. Cunningham, *Leisure in the Industrial Revolution c.1780–c.1880* (London, 1980); P. Summerfield, 'The Effingham Arms and the Empire: Deliberate Selection in the Evolution of Music Hall in London', in E. and S. Yeo (eds.), *Popular Culture and Class Conflict 1590–1914* (Sussex, 1981), pp. 209–40; B. Waites, 'The Music Hall', in *Popular Culture*, Block 2, ed. Open University Press (Milton Keynes, 1981), pp. 43–76; P. Bailey, 'Custom, Capital and Culture in the Victorian Music Hall', in R. D. Storch (ed.), *Popular Culture in Nineteenth-Century Britain: Continuity and Change* (London, 1982), pp. 180–208; J. K. Walton and J. Walvin (eds.), *Leisure in Britain 1780–1939* (Manchester, 1983); P. Bailey (ed.), *Music Hall*; same, 'Leisure, culture and the historian: reviewing the first generation of leisure historiography in Britain', *Leisure Studies* 8 (1989), pp. 107–27.

10 Stedman Jones, 'Working-Class Culture', and Vicinus, *The Industrial Muse*.
11 Bailey, *Leisure and Class;* Summerfield, 'Effingham Arms'; Cunningham, *Leisure*.
12 For a summary of this debate see Bailey, *Leisure* (new introduction 1987) and U. Schneider, 'Literaturbericht zum Stand der Music Hall-Forschung', *Gulliver* 34 (1993), pp. 152–9.
13 Summerfield, 'Effingham Arms'.
14 Bailey, *Music Hall*, p. xiv.
15 *ibid.*, p. xvi.
16 Bailey, *Leisure*, p. 151.
17 Bailey, *Music Hall*, p. 34.
18 Bailey, *Custom*, pp. 203–4 and *Leisure*, p. 150.
19 P. Joyce, *Visions of the People. Industrial England and the Question of Class 1848–1914* (Cambridge, 1991), p. 17.
20 P. Bailey, 'Conspiracies of Meaning: Music Hall and the Knowingness of Popular Culture', *Past and Present* 144 (1994), p. 168.
21 G. J. Mellor, *The Northern Music Hall* (Newcastle, 1970).
22 M. B. Smith, 'Victorian Entertainment in the Lancashire Cotton Towns', in S. P. Bell, *Victorian Lancashire* (Newton Abbot, 1974), pp. 169–85.
23 For Bailey see note 9; also R. Poole, *Popular Leisure and the Music Hall in Nineteenth-Century Bolton* (Lancashire, 1982); D. A. Reid, 'Labour, leisure and politics in Birmingham c.1800–1875', unpublished thesis (Birmingham, 1985); J. Crump, 'Provincial Music Hall: Promoters and Public in Leicester 1863–1929', in Bailey, *Music Hall*, pp. 53–72 and same,

'Amusements of the people. The provision of recreation in Leicester, 1850–1914' (unpublished thesis, University of Warwick, 1985); D. Harker, 'The Making of the Tyneside Concert Hall', *Popular Music* 1 (1971), pp. 27–56; C. Waters, 'Manchester Morality and London Capital: The Battle over the Palace of Varieties', in Bailey, *Music Hall*, pp. 141–61.

24 R. Storch (ed.), *Popular Culture and Custom in Nineteenth-Century England* (London, 1982), Introduction, p. 17.

The question of the interdependencies between culture, society and politics is of some relevance in Germany. The historiography of working-class culture developed comparatively late here and was, at first, reviewed rather sceptically by the dominant group of structuralist social historians. It was especially feared that an anthropologically informed study of working-class culture might 'only' be looking at one phenomenon (culture) isolated from the rest and thus fall back behind the standards achieved so far. Jürgen Kocka in particular insisted on taking into account the interdependencies between culture, social structure and politics. See J. Kocka, 'Arbeiterkultur als Forschungsthema', *Geschichte und Gesellschaft* 5 (1979), pp. 5–11, here p. 7; see also G. A. Ritter (ed.), *Arbeiterkultur* (Königstein, Taunus, 1979), p. 3. These aspects have mainly been dealt with by German historical anthropologists; see N. Schindler, 'Spuren in der Geschichte der "anderen" Zivilisation', in R. von Dülmen and N. Schindler (eds.), *Volkskultur* (Frankfurt, 1984), pp. 13–77, esp. pp. 55–66, and W. Kaschuba, 'Volkskultur', *Archiv für Sozialgeschichte* 26 (1986), pp. 361–98, esp. pp. 375–84.

For the latest research on English working-class culture (including a comparison with Germany) see D. Langewiesche, '"Arbeiterkultur", Kultur der Arbeiterbewegung im Kaiserreich and in der Weimarer Republik. Bemerkungen zum Forschungsstand', *Ergebnisse* (26, 1984), pp. 9–29; G. Storm, M. Scholing and A. Frohmann, 'Arbeiterkultur zwischen Gegenkultur und Integration. Ein Literaturbericht', *Internationale Wissenschaftliche Korrespondenz* 22 (1986), pp. 318–57; F. Walter, 'Konfliktreiche Integration. Arbeiterkultur im Kaiserreich und in der Weimarer Republik. Eine Zwischenbilanz', *Internationale Wissenschaftliche Korrespondenz* 24 (1988), pp. 54–88; D. Geary, 'Arbeiterkultur in Deutschland und Großbritannien im Vergleich', in D. Petzina (for the Institut zur Geschichte der Arbeiterbewegung) (ed.), *Fahnen, Fäuste, Körper. Symbolik und Kultur der Arbeiterbewegung* (Essen, 1986), pp. 91–9; V. Lidtke, 'Recent Literature on Workers' Culture in Germany and England', in K. Tenfelde (ed.), *Arbeiter und Arbeiterbewegung im Vergleich*, (Munich, 1986), pp. 337–62.

25 P. Joyce, *Work, Society and Politics. The Culture of the Factory in Later Victorian England* (Sussex, 1980), p. xiv.

26 *ibid.*, pp. 320, 145 and 150.

27 Yeo, *Popular Culture*, p. 129. For the Bolton conflicts see Bailey, *Leisure*, ch. 1 and Poole, chs. 2 and 3.

28 Joyce, *Work*, pp. 18 and 69.

29 Poole, *Popular Leisure*, pp. 18–19.

30 *ibid.*, pp. 25–6 and Bailey, *Leisure*, p. 52.

31 Bailey, *Leisure*, p. 5.

32 M. J. Wiener, in a review of A. P. Donajgrodzki (ed.), 'Social Control in Nineteenth Century Britain' (London, 1977), *Journal of Social History* 12 (1978–9), pp. 314–21; also P. Anderson, 'Origin of the Present Crisis', *New Left Review* 23 (1964), pp. 26–53; T. Nairn, 'The English Working Class', *New Left Review* 24 (1964), pp. 43–57; E. P. Thompson, *The Making of the English Working Class* (Harmondsworth, 1972); same, *The Poverty of Theory* (London, 1978).

33 S. Pollard, 'Englische Arbeiterkultur im Zeitalter der Industrialisierung: Forschungsergebnisse und Forschungsprobleme. Ein bibliographischer Aufsatz', *Geschichte und Gesellschaft* 5 (1979), pp. 110–66, here p. 161. Decisive impulses for this area of research came from the work of E. P. Thompson, especially his researches into class structure and consciousness, eighteenth-century popular culture, time and work-discipline in the nineteenth century. Other than *The Making of the English Working Class*: 'The Moral Economy of the English Crowd in the Eighteenth Century', *Past and Present* 50 (1971), pp. 76–136; 'Patrician Society, Plebeian

Culture', *Journal of Social History* 7 (1973–4), pp. 382–405; 'Time, Work-Discipline, and Industrial Capitalism', *Past and Present* 38 (1967), pp. 56–97. Important connected works are also: R. W. Malcolmson, *Popular Recreations in English Society 1700–1850* (Cambridge, 1973); R. D. Storch, 'The Plague of the Blue Locusts', *International Review of Social History* 20 (1975), pp. 61–90; D. A. Reid, 'The Decline of St Monday 1766–1876', *Past and Present* 71 (1976), pp. 76–101; R. McKibbin, 'Working-Class Gambling in Britain 1880–1939', *Past and Present* 82 (1979), pp. 147–78; B. Harrison, *Drink and the Victorians. The Temperance Question in England 1815–1872* (London, 1971); same, 'Religion and Recreation in Nineteenth Century England', *Past and Present* 38 (1967), pp. 98–125. H. Cunningham, 'The Metropolitan Fairs: A Case Study in the Social Control of Leisure', in Donajgrodzki, *Social Control*, pp. 163–84.

34 Donajgrodzki, *Social Control.*

35 T. Parsons, *The Social System* (Glencoe, 1963), p. 486.

36 Wiener, 'Review', p. 315.

37 For criticism of the concept of social control see the reviews of Donajgrodzki's collection by Wiener and F. M. L. Thompson, 'Social Control in Victorian Britain', *Economic History Review* 34 (1981), pp. 189–208; S. Hall, 'Cultural Studies and the Centre: some problematics and problems', in S. Hall and others (eds.), *Culture, Media, Language* (London, 1979), p. 20; G. Stedman Jones, 'Class Expression versus Social Control?', *History Workshop Journal* 4 (1977), pp. 162–70; Jones's title refers to the 1975 conference of the Society of Labour History in Sussex, where the theme was 'The Working Class and Leisure: Class Expression and/or Social Control'. Some of the contributions were later published by Eileen and Stephen Yeo, *Popular Culture.* See also A. Reid, 'Politics and Economics in the Formation of the British Working Class', *Social History* 3 (1978), pp. 347–61, here pp. 350–1; Yeo, *Popular Culture,* ch. 5. They all adopt a sceptical stance to the model. Moorhouse, on the other hand, is of the opinion 'that the term social control does not inherently require or necessitate a functionalist approach to the explanation of social life … Stedman-Jones and Reid should remember that the term is only a concept, and as such can be used in all manner of ways, as the basis of all manner of theoretical statements, some of which are part and parcel of a Marxist approach.' H. F. Moorhouse, 'History, Sociology and the Quiescence of the British Working Class', *Social History* 4 (1979), pp. 481–90, here p. 484. This view is shared by Donajgrodzki in the introduction to his volume of essays. But neither he nor Moorhouse are able to give convincing arguments to support their thesis.

38 A. Gramsci, *Zur Politik, Geschichte und Kultur* (Frankfurt, 1980), p. 277 (on the problem of political leadership); also *ibid.*, pp. 228–9 (on the challenge of the intellectuals).

39 Malcolmson, *Popular Recreations*, pp. 93, 128, 135–6, 141–3; Reid, 'St Monday'; Walvin, *Leisure*, pp. 6–7 and 34–5; Cunningham, 'Fairs'.

40 Pollard, 'Englische Arbeiterkultur', pp. 156–61 (with further literature); Bailey, *Leisure*, ch. 5; T. G. Ashplant, 'London Working Men's Clubs, 1875–1914', in Yeo, *Popular Culture*, pp. 241–70.

41 Harrison, *Drink*; Wiener, Review, p. 320 and Thompson, 'Social Control', pp. 193 and 204; also J. K. Walton and A. Wilcox (eds.), *Low Life and Moral Improvement in Mid-Victorian England: Liverpool through the Journalism of Hugh Shimmin* (Leicester, 1991).

42 H. Cunningham, *Leisure*, p. 10 and M. B. Smith, 'Victorian Entertainment'.

43 Storch, 'Problem', pp. 152–3.

44 Bailey, *Leisure*, pp. 13 and 171.

45 Thompson, 'Social Control', p. 201; Cunningham, *Leisure*, pp. 127–9; H. E. Meller, 'Cultural Provisions for the Working Classes in Urban Britain in the Second Half of the Nineteenth Century', *Bulletin of the Society for the Study of Labour History* 17 (1968), pp. 18–19 and R. D. Storch, 'The Policeman as Domestic Missionary. Urban Discipline and Popular Culture in Northern England, 1850–1880', *Journal of Social History* 9 (1975–6), pp. 481–509.

46 Yeo, Review, pp. 140–1 and Thompson, 'Social Control', p. 193.

47 Yeo, Review, p. 141.

48 Thompson, 'Social Control', p. 196; see also p. 189.
49 Gramsci's arguments were especially popular in researches into Labour aristocracy. See R. Gray, *The Labour Aristocracy in Victorian Edinburgh* (Oxford, 1976), p. 6; same, *The Aristocracy of Labour in Nineteenth-Century Britain* (London, 1981), pp. 38–41; G. Crossick, *An Artisan Elite in Victorian Society* (London, 1978), pp. 134–5 and 251–3; T. Tholfsen, *Working-Class Radicalism in Mid-Victorian England* (London, 1976); G. McLennan, '"The Labour Aristocracy" and "Incorporation": Notes on some Terms in the Social History of the Working Class', *Social History* 6 (1981), pp. 71–81. The concept also played an important role in the work of the Centre for Contemporary Cultural Studies in Birmingham; see Hall.
50 Cunningham, *Leisure*, p. 9.

1. HISTORY

1 Parliamentary Papers 1866 (373) XVI, Select Committee Report on Theatrical Licenses and Regulations, pp. 306–7.
2 John Earl, 'Building the Halls', in Bailey, *Music Hall*, pp. 1–32, here pp. 3–5.
3 Bailey, *Leisure*, p. 147 and 'Custom', p. 185; also Vicinus, *Industrial Muse*, p. 240 and Schneider, *Londoner Music Hall*, p. 20. For the early history of the halls, especially the concert rooms, see Laurence Senelick, 'Moonlighting in the Music Hall: the Double Life of Charles Rice', *Theatre Survey* 34 (1993), pp. 29–42.
4 Earl, 'Building', pp. 5–6 and Poole, *Popular Leisure*, p. 61.
5 Stedman Jones, 'Working-class Culture', p. 477.
6 Bailey, *Leisure*, p. 220.
7 James Ellis, 'Life of an Athlete' (no place or date), p. 8; *Yorkshire Owl*, 22 February 1893, p. 299.
8 Ellis, 'Life', pp. 31–3. The three Manchester halls he mentions are also named in the 1853 Select Committee Report on Public Houses (see Parliamentary Papers 1852–3 (855) XXXVII, p. 218). Burton's Casino is even mentioned in the 1849–50 Select Committee Report on the Operation of the Acts for the Sale of Beer, Parliamentary Papers 1849–50 (398) XVIII, p. 20 (with audiences between 600 and 700).
9 For Thomas Sharples see the pamphlet published by his son William in 1859 or 1860 entitled 'Star Museum' in the Bolton Reference Library. This gives a summary of the history of the Star till 1860. Also Bailey, *Leisure*, p. 31 and Poole, *Popular Leisure*, p. 51. For Pullan see *Yorkshire Busy Bee*, 17 March 1883, p. 171.
10 *Era*, 15 October 1848, p. 12, and for Towers the details in C. W. Sutton, *Newspaper Cuttings, etc. relating to the Manchester Stage*, 2 vols. (no place or date).
11 For Pullan see *Yorkshire Daily Observer*, 3 November 1903, p. 10 and – with slight differences – the magazine *Yorkshire Busy Bee*, 17 March 1883, p. 171, which gives the opening year as 1851; also G. J. Mellor, *Theatres of Bradford*, Bingley 1978, who gives the date as 1850. For Hobson see *Leeds Express*, 8 December 1883, p. 5 and for Towers, *Era*, 9 September 1849, p. 11 and 28 October 1849, p. 12.
12 K. Barker, 'Note on Balmbra's', in *Call Boy* 2 (1981), p. 10. For the Parthenon see *Era*, 3 January 1847, p. 10 and for the Casino *Era*, 13 May 1849, p. 12, 1 July 1849, p. 12 and 26 August 1849, p. 11.
13 For the singing saloons of the 1830s and 1840s see Parliamentary Papers 1852–3 (855) XXXVII, pp. 60–2 and p. 325; Bailey, *Leisure*, p. 30; Cunningham, 'Leisure', p. 167; Smith, 'Victorian Entertainment', p. 173.
14 Bailey, *Leisure*, p. 178 (for the Star); *Era*, 1 May 1859, p. 11 (for Polytechnic); *Era*, 26 August 1849, p. 11 (for Youdan's Casino); *Era*, 9 December 1849, p. 12 (for Hobson's Casino).
15 *Era*, 9 December 1849, p. 12.
16 *Era*, 20 May 1849, p. 12, 28 October 1849, p. 11 and 9 December 1849, p. 12; also *Bolton Free Press*, 5 September 1846, p. 1.

17 From 1849 onwards the *Era* reviewed the shows in Towers's Polytechnic and the Colosseum as well as in Hobson's Casino, Ben Lang's Hall and Sharples's Star in Bolton.

18 For Sharples see the advertisements in the *Bolton Chronicle* in the 1840s; for Youdan, *Era*, 26 August 1849, p. 11; and for Towers, *Era*, 1 May 1859, p. 11.

19 Watson, *Song*, p. 18.

20 For the link between pleasure gardens and music halls see esp. Scott, *Early Doors*, pp. 21–7; for the recruiting of early music-hall stars see Hibbert, pp. 34–5 and Senelick, 'Brief Life', pp. 385–6.

21 See also Scott, *Early Doors*, p. 139.

22 For the Sheffield Music Hall see *Sheffield Daily Telegraph*, 15 October 1910; H. Tatton, *Sheffield 1929–1932*, vol. II (no place or date; manuscript in Sheffield Reference Library), p. 418; E. D. Mackerness, *Somewhere Further North. A History of Music in Sheffield* (Sheffield, 1974), pp. 32–3. Some of the early programmes of the Sheffield Music Hall still exist in the Sheffield Reference Library. References to similar 'music halls' elsewhere can be found, amongst others, in adverts in the *Era* 1842 and 1843. See also Cheshire, p. 17.

23 *Era*, 27 June 1852, p. 11.

24 *Era*, 8 February 1863, p. 10. For the early programmes in the music halls, Stuart and Park, *Variety*, pp. 53–6.

25 Bailey, *Leisure*, p. 148.

26 See Parliamentary Papers 1866 (373) XVI, pp. 21 and 103.

27 Cunningham, 'Leisure', p. 170; Bailey, *Leisure*, pp. 150–1.

28 Schneider, *Londoner Music Hall*, pp. 39–40.

29 Bailey, *Leisure*, p. 148.

30 Bailey, 'Custom', p. 186; Cunningham, 'Leisure', p. 170; Schneider, *Londoner Music Hall*, pp. 39–40. The individual halls are described in J. E. Ritchie, *The Night Side of London* (London, 1857) – mostly disapprovingly – and Scott, *Early Doors*, ch. 8.

31 Bailey, *Music Hall*, pp. 36–7. This is confirmed by an evaluation of the data given in D. Howard, *London Theatres and Music Halls 1850–1950* (London, 1950), a compilation of all the metropolitan music halls and theatres of the time with information on the individual institutions, date of existence, address, size, capacity, furbishings, renovations etc.

32 *Dublin University Magazine*, August 1878, p. 192.

33 Vicinus, *Industrial Muse*, pp. 251–2 and McKechnie, *Popular Entertainment*, pp. 143–4.

34 Stuart and Park, *Variety*, pp. 190–1.

35 L. Rutherford, 'Managers in a small way: The Professionalisation of Variety Artistes, 1860–1914', in Bailey, *Music Hall*, pp. 93–117, here p. 93. For the 1907 strike see *ibid.*, pp. 108–9 and Cheshire, *Music Hall*, pp. 45–8.

36 V. Glasstone, *Victorian and Edwardian Theatres* (London, 1975), p. 75.

37 Bailey, 'Custom', p. 187.

38 Hibbert, pp. 158–61 and Mellor, *Northern Music Halls*, p. 134. The annual statistics of the *Era Almanack* give statistics on who owned what.

39 Schneider, *Londoner Music Hall*, p. 83.

40 Hibbert, *Fifty Years*, p. 160.

41 *Era Annual* 1914, pp. 73–6; Bailey, 'Leisure', p. 167.

42 F. Anstey, 'London Music Halls', *Harper's Monthly Magazine* 1891, pp. 190–202, here p. 190.

43 Summerfield, 'Effingham Arms', pp. 216–18; see also note 3.

44 Mander and Mitchenson, British Music Hall pp. 35–37; Cheshire, *Music Hall*, pp. 52–9; Schneider, *Londoner Music Hall*, pp. 91–2. In his oral-history project on working-class leisure in Salford and Manchester between 1900 and 1939, Andrew Davies noted that if poor people spent any money at all for leisure pursuits, young people tended to spend it in dance halls, men on drink, gambling and the cinema but only a few of his female respondents mentioned the music hall. See A. Davies, *Leisure, Gender and Poverty. Working-Class Culture in Salford and Manchester, 1900–1939* (Buckingham, 1992), pp. 54–8 and 83.

45 On the survival of music-hall elements in twentieth-century English drama see Raab, 'The

Music Hall'; on twentieth-century music-hall stars and their activities in radio and television see
J. Fisher, *Funny Way to Be A Hero* (London, 1973).

46 Poole, *Popular Leisure*, pp. 81–2; *Bolton Evening News*, 2 November 1933; *Bolton Chronicle*, 6 October 1860, p. 1; *Era*, 18 March 1877, p. 6.
47 *Era*, 13 May 1849, p. 12; 26 August 1849, p. 11; 15 February 1852, p. 12; 20 April 1856, p. 10; 4 September 1864, p. 12; 5 November 1865, p. 13; 9 August 1868, p. 13; *Sheffield Daily Telegraph*, 29 November 1876, p. 3; also the Bland Collection (articles, newspaper cuttings and pictures on the early music halls and theatres in Sheffield) in the Sheffield Reference Library.
48 Crump, 'Provincial Music Hall', pp. 57–8.
49 *Leeds Express*, 8 December 1883, p. 5.
50 *Leeds Bibliography* 282; *Era*, 9 December 1849, p. 12 and 25 December 1864, p. 13; *Yorkshire Busy Bee*, 20 August 1881, p. 14; *Leeds Express*, 8 December 1883, p. 5; *Era*, 2 July 1892, p. 8.
51 *Brear's Guide to Bradford and District* (Bradford, 1873), p. 66; the annual statistics in *Era Almanack*; *Yorkshire Daily Observer*, 3 November 1903, p. 10. There are various opinions on Pullan's opening date. Most authors settle for 1868 or 1869. But the music hall is mentioned in the *Era*, 11 December 1864, p. 12.
52 R. Greenhalgh, '60 Years' Local Records and Reminiscences by a Bolton Journalist' (Bolton[?] 1908 (Manuscript, Bolton Reference Library), pp. 4–5.
53 *Era*, 20 April 1856, p. 10 (for Youdan's Surrey) and *Yorkshire Busy Bee*, 20 August 1881, p. 14 (for Hobson's Museum).
54 *Sheffield Daily Telegraph*, 10 September 1858, p. 1 and 25 March 1865, p. 8.
55 *Sheffield Daily Telegraph*, 18 September 1858, p. 1; 1 September 1863, p. 1; 14 September 1863, p. 1.
56 *Bolton Free Press*, 21 March 1846, p. 1; 16 May 1846, p. 1; 21 November 1846, p. 1; *Bolton Chronicle*, 26 February 1848, p. 1; 20 December 1862, p. 1.
57 *Bolton Free Press*, 27 November 1847, p. 1; 25 September 1847, p. 1; *Bolton Chronicle*, 5 February 1848, p. 1.
58 *Era*, 23 October 1897, p. 18.
59 *Bradford Observer*, 4 January 1886, p. 7; Russell and Campagnac, 'Poor People's Music Halls', pp. 291–2.
60 See the details in the annual statistics in the *Era Almanack* and the programmes of the Star Music Hall in the 1870s.
61 For a more detailed location of halls and audiences see my article: D. Höher, 'The Composition of Music Hall Audiences', in Bailey (ed.), *Music Hall*, pp. 73–92.
62 *Era*, 17 September 1892, p. 17; *Manchester Police Returns*, 1892; *Bradford Observer*, 29 January 1891, p. 7.
63 *Liverpool Daily (Evening) Albion*, 3 December 1877, p. 2 (Colosseum); 8 December 1877, p. 2 (Alhambra und Gaiety); 12 December 1877, p. 2 (Constellation); 15 December 1877, p. 2 (an 'unmentionable'); 18 December 1877, p. 2 (Crystal Palace); 22 December 1877, p. 2 (Griffith's); 8 January 1878, p. 2 (Metropolitan).
64 For the Liverpool music halls see R. J. Broadbent, *Annals of the Liverpool Stage* (Liverpool, 1908), esp. pp. 346–9 (Parthenon) and p. 342 (Star); also *Era*, 3 January 1847, p. 10.
65 *Liverpool Daily (Evening) Albion*, 23 November 1877, p. 2.
66 *Era*, 26 January 1851, p. 12.
67 *Era Almanack* 1880 and 1881; also for the early 1860s the advertisements in the *Era*.
68 *Sheffield Era*, 13 December 1880.
69 *Free Lance*, 8 February 1868, p. 41 and 25 January 1868, p. 236. For the free-and-easies see *ibid.*, 2 March 1867, pp. 81–3.
70 *Free Lance*, 25 January 1868, p. 236.
71 For the Victoria Music Hall see *Manchester Courier and Lancashire General Advertiser*, 13 August 1868, p. 6.
72 Waters, 'Manchester', pp. 146–56.

73 I have taken the definition of 'music hall' from that used in the local press and from the statistics given in the *Era Almanack*.

74 For Kiernan, the 'pioneer in the variety theatre world of Liverpool', *Liverpool Review*, 19 December 1896, p. 5 and *ibid.*, 22 February 1896, p. 12; also *Liverpool Echo*, 23 January 1920 and Broadbent, *Annals*, pp. 368–9.

75 B. Dickinson, 'The Magic of Music Hall', *Manchester Evening News*, 17 January 1983.

76 See the statistics in the annual *Era Almanack* and in Mellor, *Northern Music Hall*.

77 *Era Annual* 1914, pp. 227 and 232–3.

78 *ibid.*, pp. 73–6.

79 The populations of the most often-mentioned towns in this chapter were (in 1000s):

	1851	1891
Liverpool	376	630
Manchester	303	505
Leeds	172	368
Sheffield	135	324
Bradford	104	266
Leicester	61	175
Bolton	61	156

Source: B. Mitchell and P. Deane, *Abstract of British Historical Statistics* (Cambridge, 1962), pp. 24–7.

80 Watson, p. 19; Russell and Campagnac, p. 290.

81 *Bolton Free Press*, 29 November 1845, p. 1; *Bolton Chronicle*, 18 January 1845, p. 2; *Bradford Observer*, 23 October 1871, p. 1.

82 Vicinus, *Industrial Muse*, ch. 5.

83 Geoghegan's itinerary can be traced esp. in the *Era*. From 1845 to 1858 he worked in the Star Hotel in Liverpool (see, amongst others, *Era*, 21 February 1858, p. 12) and from 1860 to 1864 in several music halls in Sheffield (*Era*, 21 October 1860, p. 12 and 19 June 1864, p. 12). After that he moved to Manchester and Bolton, where he worked as Chairman in the Star and as manager of the Victoria Variety Theatre. He finally bought his own music hall in Hanley. (*Era*, 4 November 1866, p. 13; 28 March 1885, p. 16 and *Bolton Journal and Guardian*, 26 January 1889).

84 *Bolton Free Press*, 6 December 1845, p. 2; *Era*, 17 March 1850, p. 11; 'Depositions relating to the Star Inn Theatre, Music Hall, and Museum, Churchgate, Bolton, 1860', p. 6, Bolton Reference Library.

85 Bailey, *Leisure*, p. 31 and Poole, *Popular Leisure,* p. 52.

86 'Catalogue of the Extensive Exhibition to be seen daily in Mr. Sharples Museum, Star Inn' (Bolton, 1845), Bolton Reference Library.

87 Thompson, *Making*, p. 322. For hand-weavers' culture see also P. Burke, *Popular Culture in Early Modern Europe* (London, 1978), pp. 37–8; Vicinus, *Industrial Muse*, pp. 38–53.

88 *Bolton Chronicle*, 21 September 1844, P. 1 and *Bolton Free Press*, 22 November 1845, p. 1.

89 Harker, 'Making', p. 32.

90 Vicinus, *Industrial Muse*, p. 267 (for Wilson) and p. 243 (Corvan). For Corvan also Harker, 'Making', pp. 47–55.

91 Vicinus, *Industrial Muse*, pp. 244 and 270; Harker, 'Making', p. 49.

92 Harker, 'Making', pp. 48–9. For itinerant musicians in Yorkshire see *Yorkshire Busy Bee*, 11 March 1882, p. 149; *Yorkshire Post and Leeds Intelligencer*, 18 January 1876, p. 8; *Bradford Observer*, 23 January 1882, p. 7.

93 For Thornton see esp. Harker, 'Making', pp. 36–7.

2. THE MUSIC-HALL PROGRAMME

1 Bailey, 'Custom', p. 204.

2 This is particularly true of the 'memoire' literature mentioned in the introduction. Scott, *Early*

Doors, is the first to go into more detail on the programme as a whole. For the content of the regional halls see Russell and Campagnac, 'Poor People's Music Halls', also Mellor, *Northern Music Hall*.

3 Voigt, *Music Hall Songs*, p. 20.
4 Above all Pulling, *They Were Singing*, and MacInnes, *Sweet.*
5 Above all Disher, *Victorian Song*; Bratton, *Victorian Popular Ballad*; Vicinus, *Industrial Muse.*
6 Senelick, 'Politics'; Stedman Jones, 'Working-class Culture'; Summerfield, 'Effingham Arms'; Russell, *Popular Music,* ch. 5.
7 See above-mentioned, also P. Bailey, 'Champagne Charlie: Performance and Ideology in the Music Hall Swell Song', in Bratton, *Music Hall*, pp. 49–69; J. Traies, 'Jones and the Working Girl: Class Marginality in Music-Hall Song 1860–1900', in Bratton, *Music Hall*, pp. 23–48; M. Pickering, 'White Skin, Black Masks: "Nigger" Minstrelsy in Victorian Britain', in Bratton, *Music Hall*, pp. 70–91 and the introduction by J. Bratton in the said volume of essays esp. p. XI. Most recently Bailey, 'Conspiracies'.
8 MacInnes, *Sweet*, p. 22.
9 Bratton, *Victorian Popular Ballad*, p. 198 and Waites, 'Music Hall', p. 64.
10 MacInnes, *Sweet*, p. 36; Stedman Jones, 'Working-class Culture', p. 492. Schneider, *Londoner Music Hall*, ch. 8, 1.
11 Waites, 'Music Hall', p. 63.
12 Bratton, *Victorian Popular Ballad*, p. 173.
13 The song is quoted in MacInnes, *Sweet*, p. 54.
14 Bratton, *Victorian Popular Ballad*, p. 188.
15 *ibid.*, pp. 167 and 189.
16 Stedman Jones, 'Working-class Culture', p. 492.
17 For the text see Vocal Music H 17780 (20), British Museum Music Library.
18 See esp. Stedman Jones, 'Working-class Culture', p. 491.
19 W. Freer, *My Life and Memories* (Glasgow, 1929), p. 37.
20 *ibid.*
21 Newton, *Idols,* p. 113.
22 Stedman Jones, 'Working-class Culture', p. 493; Bratton, *Victorian Popular Ballad*, pp. 177–9; Schneider, *Londoner Music Hall*, ch. 8, 2, esp. pp. 195 and 227.
23 For political music-hall songs see esp. Voigt, *Music Hall Songs,* ch. 3; Senelick, 'Politics'; Schneider, *Londoner Music Hall*, ch. 8, 3.
24 Both texts are quoted in Senelick, 'Politics', pp. 169 and 172.
25 Quoted *ibid.*, pp. 173–4. See also MacInnes, *Sweet*, p. 80.
26 Senelick, 'Politics', pp. 174 and 164; Schneider, *Londoner Music Hall*, pp. 207–11 and 222.
27 Stedman Jones, 'Working-class Culture', p. 494.
28 Summerfield, 'Effingham Arms', p. 231 and p. 236; Senelick, 'Politics', p. 180.
29 Voigt, *Music Hall Songs,* p. 120 and Senelick, 'Politics', p. 180.
30 Schneider, *Londoner Music Hall*, pp. 135 and 10 and ch. 6; Bailey, 'Champagne'.
31 For the minstrel shows see esp. H. Reynolds, *Minstrel Memories* (London, 1928), pp. 45–7 and p. 71; MacInnes, *Sweet*, p. 33; Schneider, *Londoner Music Hall*, pp. 135 and 145; Scholes, *Mirror*, pp. 514–15; Pickering, 'White Skin'.
32 See Harry Lauder's recollections of his first appearances in London, H. Lauder, *Roamin' in the Gloamin'* (London, 1928), pp. 116–23.
33 F. Anstey, *Mr. Punch's Model Music-Hall Songs and Dramas* (London, 1892), pp. 87–9.
34 Bratton, *Victorian Popular Ballad*, pp. 184–6.
35 See esp. Schneider, *Londoner Music Hall*, pp. 169–71 and Waites, 'Music Hall', pp. 63–5.
36 Schneider, *Londoner Music Hall*, p. 171.
37 Pulling, *They Were Singing*, p. 25. For detailed social aspects of the character, Bailey, 'Champagne', esp. pp. 54–5.
38 Scott, *Early Doors*, pp. 150–2; Pulling, *They Were Singing,* pp. 25–7; Schneider, *Londoner Music Hall*, p. 163.

39 Bailey, 'Champagne', p. 69. See also Scott, *Early Doors*, p. 150 and Waites, 'Music Hall', p. 69.
40 Pulling, *They Were Singing*, p. 27.
41 Scott, *Early Doors*, pp. 150–2; Vicinus, *Industrial Muse*, p. 259; Schneider, *Londoner Music Hall*, p. 160 and above all Bailey, 'Champagne', pp. 50–2.
42 *Dublin University Magazine*, August 1874, p. 235.
43 Vicinus, *Industrial Muse*, p. 259.
44 *ibid.*
45 Bailey, 'Champagne', pp. 55, 60 and 66.
46 *ibid.*, pp. 64–6.
47 Scott, *Early Doors*, p. 151. A somewhat later imitation has recently been discovered in Edgar Wallace's performance of the man-about-town; see D. Glover, 'Looking For Edgar Wallace: The Author as Consumer', *History Workshop Journal* 37 (1994), pp. 143–64.
48 Pulling, *They Were Singing*, p. 26.
49 Quoted in Bailey, 'Champagne', p. 65.
50 *ibid.*, p. 64; Schneider, *Londoner Music Hall*, ch. 6, 5; S. Maitland, *Vesta Tilley* (London, 1986); E. Aston, 'Male Impersonation in the Music Hall. The Case of Vesta Tilley', *New Theatre Quarterly* 4 (1988), pp. 247–57.
51 Bailey, 'Champagne', p. 54.
52 J. Greenwood, *The Wilds of London* (London, 1874), p. 90.
53 Apart from Bailey's analysis of the swell see also the contributions of Traies and Pickering: also Bratton in Bratton (ed.), *Performance* and same, *Victorian Popular Ballad*.
54 Joyce, *Visions*, p. 225.
55 Bailey, 'Conspiracies'.
56 *ibid.*, p. 151.
57 *ibid.*, pp. 156 and 158.
58 *ibid.*, p. 167; M. Mason, *The Making of Victorian Sexuality* (Oxford, 1994), pp. 132–3.
59 I have based my analysis on the programmes of the following halls, which for the given years are relatively complete.

Star and Millstone Concert Hall, Bolton 1840s
Surrey Music Hall, Sheffield 1850s
Princess's Concert Hall, Leeds 1860s
People's Concert Hall, Manchester 1860s to 1880s
Pullan's Music Hall, Bradford 1870s
Circus of Varieties, Rochdale 1880s to 1890s
Star Music Hall, Bradford 1880s to 1890s
Folly, Grand and Tivoli, Manchester 1880s to 1890s.

My choice can be regarded as representative because (1) every hall changed its artistes after one or two weeks so that – apart from individual owner's preferences, like Youdan's for opera – there is a definite resemblance between the programmes of all halls in a single class over the same period of time and (2) the majority of halls mentioned here were the most important halls in their towns.
60 For the history of the fairs see esp. Cunningham, 'Metropolitan Fairs'; for the history of the circus see G. Sanger, *Seventy Years a Showman* (London, 1927).
61 Glasstone, *Victorian*, p. 50.
62 See esp. *Bolton Chronicle*, 5 February 1848, p. 1.
63 *ibid.*, 19 September 1846, p. 1.
64 Stuart and Park, *Variety*, p. 53 for the premiere of Gounod's 'Faust' and *Sheffield Daily Telegraph*, 20 September 1858, p. 1 for Youdan's operatically orientated programmes.
65 Russell, *Popular Music*, pp. 6–8 and 64–9.
66 For the Star see *Bolton Chronicle*, 13 February 1847, p. 1. The Millstone poster is kept in the poster collection of the Bolton Reference Library.
67 *Bolton Chronicle*, 28 September 1844, and 9 December 1848, p. 1.

68 A. Briggs, *Victorian Things* (London, 1990), p. 370.
69 *Bradford Observer*, 19 August 1875, p. 8 and the programme advertisements of the Mechanics' Institutes in the same newspaper, 13 September 1873, p. 1 and 27 October 1873, p. 1. In April 1881 the Bradford Mechanics' Institute presented a 'Grand Miscellaneous Entertainment', at which a member of the Pullan family played the piano. See the programme of 8 April 1881 in Bradford City Library.
70 Bailey, *Leisure*, p. 121 and Ashplant, *London*, pp. 243–51.
71 McKechnie, *Popular Entertainment Through the Ages* (New York and London, 1969), pp. 178–80 and pp. 193–4; Mellor, *Northern Music Hall*, pp. 39–42; Howard, *London Theatres*, where the developments with respect to the London halls can be clearly followed.
72 *Yorkshire Post and Leeds Intelligencer*, 24 February 1866, p. 1.
73 *ibid.*, p. 1; see also *ibid.*, 26 December 1866, p. 1.
74 J. Bratton, 'Theatre of War: the Crimea on the London stage 1854–5', in D. Bradby, L. James and B. Sharratt (eds.), *Performance and politics in popular drama* (Cambridge, 1980), pp. 119–37, here p. 119.
75 For more details see part II this book.
76 *Yorkshire Post and Leeds Intelligencer*, 28 August 1866, p. 1; *Bradford Observer*, 23 October 1871, p. 1.
77 Booth, *London Town*, p. 149; M. Disher, *The Personality of the Alhambra* (London, 1937), p. 7.
78 Advertisements for ballet in Manchester's music halls can be found in esp. *Free Lance*, 15 February 1868 and 15 August 1868; *City Lantern* 4 (1877–8), p. 72.
79 For the Palace see *Era*, 12 March 1892, p. 17; and for the Rochdale Circus of Varieties the *Rochdale Times*, 22 February 1890, p. 1 and the manager's bookings diary, 'Circus of Varieties Bookings', DBC RCV/1, Rochdale Ref. Library. Charlie Chaplin was booked to appear on 12 March 1894.
80 *Bradford Observer*, 3 and 31 July 1871, p. 1 and the programmes of the 1870s.
81 See esp. *Free Lance*, 23 May 1868 or *City Lantern* 6 (1879–80), p. 56.
82 See the programme advertisements in the *Sheffield Era*, 1879 and 1880.
83 *Bolton Free Press*, 23 May 1846, p. 1.

3. THE AUDIENCE

1 *The Times*, 24 January 1910, p. 4. An earlier version of this section on audiences was published by Open University Press (see Höher, 'Composition').
2 Anstey, 'London Music Halls', p. 190.
3 See the details in Ritchie on the individual halls; J. Bratton, *Wilton's Music Hall* (Cambridge, 1980), p. 17; Schneider, *Londoner Music Hall*, pp. 40–1.
4 Entrance prices are based on the details in Parliamentary Papers 1866 (373) XVI, pp. 51 and 56; also in the advertisements in the *Era Almanack* 1868–72.
5 *ibid.*; Bailey, *Leisure*, pp. 155–6; Bratton, *Wilton's*, p. 14.
6 London County Council (LCC), Presented Papers: Theatres and Music Hall Committee, LCC/MIN/10, 782: Canterbury Music Hall, Reports of February and August 1891.
7 The most detailed reports on music-hall fires and panics can be found in *The Times*, the *Era*, in the local press and in the fire statistics in Parliamentary Papers 1892 (240) XVIII, Select Committee Report on Theatres and Places of Entertainment, pp. 519–20.
   For the panics see esp. *Supplement to the Sheffield and Rotherham Independent*, 18 September 1858, p. 10; 25 September 1858, p. 12; *Dundee Advertiser*, 4 January 1865, pp. 2–3; *Times*, 5 January 1865, p. 7; *Manchester Courier and Lancashire General Advertiser*, 3 August 1868, p. 3; 13 August 1868, p. 6; *Liverpool Weekly Albion*, 19 October 1878, p. 2; *Glasgow Weekly Herald*, 8 November 1884, p. 3; *Aberdeen Evening Express*, 1 October.1896, pp. 2 and 4; *Aberdeen Weekly Journal*, 7 October 1896, p. 5. Most statements said that victims were

sitting in definite areas of the hall. Evidence to the enquiries, however, was in the main provided by witnesses who had been sitting in all areas of the hall. Thus the statements enable one to reestablish the whole audience and their seating habits in any one hall, rather than just a part.

For Manchester's music-hall audiences see also G. Wewiora, 'Manchester Music-Hall Audiences in the 1880s', *Manchester Review* 12 (1973), pp. 124–8.

8 Youdan's Surrey was the largest music hall in Sheffield. Springthorpe's was Dundee's only hall in 1865, see *Dundee Advertiser*, 7 January 1865, p. 3. The People's Palace in Aberdeen was one of two halls in the town, see *Era Almanack* 1896.

9 The entrance prices for the music halls in Manchester and Liverpool can be found in the following articles: *Free Lance*, 25 January 1868, p. 236 (People's, Manchester) and 22 April 1871, p. 125 (Alexandra, Manchester), *Manchester Courier*, 13 August 1868, p. 6 (Victoria, Manchester), *Bolton Chronicle*, 14 February 1863, p. 1 (London, Manchester); *Liverpool Daily (Evening) Albion*, 23 November 1877, p. 2 and the following articles in the series.

10 B. Messenger, *Picking Up the Linen Threads* (Belfast, 1980), pp. 6–7 and p. 45. Davies, 'Leisure', p. 129, also gives examples on how elements of the music-hall programme were picked up, transformed and integrated into everyday popular culture.

11 *North British Daily Mail*, 2 March 1875, p. 4.

12 *Aberdeen Evening Express*, 1 October 1896, p. 2; *Aberdeen Weekly Journal*, 7 October 1896, p. 5; *Weekly Free Press and Aberdeen Herald*, 3 October 1896, p. 8.

13 J. H. Marshall, *The 'Social Evil' in Bradford* (Bradford, 1859), p. 8.

14 'Depositions relating to the Star in Bolton', p. 6.

15 *Bradford Observer*, 24 August 1875, p. 3.

16 *Scotsman*, 4 January 1865, p. 2.

17 See Parliamentary Papers 1852–3 (855) XXXVII, p. 454.

18 *Supplement to the Sheffield and Rotherham Independent*, 18 August 1858, p. 10; 'Depositions relating to the Star in Bolton'.

19 *Liverpool Daily (Evening) Albion*, 3 December 1877, p. 2.

20 *Liverpool Review*, 17 October 1883, p. 10 and *Free Lance*, 22 November 1866, p. 5.

21 B. Orchard, *The Clerks of Liverpool* (Liverpool, 1871), p. 16; *City Jackdaw*, 5 May 1876, p. 226; *City Lantern*, 1 December 1876, p. 79.

22 *ibid*. See also G. Crossick (ed.), *The Lower Middle Class in Britain 1870–1914* (London, 1977); J. Kocka (ed.) *Angestellte im europäischen Vergleich* (Göttingen, 1981).

23 For the 'milieu' see G. Crossick, 'The Petite Bourgeoisie in Nineteenth-Century Europe: Problems and Research', in K. Tenfelde (ed.), *Arbeiter und Arbeiterbewegung im Vergleich* (München, 1986), pp. 227–77, here pp. 256–9.

24 *Glasgow Herald*, 4 March 1875, p. 7.

25 Mander and Mitchenson, *British Music Hall*, p. 26.

26 See details in the *Manchester Programme* and for the Palace see Waters, 'Manchester', p. 153.

27 *Liverpool Review*, 15 October 1892, p. 14 and 21 May 1892, p. 12; also Parliamentary Papers 1892 (240) XVIII, p. 244 for Liverpool. For Manchester see *Manchester Amusements* (March, 1893) and the contemporary music-hall programmes in the Theatre Collection of Manchester City Library.

28 J. Jerome, 'Variety Patter', *The Idler* (March, 1892), pp. 119–35.

29 For the early writers' interpretation of chorus singing and riotous behaviour see Booth, *Fifty Years*.

30 Bailey, 'Custom', p. 193.

31 *Era*, 19 March 1887, p. 13; 2 February 1889, p. 11; 9 February 1889, p. 11; 19 April 1890, pp. 13–4; Bailey, 'Custom', p. 193.

32 Bailey, 'Custom'; and D. Reid, 'Popular Theatre in Victorian Birmingham', in Bradby *et al.*, *Performance*, pp. 65–89.

33 Bailey, 'Custom', p. 193.

34 Lauder, *Roamin'*, pp. 45–8, 56–7 and 80–2.

35 F. M. L. Thompson, *The Rise of Respectable Society. A Social History of Victorian Britain, 1830–1900* (London, 1988), p. 288.

36 *Liverpool Weekly Albion*, 19 October 1878, p. 2.
37 T. Wright, *Some Habits and Customs of the Working Classes* (London, 1867), p. 198.
38 V. Tilley, 'Concerning Audiences', *Era Almanack* 1899, p. 67; Russell and Campagnac, p. 291.
39 M. Brown, *Views and Opinions* (London, 1866), p. 255.
40 *Bradford Observer*, 4 January 1886, p. 7.
41 C. Aspin (ed.), *Angus Bethune Reach: Manchester and the Textile Districts in 1849* (Helmshore, 1972), p. 59.
42 Russell, *Popular Music*, p. 30.
43 J. Burnley, *Phases of Bradford Life* (London, 1872), p. 55.
44 *Manchester Courier*, 13 August 1868, p. 6; *Weekly Free Press and Aberdeen Herald*, 3 October 1896, p. 8.
45 Bailey, *Music Hall*, pp. 45–6.
46 *Bolton Chronicle*, 2 January 1859, p. 8; Poole, *Popular Leisure*, p. 66; *Era*, 29 June 1856, p. 10; 18 July 1858, p. 12; *Era*, 19 September 1896, p. 19 (for Huddersfield).
47 *Era*, 16 March 1895, p. 16; *Manchester Programme*, 8 May 1899, p. 1.
48 *Bradford Observer*, 5 February 1891, p. 7.

4. 1840–1865: RIVALRY IN LEISURE

1 R. Storch, 'The Problem of Working-Class Leisure', in Donajgrodzki, *Social Control*, pp. 138–62, here p. 138.
2 For London see Summerfield, 'Effingham Arms'; S. Pennybacker, 'It Was Not What She Said But The Way In What She Said It: The London County Council and the Music Halls', in Bailey (ed.), *Music Hall*, pp. 120–40; Schneider, *Londoner Music Hall*, ch. 3. For the regions see Waters, *British Socialists*; Poole, *Popular Leisure*, and Bailey, *Leisure*.
3 J. Redlich and F. Hirst, *The History of Local Government in England* (London, 1958), p. 118. Today there are certain doubts about the middle-class 'takeover of power' in the 1830s after John Vincent in particular showed that the social composition of Parliament was very little changed by the 1832 Electoral Reform Act. See J. Vincent, *The Formation of the Liberal Party 1857–1868* (London, 1966), pp. 1–5. All the same the old elite took account of the ideas and needs of the rising middle classes and many of the new acts were accommodated to a new middle-class order. See H. Perkin, *The Origins of Modern English Society 1780–1880* (London, 1971), p. 271 and G. Clark, *The Making of Victorian England* (London, 1962), p. 7.
4 Parliamentary Papers 1835 (116) XXIII-XXVI. Royal Commission Reports on Municipal Corporations in England and Wales.
5 The 1833 Royal Commission visited the towns over a period of 18 months and presented its final report to Parliament in March 1835 with a supplement which amounted to almost 3,500 pages (Parliamentary Papers 1835 (116) XXIII-XXVI, Royal Commission Reports on Municipal Corporations in England and Wales). On the work of the Commission see I. Jennings, 'The Municipal Revolution', in H. J. Laski *et al.* (eds.), *A Century of Municipal Progress 1835–1935* (Westport CT, 1978 1935 repr.), pp. 55–65.
6 W. Odgers, *Local Government* (London, 1899), p. 6; Asa Briggs, *Victorian Cities* (Harmondsworth, 1977 edn.), p. 193; P. J. Waller, *Town, City and Nation. England 1850–1914* (Oxford, 1983), p. 245.
7 Proponents of the 'municipal revolution' theory were esp. the Webbs and amongst earlier writers esp. Odgers and Jennings.
8 Briggs, *Victorian Cities*, p. 89. On the administration of non-incorporated and 'unreformed' cities see A. Elliott, 'Municipal Government in Bradford in the mid-Nineteenth Century', in D. Fraser (ed.), *Municipal Reform and the Industrial City* (Leicester, 1982), pp. 111–61; Odgers, *Local Government*, p. 54 and Redlich and Hirst, *History*, p. 168 on Vestrys and Highway Surveyors; D. Fraser, *Urban Politics in Victorian England* (Leicester, 1973), p. 103 on Highway Surveyors and p. 91 on Improvement Commissions; E. Burney, *JP, Magistrate, Court and*

Community (London, 1979), pp. 48–50 on Justices of the Peace. See also Halevy, 'Before 1835', pp. 25–36.

9 For the Local Acts see E. P. Hennock, 'Central/Local Government Relations in England: An Outline', *Urban History Yearbook* (1982), pp. 38–49, here p. 39; and D. Fraser, *Power and Authority in the Victorian City* (Oxford, 1979), p. 151.

10 See H. Hanham, *Elections and Party Management* (Hassocks, 1978 edn.), pp. 302–3. on the differences between the textile towns in the area of Greater Manchester. For a general study see J. Garrard, 'Social History, Political History and Political Science: The Study of Power', *Journal of Social History* 16 (1982–3), pp. 105–21, here p. 111; J. Davies, 'The Problem of London Local Government Reform, 1880–1900', unpublished thesis Oxford 1983, p. 21ff.

11 *Bolton Chronicle*, 22 October 1842, pp. 2.

12 Poole, *Popular Leisure,* p. 54.

13 *Bolton Chronicle*, 22 October 1842, p. 2.

14 *Bolton Chronicle*, 8 October 1842, p. 2.

15 *Bolton Chronicle*, 21 and 28 January 1843, p. 2; Bailey, *Leisure*, p. 19 and Poole, *Popular Leisure,* p. 54.

16 *Bolton Chronicle*, 31 August 1844, and 29 September 1844, p. 3.

17 *ibid.*; Poole, *Popular Leisure,* p. 55; Harrison, *Drink*, p. 329.

18 *Bolton Chronicle*, 31 August 1844, p. 3 and Harrison, *Drink.* There is a link here between the arguments used by the opponents of the Star and the Lord's Day Observance debates instigated by the Temperance movement and the Sabbatarians which went on for several decades. Even as late as 1868 when pub and beer-house opening hours had long been shortened there was a lengthy campaign for complete closure on Sundays in Bolton. See Parliamentary Papers 1867–8 (402) XIV, Select Committee Report on the Sale of Liquors on Sunday Bill, pp. 192–3.

19 The magistrates either issued 'wine' or 'wine and/or spirit' licences. Following the introduction of the Beer Act in 1830 the Treasury was responsible for beer licences. In principle any rate-payer could apply for a licence – and got it too. The local authorities were powerless to control the type and number of applicants. (See Harrison, *Drink*, pp. 70 and 79.)

20 J. Taylor, *Autobiography of a Lancashire Lawyer*, ed. James Clegg (Bolton, 1883).

21 Thompson, 'Social Control', p. 190.

22 *Bolton Free Press*, 28 September 1844, p. 3.

23 D. Smith, *Conflict and Compromise* (London, 1982), p. 50.

24 *Bolton Chronicle*, 28 September 1844, p. 1.

25 *ibid.*

26 Fraser, *Power,* p. 86; Poole, *Popular Leisure,* p. 2; H. Hamer, *Bolton 1838–1939* (Bolton, 1938), pp. 22–5 and P. Philipps, *The Sectarian Spirit* (Toronto, 1982), pp. 28–9.

27 J. Garrard, *Leadership and Power in Victorian Industrial Towns* (Manchester, 1983), p. 11.

28 Garrard, *Leadership*, p. 166; Halevy, 'Before 1835', pp. 18 and 23; E. Moir, *The Justice of the Peace* (Harmondsworth, 1969), pp. 167 and 179.

29 In 1849 Bolton had 179 beer-houses, in 1852 201 and in 1854 221 – the number of pubs varied between 117 and 118. See Parliamentary Papers 1852–3 (855) XXXVII, pp. 247–8 and *Bolton Chronicle*, 29 August 1857, p. 8.

30 *Era*, 5 September 1852.

31 *Bolton Chronicle*, 2 September 1854, p. 5.

32 The movements and developments in the USA were the models. In 1851 the State of Maine had introduced a prohibition law. See Harrison, *Drink*, pp. 195–6; S. Petrow, *Policing Morals. The Metropolitan Police and the Home Office 1870–1914* (Oxford, 1949), p. 180.

33 *Bolton Chronicle*, 2 September 1854, p. 5.

34 Harrison, *Drink*, pp. 179 and 184; L. Shiman, *Crusade against Drink in Victorian England* (London, 1988), pp. 75–6.

35 Harrison, *Drink*, p. 91 and ch. 5; Harrison, 'Religion', pp. 107–8 and B. Harrison, 'Temperance Societies', *Local Historian* 8 (1968), pp. 135–8.

36 Harrison, *Drink*, pp. 129f; Shiman, *Crusade,* pp. 10 and 33.

37 *ibid.*, pp. 135–7, 267 and 318. Also Harrison, 'Religion', pp. 112 and 121–2.
38 Harrison, *Drink*, pp. 194–5.
39 *Bolton Chronicle*, 4 September 1852.
40 *ibid.*, 18 September 1852.
41 *ibid.*, 4 September 1852.
42 *Era*, 29 August 1852, p. 11.
43 The minutes of 1852 no longer exist. But there are reports on the meeting of 19 August 1852 and detailed and controversial debates in readers' letters in the *Bolton Chronicle* between 28 August and 9 October 1852; and in the *Era* between 29 August and 12 September 1852. Similar minutes of those arrested – again mostly young people – in 1860 can be found under the title: 'Depositions relating to the Star Inn Theatre, Music Hall, and Museum, Churchgate, Bolton' in the Bolton Reference Library. The statements of the youths give credible and authentic-sounding descriptions of aspects of their lives in Bolton around the middle of the century. They only become stereotyped when dealing with the role of the Star. See Poole, *Popular Leisure*, p. 58.
44 *Era*, 5 September 1852, p. 12.
45 *Bolton Chronicle*, 11 and 18 September 1852. For the question of the treatment of young people see Parliamentary Papers 1852–3 (855) XXXVII, p. 454.
46 *Bolton Chronicle*, 23 November 1844, p. 2.
47 *Bolton Chronicle*, 22 January 1859, p. 8 and Poole, p. 66.
48 *Bolton Chronicle*, 2 October 1852.
49 *ibid.*, 18 September 1852.
50 *ibid.*, 28 April 1860, p. 5
51 *ibid.*
52 Star Museum Pamphlet ca.1859/60, Bolton Reference Library.
53 The Bolton Theatre Royal is mentioned as belonging to Sharples, see *Bolton Chronicle*, 16 February 1856, p. 5.
54 His profession as councillor was given as 'beer-house keeper'; see the list of councillors in J. Furness, *Record of Municipal Affairs in Sheffield Since the Incorporation of the Borough in 1843 to the Celebration of the Jubilee in 1893* (Sheffield, 1893). For personal details see obituary in *Sheffield Daily Telegraph*, 29 November 1876, p. 3 and K. Barker, 'Thomas Youdan of Sheffield', *Theatrephile* 2, 6 (1985), pp. 9–12.
55 See the report in the *Sheffield and Rotherham Independent*, 25 September 1858, p. 5. Of the other papers in Sheffield the *Sheffield Daily Telegraph* in particular was a proponent of the conspiracy theory (cf. 14 September 1858, p. 2) and the *Sheffield Daily News* of the gas explosion. (see 15 and 25 September 1958, p. 2).
56 *Suppl. to The Sheffield and Rotherham Independent*, 30 October 1858, p. 12 and *Sheffield and Rotherham Independent*, 8 January 1859, pp. 6 and 8. The rape was not a subject of the action.
57 *Era*, 10 December 1854, p. 11.
58 The list is largely based on reports in the *Era*, 29 December 1850, p. 11; 2 January 1853, p. 9; 11 July 1852, p. 11; 29 January 1865, p. 6; 17 March 1872, p. 7; 11 June 1881, p. 5. It is, however, probably incomplete.
59 Barker, 'Thomas Youdan', p. 9.
60 *Sheffield Daily Telegraph*, 5 September 1863, p. 8.
61 *Era*, 6 January 1856, p. 11.
62 *Era*, 24 January 1858, p. 13.
63 For the early discussion of the issue see Parliamentary Papers: 1808 (182) and (323) II, Select Committee Reports on Laws Relating to Lotteries; 1834 (279) and (560) XVIII, Select Committee Reports on the Glasgow Lottery; and 1844 (297), (468), (544) and (604) VI, Select Committee Reports on Statutes Against Gaming. For later nineteenth-century gambling see McKibbin, 'Working-class Gambling' and Davies, *Leisure*, p. 5. On gambling legislature see Petrow, *Policing Morals*, pp. 265 and 272.
64 See, for example, *Era*, 2 February 1879, p. 4 and 19 December 1880, p. 4.

65 *Era*, 10 December 1854, p. 11 and 24 January 1858, p. 13; Barker, 'Thomas Youdan', p. 13.
66 See Parliamentary Papers 1831–2 (679) VII, Select Committee Report on Laws affecting Dramatic Literature.
67 *ibid.*, p. V.
68 *ibid.*, p. 5.
69 See 6&7 Vict.c.68, Para.XXIII.
70 See Parliamentary Papers 1866 (373) XVI, p. 183.
71 *ibid.*, pp. 280–3.
72 See Parliamentary Papers 1866 (373) XVI and 1892 (240) XVIII.
73 For a more detailed description of theatre licensing see Cheshire, *Music Hall*, ch. 7; R. Findlater, *Banned! A Review of Theatrical Censorship in Britain* (London, 1967), pp. 30, 46 and 60–1; W. Geary, *The Law of Theatres and Music Halls* (London, 1885), introduction; and W. Nicholson, *The Struggle for a Free Stage in London* (London, 1906), pp. 139–40.
74 This was the view of e.g. C. Norton, magistrate at the Lambeth magistrates courts and Sir T. Henry, presiding magistrate at the Bow Street magistrates courts, see Parliamentary Papers 1866 (373) XVI, pp. 51–2 and p. 33.
75 *Era*, 9 March 1862, p. 6.
76 *ibid.*
77 *Sheffield Register* and Barker, 'Thomas Youdan', p. 11.
78 *Suppl. to The Sheffield and Rotherham Independent*, 16 January 1858, p. 10.
79 *ibid.*
80 *Era*, 29 June 1856, p. 10.
81 *Era*, 18 July 1858, p. 12.
82 'Star Music Hall', Pamphlet 1859–60, Bolton Reference Library.
83 *Era*, 6 July 1856, p. 11 and *Sheffield Daily Telegraph*, 28 March 1865, p. 6.
84 *Era*, 18 July 1858, p. 11; 27 September 1857, p. 12.
85 F. Engels, *Die Lage der arbeitenden Klasse in England* (1845; repr. Munich, 1977), p. 62.
86 Briggs, *Victorian Cities*, p. 36; S. Pollard, *A History of Labour in Sheffield* (Liverpool, 1959), p. 3; Waller, *Town*, p. 76; G. Lloyd, *The Cutlery Trades* (London, 1913), pp. 191–3; Fraser, *Urban Politics*, p. 201.
87 Fraser, *Power*, p. 139; also Pollard, *History*, p. 42.
88 G. Jones, 'Civic Administration', in D. Linton (ed.), *Sheffield and Its Region* (Sheffield, 1956), pp. 181–3.
89 Pollard, *History*, p. 43 and D. Fraser, *Municipal Reform*, p. 7; Fraser stresses here that the intellectual and monied upper classes in the town distanced themselves from the council.
90 *ibid.*, p. 49; Fraser, *Power*, p. 140. Both give the number of seats in the council as forty-six. In fact it was fifty-six: see Furness, p. 11; Smith, *Conflict*, p. 76.
91 Pollard, *History*, p. 42.
92 Smith, *Conflict*, p. 241; Pollard, *History*, pp. 10–11.
93 Pollard, *History*, p. 29 and Furness, p. 7.
94 These were the Police Commissioners, the Highway Board, the Board of Guardians, the Vestrys, the magistrates and the Cutlery Company; see Pollard, *History*, pp. 8–9.
95 Briggs, *Victorian Cities*, p. 36.
96 *ibid.*, p. 237.
97 Smith, *Conflict*, p. 76.
98 S. Pollard, 'The Ethics of the Sheffield Outrages', *Transactions of the Hunter Archaeological Society*, VII (1951–7), pp. 118–39, here p. 124. For the Trade Societies see also Lloyd, *Cutlery Trades*, chs. 10 and 12; and for the connection between industrial differentiation and the lack of municipal solidarity: Smith, *Conflict*, p. 163.
99 Harrison, *Drink*, pp. 134–8 and C. Reid, 'Temperance, Teetotalism and Local Culture. The Early Temperance Movement in Sheffield', *Northern History* 13 (1977), pp. 248–64.
100 Reid, 'Temperance', pp. 257 and 263.
101 *ibid.*, pp. 261 and 249.

102 Pollard, *History*, p. 30.
103 *ibid.* and *Sheffield Local Register*: in 1859 the magistrates refused thirty-two out of forty applications, and in 1866 they granted only two out of twenty-two applications. For the correspondence between the mayor and the Home Office see Home Office Papers HO 43/96 and 43/109, Public Record Office, London.
104 C. Reid, 'Middle-Class Values and Working-Class Culture in Nineteenth-Century Sheffield – the Pursuit of Respectability', in S. Pollard and C. Holmes (eds.), *Essays in the Economic and Social History of South Yorkshire* (Sheffield, 1976), pp. 275–95, here pp. 284–6; Pollard, *History*, pp. 34–6 and for education in Sheffield: Smith, *Conflict*, chs. 5 and 6.
105 *Sheffield and Rotherham Independent*, 19 January 1861, p. 2.
106 *ibid.*, 7 April 1865, p. 3.
107 *Sheffield Daily Telegraph*, 28 March 1865, p. 6.
108 *Sheffield Times*, 1 April 1865, p. 6.
109 *Sheffield Daily Telegraph*, 25 March 1865, p. 8 and Smith, *Conflict*, p. 188.
110 Material on the Alexandra is kept in the Bland Collection, Sheffield Archives. See also *Sheffield Daily Telegraph*, 29 November 1876, p. 3; J. Stainton, *The Making of Sheffield 1865–1914* (Sheffield, 1924), p. 247; Barker, 'Thomas Youdan', pp. 9–12.
111 For Brougham see *Dictionary of National Biography* (1937–8) and Harrison, *Drink*, pp. 197 and 237. For the Social Science Association see Petrow, pp. 19 and 50; Mason, *Making*, p. 230.
112 Bailey, *Leisure*, pp. 9–11; Cunningham, *Leisure*, p. 84; Walvin, *Leisure*, pp. 34–5; Harrison, *Drink*, p. 45.
113 W. Bennett, *The History of Burnley*, vol. III (Burnley, 1948), p. 342.
114 Pollard, 'Englische Arbeiterkultur', p. 161.

5. 1860–1877: THE 'DEMON DRINK'

1 *Era*, 17 August 1851, p. 12 (for Manchester); and Parliamentary Papers 1852–3 (855) XXXVII, p. 226 (for Liverpool).
2 See HO 32/102, p. 284 (for Norwich), p. 426 (for Bury), p. 312 (for Huddersfield), p. 163 (for Preston) and p. 300 (for Leeds); Parliamentary Papers 1866 (373) XVI, p. 259 (for Birmingham) and p. 254 (for Oldham). Further details can be found in Geary, *Law*; his compilation of local licensing laws is however incomplete.
3 *Era*, 29 September 1861, p. 7 (for Birmingham) and *Bolton Evening News*, 25 January 1873, p. 3 (for Oldham.) In both towns music-hall opponents enjoyed only a limited success. Birmingham's magistrates did not issue music licences to the proprietors of gin palaces, but they did so to pub owners.
4 See Domestic Entry Books, HO 43/102, p. 300.
5 *Leeds Temperance Society Annual Report* 1868, p. 11.
6 Fraser, *Power*, pp. 51–3 and Briggs, *Victorian Cities*, p. 148.
7 E. Hennock, *Fit and Proper Persons* (London, 1973), p. 179; also 'The Social Composition of Borough Councils in Two Large Cities', in H. Dyos (ed.), *The Study of Urban History* (London, 1976 edn.), pp. 315–36, here p. 330; D. Fraser, 'Politics and Society in the Nineteenth Century', in D. Fraser (ed.), *A History of Modern Leeds* (Manchester, 1980), pp. 270–300, here p. 270; same, *Urban Politics in Victorian England* (Leicester, 1973), pp. 118 and 129–31.
8 A. Taylor, 'Victorian Leeds. An Overview', in Fraser, *History*, pp. 388–407, here p. 401 and N. Yates, 'The Religious Life of Modern Leeds', in Fraser, *History*, pp. 250–69, here pp. 250–1.
9 Hennock, *Fit*, p. 181.
10 *ibid.*, and Fraser, 'Politics', p. 283–4.
11 Hennock, *Fit*, p. 201. Later the conservatives' share grew once again, see *ibid.*
12 Fraser, 'Politics', p. 284.
13 Hennock, *Fit*, p. 215 and Fraser, *Urban Politics*, p. 133.
14 *Leeds Mercury*, 25 September 1862, p. 3.

15 R. Morris, 'Middle-Class Culture 1700–1914', in Fraser, *History*, pp. 200–22, here pp. 210–17.
16 Taylor, *Victorian Leeds*, p. 402.
17 For the chorus movement see Nettel, *The Englishman Makes Music,* and Russell, *Popular Music.*
18 J. Harrison, 'Chartism in Leeds', in A. Briggs (ed.), *Chartist Studies* (London, 1977, 1959 repr.), pp. 65–98, here p. 65.
19 *ibid.*, pp. 71–2; Fraser, 'Politics', p. 287; T. Woodhouse, 'The Working Class', in Fraser, *History*, pp. 353–88, here p. 354.
20 Harrison, 'Chartism', p. 81.
21 Harrison, *Drink*, pp. 247 and 259.
22 Briggs, *Victorian Cities*, ch.4.
23 *Leeds Records*: Corporation/Justices, Special Sessions 1864–76, LC/J/6.
24 See § 102 of the Leeds Improvement Act of 1866, in Geary, *Law,* p. 182.
25 Information on magistrates and councillors in Leeds in M. Merrimac, *Pen-and-Ink Photographs of Members of the Leeds Town Council* (Leeds, 1862); J. Mayhall, *The Annals of Yorkshire*, vol. III (Leeds, no date); Sykes Collection; *Local Notes and Queries; Leeds and Yorkshire Biography; Leeds Biographer; Leeds Obituary Notices* – all in Leeds Local History Library.
26 *Era*, 6 January 1867, p. 5; LC/J/6, Report on the sessions 4 January 1867; *Leeds Mercury*, 5 January 1867, p. 7.
27 *Yorkshire Post and Leeds Intelligencer*, 5 January 1867, p. 8.
28 Police report 5 April 1867, in LC/J/6.
29 The details for the table come from LC/J/6; see also *Yorkshire Post and Leeds Intelligencer*, 6 April 1867, p. 5.
30 See police report 3 January 1868, in LC/J/6.
31 *Leeds Temperance Society Annual Report* 1868, p. 11.
32 See LC/J/6, report 2 July 1869.
33 *Leeds Temperance Society Annual Report* 1870, p. 6, 1871, p. 5 and 1872, p. 5.
34 *ibid.*, 1868, pp. 10–13.
35 Taylor, 'Victorian Leeds', p. 402.
36 *Leeds Express*, 8 December 1883, p. 5.
37 *Era*, 11 July 1852, p. 11.
38 *Yorkshire Busy Bee*, Pantomime No. 1882–3, p. 28. The *Leeds Express* dates the change as 1856, see 8 December 1883, p. 5.
39 *ibid.*, and LC/J/6.
40 *Leeds Express*, 8 December 1883, p. 5; *Era*, 30 September 1866, p. 13; Hennock, *Fit*, p. 218.
41 Harrison, *Drink*, pp. 199 and 260.
42 Circular letter of the 'Representative Committee of the Temperance Organisations of the Borough of Bradford', 4 January 1876, Bradford Central Library and Archives.
43 P. Waller, *Democracy and Sectarianism. A Political and Social History of Liverpool* (Liverpool, 1981), p. 24 and B. White, *A History of the Corporation of Liverpool 1835–1914* (Liverpool, 1951), p. 105. For Liverpool Vigilance Committee see W. Cockcroft, 'The Liverpool Police Force 1836–1902', in S. P. Bell (ed.), *Victorian Lancashire* (Newton Abbott, 1974), pp. 150–68, here p. 156.
44 See Parliamentary Papers 1878–9 (113) X, Select Committee Report on Intemperance, p. XLIV; and 1877 (171) XI, Select Committee Report on Intemperance, pp. 229–30. In 1855 the Gothenburg municipal authority began cutting down on the number of alcohol licences and licensees. Using the licensing fees it then set up its own spirits company in cooperation with leading citizens in the town. In the course of time this company became the only licence holder in the town thus ensuring that no individual person could profit from the sale of alcohol. The number of distilleries is said to have shrunk from 30,000 to 500. This did not, however, take account of beer as did the plans in England. In 1877 Chamberlain, then an MP tried to introduce the 'Gothenburg System' into England with a modification which would have allowed the

municipal authority to be a direct licensee without having to set up its own spirits company. See Parliamentary Papers 1878–9 (113) X, p. XLIII.

45 Taylor, *Victorian Leeds*, p. 394. Fraser, *Urban Politics*, pp. 124–5 (for the composition of the parties on the council).

46 Hennock, *Fit*, pp. 215–20.

47 *Leeds Monthly Record of Current Events* 1875, pp. 125–6. In the USA women held daily prayers in front of pubs and saloons. See P. Winskill, *The Temperance Movement and its Workers*, vol. III, p. 255.

48 *ibid.*, p. 254; *Leeds Record of Current Events 1876*, p. 12; *Sheffield Local Register*, 26 August 1875.

49 *Leeds Record of Current Events* 1879, p. 20 and police report of 1888 in *Leeds Mercury*, 24 August 1888, p. 7.

50 *Leeds Monthly Record* 1876, p. 127.

51 Storch, 'Policeman', p. 485.

52 The report appears in *Yorkshire Post and Leeds Intelligencer*, 8 January 1876, p. 8.

53 *Leeds Mercury*, 5 January 1877, p. 3. This explains why in 1877 there were only 279 reapplications of which 100 were for pubs, 141 for beerhouses and 13 for institutions not serving alcohol (see *ibid.*).

54 *Yorkshire Post and Leeds Intelligencer*, 8 January 1876, p. 8.

55 *Leeds Record* 1877, II, p. 5. The three music halls were the Seven Stars Concert Hall, whose proprietor withdrew his application during the magistrates' sessions, the Angel Inn Concert Hall belonging to John Brooke and the Rose and Crown Concert Hall belonging to Joseph Binks. The last named was a pub which was over a hundred years old and where the middle classes of Leeds had organised concerts and dances in the eighteenth century. See *Leeds Bibliography* No.282; Morris, 'Middle-Class Culture', p. 202. Both Binks and Brooke tried unsuccessfully to get their licences back in April 1876. (See LC/J/6, report on the sessions 6 April 1876.) Nor do they seem to have been any more successful in 1877, for the report on the licensing sessions in the *Leeds Mercury* mentions only two 'Concert Halls'. See *ibid.*, 5 January 1877, p. 3.

56 Brooke later succeeded. The Angel Concert Hall is included in the annual music-hall statistics of the *Era Almanack* until 1886. A further rejection of an application in 1894 leads one to suppose that the hall even continued in business until then. (See *Leeds Mercury Weekly Supplement*, 15 December 1894, p. 7.) Its proprietor still did not give up but documents show only rejections until 1899. (See Leeds Council Meeting Minutes, 11 January 1895, p. 8; 6 January 1897, p. 10; 5 January 1898, p. 10; and 4 January 1899, p. 11.)

57 *Yorkshire Post and Leeds Intelligencer*, 8 January 1876, p. 8; LC/J/6, 1864–76, report on the sessions of 7 January 1876.

58 *Leeds Mercury*, 5 January 1877, p. 3.

59 Special and Licensing Sessions 1885–93, LC/J/7, report 13 August 1886.

60 *ibid.*, report on sessions 7 January 1887.

61 *Leeds Mercury*, 8 January 1876, p. 7.

62 See Parliamentary Papers: 1877 (171), (271) and (418) XI; 1878 (338) XIV, Select Committee Reports on Intemperance; also 1878–9 (113) X.

63 See Parliamentary Papers: 1877 (418) XI, p. 365 and 1878–9 (113) X, p. LXI.

64 *Liverpool Daily (Evening) Albion*, 23 November 1877, p. 2.

65 *Era*, 11 April 1875, p. 3; 4 November 1877, p. 3.

66 *Liverpool Daily (Evening) Albion*, 23 November 1877, p. 2.

67 *ibid.*, 15 December 1877, p. 2.

68 *ibid.*, 12 December 1877, p. 2; for the other singing saloons and music halls see *ibid.*, 18 and 22 December 1877, p. 2.

69 *ibid.*, 8 December 1877, p. 2.

70 *Era*, 4 November 1877, p. 3.

71 *Liverpool Daily Courier*, 23 November 1877, p. 7.

72 *Liverpool Daily (Evening) Albion*, 23 November 1877, p. 4.
73 For Liverpool's administration see Fraser, *Urban Politics*, pp. 140–1 and for its 'free licensing policy' see Harrison, *Drink*, p. 251. That the chief magistrate was himself a pub owner is mentioned in Waller, *Democracy*, p. 98. On the connection between the elite and breweries see Cockcroft, 'Liverpool Police', p. 155.
74 For Leybourne and Vance see Hibbert, *Fifty Years*, p. 93; Disher, *Victorian Song*, pp. 161–2; Schneider, *Londoner Music Hall*, p. 160. For Geoghegan see *Era*, 21 February 1858, p. 12; 21 October 1860, p. 12; 28 October 1868, p. 12; and 28 March 1885, p. 16.
75 The songs quoted here are 'John Barleycorn Is A Hero Bold' (Song Collection of the British Museum Music Library, Vocal Music H 2481) and 'Roger Ruff And A Drop Of Good Beer' (*ibid.*, H 1771).
76 Harrison, *Drink*, p. 21.
77 On the difference between 'social' and 'narcotic' drinking see J. S. Roberts, 'Der Alkoholkonsum deutscher Arbeiter im 19. Jahrhundert', *Geschichte und Gesellschaft* 6 (1980), pp. 222–3.
78 *Liverpool Daily (Evening) Albion*, 18 December 1877, p. 2 and Parliamentary Papers 1866 (373) XVI, pp. 34, 38, 51 and 53.
79 *Bolton Evening News*, 19 February 1873, p. 3.
80 See esp. Bailey, *Leisure*, p. 166.
81 *Bolton Chronicle*, 1 February 1873, p. 3.
82 The same holds true for the controversies around the pubs where outside pressure did not lead to a change in drinking habits. The reasons lie rather in the development of the railways which weakened the function of pubs as communication centres, improved living conditions which made pubs superfluous as places of refuge, and greater leisure opportunities as acceptable alternatives to pubs. See Harrison, *Drink*, pp. 319–39.

6. 1875–1888: PROGRAMMES AND PURIFIERS

1 *Dublin University Magazine*, August 1874, p. 233.
2 *Sheffield Daily Telegraph*, 5 February 1876, p. 6.
3 *North British Daily Mail*, 22 February 1875, p. 4. See also *ibid.*, 13 March 1875, p. 5 and 24 February 1875, p. 4; see the petition entitled 'To the Honourable Lord Provost and Magistrates of the City of Glasgow. The Memorial of the several Persons whose Names are hereunto subscribed, Citizens of Glasgow', 24 February 1875, Strathclyde Regional Archives; the 'Report of Visits to Music Halls on 27 February 1875' by Police Superintendent Brown, Strathclyde Regional Archives and *Era*, 14 February 1875, p. 7.
4 *North British Daily Mail*, 26 February 1875, p. 4.
5 'Memorial', 24 February 1875; *Era*, 7 March 1875, p. 4; *League Journal*, 6 March 1875, p. 1; *North British Daily Mail*, 2 March 1875, p. 5.
6 None of the names appear in the list of members of the magistrates and council.
7 See note 3.
8 *North British Daily Mail*, 27 February 1875, p. 2.
9 Orchard, chs 6 and 7; G. Anderson, *Victorian Clerks* (Manchester, 1976), p. 34 and same, 'The Social Economy of Late Victorian Clerks', in Crossick, *Lower Middle Class*, p. 121.
10 Bailey, *Leisure*, p. 161.
11 *North British Daily Mail*, 2 March 1875, p. 4.
12 *ibid.*, p. 5.
13 *North British Daily Mail*, 24 April 1875, p. 5 and *League Journal*, 1 May 1875, p. 138. Checkland, writing of Glasgow's elite between 1870 and 1914, claims they were abstinent and puritanical, that they censored art exhibitions and practised heavy social discipline. See S. G. Checkland, *The Upas Tree. Glasgow 1875–1975* (Glasgow, 1976), p. 29. The events and decisions of 1875 do not support this.

14 *Era*, 14 February 1875, p. 7.
15 See police report 9 March 1875, Strathclyde Regional Archives.
16 Illustrated in a letter from Brown's manager to the Glasgow Chief of Police, Strathclyde Regional Archives.
17 *Glasgow Herald*, 8 March 1875, p. 4.
18 *Dublin University Magazine*, August 1874, p. 240.
19 *North British Daily Mail*, 5 March 1875, p. 4.
20 *ibid.*
21 *Glasgow Weekly Mail*, 13 March 1875, p. 5.
22 *North British Daily Mail*, 8 March 1875, p. 4.
23 *Glasgow Weekly Mail*, 27 February 1875, p. 4.
24 *Glasgow Weekly Herald*, 27 February 1875, p. 4. For Glasgow popular culture see also E. King, 'Popular Culture in Glasgow', in R. A. Cage (ed.), *The Working Class in Glasgow 1750–1914* (London, 1987), pp. 142–87.
25 See *Bolton Chronicle*, 29 January 1876, p. 5; *Era*, 3 February 1876, p. 9; Hanham, *Elections*, p. 312.
26 For information on licensing laws in the regions see Geary, *Law*, even if incomplete, e.g. Bradford and Manchester are missing.
27 W. Cudworth, *Historical Notes on the Bradford Corporation* (Bradford, 1881), pp. 218–19.
28 *Bradford Daily Telegraph*, 14 January 1882, p. 3.
29 *Bradford Observer*, 23 January 1882, p. 7.
30 *ibid.*, 2 February 1882, p. 7.
31 *Yorkshire Busy Bee*, 11 March 1882, p. 149 and *Bradford Observer*, 23 January 1882, p. 7.
32 *Bradford Observer*, 2 February 1882, p. 7; 19 January 1882, p. 7; 23 January 1882, p. 7; 26 January 1882, p. 6.
33 *Bradford Observer*, 23 January 1882, p. 7.
34 *ibid.*
35 *Yorkshire Busy Bee*, 11 March 1882, p. 149.
36 *Bradford Observer*, 19 January 1882, p. 7.
37 *Sheffield and Rotherham Independent*, 18 October 1883, p. 5; also *ibid.*, 6 September 1883, p. 2 and 14 September 1883, p. 3.
38 *Sheffield and Rotherham Independent*, 6 September 1883, p. 2.
39 Reid, 'Temperance', p. 249.
40 For the composition of the bench see Furness, *Record*. Counter to the general trend the number of pubs in Sheffield in relationship to the population even increased in the 1880s. (See Chief Constable Returns for 1886, 1887 and 1889 in *Sheffield Annual Record* 1886, p. 52; 1887, p. 110; and 1889, pp. 242–3.)
41 *Sheffield and Rotherham Independent*, 21 September 1883, p. 3.
42 *ibid.*, 14 September 1883, p. 3 and 21 September 1883, p. 3.
43 *ibid.*, 22 September 1883, p. 2.
44 *ibid*, 21 September 1883, p. 3.
45 *ibid.*
46 *ibid.*
47 *ibid.*, 22 September 1883, p. 2.
48 For this discussion see *ibid.*, and 21 September 1883, p. 3.
49 *ibid*, 21 September 1883, p. 3.
50 *ibid*, 29 November 1883, p. 2.
51 Pollard, *History*, p. 132 and Smith, *Conflict*, p. 245.
52 Smith, *Conflict*, pp. 67 and 259.
53 Reid, 'Middle Class Values', p. 276; Smith, *Conflict*, pp. 163 and 260.
54 *Sheffield Annual Record*, 1886 and Pollard, *History*, p. 120.
55 Shiman, *Crusade*, p. 204.
56 A. Briggs, 'The Victorian City', *Victorian Studies* 11 (1967–8), pp. 711–30, here p. 149; D. G.

Wright, 'Mid-Victorian Bradford: 1850–80', *The Bradford Antiquary*, New Series Part XLVII (1982), pp. 65–86, here p. 65.

57 Wright, 'Mid-Victorian Bradford'; A. Elliott, 'The Incorporation of Bradford', *Northern History* 15 (1979), pp. 156–75; Fraser, *Power*, pp. 130–8; D. G. Wright and J. Jowitt (eds.), *Victorian Bradford* (Bradford, 1981).

58 T. Jowitt, 'A Review of Recent Writing on the History of the Town', in Wright and Jowitt, *Bradford*, pp. 245–56.

59 E. Hunt, *British Labour History 1815–1914* (London, 1981), p. 271; see also Hanham, *Elections*, p. XV.

60 G. Cole, *A Short History of the British Working-Class Movement 1789–1947* (London, 1948), pp. 224–33. Also J. Hinton, *Labour and Socialism* (Brighton, 1983), pp. 26 and 35 and Hunt, *British Labour History*, pp. 272–4.

61 Gladstone's government fell in 1886 over the Home Rule question in Ireland. The Liberal Party was also split on this issue and the so-called Liberal Unionists went over into the Conservative camp. The latter ruled from 1886 until 1906, with a short break from 1892 to 1895. See Clark, *Making*, pp. 234–5.

62 Cole, pp. 233–6 and Yeo, 'A New Life: The Religion of Socialism in Britain 1883–1896', *History Workshop* 4 (1977), pp. 5–56. Here pp. 7–8.

63 S. and B. Webb: *The History of Trade Unionism 1660–1920* (London, 1920), pp. 380–9; Cole, pp. 239–41; Hunt, p. 295 and K. Brown, *The English Labour Movement 1700–1951* (Dublin 1982), pp. 173–4. For the 'New Unions' see also the essays in E. Hobsbawm, *Labouring Men* (1964; repr. London, 1976). For a comparison between the English and German trades union movement see W. Mommsen and H. Husung (eds.), *The Development of Trade Unionism in Great Britain and Germany 1880–1914* (London, 1985).

64 Cole, pp. 247f. The influence of the socialist movement(s) on the new unions is now seen as being less direct. See Brown, *English Labour*, p. 175.

65 E. P. Thompson, 'Homage to Tom Maguire', in A. Briggs and J. Saville (eds.), *Essays in Labour History*, vol. I (London, 1960), pp. 276–316, here p. 286. For the founding of the ILP in Bradford see J. Reynolds and K. Laybourn, 'The Emergence of the Independent Labour Party in Bradford', *International Review of Social History* 20 (1975), pp. 313–46 and same: *Liberalism and the Rise of Labour* (London, 1984), p. 203. Above all they stress the role of the unions in the pre-history of the founding of the ILP. See also Cole, *Short*, pp. 250–1 and Brown, *English Labour*, pp. 179–80. For the relationship between the ILP to the unions and to local political structures see the detailed research by D. Howell, *British Workers and the Independent Labour Party 1888–1906* (Manchester, 1983).

66 Thompson, 'Homage', p. 281; J. Young, *Socialism and the English Working Class. A History of English Labour* (New York, 1989), pp. 29 and 220.

67 *Bradford Observer*, 24 January 1884, p. 6; 29 January 1885, p. 7; 27 January 1887, p. 7; 26 January 1888, p. 7.

68 See the adverts of the various music saloons in the Star music-hall programmes of September 1892 and 1894, Bradford Central Library and Archives.

69 *Bradford Observer*, 5 February 1891, p. 7; Russell, *Popular Music*, p. 58.

70 *Sheffield Weekly Telegraph*, 16 August 1884, p. 8; 27 September 1884, p. 8. *Manchester Courier and Lancashire General Advertiser*, 14 November 1883, p. 3 and *Manchester Weekly Times*, 15 October 1887, p. 7; Statistical Returns of the Manchester Police, Manchester 1892, Nr. 18 and 19.

71 Harrison, *Drink*, p. 297.

72 E. H. Hall, *Coffee Taverns, Cocoa Houses, Coffee Palaces* (London, 1897), pp. 34 and 38–9.

73 Schneider, *Londoner Music Hall*, pp. 63–4.

74 Bailey, *Leisure*, pp. 106–18; R. Price, 'The Working Men's Club Movement and Victorian Social Reform Ideology', in *Victorian Studies* 15 (1971–2), pp. 117–47; Hall, *Coffee Taverns*, pp. 42–3, 52 and 57.

75 Harrison, *Drink*, p. 304.

76 *Era*, 20 July 1879, p. 4.
77 Schneider, *Londoner Music Hall*, p. 65.
78 *Era*, 12 December 1880, p. 4 and Bailey, *Leisure*, p. 163.
79 Quoted in Bailey, *Leisure*, p. 163.
80 *Punch*, 13 September 1879, p. 110.
81 *ibid.*, 2 November 1895, p. 210.

7. THE SPECIAL CASE OF LONDON, 1840–1888

1 Briggs, *Victorian Cities*, pp. 312 and 318; Waller, *Town*, p. 24; P. Thompson, *Socialists, Liberals and Labour* (London, 1967), pp. 14–15; G. Stedman Jones, *Outcast London* (Oxford, 1971), p. 193; G. Crossick, 'The Labour Aristocracy and Its Values', *Victorian Studies* 19 (1975–6), pp. 301–28.
2 Harrison, *Drink*, pp. 59 and 347. Also D. Fahey, 'Brewers, Publicans, and Working-Class Drinkers: Pressure Group Politics in Late Victorian and Edwardian England', *Histoire Sociale – Social History* 13 (1980), pp. 85–103.
3 Waller, *Town*, p. 26; Stedman Jones, *Outcast*, p. 22; S. Alexander, 'Women's Work in Nineteenth-Century London. A Study of the Years 1820–1850', in J. Mitchell and A. Oakley (eds.), *The Rights and Wrongs of Women* (1976; repr. London, 1983), pp. 59–111.
4 It is impossible to give exact figures because of the difficulty of defining prostitution and because for many women it was only a temporary activity or undertaken as a means of earning a little more money. See H. Mayhew, *London Labour and the London Poor* (1862; repr. London, 1967), vol. IV. The section on London prostitutes was written by Bracebridge Hemyng. See also J. Walkowitz, *Prostitution and Victorian Society* (Cambridge, 1980), esp. part 1, pp. 14–18; E. Bristow, *Vice and Vigilance* (Dublin, 1977), p. 56. Details on prostitutes' backgrounds are generally based on Mayhew (Hemyng) who was able to establish the background of arrested prostitutes from police files. They included: 646 milliners, 418 laundresses, 400 domestic servants, 249 workers in the shoe industry, 215 tailors as well as several small groups of thirty to seventy persons also from the clothing industry. See Mayhew, *London Labour*, pp. 263 and 255–7.
5 Walkowitz, *Prostitution*, part I, esp. pp. 21–3; Mayhew, pp. 218–19 and 223; J. Greenwood, *The Seven Curses of London* (London, 1869), pp. 314–23; *Punch*, 28 August 1862, pp. 79–80.
6 Mayhew, *London Labour*, p. 211.
7 *The Times*, 10 October 1874, p. 11.
8 *ibid.*, 9 October 1858, p. 9.
9 *Era*, 15 October 1871, p. 12; *The Times*, 10 October 1874, p. 11 and 11 October 1878, p. 9.
10 *The Times*, 15 October 1881, p. 7; 14 October 1882, p. 10; 13 October 1883, p. 12.
11 *ibid.*, 1 November 1869, p. 5.
12 Storch, 'Policeman', p. 486; Petrow, pp. 295–6; Parliamentary Papers: 1866 (373) XVI, pp. 45–7 and 311; 1892 (240) XVIII, p. 266.
13 Halevy, 'Before 1835', p. 26 and H. Finer, 'The Police and Public Safety', in Laski *et al.*, pp. 271–98, here p. 278. For police history see also: C. Reith, *A Short History of the British Police* (Oxford, 1948); T. Critchley, *A History of Police in England and Wales* (London, 1967); D. Ascoli, *The Queen's Peace. The Origins and Development of the Metropolitan Police 1829–1979* (London, 1979). Also the critical studies by Storch; J. Field, 'Police, Power and Community in a Provincial English Town', in V. Bailey (ed.), *Policing and Punishment in Nineteenth Century Britain* (London, 1981), pp. 42–64; C. Steedman, *Policing the Victorian Community* (London, 1984); S. Petrow, *Policing Morals. The Metropolitan Police and the Home Office 1870–1914* (Oxford, 1994).
14 *Era*, 26 January 1879 and 27 April 1879, both p. 4; Middlesex Record, MR/LMD 7/13: Orders, Reports, Regulations, etc; Greater London Council Record Office. For internal differences between magistrates and the Home Office, and also magistrates and police see also Ascoli, *Queen's Peace*; Field, 'Police', p. 54.

15 *Era*, 15 October 1871, p. 12; 7 February 1891, p. 16; Parliamentary Papers 1866 (373) XVI, pp. 39, 47 and 311. *The Bat*, 31 March 1885, p. 6; Field, 'Police', p. 53; Ascoli, *Queen's Peace*, pp. 143–7.

16 *The Times*, 11 October 1878, p. 7; *Era*, 15 October 1871, p. 12.

17 *The Times*, 15 October 1881, p. 7.

18 *The Times*, 9 October 1858, p. 9 and 9 October 1874, p. 10; Greenwood, *Seven Curses*, pp. 275–7; Bristow, p. 168.

19 *Era*, 18 October 1868, p. 5; *The Times*, 9 October 1869, p. 9.

20 *The Times*, 15 October 1881, p. 7 and 14 October 1882, p. 10.

21 For Cremorne Gardens see Parliamentary Papers 1866 (373) XVI, p. 131 and R. Altick, *The Shows of London* (Cambridge MA, 1978), p. 322; 'Petitions to the Justices...', MR/LMD 11/9; *The Times*, 10 October 1857, p. 9; 13 October 1860, p. 9; 5 October 1877, p. 7; Howard, *London Theatres*. For Highbury Barn see *The Times*, 6 October 1854, p. 9; 12 October 1855, p. 9 and 15 October 1870, p. 11; also the corresponding entry in Howard.

22 *The Times*, 14 October 1850, p. 7 and *Era*, 2 March 1851, p. 12; MR/LMD 5/1 and 5/8: Record of Applications for Music and Dancing Licence granted or refused 1850–1857; also *The Times*, 9 October 1857, p. 10 (with slightly differing numbers).

23 *The Times*, 7 October 1865, p. 11.

24 *Era*, 18 October 1868, p. 5.

25 *The Times*, 14 October 1870, p. 12 and *Era*, 16 October 1870, p. 5.

26 Waller, *Town*, pp. 38–40; Nettel, *Seven Centuries*, pp. 131–3; Stuart and Park, *Variety*, pp. 14, 40–2; Scott, *Early Doors*, pp. 9–19; Cheshire, *Music Hall*, pp. 11–19; and Schneider, *Londoner Music Hall*, ch. 2, 2.

27 MR/LMD 11/1 'Petitions to the Justices...'; also *The Times*, 6 October 1860, p. 11 and 13 October 1860, p. 9.

28 See MR/LMD 11/5–8; Parliamentary Papers 1866 (373) XVI, pp. 19, 94–5 and 203–5; 'The Empire, Leicester Square 1887', MR/LMD 24/3.

29 *The Times*, 13 October 1887, p. 8.

30 See also Schneider, *Londoner Music Hall*, pp. 50–61.

31 § II of the Disorderly Houses Act 1751 (in force 1752).

32 *Era*, 3 March 1861, p. 10.

33 *ibid.*, 10 March 1861, p. 10.

34 Schneider, *Londoner Music Hall*, pp. 51–2; *Era*, 3 March 1861, p. 10; Parliamentary Papers 1866 (373) XVI, p. 100.

35 Parliamentary Papers 1866 (373) XVI, p. 308.

36 *ibid.*, pp. 100 and 165–6.

37 Bailey, *Leisure*, p. 149; Cunningham, 'Leisure', p. 170; Rutherford, 'Managers', pp. 93–117. For the pre-history of the parliamentary enquiry see Parliamentary Papers 1866 (373) XVI, pp. 99 and 308.

38 See HO 43/102, p. 271 and HO 43/106, p. 101.

39 See Parliamentary Papers 1866 (373) XVI, pp. 183–5, 210 and 97.

40 *ibid.*, p. III.

41 In spring 1867 there was another exchange of letters between the London Music Halls Protection Society and the Home Office but this too soon came to nothing. See HO 43/109, pp. 172, 274 and 327 and HO 43/110, p. 53.

42 *Era*, 4 November 1866, p. 15; 27 January 1867, p. 5; 11 December 1870, p. 12; *The Times*, 30 October 1871, p. 9; *Era*, 15 February 1880, p. 5; and *The Times*, 15 October 1880, p. 10.

43 See the theatre programmes in the John Johnson Collection in the Bodleian Library, Oxford and Schneider, *Londoner Music Hall*, pp. 57–60. For the poaching of music-hall artistes by the theatres see Mander and Mitchenson, *British Music Hall*, p. 26; Bailey, *Music Hall*, p. XI.

44 Rutherford, esp. pp. 96 and 116; Parliamentary Papers 1892 (240) XVIII, pp. 97, 197 and 298.

45 *Era*, 12 October 1889, p. 16.

46 Schneider, *Londoner Music Hall*, p. 54; Parliamentary Papers 1892 (240) XVIII, p. ii.

47 *ibid.*, p. 80; *Era*, 10 February 1883, p. 5 and MR/LMD 10, 'The Regulation of Music Halls. A Summary of the Attempts made by the Music Hall Proprietors to obtain an Improvement of the Law regulating Places of Public Entertainment', p. 20. Home Office documents show that there was another bill in 1876 (the Public Entertainment Bill) after the Lords enquired into the question of licensing in 1875. See MR/LMD 10, pp. 6f and J. Hollingshead, *Theatrical Licences* (London, 1875), p. 3. This bill was so short-lived that most studies do not even bother to mention it.

48 See Parliamentary Papers 1892 (240) XVIII, pp. 99–100, 198 and 297 (for the music-hall proprietors) and p. 52 (for the theatre owners).

49 See *ibid.*, p. VI.

50 Cheshire, *Music Hall*, p. 93; Mander and Mitchenson, *British Music Hall*, p. 18; Schneider, *Londoner Music Hall*, p. 56.

51 *Era*, 12 October 1889, p. 16.

52 The official title is 25 Geo II, c.36: 'An Act for better preventing Thefts and Robberies, and for Regulating Places of Entertainment, and punishing Persons keeping Disorderly Houses.' It can be found quoted in its entirety in Parliamentary Papers 1866 (373) XVI, pp. 283–6. See also A. Strong, *Dramatic and Musical Law* (London, 1898), pp. 58–62 and S. Isaacs, *The Law Relating to Theatres, Music-Halls, and Other Public Entertainments* (London, 1927), pp. 34–9.

53 Disorderly Houses Act, § II. Thus there were counties (Middlesex, Kent and Surrey), in only a part of which the law was applicable and this situation continued unchanged for a long time. The law was only made applicable to the whole of Middlesex in 1894, and in the Home Counties in 1926 (see Isaacs, *Law*, p. 39).

54 Odgers, *Local Government;* Briggs, *Victorian Cities*, ch. 8; D. Owen, *The Government of Victorian London* (London, 1982); K. Young and P. Garside, *Metropolitan London* (London, 1982); J. Davies, 'The Problem of London Local Government Reform' (unpublished thesis, University of Oxford, 1983).

55 Parliamentary Papers 1866 (373) XVI, p. 23; see also *ibid.*, pp. 67–8.

56 London was nonetheless the first city to get a police force in 1829 following the Metropolitan Police Act introduced by Robert Peel. The law established a Metropolitan Police District centred on Charing Cross (but not including the City, which had its own police force and wanted to keep it) within a radius of seven (from 1839, fourteen) miles. This area was under the control of two magistrates acting as Commissioners, one of whom in 1829 was Richard Mayne. They were directly responsible to the Home Office (see Finer, pp. 272–3 and 277–8).

57 J. Adams, 'A Letter to the Justices of the Peace of the County of Middlesex on the Subject of Licences for Public Music and Dancing', London, 1850, p. 17.

58 *ibid.*, pp. 21 and 12.

59 See Parliamentary Papers 1866 (373) XVI, pp. 45 and 39.

60 *ibid.*, pp. 42–3.

61 *ibid.*, pp. 39–40.

62 The official titles of both acts are 41 & 42 Vict., c. 32 and 42 & 43 Vict., c.34.

63 H. Cunningham, 'Leisure', in J. Benson (ed.), *The Working Class in England* (London, 1985), pp. 133–64, here p. 139.

64 Summerfield, 'Effingham Arms', p. 216.

65 *ibid.*, pp. 212–14.

66 *Era*, 9 October 1842, p. 6.

67 *Era*, 21 October 1860, p. 9; *The Times*, 7 October and 12 October 1865, p. 11.

68 MR/LMD 7/6: Orders...; for the years before see MR/LMD 4/157–76: Police Returns 1849; MR/LMD 9/388–400: Police and Justices Returns 1856 and MR/LMD 17/1–8: Police Reports 1862.

69 Unless otherwise stated, these and the following figures are based on D. Howard. Details of the licensing practices of the magistrates 1850–7 can be found in MR/LMD 5/1–8, 'Record of Applications for Music and Dancing Licence granted or refused 1850–1857'.

70 *The Times*, 6 October 1854, p. 9 and 9 October 1857, p. 10.

71 For details of the number of renewal applications see *The Times*, 10 October 1862, p. 9; 9 October 1863, p. 9; 7 October 1864, p. 9.

72 *ibid.*, 8 October 1864, p. 11.

73 *ibid.*, 7 October 1864, p. 9; 8 October 1864, p. 11.

74 MR/LMD 17/1a: Metropolitan Police and MR/LMD 17/3 and 4: Police Reports 1862.

75 See the details in D. Howard and those in the *The Times*, 14 October 1870, p. 12 and *Era*, 16 October 1870, p. 5.

76 Details in D. Howard.

77 See MR/LMD 3/30: Metropolitan Board of Work Regulations 1879 and *Era*, 1 September 1878, p. 4; 22 August 1885, p. 15; 13 March 1886, p. 15.

78 *The Times*, 13 October 1882, p. 10.

79 MR/LMD 7/16: Regulations 1878 and *Era*, 13 April 1879, p. 4.

80 *The Times*, 8 October 1886, p. 3; 8 October 1887, p. 4 and MR/LMD 27/1–26, 'Letters from Metropolitan Board of Works to Clerk of the Peace, 1887 and 1888'.

81 D. Howard, *London Theatres*, Nrs. 48, 50, 111, 287, 392 and 673.

82 *Era*, 12 August 1882, p. 4 and 21 April 1888, p. 9; MR/LMD 22/1–21: Reports from Metropolitan Board of Works 1886; *Era*, 20 May 1882, p. 4; 13 February 1886, p. 10; 9 April 1887, p. 16.

83 *Era*, 27 May 1882, p. 13; 13 March 1886, p. 15; 20 March 1886, pp. 9 and 15; 12 February 1887, p. 9; 4 February 1888, p. 13; 21 April 1888, p. 9.

84 Cunningham, 'Leisure', p. 139.

85 Adams, *Letter*, p. 23; *Era*, 18 October 1868, p. 5.

86 *ibid.*, p. 23.

87 *Era*, 18 October 1868, p. 5.

88 Parliamentary Papers 1866 (373) XVI, pp. 16, 245 and 51.

89 For example *Era*, 15 October 1871, p. 9.

90 *ibid.*

91 See Parliamentary Papers 1866 (373) XVI, p. 102.

92 J. Hollingshead, *Plain English* (London, 1880), pp. 5–6.

93 See Parliamentary Papers 1866 (373) XVI, pp. 16, 231, 67–8., 71, 34, 38, 52–3.

8. CONTROVERSIES IN THE 1890s

1 For Charrington see G. Thorne (pseudonym for C. A. Gull), *The Great Acceptance. The Life Story of F. N. Charrington* (London, 1912), pp. 20–2.

2 *ibid.*, p. 224.

3 Bristow, *Vice*, p. 105.

4 Thorne, *Acceptance*, pp. 61–2; and *The Times*, 15 October 1881, p. 7.

5 Thorne, *Acceptance*, pp. 110–11.

6 *ibid.*, pp. 115–16 and 125.

7 For Lusby's provoked attacks on Charrington see *The Times*, 15 October 1881, p. 7; *Era*, 5 August 1882, p. 4; 12 August 1882, p. 4; 21 October 1882, p. 4.

8 Bailey, *Leisure*, p. 162.

9 *The Times*, 14 October 1882, p. 10. For the attitude of the police to Lusby's and Charrington see also *The Times*, 15 October 1881, p. 7; *Era*, 11 August 1883, p. 4; *The Times*, 13 October 1883, p. 12.

10 *Era*, 13 February 1882 and 21 October 1882, p. 4; *The Times*, 13 October 1883, p. 12.

11 *The Times*, 13 October 1883, p. 12; *Era*, 11 October 1884, p. 9; 30 May 1885, p. 10 and 25 June 1885, p. 10.

12 Walkowitz, *Prostitution*, p. 1.

13 *ibid.*, p. 2 ; Bristow, *Vice*, p. 77; P. McHugh, *Prostitution and Victorian Social Reform* (London, 1980), esp. ch. 5. A summary of the contemporary debates can be found in K. Nield (ed.),

Prostitution in the Victorian Age. Debates on the Issue from Nineteenth Century Critical Journals (Farnborough, 1973).

14 Walkowitz, *Prostitution*, p. 2. For J. Butler see also McHugh, *Prostitution*, p. 29.

15 Bristow, *Vice*, pp. 77, 126, 133 and 155; Walkowitz, *Prostitution*, p. 252.

16 Bristow, *Vice*, p. 210; McHugh, *Prostitution*, pp. 28f; Bailey, *Leisure*, p. 162. According to Bailey the Methodist Times was the principal supporter of Charrington's battle against Lusby's.

17 *Manchester Courier*, 18 February 1891, p. 8; *Manchester Weekly Times*, 21 September 1889, p. 5 and 5 October 1889, p. 8; *Era*, 12 March 1892, p. 17; and Waters, 'Manchester'. Details on persons and organisations can be found in Winskill, vols. II-IV.

18 *Manchester Weekly Times*, 21 September 1889, p. 5.

19 *Era*, 24 July 1859, p. 12; 9 September 1866, p. 14; 11 November 1866, p. 13.

20 *Liverpool Courier*, 31 October 1891, p. 3.

21 (Liverpool) *Evening Express*, 14 November 1892, p. 3. For reformers see B. G. Orchard, *Liverpool's Legion of Honour* (Birkenhead, 1893), pp. 136, 344 and 468–9.

22 *Era*, 29 July 1893, p. 10.

23 Official title: 51 & 52 Vict. c.41.

24 E. Griffith, *The Modern Development of City Government in the United Kingdom and the United States* (1926; repr. New York, 1969), p. 198.

25 Isaacs, *Law*, pp. 35–42 and 363–4; Redlich and Hirst, *History*, p. 203.

26 Hanham, pp. 284–5; Waller, *Democracy*, pp. 12–13.

27 Waller, *Democracy*, pp. 23–4. For the Liverpool licensing laws see White, *History*, p. 108 and Waller, *Democracy*, p. 112. For contemporary discussions see the 'Domestic Entry Books' of the Home Office, HO 43/98, pp. 190 and 331 and HO 43/104, p. 231; also *Era*, 22 July 1866, p. 7 and 12 August 1866, p. 7. The liberal licensing law was supposed to be changed in 1867. Teetotallers and Sabbatarians were the main groups behind the change. See *Era*, 13 January 1867, p. 7; and 7 April 1867, p. 7.

28 Waller, *Democracy*, pp. 106–7.

29 *Era*, 19 August 1866 and 2 September 1866, p. 7. For the events of 1875 see White, *History*, pp. 105 and 108; Cockroft, 'Liverpool', p. 156; Waller, *Democracy*, p. 23.

30 For the problems of the police with the temperance movement see the memoires of Liverpool Head of Police, W. Nott-Bower, *Fifty-two Years a Policeman* (London, 1926), esp. ch. 10, pp. 134 and 140.

31 H. Carter, *The English Temperance Movement*, vol. I (London, 1933), p. 186.

32 A. Dingle, *The Campaign for Prohibition in Victorian England. The United Kingdom Alliance* (London, 1980), p. 10.

33 See Waller, *Democracy*, p. 97. For the Liverpool Temperance Movement around 1890 see also *Liverpool Review*, 2 April 1892, p. 14.

34 Bristow, *Vice*, p. 162; White, *History*, p. 101; Waller, *Democracy*, p. 114.

35 *Liverpool Daily Post*, 28 October 1892, p. 3 and for all entertainment licences, 'Register of Licences for Public Dancing, Singing, and Music, and of Theatrical and Cinematographic Licences', 347 Jus 1/5/1 (January 1890 to October 1892) and Jus 1/5/2 (October 1892 to October 1904), Liverpool Archives. The attitude of the Liverpool magistrates to music halls is not so easy to establish as that of the members of the LCC licensing committee. The newspapers quote very few personal opinions and B. G. Orchard's *Liverpool's Legion of Honour*, which deals with the social origins, careers and political leanings of Liverpool VIPs contains practically no information on this particular subject. The only information which can be culled from the news-paper lists of those magistrates who were present at the various sittings shows that the group of magistrates who were nominated after 1889 showed an overproportionally large interest in the issuing of licences. They comprised only 19 per cent of JPs as a whole, but 33 to 46 per cent of the magistrates present at the 1891–2 sessions. Their presence coincides with increasing prob-lems for some music halls in the city, especially after 1892 (see esp. *Liverpool Mercury*, 31 March 1892, p. 5; *Era*, 9 April 1892, p. 17).

36 *Reynold's Newspaper*, 13 January 1889, quoted in Waller, *Town*, p. 59. For the history of the

LCC see W. Saunders, *History of the First London County Council 1889–1890–1891* (London, 1892), p. xlix; G. Gibbon and R. Bell, *History of the London County Council* (London, 1939), pp. 86–7; Thompson, *Socialists*, p. 144–7; I. Britain, *Fabianism and Culture* (Cambridge, 1982), pp. 228–9 and 235–40.

37 Gibbon and Bell, *History*, p. 94; Pennybacker, 'It Was Not', pp. 119–20.

38 Gibbon and Bell, *History*, p. 94.

39 Bristow, *Vice*, pp. 209–11. For Charrington's work on the LCC see Thorne, *Acceptance*, pp. 135–46. For the composition of the LCC licensing committee see Schneider, *Londoner Music Hall*, p. 68 and Pennybacker, 'It Was Not', pp. 122–3.

40 Bristow, *Vice*, p. 211.

41 E. S. Turner, *Roads to Ruin. The Shocking History of Social Reform* (London, 1950), pp. 215–17. A collection of newspaper cuttings which documents the vast amount of public discussion around the Empire can be found in the appendix to a work by Mrs Ormiston Chant, the main opponent of the Empire. It contains articles from the following newspapers and magazines: *England, Standard, Westminster Gazette, Echo, Morning Post, Sportsman, Morning Leader, Daily Telegraph, Music Hall, Today, Pall Mall Gazette, Word And Work, Morning, Reynold's Weekly, Methodist Times, Sportsman, Western Daily Press, Sporting Life*. See L. O. Chant: *Why We Attacked the Empire* (London, 1895). The following publications were also involved in the debate: *Ally Sloper, Punch, Daily Chronicle, Liverpool Post* and *The Times* (see Turner, pp. 222–6) as well as the *Saturday Review, Era, Theatre* and *Church Reformer*.

42 Booth, *London Town*, p. 142.

43 Turner, *Roads*, pp. 214–15 and 222; Bristow, *Vice*, pp. 210–11.

44 I. Bevan, *Royal Performance* (London, 1954), pp. 212–13. Of modern music-hall historians Ulrich Schneider mentions Mrs Ormiston Chant only in the context of the Social Purity movement. Peter Bailey and Chris Waters see her merely as a precursor of Mrs Mary Whitehouse, the English campaigner for cleaning up television. Schneider, *Londoner Music Hall*, pp. 70–71; Bailey, *Music Hall*, p. XII; and Waters, 'Manchester', p. 157.

45 Chant, *Why*, p. 7. For her attitudes to music halls see *Era*, 30 October 1897, p. 19 and Bristow, *Vice*, p. 201.

46 Turner, *Roads*, p. 226; *Era*, 20 October 1894, pp. 17–18 and 27 October 1894, p. 17; Pennybacker, 'It Was Not', pp. 132–3.

47 For Burns see Cole, *Short*, p. 251; K. Brown, *John Burns* (London, 1977), esp. pp. 57–61; Petrow, *Policing*, p. 137. For the delicate relationship between working-class movements and working-class leisure see C. Waters, *British Socialists and the Politics of Popular Culture, 1884–1914* (Manchester, 1990).

48 Burns's address to the LCC is printed in Chant, 'It Was Not', pp. 21–2.

49 *Era*, 10 November 1894, p. 17 and Turner, *Roads*, pp. 226–7.

50 Turner, *Roads*, pp. 228–9; Summerfield, 'Effingham Arms', p. 219.

51 *Era*, 18 July 1916, p. 4 and 24 July 1916, p. 8; *Contemporary Review* 110 (1916), pp. 611–20; B. Ross, 'The Empire, Leicester Square', *Call Boy* 3 (1979), p. 8.

52 See esp. Bailey, *Leisure*, p. 162.

53 Parliamentary Papers 1892 (240) XVIII, p. 87.

54 For Liverpool see 'Liverpool Corporation Act 1889' (52 & 53 Vict. C.lxxv) part IV; for Manchester see Waters, 'Manchester', p. 144. Also *Era*, 16 August 1890, p. 13 and Parliamentary Papers 1892 (240) XVIII, p. III.

55 Waters, 'Manchester', pp. 156–7.

56 For Manchester theatre licences see 'Stage Plays. Register of Licences 1889–1934', M 192/1, Manchester Central Reference Library.

57 *Liverpool Courier*, 2 October 1891, p. 7; *Liverpool Daily Post*, 28 October 1892, p. 3. For Manchester see 'Stage Plays'.

58 For the debates on texts see (for 1889) *Era*, 5 October 1889, pp. 13–14 and 12 October 1889, pp. 15–16 – and for succeeding years licensing reports of October. For the controversies around

the 'Anti-Gagging' clause of the LCC Theatres Bill 1890 see *Era*, 8 March 1890, p. 16; 15 March 1890, p. 14; and 22 March 1890, p. 13.

59 *Era*, 21 February 1891, p. 17.

60 *ibid.*, 15 March 1890, p. 14.

61 Saunders, *History,* p. 370.

62 Parliamentary Papers 1892 (240) XVIII, pp. 142–3, 122f, 128–9, 272; Summerfield, 'Effingham Arms'.

63 Parliamentary Papers 1892 (240) XVIII, pp. 89–94, 203, 448. The complete case is described on pp. 446–9.

64 A detailed description of the case can be found in Parliamentary Papers 1892 (240) XVIII, pp. 491–6, 471, 357–8, 92f; also Saunders, *History,* pp. 543–7, 550, 572 and 600.

65 Parliamentary Papers 1892 (240) XVIII, p. 93.

66 *ibid.*, pp. 491–3.

67 *ibid.*, p. 493. See also LCC/MIN/10, 772, 'Angel and Crown, 1889–1903'.

68 The verdict is printed in Parliamentary Papers 1892 (240) XVIII, pp. 494–6. See also *Era*, 26 December 1891, p. 7; Saunders, pp. 603–5.

69 *Era*, 31 October 1891, p. 17 and 26 December 1891, p. 7.

70 Saunders, *History,* p. 111.

71 Quoted in the *Era*, 18 March 1893, p. 12.

72 Saunders, *History,* p. XIII; Gibbon and Bell, *History,* p. 569.

73 Bristow, *Vice,* pp. 209–15.

74 Schneider, *Londoner Music Hall*, p. 71; Petrow, *Policing,* pp. 298–9.

75 Pennybacker, 'It Was Not', p. 120.

76 Schneider, *Londoner Music Hall*, p. 72; Pennybacker, 'It Was Not', pp. 136–7; Bailey, 'Custom', p. 204; Summerfield, 'Effingham Arms', p. 224.

77 As early as the 1870s Brown in Glasgow had introduced House Rules for his artistes and singers instructing them to refrain from all forms of obscenity 'either in song, saying, or gesture, when on stage'. He also retained the right of censorship. There is one copy of these house rules in the Strathclyde Regional Archives. House rules like this were common everywhere in the 1880s. Most of them were not introduced as a reaction to the introduction of licensing laws. Garcia in Manchester had house rules before Manchester began to license its halls.

78 Bailey, *Leisure*, pp. 165–8.

79 *ibid.*, p. 204.

80 *Era*, 1 March 1863, p. 10; 17 May 1863, p. 12; 28 August 1864, p. 9; and 30 March 1879, p. 4.

81 *ibid.*, 28 February 1875, p. 3.

82 *Era*, 26 October 1873, p. 4; also *Era*, 25 November 1877, p. 4; 13 April 1879, p. 4; and 17 October 1885, p. 10.

83 *Toby*, 29 November 1884, p. 135. See also F. Low, 'Society and Music Halls. The Decline of Innuendo', *Music Hall*, 16 February 1889, p. 6.

84 *Era*, 3 February 1876, p. 9 and 7 March 1875, p. 6.

85 *Era Almanack* 1919, p. 33; Mellor, *Northern Music Hall*, pp. 136 and 152.

86 Hibbert, p. 232.

87 Summerfield, 'Effingham Arms', p. 225.

88 Macqueen-Pope, *Indiscreet Guide*, p. 75.

89 And this is how the big stars of the time have been remembered. See Newton, pp. 97–8; Booth, *Days*, pp. 59–61; Macqueen-Pope, *Indiscreet Guide*, p. 39; Beaver, pp. 93–4. Schneider has drawn attention to the aesthetic implications of the atmosphere which are often ignored: 'Whereas some artists and intellectuals took most pleasure in erotic liberties ... others discovered dance as an art form ... the dancers became key figures in a new aesthetic' (*Londoner Music Hall*, p. 351). The hallmarks of such an aesthetic were naturalness and improvisation.

90 Macqueen-Pope, *Queen*, p. 38.

91 *ibid.*, pp. 44 and 131; Bailey, 'Custom', pp. 194–5; Vicinus, *Industrial Muse*, p. 264.

92 Macqueen-Pope, *Queen*, p. 38; Bailey, *Leisure*, p. 168.

93 Beaver, *Spice,* p. 95 and Lee, *Folksong,* p. 111.

94 Pennybacker, 'It Was Not', p. 136–7. The progressives only maintained power until 1907.

95 *Echo*, 28 October 1892, 'Newscuttings', 347 Jus 2, vol. II, p. 28.

96 *Era*, 17 September 1892, p. 17. See also the 1892 police report which summarises developments during the previous ten years, 'Criminal and Miscellaneous Statistical Returns of the Manchester Police', Manchester 1892. This was, however, not the case in all regional towns. Birmingham like London tried to reduce its pub music halls and Macclesfield closed its pub music halls in 1901. *Era*, 17 September 1892, p. 17 (for Birmingham) and a note 9 December 1901 in *Scrap Books*, vol. 42, pp. 40–1, Manchester City Library, Arts Library, 1892.

97 *Manchester Weekly Times*, 21 September 1889, p. 2; Waters, 'Manchester', p. 142 .

98 *Manchester Weekly Times*, 21 September 1889, p. 2.

99 Gallery prices are not taken into account since here neither seat-prices nor the size of boxes are clear. The prices of the different seating areas come from contemporary programmes in the Manchester Local History Library (Folly) and adverts in the *Liverpool Courier* (Star).

100 For the Palace see *Manchester Amusement*, March 1893 and Waters, 'Manchester', p. 153.

101 *Manchester Courier*, 17 March 1891, p. 6.

102 *ibid.* and 20 March 1891, p. 8; Waters, 'Manchester', p. 145.

103 Waters, 'Manchester', p. 156.

104 *Manchester Courier*, 25 March 1891, pp. 5–6 and *Era*, 28 March 1891, p. 15.

105 *Manchester Guardian*, 19 May 1891, p. 5; Waters, 'Manchester', p. 145 .

106 *Era*, 26 January 1851, p. 12; *Era*, 4 November 1877, p. 3; *Liverpool Daily Courier*, 23 November 1877, p. 7; *Era*, 1 December 1878, p. 4. See *Liverpool Weekly Albion*, 19 October 1878, p. 2 and *Era*, 1 December 1878, p. 4. Indications that the Colosseum and Grand – both in Liverpool's Paradise Street – are identical can be found in *Era*, 29 November 1884, p. 8.

107 (Liverpool) *Evening Express*, 14 and 21 November 1892, p. 3.

108 *ibid.*

109 (Liverpool) *Evening Express*, 27 October 1892, p. 3 and *Liverpool Daily Post*, 28 October 1892, p. 3. For the background to Matkin's election as magistrate see White, *History*, pp. 102–3 and Waller, *Democracy*, ch. 7.

110 (Liverpool) *Evening Express*, 28 October 1892, p. 4.

111 *ibid.*, 15 December 1892, p. 4.

112 *Era*, 29 July 1893, p. 10 and 20 October 1894, p. 9. Nor did successive persons have much luck with the Grand; see *Liverpool Courier*, 31 October 1894 and 28 November 1894.

CONCLUSION

1 Geary, 'Arbeiterkultur', p. 92.

2 Joyce, *Visions*, p. 15.

3 Ross McKibbin, *The Ideologies of Class. Social Relations in Britain 1880–1950* (Oxford, 1991), p. 301.

4 C. Eisenberg, 'The Comparative View in Labour History. Old and New Interpretations of the English and German Labour Movements before 1914', *International Review of Social History* 34 (1989), pp. 403–28, here pp. 425–8.

Bibliography

PRIMARY SOURCES

Archives

Bolton reference library

'Catalogue of the Extensive Exhibition to be Seen Daily in Mr Sharples Museum, Star Inn', Bolton 1845
Collection of local theatre playbills, *c.* 1815–70
'Depositions relating to the Star Inn Theatre, Music Hall, and Museum, Churchgate', Bolton 1860
'Star Museum', pamphlet *c.* 1859–60
Star Music Hall account book 1847–50
Uncatalogued poster collection
Poole, Robert, 'Leisure in Bolton. A Study Undertaken for the Bolton Research Award in 1980-81', undated MS

Bradford Central Library and Archives

Information sheet on Bermondsey Hotel
Music-hall programmes (Deed box 26, cases 3.2–3.4; 3.7f)
Pub survey by local Temperance Organisations 1875–6 (Deed box 16, case 39)
'A Publican'. To the magistrates of the Borough of Bradford on the proceedings at the late Brewster Sessions, Bradford 1858
Pullan's Music Hall programmes 1873
Prior, Michele, 'Bradford's Music Hall Days', undated MS
Scruton, William, 'Bradford Scenes, Characters, and Events: and other local Articles', 1900, Newspaper-cuttings collection

Glasgow, Strathclyde regional archives

Letter from an employer of Brown's Music Hall to the Glasgow Chief Constable on stage costumes, March 1875
'To the Honourable Lord Provost and Magistrates of the City of Glasgow. The Memorial of the several Persons whose Names are here unto subscribed, Citizens of Glasgow', Glasgow, 1875
Two police reports on the audience and programmes in the city's music halls, 1 March 1875 and 9 March 1875

Bibliography

Leeds district archives

Leeds records: Corporation /Justices (LC/J):
  Special Sessions 1864–76 (LC/J/6)
  Special and Licensing Sessions 1885–93 (LC/J/7)

Leeds local history library

Leeds copy minutes 1894–8
Leeds Council proceedings 1889–99
The Leeds Monthly Record of Current Events, January 1875 – November 1876
The Leeds Record of Current Events, vols. I (1875) – V (1879)
Leeds Temperance Society annual reports, 1850, 1854, 1868, 1870-2, 1875, 1878, 1880, 1882–93, 1895–6, 1898–1900
Newspaper-cuttings collection:
  Leeds Obituary Notices, vol. IV
  Leeds People, vol. II
  Leeds and Yorkshire Biography, vol. III
  Local Notes and Queries, Leeds and Yorkshire, 1893
  Scott, Leeds Past and Present, vol. II
  Sykes Collection, vol. I

Liverpool archives

Newscuttings relating to matters dealt with by the Magistrates (347 Jus 2)
Register of Alcohol Licences (347 Jus 1/1)
Register of licences for public dancing, singing, and music, and of theatrical and cine-matograph licences, 1890–1920 (347 Jus 1/5/1–3)

Liverpool local history library

Miscellaneous theatre programmes, 1877–1912
Theatrical periodicals, 1862–77

London, British Museum

Song Collections:
  Songs (G 426 qq (9) and H 1650 pp (1))
  Vocal music (H 1771f; H 1775; H 1778; H 1783; H 1788; H 2481)

London, Greater London Council record office

London County Council: Theatres and music hall committee, presented papers (LCC/MIN/10,772; 10,774; 10,782; 10,790; 10,824; 10,828; 10,832; 10,853; 10,868; 10,871; 10,876; 10,885)
Middlesex records:
  Miscellaneous applications for licences, etc., 1841–95 (MR/LMD 3/1–68)
  Applications for new and renewed licences 1849 (MR/LMD 4/1–176)
  Record of applications for music and dancing licences granted or refused 1850–7 (MR/LMD 5/1–8)

Orders, reports, regulations, etc., printed applications for licence (MR/LMD 7/1–48);
Applications for new and renewed licences 1856 (MR/LMD 9/1–400)
'The Regulation of Music Halls. A Summary of the Attempts Made by the Music Hall
Proprietors to Obtain an Improvement of the Law Regulating Places of Public
Entertainment 1883. With some Opinions of the Press' (MR/LMD 10)
Petitions to the Justices against the granting of music and dancing licences 1860
(MR/LMD 11/1–25)
Police reports 1862–73 (MR/LMD 17/1–15)
Report from Metropolitan Board of Works 1886 (MR/LMD 22/1–21)
'The State of the London Theatres and Music Halls', 1887 (MR/LMD 23)
The Empire, Leicester Square 1887 (MR/LMD 24/1–7)
Justices' and police reports 1863, 1866, 1867 (MR/LMD 25/1–51)
Letters from Metropolitan Board of Works to Clerk of the Peace, 1887 and 1888
(MR/LMD 27/1–26)
Justices' reports 1888 (MR/LMD 29/1–16)

London, Public Record Office

Home Office papers:
Domestic entry books (HO 43/94–111)
Home Office out-letters (HO 43/155–160)

Manchester archives department

Records of the Palace Theatre, Manchester, deposited 23 January 1980: minutes of direc-
tors' meeting, 1889–93
'A Reminiscence of Music Hall and Variety Entertainments, 1864–5–6', 1908
Stage plays. Register of licences 1889–1934 (M 192/1)

Manchester local history library

Criminal and miscellaneous statistical Returns of the Manchester Police for the year
ended the 29 September 1891, Manchester 1892
Proceedings of the Council 1867–8, 1870, 1882–3, 1888–98
Theatre collection: music hall programmes
Newspaper-cuttings collection:
Scrap-books 1866–1907
Sutton, C. W., 'Newspaper Cuttings, etc., relating to the Manchester Stage', 2 vols.
Tagg, Brian, 'Notes and Extracts, etc. relating to Harry Liston'

Oxford, Bodleian library

John Johnson Collection

Rochdale, local studies library

Circus of Varieties Bookings 1884–97 (DBC RCV/1)
Circus of Varieties, Rochdale. Correspondence 1897–1903 (DBC RCV/2)

Sheffield archives

Bland Collection (B.C.15)
Canterbury Music Hall Programme, 1864
Newspaper-cuttings collection:
Newspaper cuttings relating to Sheffield and District, vols. II, IX, XII, XXIX, IL
Tatton, H., 'Sheffield 1929–1932', vol II undated MS

Parliamentary papers

PP 1831–32 (679) VII, Select Committee Report on the Laws affecting Dramatic
    Literature
PP 1835 (116) XXIII-XVI, Royal Commission Reports on Municipal Corporations in
    England and Wales
PP 1849–50 (398) XVIII, Select Committee Report on the Acts for the Sale of Beer
PP 1852–53 (855) XXXVII, Select Committee Report on Public Houses, Hotels, Beer-
    Shops, Dancing Saloons, Coffee-Houses, Theatres, Temperance Hotels, and Places
    of Public Entertainment
PP 1854 (367) XIV, Select Committee Report on Public Houses
PP 1866 (373) XVI, Select Committee Report on Theatrical Licenses and Regulations
PP 1866 (373–1) XVI, Index to the Select Committee Report on Theatrical Licenses and
    Regulations
PP 1867–68 (402) XIV, Select Committee Special Report on the Sale of Liquors on
    Sunday Bill
PP 1867–68 (402–1) XIV, Index to the Select Committee Report on the Sale of Liquors
    on Sunday Bill
PP 1876 (321) XI, Select Committee Report on the Metropolitan Fire Brigade
PP 1877 (342) XIV, Select Committee Report on the Metropolitan Fire Brigade
PP 1877 (171) XI, Select Committee First Report on Intemperance
PP 1877 (271) XI, Select Committee Second Report on Intemperance
PP 1877 (418) XI, Select Committee Third Report on Intemperance
PP 1878–79 (113) X, Select Committee Report on Intemperance
PP 1888 (c.5560) LVI, Royal Commission Interim Report on the Metropolitan Board of
    Works
PP 1892 (240) XVIII, Select Committee Report on Theatres and Places of Entertainment

Newspapers and magazines

Only those which have been evaluated over a lengthy period are mentioned here.
Bolton Chronicle, Bolton, 1825–35; 1846–77
Bolton Free Press, Bolton, 1835–47
Bolton Weekly Journal, Bolton, 1883–6
Bradford Observer, Bradford, 1869–75; 1882–99 (mainly reports on the licensing ses-
    sions in January and February)
The Curtain, Liverpool, 1862–3
The Era, London, 1838–1900
The Era (Dramatic and Musical) Almanack, London, 1868–1919
Evening Express, Liverpool, October–November 1878; 1891–2
Footlights, Liverpool, 1864

Leeds Mercury, Leeds, 1866–7; 1876–80 (for the annual licensing sessions in January)
Liverpool Courier, Liverpool, 1891–4
The Liverpool Critic, Liverpool, 1877
Liverpool Daily (Evening) Albion, Liverpool, November 1877– November 1878
Liverpool Daily Post, Liverpool, 1890-3
The Liverpool Era, Liverpool, 1864
Liverpool Lantern, Liverpool, 1878
Liverpool Review, Liverpool, November 1883; 1888–93; 1896
Manchester Courier, Manchester, August 1868; 1882–3; 1891–3
The Manchester Programme of Entertainment and Pleasure, Manchester, 1897–9
The Musical and Dramatic World, Liverpool, 1881
The Play, Liverpool, 1867
Rochdale Times, Rochdale, 1885; 1887–90; 1895–6
Sheffield and Rotherham Independent, Sheffield, 1882–9
Sheffield Daily Telegraph, Sheffield, 1858; 1861; 1863; 1865; 1875–7
The Sheffield Era, Sheffield, 1879–81
Sheffield Weekly Telegraph, Sheffield, 1884–9 (August and September respectively for the reports on the annual licensing sessions)
The Star, Liverpool, 1865 and 1867
The Times, London, 1849–1900 (mainly for the annual licensing sessions in October and the annual reports of the fire-service in December and January)
Toby, 1883–5.
Weekly Times, Manchester, 1882–90, fourth Quarter
The Yorkshire Busy Bee, 1881–3
Yorkshire Owl, 1892–8
Yorkshire Post and Leeds Intelligencer, Leeds, 1866–7; 1870; 1876 and 1890

Memoirs and reminiscences

Anstey, F., *A Long Retrospect* (London, 1936)
Bedford, Paul, *Recollections and Wanderings of Paul Bedford. Facts, not Fancies* (London, 1864)
Booth, John Bennion, *The Days We Knew* (London, 1943)
  Life, Laughter and Brass Hats (Gateshead on Tyne, 1939)
  London Town (London, 1929)
  ed., *The Old Music Hall: Fifty Years Memories and Contrasts. A Composite Picture of the Period 1882–1932. By twenty-seven Contributors to The Times* (London, 1932)
  Old Pink 'Un Days (London, 1925)
  'Master' and Men. Pink 'Un Yesterdays (London, 1927)
  Palmy Days (London, 1957)
  Pink Parade (London, 1933)
  A Pink 'Un Remembers (London, 1937)
Coward, Henry, *Reminiscences of Henry Coward* (London, 1919)
Croxten, Arthur, *Crowded Nights – and Days. An Unconventional Pageant* (London, 1934)
Desmond, Shaw, *The Edwardian Story* (London, 1949)
Doran, F. P., *Diary (Notes on various aspects of Manchester)* (Manchester[?], 1960)
Dunville, Ted E., *The Autobiography of an Excentric Comedian* (London, 1912)

Ellis, James, *Life of an Athlete* (n.p., n.d.)

Finck, Herman, *My Melodious Memories* (London, 1937)

Fish, William Frederick, *The Autobiography of a Counter Jumper* (London, 1929)

Freer, Walter, *My Life and Memories* (Glasgow, 1929)

Frost, Thomas, *Reminiscences of a Country Journalist* (London, 1886)

Greenhalgh, Robert, '60 Years' Local Records and Reminiscences by a Bolton Journalist', Bolton MS 1908

Harris, Harry, *Under Oars. Reminiscences of a Thames Lighterman 1894–1909* (London, 1978)

Hayes, Louis M., *Reminiscences of Manchester And Some of Its Local Surroundings From the Year 1840* (London and Manchester, 1905)

Heaton, William, *The Old Soldier; The Wandering Lover; and Other Poems; Together with a Sketch of the Author's Life* (London, 1857)

Hibbert, H. G., *Fifty Years of a Londoner's Life* (London, 1916)

Hird, Horace, *Bradford Remembrances* (Bradford, 1972)

Hollingshead, John, *My Lifetime*, 2 vols. (London, 1895)

Keating, Joseph, *My Struggle for Life* (London, 1916)

Lauder, Sir Harry, *Roamin' in the Gloamin'* (London, 1928)

Macqueen-Pope, W., *Carriages at Eleven. The Story of the Edwardian Theatre* (London, 1947)

 Ghosts and Greasepaint. A Story of the Days that Were (London, 1951)

Mathews, Charles, *Memoirs of Charles Mathews, Comedian, by Mrs. Mathews* (London, 1838–9)

Newton, H. Chance, *Idols of the 'Halls'. Being my Music-Hall Memories* (London, 1928)

Nott-Bower, William, *Fifty-two Years a Policeman* (London, 1926)

Parry, Edward Abbott, *What the Judge saw. Being twenty-five years in Manchester. By One Who Has Done It* (London, 1912)

 1901–1939 (Wakefield, 1978)

Rendle, T. McDonald, *Swings and Roundabouts. A Yokel in London* (London, 1919)

Reynolds, Harry, *Minstrel Memories. The Story of Burnt Cork Minstrelsy in Great Britain from 1836 to 1927* (London, 1928)

Sanger, 'Lord' George, *Seventy Years a Showman* (London, 1927)

Slugg, J. T., *Reminiscences of Manchester. Fifty Years Ago* (Manchester, 1881)

Taylor, John, *Autobiography of a Lancashire Lawyer. Being the Life and Recollection of John Taylor, Attorney-at-Law, and First Coroner of the Borough of Bolton* (Bolton, 1883)

Teasdale, Harvey, *The Life and Adventures of Harvey Teasdale* (Sheffield, 1881).

SECONDARY SOURCES

Abrams, Lynn C., 'Aspects of popular culture, leisure and recreation in Imperial Germany with particular reference to Bochum and Düsseldorf', PhD thesis (University of East Anglia, Norwich, 1988 [Microfilm])

Adams, John, *A Letter to the Justices of the Peace of the County of Middlesex on the Subject of Licences for Public Music and Dancing* (London, 1850)

Alexander, Sally, 'Women's Work in Nineteenth-Century London. A Study of the Years 1820–1850', in Juliet Mitchell and Ann Oakley, eds., *The Rights and Wrongs of Women* (Harmondsworth, 1976; repr. London, 1983)

Altick, R. D., *The Shows of London* (Cambridge MA, 1978)

Anderson, Gregory, 'Angestellte in England 1850–1914', in Kocka, ed., *Angestellte*
  'The Social Economy of the Late-Victorian Clerks', in Crossick, ed., *The Lower Middle Class*
  Victorian Clerks (Manchester, 1976)
Anderson, Perry, 'Origins of the Present Crisis', *New Left Review* 23 (1964)
Anstey, F., 'London Music Halls', *Harper's Monthly Magazine* (1891)
  Mr. Punch's Model Music-Hall Songs and Dramas (London, 1892)
Archer, William, 'The County Council and the Music Halls', *Contemporary Review* 67 (1895)
Ascoli, David, *The Queen's Peace. The Origins and Development of the Metropolitan Police 1829–1979* (London, 1979)
Ashplant, T. G., 'London Working Men's Clubs, 1875–1914', in Stephen and Eileen Yeo, eds., *Popular Culture*
Aspin, C., ed., *Angus Bethune Reach: Manchester and the Textile Districts in 1849* (Helmshore, 1972)
Bailey, Peter, 'A Community of Friends: Business and Good Fellowship in London Music Hall Management, *c.* 1860–1885', in same, ed., *Music Hall*
  'Champagne Charlie: Performance and Ideology in the Music-Hall Swell Song', in Bratton, ed., *Music Hall*
  'Conspiracies of Meaning: Music Hall and the Knowingness of Popular Culture', *Past and Present* 144 (1994)
  'Custom, Capital and Culture in the Victorian Music Hall', in Robert Storch, ed., *Popular Culture Leisure and Class in Victorian England.*
  Rational Recreation and the Contest for Control, 1830–1885 (London, 1978)
  'Leisure, Culture and the Historian: Reviewing the First Generation of Leisure Historiography in Britain', *Leisure Studies* 8 (1989)
  'A Mingled Mass of Perfectly Legitimate Pleasures: The Victorian Middle Class and the Problem of Leisure', *Victorian Studies* 21 (1977–8)
  ed., *Music Hall. The Business of Pleasure* (Milton Keynes, 1986)
  'Will the Real Bill Banks Please Stand Up? Towards a Role Analysis of Mid-Victorian Working-Class Respectability', *Journal of Social History* 12 (1978–9)
Bailey, Victor, 'The Metropolitan Police, the Home Office and the Threat of Outcast London', in same, ed., *Policing*
Barber, Brian J., 'Aspects of Municipal Government, 1835–1914', in Fraser, ed., *Modern Leeds*
  'Municipal Government in Leeds 1835–1914', in Fraser, ed., *Municipal Reform*
Barker, Clive, 'The Audiences of the Britannia Theatre, Hoxton', *Theatre Quarterly* 9 (1979)
Barker, Kathleen, *Early Music Hall in Bristol* (Bristol, 1979)
  'Harvey Teasdale, Clown of Theatre, Circus and Music Hall', *Nineteenth Century Theatre Research* 12 (1984)
  'Thirty Years of Struggle. Entertainment in Provincial Towns between 1840 and 1870', *Theatre Notebook* 39 (1985)
  'Thomas Youdan of Sheffield', *Theatrephile* 2 (1985)
Bausinger, Hermann, 'Verbürgerlichung – Folgen eines Interpretaments', in Wiegelmann, ed., *Kultureller Wandel*
Bausinger, Hermann, Utz Jeggle, Gottfried Korff and Martin Scharfe, *Grundzüge der Volkskunde* (Darmstadt, 1978)
Beaver, Patrick, *The Spice of Life. Pleasures of the Victorian Age* (London, 1979)

Bell, S. P., ed., *Victorian Lancashire* (Newton Abbot, 1974)

Bennett, Anthony, 'Sources of Popular Song in Early Nineteenth-Century Britain: Problems and Methods of Research', *Popular Music* 2 (1982)

Bennett, Tony, *Popular Culture: History and Theory* (Milton Keynes, 1981)

Bennett, Tony, Graham Martin, Colin Mercer and Janet Wollacot, *Culture, Ideology and Social Process* (Milton Keynes, 1981; repr. 1983)

Benson, John, ed., *The Working Class in England 1875–1914* (London, 1985)

Beresford, M. W. and G. R. J. Jones, eds., *Leeds and its Region* (Leeds, 1967)

Bertram, J., 'Some Old Time Sheffield Theatres and Music Halls', *Prest 1* 1 (1947)

Best, Geoffrey, *Mid-Victorian Britain 1851–1875* (London, 1971)

Black, Adam and Charles Black, *Black's Guide to Glasgow and its Environs* (London, 1900)

   Black's Guide to Manchester and Salford (Edinburgh, 1868)

Blakeley, J. W., ed., *Some Scarborough Faces (Past and Present): Being a Series of Interviews. Illustrated with Photographs* (Scarborough, 1901)

Booth, John Bennion, ed., *Seventy Years of Song* (London, 1943)

Booth, Michael, *Victorian Spectacular Theatre 1850–1910* (London, 1981)

Bradby, David, Louis James and Bernhard Sharrat, *Performance and Politics in Popular Drama* (Cambridge, 1980; repr. 1981)

Bradford: Past and Present, (Bradford[?], 1890)

Bratton, Jacqueline S., ed., *Music Hall. Performance and Style* (Milton Keynes, 1986)

   'Theatre of War: the Crimea on the London Stage 1854–5', in Bradby *et al.*, eds., *Performance*

   The Victorian Popular Ballad (London, 1975)

   Wilton's Music Hall (Cambridge, 1980)

Brear's Guide to Bradford and District (Bradford, 1873)

Bridges-Adams, William, *The British Theatre* (London, 1947)

Briggs, Asa, *Victorian Cities* (London, 1963)

   'The Victorian City. Quantity and Quality', *Victorian Studies* 11 (1967–8)

   Victorian Things (London, 1990)

Bristow, Edward J., *Vice and Vigilance. Purity Movements in Britain since 1700* (Dublin, 1977)

Britain, Ian, *Fabianism and Culture. A Study in British Socialism and the Arts, c. 1884–1918* (Cambridge, 1982)

Broadbent, R. J., *Annals of the Liverpool Stage From the Earliest Period to the Present Time Together with some Account of the Theatres and Music Halls in Bootle and Birkenhead* (Liverpool, 1908)

Brown, Kenneth D., *The English Labour Movement 1700–1951* (Dublin, 1982)

   John Burns (London, 1977)

Browne, Matthew, *Views and Opinions* (London, 1866)

Burke, Peter, 'The "discovery" of popular culture', in Samuel, ed., *People's History*

Burke, Thomas, *The Real East End* (London, 1930)

Burney, Elizabeth, *J.P., Magistrate, Court and Community* (London, 1979)

Burnley, James, *Phases of Bradford Life* (London, 1872)

Burton, Pamela, 'Sheffield – and the Theatre', *Hallamshire Teacher* (July 1968)

Busby, Roy, *British Music Hall. An Illustrated Who's Who From 1850 to the Present Day* (London, 1976)

Cannadine, David, 'Victorian cities: How Different?', *Social History* 2 (1977)

Lords and Landlords: The Aristocracy and the Towns 1774–1967 (Leicester, 1980)

Patricians, power and politics in nineteenth-century towns (Leicester, 1982)

Cannadine, David and David Reeder, eds., *Exploring the Urban Past. Essays in Urban History by H. J. Dyos* (Cambridge, 1982)

Carter, Henry, *The English Temperance Movement: A Study in Objectives, vol. I: The Formative Period 1830–1899* (London, 1933)

The Centenary Book of Bradford (Bradford, 1947)

Chant, Laura Ormiston, *Why We Attacked the Empire* (London, 1895)

Checkland, S. G., *The Upas Tree. Glasgow 1875–1975* (Glasgow, 1976)

Cheshire, D. F., *Music Hall in Britain* (Newton Abbot, 1974)

Clark, George Kitson, *The Making of Victorian England* (London, 1962)

Clarke, J., Chas Critcher and Richard Johnson, *Working Class Culture: Studies in History and Theory* (London, 1979)

Cockroft, W. R., 'The Liverpool Police Force, 1836–1902', in Bell, ed., *Victorian Lancashire*

Cole, George Douglas Conrad, *A Short History of the British Working-Class Movement 1789–1947* (London, 1948)

Colls, Robert, *The Colliers Rant: Song and Culture in the Industrial Village* (London, 1977)

Connell, E .J. and M. Ward, 'Industrial development, 1780–1914', in Fraser, ed., *Modern Leeds*

Courtneidge, Robert, 'The Amusements of Manchester', in Sutton, ed., *Handbook to Manchester*

Critchley T. A., *A History of Police in England and Wales 1900–1966* (London, 1967)

Cross, A. N., *A Select Gazeteer of Local Government Areas for Greater Manchester County* (Manchester[?], 1982)

Crossick, Geoffrey 'Angestellte: Überlegungen am englischen Beispiel', in Kocka, ed., *Angestellte*

An Artisan Elite in Victorian Society. Kentish London 1840–1880 (London, 1978)

'The Labour Aristocracy and its Values: A Study of Mid-Victorian Kentish London', *Victoran Studies* 19 (1975–6)

ed., *The Lower Middle Class in Britain 1870–1914* (London, 1977)

'The Petite Bourgeoisie in Nineteenth-century Britain: the urban and liberal case', in Crossick and Haupt, eds., *Shopkeepers*

'The Petite Bourgeoisie in Nineteenth-Century Europe: Problems and Research', in Tenfelde, ed., *Arbeiter*

Crossick, Geoffrey and Heinz-Gerhard Haupt, eds., 'Shopkeepers, Master Artisans and the Historian: the Petite Bourgeoisie in Comparative Focus', in same, eds., *Shopkeepers and Master Artisans in Nineteenth-Century Europe* (London, 1984)

Crump, Jeremy, 'Amusements of the People. The Provision of Recreation in Leicester, 1850–1914', unpublished thesis (University of Warwick, 1985)

'Provincial Music Hall: Promoters and Public in Leicester, 1863–1929', in Peter Bailey, ed., *Music Hall*

Cudworth, William, *Condition of the Industrial Classes of Bradford and District* (Bradford, 1887; repr. Queensbury, 1977)

Historical Notes on the Bradford Corporation, with Records of the Lighting and Watching Commissioners and Board of Highway Surveyors (Bradford, 1881)

Bibliography

Cunningham, Hugh, 'Leisure', in Benson, ed., *The Working Class Leisure in the Industrial Revolution c. 1780 – c. 1880* (London, 1980)

'The Metropolitan Fairs: A Case Study in the Social Control of Leisure', in Donajgrodzki, ed., *Social Control*

Davie, A. F., 'The Administration of Lancashire, 1838–1889', in Bell, ed., *Victorian Lancashire*

Davies, Alfred T., *A Survey of Liverpool's 144 Lapsed Licenses, and What It Teaches* (Nottingham, 1897)

Davies, Andrew, *Leisure, Gender and Poverty. Working-Class Culture in Salford and Manchester, 1900-1939* (Buckingham, 1992)

Davies, John H., 'The Problem of London Local Government Reform, 1880-1900', thesis (University of Oxford, 1983)

Davison, Peter, *Songs of the British Music Hall* (New York, 1971)

Degen, Günther, 'Zur Geschichte und Gegenwart der Gewerkschaftsbewegung in Großbritannien. Ein Literaturbericht', *Internationale Wissenschaftliche Korrespondenz* 12 (1976)

Denton's Yearbook and Parlour Almanac for 1872 (Bradford, 1872)

Denton's Yearbook and Parlour Almanac for 1886 (Bradford, 1886)

Dickens, Charles, 'The Magistrates and the Music Halls', *The Theatre* 2 (1 March 1879)

Dickinson, Bob, 'In the Audience', *Oral History Journal* 11 (1983)

'The Magic of Music Hall', *Manchester Evening News* (17 January 1983)

Dingle, A. E., *The Campaign For Prohibition in Victorian England: The United Kingdom Alliance 1872–1895* (London, 1980)

Disher, Maurice Willson, *Fairs, Circuses and Music Halls* (London, 1942)

The Personality of the Alhambra (London, 1937)

Victorian Song. From Dive to Drawing Room (London, 1955)

Winkles and Champagne. Comedies and Tragedies of the Music Hall (London, 1938; repr. 1974)

Donajgrodzki, Antony P., ed., *Social Control in Nineteenth-Century Britain* (London, 1977)

Donelly, F. K., 'Ideology and Early English Working-Class History: Edward Thompson and his Critics', *Social History* 1 (1976)

Dunbabin, J. P. D., 'Expectations of the New County Councils, and their Realization', *Historical Journal* 8 (1965)

Dyos, H.J., 'Greater and Greater London: Metropolis and Provinces in the Nineteenth and Twentieth Centuries', in Cannadine and Reeder, eds., *Exploring*

'Urbanity and Suburbanity', in Cannadine and Reeder, eds., *Exploring*

Earl, John, 'Building the Halls', in Bailey, ed., *Music Hall*

Eisenberg, Christiane, 'The Comparative View in Labour History. Old and New Interpretations of the English and German Labour Movements Before 1914', *International Review of Social History* 23 (1989)

Elbourne, Roger, *Music and Tradition in Early Industrial Lancashire 1780-1840* (Trowbridge, 1980)

'Singing Away to the Click of the Shuttle. Musical Life in the Handloom Weaving Communities of Lancashire', *Local Historian* 12 (1976)

Eley, Geoff and Keith Nield, 'Why Does Social History Ignore Politics?', *Social History* 5 (1980)

Elliott, Adrian, 'The incorporation of Bradford', *Northern History* 15 (1979)

'Municipal Government in Bradford in the mid-Nineteenth Century', in Fraser, ed., *Municipal Reform*

Engels, Friedrich, *Die Lage der arbeitenden Klasse in England* (Munich, 1845; 1977 edn)

Evans-Pritchard, E. E., *Anthropology and History* (Manchester, 1961)
Social Anthropology (London, 1964)

Fahey, David M., 'Brewers, Publicans, and Working-Class Drinkers: Pressure Group Politics in Late Victorian and Edwardian England', *Histoire Sociale-Social History* 13 (1980)
'The Politics of Drink: Pressure Groups and the British Liberal Party, 1883–1908', *Social Science* 54 (1979)

Field, John, 'Police, Power and Community in a Provincial English Town: Portsmouth 1815–1875', in Bailey, ed., *Policing and Punishment*

Findlater, Richard, *Banned! A Review of Theatrical Censorship in Britain* (London, 1967)

Finer, H., 'The Police and Public Safety', in Laski, *et al.*, eds., *A Century*

Fitzgerald, Percy, 'Music Hall Land', *National Review* 15 (1890)
Music-Hall Land. An Account of the Natives, Male and Female, Pastimes, Songs, Antics, and General Oddities of that Strange Country (London, 1891)

Foster, John, *Class Struggle and the Industrial Revolution. Early Industrial Capitalism in three English Towns* (London, 1974)

Fraser, Derek, ed., *A History of Modern Leeds* (Manchester, 1980)
Municipal Reform and the Industrial City (Leicester, 1982)
'Politics and the Victorian City', *Urban History Yearbook* (1979)
Power and Authority in the Victorian City (Oxford, 1979)
Urban Politics in Victorian England. The structure of politics in Victorian cities (Leicester, 1973)

Furness, J. M., *Record of Municipal Affairs in Sheffield since the Incorporation of the Borough in 1843 to the Celebration of the Jubilee in 1893* (Sheffield, 1893)

Garrard, John, *Leadership and Power in Victorian Industrial Towns 1830-80* (Manchester, 1983)
'Social History, Political History and Political Science: the Study of Power', *Journal of Social History* 16 (1982–3)

Gaskell, S. Martin, 'Housing and the Lower Middle Class, 1870-1914', in Crossick, ed., *The Lower Middle Class*

Geary, Dick, 'Arbeiterkultur in Deutschland und Großbritannien im Vergleich', in D. Petzina, *Fahnen, Fäuste, Körper. Symbolik und Kultur der Arbeiterbewegung* (Essen, 1986)

Geary, W. N. M., *The Law of Theatres and Music Halls including Contracts and Precedents of Contracts. With Historical Introduction by James Williams* (London, 1885)

Gibbon, Gwilym and Reginald Bell, *History of the London County Council 1889–1939* (London, 1939)

Glasstone, Victor, *Victorian and Edwardian Theatres* (London, 1975)

Glover, David, 'Looking for Edgar Wallace: the Author as Consumer', *History Workshop Journal* 37 (1994)

Gramsci, Antonio, *Zu Politik, Geschichte und Kultur* (Frankfurt, 1980)

Gray, Robert, *The Aristocracy of Labour in Nineteenth-Century Britain c. 1850–1914* (London, 1981)

The Labour Aristocracy in Victorian Edinburgh (Oxford, 1976)

'Religion, Culture and Social Class in Late Nineteenth and Early Twentieth Century Edinburgh', in Crossick, ed., *The Lower Middle Class*

'Styles of Life, the "Labour Aristocracy" and Class Relations in later Nineteenth Century Edinburgh', *International Review of Social History* 18 (1973)

Green's Handy Guide to Leeds (Leeds, n.d.)

Greenwood, James, *Low Life Deeps. An Account of the Strange Fish to be Found There* (London, 1876)

The Seven Curses of London (London, 1869)

In Strange Company. The Notebook of a Roving Correspondent (London, 1873)

The Wilds of London (London, 1874)

Griffith, Ernest S., *The Modern Development of City Government in the United Kingdom and the United States*, 2 vols. (Maryland, 1926; repr. New York, 1969)

Groh, Dieter, 'Base-processes and the problem of organization: outline of a social history research project', *Social History* 4 (1979)

Introduction, in same, ed., *E. P. Thompson. Plebeiische Kultur und moralische Ökonomie. Aufsatze zur englischen Sozialgeschichte des 18. und 19. Jahrhunderts* (Frankfurt, 1980)

The Guide to Leeds and its Amusements (Leeds, 1870)

Haddon, Archibald, *The Story of the Music Hall from Cave of Harmony to Cabaret* (London, 1924)

Halevy, Elie, 'Before 1835', in Laski *et al.*, eds., *A Century*

Hall, Catherine, 'The Early Formation of Victorian Domestic Ideology', in Sandra Burman, ed., *Fit Work for Women* (London, 1979)

Hall, Edward Hepple, *Coffee Taverns, Cocoa Houses, Coffee Palaces* (London, 1879)

Hall, Stuart, 'Cultural Studies and the Centre: some problematics and problems', in Stuart Hall, Dorothy Hobson, Andrew Lowe and Paul Willis, eds., *Culture, Media, Language* (London, 1981)

'Notes on deconstructing "the popular"', in Samuel, ed., *People's History*

Hamer, Harold, *Bolton 1838–1938. A Centenary Record of Municipal Progress* (Bolton, 1938)

Hammond, J. L., 'The Social Background: 1835–1935', in Laski, *et al.*, eds., *A Century*

Hanham, H. J., *Elections and Party Management. Politics in the time of Disraeli and Gladstone* (1959; repr. Hassocks, 1978)

Harker, Dave, 'The Making of the Tyneside Concert Hall', *Popular Music* 1 (1981)

Harrison, Brian, *Drink and the Victorians. The Temperance Question in England 1815–1872* (London, 1971)

Peaceable Kingdom. Stability and Change in Modern Britain (Oxford, 1982)

'Pubs', in H. J. Dyos and Michael Wolff, eds., *The Victorian City*, vol. I (London, 1976)

'Religion and Recreation in Nineteenth Century England', *Past and Present* 38 (1967)

'State Intervention and Moral Reform in Nineteenth-Century England', in Patricia Hollis, ed., *Pressure from Without in Early Victorian England* (London, 1974)

'Temperance Societies', *Local Historian* 8 (1968)

'Traditions of Respectability in British Labour History', in same, ed., *Peaceable Kingdom*

'Underneath the Victorians', *Victorian Studies* 10 (1966–7)

Harrison, J. F. C., 'Chartism in Leeds', in Asa Briggs, ed., *Chartist Studies* (London, 1959; repr. 1977)

Haweis, H. R., *Music and Morals* (London, 1873)

Hebdige, Dick, *Subculture: The Meaning of Style* (London, 1979)

'Towards a Cartography of Taste 1935–1962', in Waites *et al.*, eds., *Popular Culture*

Hennock, E. P., 'Central /Local Government Relations in England: An Outline', *Urban History Yearbook* (1982)

Fit and Proper Persons (London, 1973)

'The Social Composition of Borough Councils in Two Large Cities, 1835–1914', in H. J. Dyos, ed., *The Study of Urban History* (London,1968; repr. 1976)

Hewitt, Archie, 'Sheffield Theatres and Music Halls', *Contact* (February 1978)

Hinton, James, *Labour and Socialism. A History of the British Labour Movement 1867–1974* (Brighton, 1973)

Hobsbawm, Eric J., 'The labour aristocracy in Nineteenth-Century Britain', in same, *Labouring Men* (London, 1964)

'Men and Women in Socialist Iconography', *History Workshop Journal* 6 (1978)

Höher, Dagmar, 'The Composition of Music Hall Audiences', in Peter Bailey, ed., *Music Hall*

Hole, James, *The Working Classes of Leeds* (London, 1863)

Hollingshead, John, *Plain English* (London, 1880)

Theatrical Licences (London, 1875)

Houghton, Walter E., *The Victorian Frame of Mind 1830–1870* (New Haven and London, 1957; repr. 1968)

Howard, Diana, *London Theatres and Music Halls 1850–1950* (London, 1970)

Howell, David, *British Workers and the Independent Labour Party 1888–1906* (Manchester, 1983)

Huck, Gerhard, 'Freizeit als Forschungsproblem', in same, ed., *Sozialgeschichte der Freizeit* (Wuppertal, 1980)

Hunt, E. H., *British Labour History 1815–1914* (London, 1981)

Irving, Gordon, *The Good Auld Days. The Story of Scotland's Entertainers from Music Hall to Television* (London, 1977)

Great Scot. The Life Story of Sir Harry Lauder, Legendary Laird of the Music Hall (London, 1968)

Isaacs, Sidney C., *The Law relating to Theatres, Music-Halls, and other Public Entertainments, and the Performers therein, including the Law of Musical and Dramatic Copyright* (London, 1927)

Jackson, Rosemary, *Fantasy: the Literature of Subversion* (London, 1981)

Jennings, Ivor W., 'The Municipal Revolution', in Laski *et al.*, eds., *A Century*

Jerome, Jerome K., 'Variety Patter', *The Idler* (March 1892)

Jevons, W. Stanley, 'Methods of Social Reform: Amusements of the People', *Contemporary Review* 33 (1878)

Johnson, Richard, 'Barrington Moore, Perry Anderson and English social development', in Hall *et al.*, eds., *Culture, Media, Language*

'Educating the Educators: "Experts" and the State 1833–9', in Donajgrodzki, ed., *Social Control*

Jones, G. P., 'Civic Administration', in Linton, ed., *Sheffield*

Jordan, E. D. and M. J. B. Baddeley, eds., *Black's Guide to Liverpool and Environs* (London, 1900)

Jowitt, Tony, 'A Review of Recent Writing on the History of the Town', in Wright and Jowitt, eds., *Victorian Bradford*

Joyce, Patrick, *Visions of the People. Industrial England and Questions of Class 1848–1914* (Cambridge, 1991)

    Work, Society and Politics. The Culture of the Factory in Later Victorian England (Sussex, 1980)

Klingender, F. D., *The Condition of Clerical Labour in Britain* (London, 1935)

Kocka, Jürgen, ed., *Angestellte im europäischen Vergleich. Die Herausbildung angestell-ter Mittelschichten seit dem späten 19. Jahrhundert* (Göttingen, 1981)

    'Arbeiterkultur als Forschungsthema. Einleitende Bemerkungen', *Geschichte und Gesellschaft* 5 (1979)

Kosok, Elisabeth, 'Arbeiterfreizeit und Arbeiterkultur im Ruhrgebiet. Eine Untersuchung ihrer Erscheinungsformen und Wandlungsprozesse 1850–1914', unpublished thesis (University of Bochum, 1989)

Langewiesche, Dieter, 'Arbeiterkultur in Österreich: Aspekte, Tendenzen und Thesen', in Ritter, ed., *Arbeiterkultur*

    'Arbeiterkultur, Kultur der Arbeiterbewegung im Kaiserreich und in der Weimarer Republik', *Ergebnisse* 26 (1984)

Laski, Harold J., W. Ivor Jennings and William A. Robson, eds., *A Century of Municipal Progress 1835–1935* (London, 1935; repr. Westport CT, 1978)

Laybourn, Keith and Jack Reynolds, *Liberalism and the Rise of Labour 1890-1918* (London, 1984)

Lee, Edward, *Folksong and Music Hall* (London, 1982)

    Music of the People. A Study of Popular Music in Great Britain (London, 1970)

Leeds Biographer (Leeds, n.d.)

Lepenies, Wolf, 'Arbeiterkultur. Wissenschaftssoziologische Anmerkungen zur Konjunktur eines Begriffes', *Geschichte und Gesellschaft* 5 (1979)

    'Probleme einer Historischen Anthropologie', in Reinhard Rürup, ed., *Historische Sozialwissenschaft* (Göttingen, 1977)

Liddington, Jill, 'Birmingham: Leisure and Popular Culture. Oral History Society Autumn Conference, Birmingham 27–28 October 1978', *Oral History* 7 (1979)

Liddington, Jill and Jill Norris, *One hand tied behind us … The rise of the women's suf-frage movement* (London, 1978)

Lidtke, Vernon, 'Recent Literature on Workers' Culture in Germany and England', in Tenfelde, ed., *Arbeiter*

Linton, David C., ed., *Sheffield and its Region. A Scientific and Historical Survey* (Sheffield, 1956)

Liverpool Life: Its Pleasures, Practices, and Pastimes. First Series. Reprinted from 'The Liverpool Mercury' (Liverpool, 1856)

Liverpool Life: Its Pleasures, Practices, and Pastimes. Second Series. Reprinted from 'The Liverpool Mercury' (Liverpool, 1857)

Lloyd, G. I. H., *The Cutlery Trades. An Historical Essay in the Economics of Small-Scale Production* (London, 1913)

Low, F. Percy, 'Society and Music Halls. The Decline of Innuendo', *Music Hall* (16 July 1889)

MacInnes, Colin, *Sweet Saturday Night* (London, 1967)

Mackerness, E. D., *A Social History of English Music* (London, 1964)

    Somewhere Further North. A History of Music in Sheffield (Sheffield, 1974)

Macleod, Stella, 'The Changing Face of the Bradford Borough Bench 1848–1980', unpublished examination paper (University of Bradford, 1980)

Macqueen-Pope, W., *An Indiscreet Guide to Theatreland* (London, 1949)

    The Melodies linger on. The Story of the Music Hall (London, 1951)

    'The Men who wrote the Songs', in Booth, ed., *Seventy Years*

    Queen of the Music Halls. Being the dramatic story of Marie Lloyd (Norwich, 1957)

Maitland, Sara, *Vesta Tilley* (London, 1986)

Malcolmson, Robert W., *Popular Recreation in English Society 1700–1850* (Cambridge, 1973)

Mander, Raymond and Joe Mitchenson, *British Music Hall. A Story in Pictures* (London, 1965)

Mangold, Werner, 'Angestelltengeschichte und Angestelltensoziologie in Deutschland, England und Frankreich', in Kocka, ed., *Angestellte*

Manning, Harold, 'Holder's and Day's: Two Early Birmingham Music Halls', *Alta* 2 (1969)

Margetson, Stella, *Fifty Years of Victorian London. From the Great Exhibition to the Queen's Death* (London, 1969)

Marshall, J. H., *The 'social evil' in Bradford; its Extent, Causes, and Remedy (Repr. from the Bradford Review). Being a Paper read at the Annual congress of the National Association For the Promotion of Social Science, held at Bradford, October 1859* (Bradford, 1859)

Mason, Michael, *The Making of Victorian Sexuality* (Oxford, 1994)

Mason, Tim, 'The Domestication of Female Socialist Icons: a Note in Reply to Eric Hobsbawm', *History Workshop Journal* 7 (1979)

May, F. B., 'Victorian and Edwardian Ilfracombe', in Walton and Walvin, eds., *Leisure*.

Mayhall, John, *The Annals of Yorkshire, From the Earliest Period to the Present Time*, vol. III (Leeds, n.d.)

Mayhew, Henry, *London Labour and the London Poor*, vol. IV (London, 1861–2; repr. 1967)

McCabe, A. T., 'The Standard of Living on Merseyside, 1850–1875', in Bell, ed., *Victorian Lancashire*

McHugh, Paul, *Prostitution and Victorian Social Reform* (London, 1980)

McKechnie, Samuel, *Popular Entertainment Through the Ages* (New York and London, 1969)

McKibbin, Ross, *The Ideologies of Class. Social Relations in Britain 1880-1950* (Oxford, 1990)

    'Working-Class Gambling in Britain 1880–1939', *Past and Present* 82 (1979)

McLennan, Gregor, 'The "Labour Aristocracy" and "Incorporation": Notes on Some Terms in the Social History of the Working Class', *Social History* 6 (1981)

Meacham, Standish, *A Life Apart. The English Working Class 1890–1914* (London, 1977)

Meller, Helen E., 'Cultural Provisions for the Working Classes in Urban Britain in the Second Half of the Nineteenth Century', *Bulletin of the Society for the Study of Labour History* 17 (1968)

    Leisure and the Changing City, 1870-1914 (London, 1976)

Mellor, Geoffrey J., 'A Galaxy of Yorkshire Music Halls', *The Dalesman* 27 (November 1965)

    'A Hundred Years of the City Varieties', *The Dalesman* 27 (May 1965)

    The Northern Music Hall (Newcastle, 1970)

    Theatres of Bradford, with an Introduction by Mr. Roger W. Suddards and a Theatrical Portrait by Mr. Peter Holdsworth (Brigley, 1978)

Merrimac, Miles, *Pen-and-ink Photographs of Members of the Leeds Town Council* (Leeds, 1862)

Messenger, Betty, *Picking Up the Linen Threads. A Study in Industrial Folklore* (Belfast, 1980)

Middleton, Richard, 'Popular Music of the Lower Classes', in Temperley, ed., *Music in Britain*

Midwinter, Eric, 'Central and Local Government in Mid-Nineteenth-Century Lancashire', *Northern History* 3 (1968)

Mitchell, Brian R. and Phyllis Deane, *Abstract of British Historical Statistics* (Cambridge, 1962)

Moir, Esther, *The Justice of the Peace* (Harmondsworth, 1969)

Mommsen, Wolfgang and Hans G. Husung, eds., *The Development of Trade Unionism in Great Britain and Germany 1880–1914* (London, 1985)

Moorhouse. H. F., 'History, Sociology and the Quiescence of the British Working Class: a Reply to Reid', *Social History* 4 (1979)

'The Marxist theory of the Labour Aristocracy', *Social History* 3 (1978)

'The Significance of the Labour Aristocracy', *Social History* 6 (1981)

Morris, R. J., 'Middle-Class Culture, 1700–1914', in Fraser, ed., *Modern Leeds*

Musson, A. E., 'Class Struggle and the Labour Aristocracy, 1830-1860', *Social History* 1 (1976)

Nairn, Tom, 'The English Working Class', *New Left Review* 24 (1964)

Nettel, Reginald, *The Englishman Makes Music* (London, 1952)

Music in the Five Towns 1840–1914 (Oxford, 1945)

Seven Centuries of Popular Song. A Social History of Urban Ditties (London, 1956)

Sing a Song of England. A Social History of Traditional Song (London, 1954)

Nicholson, Watson, *The Struggle for a Free Stage in London* (London, 1906)

Nield, Keith, ed., *Prostitution in the Victorian Age. Debates on the Issue from Nineteenth Century Critical Journals* (Farnborough, 1973)

Nield, Kenneth, 'A Symptomatic Dispute? Notes on the Relation between Marxian Theory and Historical Practice in Britain', *Social Research* 47 (1980)

Odgers, William Blake, *Local Government* (London, 1899)

Orchard, B. Guinness, *The Clerks of Liverpool* (Liverpool, 1871)

Liverpool's Legion of Honour (Birkenhead, 1893)

O'Rourke, Eva, *Lambeth and Music Halls. A Treasury of Music Hall Memorabilia* (London, 1976)

Owen, David, *The Government of Victorian London 1855–1889* (Cambridge MA and London, 1982)

Parkin, Wilf, *Salford Theatres and Music Halls (1880–1980)* (Salford, 1980)

Parsons, Talcott, *The Social System* (Glencoe, 1963)

Patterson, A. Temple, *Radical Leicester. A History of Leicester 1780–1850* (Leicester, 1954)

Pearsall, Ronald, *Victorian Popular Music* (Newton Abbott, 1973)

Peckham, Morse, 'Victorian Counterculture', *Victorian Studies* 18 (1974–5)

Pelling, Henry, *Popular Politics and Society in Late Victorian Britain* (London, 1968)

Pennell, Elizabeth Robin, 'The Pedigree of the Music Hall', *Contemporary Review* 63 (1893)

Pennybacker, Susan, '"It Was Not What She Said, But The Way In Which She Said It'": The London County Council and the Music Halls', in Peter Bailey, ed., *Music Hall*

Perkin, Harold, 'Social History in Britain', *Journal of Social History* 10 (1976–7)

Petrow, Stefan, *Policing Morals. The Metropolitan Police and the Home Office 1870–1914* (Oxford, 1994)

Phillips, Paul T., *The Sectarian Spirit: Sectarianism, Society, and Politics in Victorian Cotton Towns* (Toronto, 1982)

Phillips, Watts, *The Wild Tribes of London* (London, 1855)

Pickering, Michael, 'White Skin, Black Masks: "Nigger" Minstrelsy in Victorian Britain', in Bratton, ed., *Music Hall*

Pollard, Sidney, 'Englische Arbeiterkultur im Zeitalter der Industrialisierung: Forschungsergebnisse und Forschungsprobleme. Ein bibliographischer Aufsatz', *Geschichte und Gesellschaft* 5 (1979)

'The Ethics of the Sheffield Outrages', *Transactions of the Hunter Archaeological Society* 7 (1951–7)

A History of Labour in Sheffield (Liverpool, 1959)

Pollard, Sidney and Colin Holmes, eds., *Essays in the Economic and Social History of South Yorkshire* (Sheffield, 1976)

Poole, Robert, *Popular Leisure and the Music Hall in Nineteenth-Century Bolton* (Lancaster, 1982)

Porter's Topographical and Commercial Directory of Leeds and Neighbourhood (Leeds, 1872–3)

Price, Richard, 'The Labour Process and Labour History', *Social History* 8 (1983)

'The Making of Working-Class History', *Victorian Studies* 20 (1976–7)

'The Working Men's Club Movement and Victorian Social Reform Ideology', *Victorian Studies* 15 (1971–2)

'Society, Status and Jingoism: The Social Roots of Lower Middle Class Patriotism, 1870-1900', in Crossick, ed., *The Lower Middle Class*

Proctor, Richard Wright, *Manchester in Holiday Dress* (London, 1866)

Pulling, Christopher, *They Were Singing. And What They Sang About* (London, 1952)

Raab, Michael, *'The Music Hall is Dying': Die Thematisierung der Unterhaltungs-industrie im englischen Gegenwartsdrama* (Tübingen, 1989)

Redford, Arthur (assisted by Ina Stafford Russell), *The History of Local Government in Manchester*, 3 vols. (London, 1939–40)

Redlich, Josef and Francis W. Hirst, *The History of Local Government in England* (London, 1903; repr. 1958)

Reid, Alastair, 'Politics and Economics in the Formation of the British Working Class: A Response to H. F. Moorhouse', *Social History* 3 (1978–9)

Reid, Caroline, 'Middle-Class Values and Working-Class Culture in Nineteenth-Century Sheffield – The Pursuit of Respectability', in Pollard and Holmes, eds., *Essays*

'Temperance, Teetotalism and Local Culture. The Early Temperance Movement in Sheffield', *Northern History* 13 (1977)

Reid, Douglas A., 'The Decline of St Monday 1766–1876', *Past and Present* 71 (1976)

'Interpreting the Festival Calendar. Wakes and Fairs as Carnivals', in Storch, ed., *Popular Culture*

'Labour, Leisure and Politics in Birmingham *c.* 1800–1874', unpublished thesis (Birmingham, 1985)

'Popular Theatre in Victorian Birmingham', in Bradby *et al.*, eds., *Performance and Politics*

Reith, Charles, *A Short History of the British Police* (Oxford, 1948)

Reynolds, J. and K. Laybourn, 'The Emergence of the Independent Labour Party in Bradford', *International Review of Social History* 20 (1975)

Richard, Kenneth and Peter Morrison, *Nineteenth Century British Theatre* (London, 1971)

Richie, J. Ewing, *The Night Side of London* (London, 1857)

Ritter, Gerhard A., ed., *Arbeiterkultur* (Königstein, Taunus, 1979)

Roberts, James S., 'Der Alkoholkonsum deutscher Arbeiter im 19. Jahrhundert', *Geschichte und Gesellschaft* 6 (1980)

Robson, William A., *The Development of Local Government* (London, 1954; repr. Westport CT, 1978)

Ross, Bert, 'The Empire, Leicester Square I-IV', *Call Boy* 4 (1978); 1, 2 and 3 (1979)

Ross, Edward Alsworth, *Social Control and the Foundation of Sociology* (Boston, 1959)

Rowbotham, Sheila, 'Anarchism in Sheffield in the 1890s', in Pollard and Holmes, eds., *Essays*

Russell, C. E. B. and E. T. Campagnac, 'Poor People's Music-Halls in Lancashire', *Economic Review* (July 1900)

Russell, Dave, *Popular Music in England, 1840–1914. A social history* (Manchester, 1987)

Rutherford, Lois, 'Managers in a Small Way: The Professionalisation of Variety Artistes, 1860-1914', in Peter Bailey, ed., *Music Hall*

Ryan, Rachel, *A Biography of Manchester* (London, 1937)

Samuel, Raphael, 'Local History and Oral History', *History Workshop Journal* 1 (1976–7) ed., *People's History and Socialist Theory* (London, 1981)
  'Wahrheit ist parteiisch. Zur Entstehung des History Workshop', *Journal für Geschichte* 3 (1981)

Saunders, William, *History of the First London County Council 1889–1890–1891* (London, 1892)

Schneider, Ulrich, 'Joyce und die Music Hall', in Ulrich Bertram and Dieter Petzold, eds., *Erlanger Anglistik und Amerikanistik in Vergangenheit und Gegenwart* (Erlangen, 1990)
  'Let's all go to the Music Hall: die Music Hall und ihre Songs', *Anglistik und Englischunterricht* 15 (1981)
  Die Londoner Music Hall und ihre Songs 1850-1920 (Tübingen, 1984)
  'A Rollicking Rattling Song of the Halls: Joyce and the Music Hall', in Ruth Bauerle, ed., *Picking up Airs: Hearing the Music in Joyce's Text* (Urbana, 1993)
  'That Exquisite Sense of the Frivolous. Die Music Hall im England der neunziger Jahre', in Manfred Pfister and Bernd Schulte-Middelich, eds., *Die 'Nineties': Der englische Fin de Siecle zwischen Dekadenz und Sozialkritik* (Munich, 1983)
  Zum Stand der Music Hall-Forschung', *Gulliver* 34 (1993)

Scholes, Percy A., *The Mirror of Music 1844–1944. A Century of Musical Life in Britain as reflected in the Pages of the Musical Times*, 2 vols. (Oxford, 1947)

Scott, Harold, *The Early Doors: Origins of the Music Hall* (London, 1946)

Scruton, William, *Bradford Fifty Years Ago. A Jubilee Memorial of the Bradford Corporation and A literary and Pictorial Record of Bradford During the Fifty Years of its Incorporation* (Bradford, 1897)
  Bradford Scenes, Characters, and Events: and other Local Articles (Bradford[?], 1900)
  Pen and Pencil Pictures of Bradford (Bradford,1889)

Senelick, Laurence, 'A Brief Life and Times of the Victorian Music-Hall', *Harvard Library Bulletin* 19 (1971)

'Moonlighting in the Music Hall: The Double Life of Charles Rice', *Theatre Survey* 34 (1993)

'Politics as Entertainment: Victorian Music-Hall Songs', *Victorian Studies* 19 (1975–6)

Senelick, Lawrence, David Cheshire and Ulrich Schneider, *British Music-Hall 1840–1923. A Bibliography and Guide to Sources, with a Supplement on European Music-Hall* (Hamden, CT, 1981)

Shaw, William Arthur, *Manchester, Old and New*, 3 vols. (Manchester, 1895)

Sheffield as it is: Being an Historical and Descriptive Handbook and Stranger's Guide to the Show Rooms, Warehouses, and Manufactories: The Splendidly Picturesque Scenery and Noblemen's Mansions in its Neighbourhood and to every other Object of Interest in the Town and Locality (Sheffield, 1852)

Sheffield 'City' 1901. Almanack and Diary (Sheffield,1902)

The Sheffield and Rotherham Red Book and Almanac, 1870 (Sheffield, 1871)

Shiman, Lilian Lewis, *Crusade against Drink in Victorian England* (London, 1988)

Short, Ernest and Arthur Compton-Rickett, *Ring up the Curtain. Being A Pageant of English Entertainment Covering Half a Century* (London, 1938)

Short, Ernest, *Sixty Years of Theatre* (London, 1951)

Simon, Shena D., *A Century of City Government. Manchester 1838–1938* (London, 1938)

Simon, George R., *How the Poor Live and Horrible London* (London, 1889)

Smith, Dennis, *Conflict and Compromise. Class Formation in English Society 1830–1914. A Comparative Study of Birmingham and Sheffield* (London, 1982)

Smith, Joan, 'Labour Tradition in Glasgow and Liverpool', *History Workshop Journal* 17 (1984)

Smith, M. B., 'Victorian Entertainment in the Lancashire Cotton Towns', in Bell, ed., *Victorian Lancashire*

The Society for Theatre Research Manchester Group Exhibition 'Two Hundred Years of Theatre in Manchester' (Manchester, 1952)

Stainton, J. H., *The Making of Sheffield 1865–1914* (Sheffield, 1924)

Stedman Jones, Gareth, 'Class Experience versus Social Control?', *History Workshop Journal* 4 (1977)

'Class Struggle and the Industrial Revolution', *New Left Review* 90 (1975)

'Working-Class Culture and Working-Class Politics in London, 1870–1900. Votes on the Remaking of a Working Class', *Journal of Social History* 7 (1974), pp. 460–508

Outcast London (Oxford, 1971)

Steedman, Carolyn, *Policing the Victorian Community. The Formation of English Provincial Police Forces, 1856–80* (London, 1984)

Stephan, Cora, 'Zugluft in Marmorhallen. Neue Perspektiven der Forschung und ihre Chancen', *Journal für Geschichte* 3 (1981)

Storch, Robert D., 'The Plague of the Blue Locusts. Police Reform and Popular Resistance in Northern England, 1840-57', *International Review of Social History* 20 (1975)

'The Policeman as Domestic Missionary: Urban Discipline and Popular Culture in Northern England, 1850-1880', *Journal of Social History* 9 (1975–6)

ed., *Popular Culture and Custom in Nineteenth-Century England* (London, 1982)

'The Problem of Working-Class Leisure. Some Roots of Middle-Class Moral Reform in the Industrial North, 1825–50', in Donajgrodzki, ed., *Social control*

Storm, Gerd, Michael Scholing and Armin Frohmann, 'Arbeiterkultur zwischen Gegenkultur und Integration. Ein Literaturbericht', *Internationale Wissenschaftliche Korrespondenz* 22 (1986)

The Stranger's Guide to the Town of Sheffield and the Surrounding District (Sheffield, 1852)

Strong, Albert Ambrose, *Dramatic and Musical Law. Being a Digest of the Law Relating to Theatres and Music-Halls and Containing Chapters on Theatrical Contracts, Theatrical, Music and Dancing and Excise Licences, Dramatic and Musical Copyright, &c. with an Appendix Containing the Acts of Parliament Relating Thereto and the Regulations of the London County Council and the Lord Chamberlain* (London, 1898)

Stuart, Charles Douglas and A. J. Park, *The Variety Stage. A History of the Music Halls From the Earliest Period to the Present Time* (London, 1895)

Summerfield, Penelope, 'The Effingham Arms and the Empire: Deliberate Selection in the Evolution of Music Hall in London', in Yeo and Yeo, eds., *Popular Culture*

Sutton, C. W., ed., *Handbook and Guide to Manchester* (Manchester and London, 1907)

Taylor, Arthur J., 'Victorian Leeds: an Overview', in Fraser, ed., *Modern Leeds*

Taylor, John, *Illustrated Guide to Sheffield and the Surrounding District* (Sheffield, 1879)

Temperley, Nicholas, ed., *Music in Britain. The Romantic Age, 1800–1914* (London, 1981)

Tenfelde, Klaus, 'Anmerkungen zur Arbeiterkultur', in Wolfgang Ruppert, ed., *Erinnerungsarbeit* (Opladen, 1982)

ed., *Arbeiter und Arbeiterbewegung im Vergleich* (Munich, 1986)

Tholfson, Trygve R., *Working-class Radicalism in Mid-Victorian England* (London, 1976)

Thomas, Keith, 'History and Anthropology', *Past and Present* 24 (1963)

'Work and Leisure in Pre-Industrial Society', *Past and Present* 29 (1964) and 30 (1965)

Thomlinson, Walter, *Bye-Ways of Manchester Life* (Manchester, 1887)

Thompson, Edward Palmer, 'Homage to Tom Maguire', in Asa Briggs and John Saville, eds., *Essays in Labour History In Memory of G. D. H. Cole*, vol. I (London, 1960)

The Making of the English Working Class (Harmondsworth, 1963; repr. 1972)

'The Moral Economy of the English Crowd in the Eighteenth Century', *Past and Present* 50 (1971)

'Patrician Society, Plebeian Culture', *Journal of Social History* 7 (1973–4)

The Poverty of Theory and other Essays (London, 1978)

'Time, Work-Discipline, and Industrial Capitalism', *Past and Present* 38 (1967)

'Volkskunde, Anthropologie und Sozialgeschichte', in Groh, ed., *E. P. Thompson*

'Working-Class Culture – The Transition to Industrialism', *Bulletin of the Society for the Study of Labour History*, 9 (1964)

Thompson, F. M. L., *The Rise of Respectable Society. A Social History of Victorian Britain, 1830-1900* (London, 1988)

'Social Control in Victorian Britain', *Economic History Review* 34 (1981)

Thompson, Paul, *The Edwardians. The Remaking of British Society* (London, 1975)

Socialists, Liberals and Labour. The Struggle for London 1885–1914 (London, 1967)

Thorne, Guy, *The Great Acceptance. The Life Story of F. N. Charrington* (London, 1912)

Tracy, W. Burnett and W. T. Pike, *Manchester and Salford at the Close of the Nineteenth Century: Contemporary Biographies* (Brighton, 1898)

Traies, Jane, 'Jones and the Working Girl: Class Marginality in Music-Hall Song 1860–1900', in Bratton, ed., *Music Hall*

Trainor, Richard, 'Urban Elites in Victorian Britain', *Urban History Yearbook* (1985)

Treble, J. H., 'The Seasonal Demand for Adult Labour in Glasgow, 1890–1914', *Social History* 3 (1978)

Turner, E. S., *Roads to Ruin. The Shocking History of Social Reform* (London, 1950)

Vester, Michael, *Die Entstehung des Proletariats als Lernprozeß. Die Entstehung anti-kapitalistischer Theorie und Praxis in England 1792–1848* (Frankfurt, 1970; repr. 1975)

Vicinus, Martha, *The Industrial Muse. A Study of Nineteenth-Century British Working-Class Literature* (London, 1974)

'The Study of Victorian Popular Culture', *Victorian Studies* 18 (1974–5)

Vickers, J .Edward, *A Popular History of Sheffield. With a Guide to Places, Buildings, and Things of Interest* (Wakefield, 1978)

Vigiers, François, *Change and Apathy. Liverpool and Manchester during the Industrial Revolution* (Cambridge MA, 1970)

Vigne, Thea and Alan Howkins, 'The Small Shopkeeper in Industrial and Market Towns', in Crossick, ed., *The Lower Middle Class*

Vincent, John, *The Formation of the Liberal Party 1857–1868* (London, 1966)

Voigt, Eberhard, *Die Music-Hall-Songs und das öffentliche Leben Englands* (Greifswald, 1929)

Waites, Bernard, 'The Music Hall', in *Popular Culture, Block II: The Historical Development of Popular Culture*, ed., Open University (Milton Keynes, 1981)

Waites, Bernard, Tony Bennett and Graham Martin, eds., *Popular Culture. Past and Present* (London, 1982)

Walkowitz, Judith R., 'Male Vice and Feminist Virtue: Feminism and the Politics of Prostitution in Nineteenth Century Britain', *History Workshop Journal* 13 (1982)

Prostitution and Victorian Society. Women, Class, and the State (Cambridge, 1980)

Waller, P. J., *Democracy and Sectarianism. A Political and Social History of Liverpool 1868–1939* (Liverpool, 1981)

Town, City and Nation. England 1850–1914 (Oxford, 1983)

Walter, Franz, 'Konfliktreiche Integration. Arbeiterkultur im Kaiserreich und in der Weimarer Republik', *Internationale Wissenschaftliche Korrespondenz* 24 (1988)

Walton, John K. and James Walvin, eds., *Leisure in Britain 1780-1939* (Manchester, 1983)

Walton, John K. and Alastair Wilcox, eds., *Low Life and Moral Improvement in Mid-Victorian England: Liverpool through the Journalism of Hugh Shimmin* (Leicester, 1991)

Walvin, James, *Leisure and Society, 1830–1950* (London, 1978)

Ward, David, 'Environs and Neighbours in the "Two Nations". Residential Differentia-tion in Mid-Nineteenth-Century Leeds', *Journal of Historical Geography* 6 (1980)

Waters, Chris, *British Socialists and the Politics of Popular Culture, 1884–1914* (Manchester, 1990)

'Manchester Morality and London Capital: The Battle over the Palace of Varieties', in Peter Bailey, ed., *Music Hall*

Watson, Ian, *Song and democratic culture in Britain. An Approach to Popular Culture in Social Movements* (London, 1983)

Watters, Eugene and Matthew Murtagh, *Infinite Variety. Dan Lowrey's Music Hall 1879–97* (London, 1975)

Webb, Sidney and Beatrice, *The History of Trade Unionism, 1660-1920* (London, 1894; repr. 1920)

Weber, William, 'Die Handwerker im Londoner und Pariser Konzertleben in der Mitte des 19. Jahrhunderts', in Ritter, ed., *Arbeiterkultur*

Wewiora, George E., 'Manchester Music-Hall Audiences in the 1880s,' *Manchester Review* 12.4 (1973)

White, Brian D., *A History of the Corporation of Liverpool, 1835–1914* (Liverpool, 1951)

Wiener, Martin J., Review of Donajgrodzki, Antony P., ed., 'Social Control in Nineteenth Century Britain', *Journal of Social History* 12 (1978–9)

Williams, Raymond, *Culture and Society 1780-1950* (London, 1958)

Winskill, P. T., *The Temperance Movement and its Workers. A Record of Social, Moral, Religious, and Political Progress,* 4 vols. (Liverpool, 1892)

Woodhouse, T., 'The Working Class', in Fraser, ed., *Modern Leeds*
'The Working Class and Leisure: Class Expression and/or Social Control' (conference report), *Bulletin of the Society for the Study of Labour History* 32 (1976)

Wright's Almanac and Annual (Bradford[?], 1874)

Wright, D. G., 'Mid-Victorian Bradford: 1850–80', The Bradford Antiquary, New Series Part XLVII (1982)
and J. A. Jowitt, eds., *Victorian Bradford. Essays in Honour of Jack Reynolds* (Bradford, 1981)

Wright, Thomas, 'Bill Bank's Day Out', in Andrew Halliday, ed., *The Savage Club Papers for 1868* (London, 1868)
The Great Unwashed (London, 1868)
Some Habits and Customs of the Working Classes. By a Journeyman Engineer (London, 1867; repr. New York, 1967)

Yates, Nigel, 'The Religious Life of Victorian Leeds', in Fraser, ed., *Modern Leeds*

Yeo, Eileen and Stephen, eds., *Popular Culture and Class Conflict* (Sussex, 1981)

Yeo, Stephen, 'A New Life: The Religion of Socialism in Britain 1883–1896', *History Workshop Journal* 4 (1977)

Young, G. M., *Portrait of an Age. Victorian England* (Oxford, 1936; repr. 1977)

Young, James D., *Socialism and the English Working Class. A History of English Labour, 1883–1939* (New York and London, 1989)

Young, Ken and Patricia Garside, *Metropolitan London. Politics and Urban Change 1837–1981* (London, 1982)

Young, Percy M., *A History of British Music* (London, 1967)

Index

Pavilion, Rose and Crown, Royal
Victoria Coffee Music Hall, Stanley,
Stoll, Strange
London County Council (LCC), 25, 52,
63, 144, 145, 148, 153–4, 161–2, 163,
165, 167–8, 169, 170, 173–4, 178
licensing committee, 161, 162–3, 164,
165, 166–8, 169, 171, 173–4, 180
London Music Hall Proprietors
Association, 17, 21, 32
London Music Halls Protection Society,
143
Lord Chamberlain, the, 90, 91, 104
lotteries, 89–90, 92
Lusby's Music Hall, London, 137, 138,
156–7, 162

MacDermott, G. H., 42, 43
magistrates, *see* individual towns and
Middlesex Magistrates
Manchester, 79, 89, 90, 94, 112, 173
free-and-easies, 32
industrial structure, 64, 65
magistrates and licensing, 31, 99, 121,
165–6, 171–2, 179, 180
music halls, 1, 2, 7, 19, 20, 31, 32–4, 59,
63, 64, 65, 66–7, 68, 71, 72, 89, 90,
112, 121, 158, 165–6, 171–2
political structure, 160, 180
pub music halls, 31, 32, 165–6, 171
singing saloons, 32, 72, 176
social purity campaigns, 158, 171
temperance campaigns, 99, 158, 177
see also Alexandra, Broadhead, Palace
of Varieties, Victoria
Mander, Raymond, 4
Manningham Mills Strike, 130–1
Mason, Michael, 52
Matkin, William, 173
Mayne, Sir Richard, 137–8, 180
McDougall, John, 162
McNaghten Circuit, 33
Mellor, G. J., 6
Methodists, 12, 156, 162
Metzger, Louis, 128
Middlesex Magistrates, 21
and music halls, 146, 153–4
and licensing, 21, 135, 137, 138,

139–41, 146–7, 148–53, 155, 157,
159, 174
and police, 137–8
and prostitution, 136–40
Milner, Alfred, 126–7
Millstone Concert Hall, 54–6
Mitchenson, Joe, 4
Morgan, William, 58, 65, 70, 123, 170,
181
Morton, Charles, 17, 19, 20, 21, 25, 27,
32, 45, 54, 62–3, 140, 141–2
Moss, Edward, 23, 33
Mossman, Mr, 122
Mould, Frederick, 125, 126, 127-8
Music Hall
decline of, 25
definitions of, 2, 5–6, 7, 18, 19–21,
31–2, 51–2, 73–4, 175–6
development and history of, 1–2,
17–19, 21, 22–5, 26, 31, 32–4, 35, 61,
62, 68–9, 71, 97, 135, 148, 149–50,
155, 158, 163–4, 165, 168–70, 174,
181-2
historiography, 3-7, 17, 175
public perception of, 1, 2, 7, 13, 77–8,
97, 99, 110–11,
urban locations, 21, 31, 32–3, 62, 63

National Association of Women, 158
National Vigilance Association, 158, 162
Newcastle, 19, 33, 35
nonconformists, 12, 84, 86, 100, 101,
135–6, 155–6, 157, 162, 178
Norwich, 99
Nottingham, 90
Nunn, Bobby, 35

Oldham, 99
Orchard, B.G., 117
Oxford Music Hall, London, 21, 25, 31,
63, 137, 138, 140, 141, 153

Palace of Varieties, Manchester, 7, 59, 68,
158, 165, 166, 171–2
panics in music halls, 63–4, 88–9, 172
Parks, A. J., 3
Parnell, Charles, 42
Parsons, Talcott, 10

With the exception of the occasional local case study, music-hall history has until now been presented as the history of the London halls. This book attempts to redress the balance by setting music-hall history within a national perspective. Kift also sheds a new light on the roles of managements, performers and audiences. For example, the author confutes the commonly held assumption that most women in the halls were prostitutes and shows them to have been working women accompanied by workmates of both sexes or by their families. She argues that before the 1890s the halls catered predominantly to working-class and lower middle-class audiences of men and women of all ages and were instrumental in giving them a strong and self-confident identity. The halls' ability to sustain a distinct class-awareness was one of their greatest strengths – but this factor was also at the root of many of the controversies which surrounded them. These controversies are at the centre of the book and Kift treats them as test cases for social relations which provide fresh insights into nineteenth-century British society and politics.

DAGMAR KIFT is the custodian of the Westphalian Industrial Museum, Dortmund, Germany, and recognised as an authority on the history of the music-hall and Victorian theatre.